Spoken Multimodal Human-Computer Dialogue in Mobile Environments

Text, Speech and Language Technology

VOLUME 28

The titles published in this series are listed at the end of this volume.

Spoken Multimodal Human-Computer Dialogue in Mobile Environments

Edited by

W. Minker
University of Ulm, Germany

Dirk Bühler
University of Ulm, Germany

and

Laila Dybkjær
University of Southern Denmark, Odense, Denmark

A C.I.P. Catalogue record for this book is available from the Library of Congress.

ISBN 1-4020-3074-6 (PB)
ISBN 1-4020-3073-8 (HB)
ISBN 1-4020-3075-4 (e-book)

Published by Springer,
P.O. Box 17, 3300 AA Dordrecht, The Netherlands.

Sold and distributed in North, Central and South America
by Springer,
101 Philip Drive, Norwell, MA 02061, U.S.A.

In all other countries, sold and distributed
by Springer,
P.O. Box 322, 3300 AH Dordrecht, The Netherlands.

Printed on acid-free paper

Printed in the Netherlands

Contents

Part II System Architecture and Example Implementations

Preface

This book is based on publications from the ISCA Tutorial and Research Workshop on Multi-Modal Dialogue in Mobile Environments held at Kloster Irsee, Germany, in 2002. The workshop covered various aspects of development and evaluation of spoken multimodal dialogue systems and components with particular emphasis on mobile environments, and discussed the state-of-the-art within this area. On the development side the major aspects addressed include speech recognition, dialogue management, multimodal output generation, system architectures, full applications, and user interface issues. On the evaluation side primarily usability evaluation was addressed. A number of high quality papers from the workshop were selected to form the basis of this book.

The volume is divided into three major parts which group together the overall aspects covered by the workshop. The selected papers have all been extended, reviewed and improved after the workshop to form the backbone of the book. In addition, we have supplemented each of the three parts by an invited contribution intended to serve as an overview chapter.

Part one of the volume covers issues in multimodal spoken dialogue systems and components. The overview chapter surveys multimodal dialogue systems and links up to the other chapters in part one. These chapters discuss aspects of speech recognition, dialogue management and multimodal output generation. Part two covers system architecture and example implementations. The overview chapter provides a survey of architecture and standardisation issues while the remainder of this part discusses architectural issues mostly based on fully implemented, practical applications. Part three concerns evaluation and usability. The human factors aspect is a very important one both from a development point of view and when it comes to evaluation. The overview chapter presents the state-of-the-art in evaluation and usability and also outlines novel challenges in the area. The other chapters in this part illustrate and discuss various approaches to evaluation and usability in concrete applications or experiments that often require one or more novel challenges to be addressed.

We are convinced that computer scientists, engineers, and others who work in the area of spoken multimodal dialogue systems, no matter if in academia or in industry, may find the volume interesting and useful to their own work.

Graduate students and PhD students specialising in spoken multimodal dialogue systems more generally, or focusing on issues in such systems in mobile environments in particular, may also use this book to get a concrete idea of how far research is today in the area and of some of the major issues to consider when developing spoken multimodal dialogue systems in practice.

We would like to express our sincere gratitude to all those who helped us in preparing this book. Especially we would like to thank all reviewers who through their valuable comments and criticism helped improve the quality of the individual chapters as well as the entire book. A special thank is also due to people at the Department of Information and Technology in Ulm and at NISLab in Odense.

Wolfgang MINKER

Dirk BÜHLER

Laila DYBKJÆR

Contributing Authors

Ilse Bakx is a Researcher at the Department of Technology Management, Technical University Eindhoven, The Netherlands. She obtained her MSc degree in Psychology (cognitive ergonomics) in 2001 at University of Maastricht. Her current research is dealing with the user aspects and usability of multimodal interaction.

Niels Ole Bernsen is Professor at, and Director of, the Natural Interactive Systems Laboratory, the University of Southern Denmark. His research interests include spoken dialogue systems and natural interactive systems more generally, including embodied conversational agents, systems for learning, teaching, and entertainment, online user modelling, modality theory, systems and component evaluation, including usability evaluation, system simulation, corpus creation, coding schemes, and coding tools.

Jonas Beskow is a Researcher at the Centre for Speech Technology at KTH in Stockholm, where he received his PhD in 2003. During 1998/99 he was a Visiting Researcher at the Perceptual Science Lab at UC Santa Cruz, sponsored by a Fulbright Grant. He received his MSc in Electrical Engineering from KTH in 1995. His main research interests are in the areas of facial animation, speech synthesis and embodied conversational agents.

Dan Bohus is a PhD candidate in the Computer Science Department at Carnegie Mellon University, USA. He has graduated with a BS degree in Computer Science from Politechnica University of Timisoara, Romania. His research is focussed on increasing the robustness and reliability of spoken language systems faced with unreliable inputs.

Jonathan Bloom received his PhD in Experimental Psychology, specifically in the area of psycholinguistics, from the New School for Social Research, New York, USA, in 1999. Since then, he has spent time designing speech user interfaces for Dragon Systems and currently for SpeechWorks International. For both companies, his focus has been on the design of usable multimodal interfaces.

Dirk Bühler is a PhD student at the University of Ulm, Department of Information Technology, Germany. He holds an MSc in Computer Science with a specialisation in computational linguistics from the University of Tübingen. His research interests are the development and evaluation of user interfaces, including dialogue modelling and multimodality, domain modelling, knowledge representation, and automated reasoning. He worked at DaimlerChrysler, Research and Technology, Germany, from 2000 to 2002.

Bob Carpenter received a PhD in Cognitive Science from the University of Edinburgh, United Kingdom, in 1989. Since then, he has worked on computational linguistics, first as an Associate Professor of computational linguistics at Carnegie Mellon University, Pittsburgh, USA, then as a member of technical staff at Lucent Technologies Bell Labs, and more recently, as a programmer at SpeechWorks International, and Alias I.

Sasha Caskey is a Computer Scientist whose main research interests are in the area of human-computer interaction. In 1996 he joined The MITRE Corporation in the Intelligent Information Systems Department where he contributed to research in spoken language dialogue systems. Since 2000 he has been a Researcher in the Natural Dialog Group at SpeechWorks International, New York, USA. He has contributed to many open source initiatives including the GalaxyCommunicator software suite.

Rachel Coulston is a Researcher at the Center for Human-Computer Communication (CHCC) in the Department of Computer Science at the Oregon Health & Science University (OHSU). She holds her BA and MA in Linguistics, and does research on linguistic aspects of human interaction with interactive multimodal computer systems.

Bert Cranen is a Senior Lecturer at the Department of Language and Speech, University of Nijmegen, The Netherlands. He obtained his masters degree in Electrical Engineering in 1979. His PhD thesis in 1987 was on modelling the acoustic properties of the human voice source. His research is focussed on questions how automatic speech recognition systems can be adapted to be successfully deployed in noisy environments and in multimodal applications.

Robert Dale is Director of the Centre for Language Technology at Macquarie University, Australia, and a Professor in that University's Department of Computing. His current research interests include low-cost approaches to intelligent text processing tasks, practical natural language generation, the engineering of habitable spoken language dialogue systems, and computational, philosophical and linguistic issues in reference and anaphora.

Courtney Darves is a PhD student at the University of Oregon in the Department of Psychology. She holds an MSc in Psychology (cognitive neuroscience) and a BA in Linguistics. Her research focuses broadly on adaptive human behaviour, both in the context of human-computer interaction and more generally in terms of neural plasticity.

Laila Dybkjær is a Professor at NISLab, University of Southern Denmark. She holds a PhD degree in Computer Science from Copenhagen University. Her research interests are topics concerning design, development, and evaluation of user interfaces, including development and evaluation of interactive speech systems and multimodal systems, design and development of intelligent user interfaces, usability design, dialogue model development, dialogue theory, and corpus analysis.

Wolfgang Eckhart visited the HTBLuVA in St. Pölten, Austria, before he worked at the Alcatel Austria Voice Processing Centre. Since 2001 he is employed at Sonorys Technology GesmbH with main focus on host-based Speech Recognition. In 2001 he participated in the research of ftw. project "Speech&More".

Jens Edlund started out in computational linguistics at Stockholm University. He has been in speech technology research since 1996, at Telia Research, Stockholm, Sweden and SRI, Cambridge, United Kingdom and, since 1999, at the Centre for speech technology at KTH in Stockholm, Sweden. His reseach interests centre around dialogue systems and conversational computers.

Robert Finan studied Electronic Engineering at the University of Dublin, Ireland, Biomedical Instrumentation Engineering at the University of Dundee, United Kingdom, and Speaker Recognition at the University of Abertay, Dundee. He currently works for Mobilkom Austria AG as a Voice Services Designer. Since 2001 he participates in the research of ftw. project "Speech&More".

Sadaoki Furui is a Professor at Tokyo Institute of Technology, Department of Computer Science, Japan. He is engaged in a wide range of research on speech analysis, speech recognition, speaker recognition, speech synthesis, and multimodal human-computer interaction.

Sabine Geldof has a background in linguistics and artificial intelligence. As part of her dissertation she investigated the influence of (extra-linguistic) context on language production, more specifically in applications for wearable and mobile devices. Her post-doctoral research focuses on the use of natural language generation techniques to improve efficiency of information delivery in a task-oriented context.

Paul Heisterkamp has obtained his MA in German Philology, Philosophy and General Linguistics from Münster University, Germany, in 1986. Starting out in 1987 with the AEG research at Ulm, Germany, that later became DaimlerChrysler corporate research, he has worked on numerous national and international research projects on spoken dialogue. The current focus of his work is shifting from dialogue management and contextual interpretation to dialogue system integration in mobile environments with special respect to the aspects of multimodality in vehicle human-computer interfaces, as well as cognitive workload assessment.

Koji Iwano is an Assistant Professor at Tokyo Institute of Technology, Department of Computer Science, Japan. He received the BE degree in Information and Communication Engineering in 1995, and the ME and PhD degrees in Information Engineering in 1997 and 2000 respectively from the University of Tokyo. His research interests include speech recognition, speaker recognition, and speech synthesis.

Anthony Jameson is a Principal Researcher at DFKI, the German Research Center for Artificial Intelligence, and an adjunct Professor of Computer Science at the International University in Germany. His central interests concern interdisciplinary research on intelligent user interfaces and user-adaptive systems.

Kouichi Katsurada received the BE degree in 1995 and the PhD degree in 2000 from Osaka University, Japan. He joined Toyohashi University of Technology as a Research Associate in 2000. His current interests are in multimodal interaction and knowledge-based systems.

Andreas Kellner received his Diploma degree in Electrical Engineering from the Technical University Munich, Germany, in 1994. He has been working in the "Man-Machine Interfaces" department at the Philips Research Laboratories in Aachen since 1995. There, he was responsible for the development of spoken language dialogue systems and conversational user interfaces for various applications. He has also been involved in standardization efforts such as the W3C Voice Browser Working group. His main research areas of interests are natural language processing, dialogue management, and systems architectures.

Kerstin Klöckner studied Computational Linguistics at the University of the Saarland, Germany, where she obtained her Diploma in 2001. Since then, she has been working as a Researcher at DFKI's Evaluation Center for Language Technology Systems.

Satoshi Kobayashi received the BE degree in 1991, the ME degree in 1994 from Toyohashi University of Technology, Japan, and the PhD degree in

2000 from Shizuoka University, Japan. He joined Toyohashi University of Technology as a Research Associate in 1999. His current interests are in multimodal interaction and language communication.

Klaus Macherey received the Diploma degree in Computer Science from the Aachen University of Technology (RWTH), Germany, in 1999. Since then, he has been a Research Assistant with the Department of Computer Science of RWTH. In 2002, he was a summer student at IBM T. J. Watson Research Center, Yorktown Heights, New York, USA. His primary research interests cover speech recognition, confidence measures, natural language understanding, dialogue systems, and reinforcement learning.

Wolfgang Minker is a Professor at the University of Ulm, Department of Information Technology, Germany. He received his PhD in Engineering Science from the University of Karlsruhe, Germany, in 1997 and his PhD in Computer Science from the University of Paris-Sud, France, in 1998. He was a Researcher at the Laboratoire d'Informatique pour la Mécanique et les Sciences de l'Ingénieur (LIMSI-CNRS), France, from 1993 to 1999 and a member of the scientific staff at DaimlerChrysler, Research and Technology, Germany, from 2000 to 2002.

Yusaku Nakamura received the BE degree in 2001 from Toyohashi University of Technology, Japan. Since 2001, he has been pursuing his Masters degree at Toyohashi University of Technology. He is presently researching multimodal interaction.

Hermann Ney received the Diploma degree in Physics in 1977 from Göttingen University, Germany, and the Dr.-Ing. degree in Electrical Engineering in 1982 from Braunschweig University of Technology, Germany. He has been working in the field of speech recognition, natural language processing, and stochastic modelling for more than 20 years. In 1977, he joined Philips Research, Germany. In 1985, he was appointed Department Head. From 19988 to 1989, he was a Visiting Scientist at Bell Laboratories, Murray Hill, New Jersey. In 1993, he joined the Computer Science Department of Aachen University of Technology as a Professor.

Georg Niklfeld studied Computer Science at the TU Vienna, Linguistics/Philosophy at the University of Vienna, Austria, and Technology Management at UMIST, United Kingdom. He did research in natural language processing at ÖFAI and later was employed as development engineer at a telecom equipment manufacturer. Since 2001 he works at ftw. as Senior Researcher and Project Manager for speech processing for telecommunications applications.

Tsuneo Nitta received the BEE degree in 1969 and the Dr. Eng. degree in 1988, both from Tohoku University, Sendai, Japan. After engaging in research and development at R&D Center of Toshiba Corporation and Multimedia Engineering Laboratory, where he was a Chief Research Scientist, since 1998 he has been a Professor in Graduate School of Engineering, Toyohashi University of Technology, Japan. His current research interest includes speech recognition, multimodal interaction, and acquisition of language and concept.

Magnus Nordstrand has been a Researcher at Centre for Speech Technology at KTH in Stockholm since 2001, after MSc studies in Electrical Engineering at KTH. Basic research interests focus on facial animation and embodied conversational agents.

Sharon Oviatt is a Professor and Co-Director of the Center for Human-Computer Communication in the Department of Computer Science at the Oregon Health & Science University, USA. Her research focuses on human-computer interaction, spoken language and multimodal interfaces, and mobile and highly interactive systems. In the early 1990s, she was a pioneer in the area of pen/voice multimodal interfaces, which now are being developed widely to support map-based interactions on hand-held devices and next-generation smart phones.

Michael Phillips is the Chief Technology Officer and co-founder of SpeechWorks International. In the early 80s, he was a Researcher at Carnegie Mellon University, Pittsburgh, USA. In 1987, he joined the Spoken Language Systems group at MIT's Laboratory for Computer Science where he contributed to the development of one of the first systems to combine speech recognition and natural language processing technologies to allow users to carry on full conversations within limited domains. In 1994, he left MIT, and started SpeechWorks, licensing the technology from the group at MIT.

Roberto Pieraccini started his research on spoken language human-computer interaction in 1981 at CSELT (now Telecom Italia Lab), Torino, Italy. He then joined AT&T Bell Laboratories, Murray Hill, New Jersey, USA, in 1990 and AT&T Shannon Laboratories, Florham Park, New Jersey, in 1995. Since 1999 he is leading the Natural Dialog group at SpeechWorks International, New York.

Michael Pucher studied philosophy at the University of Vienna and computational logic at Vienna University of Technology, Austria. Since 2001 he has been working at ftw. as a Researcher. His current research interests are multimodal systems, speech synthesis and voice services for telecommunications.

Alexander Rudnicky is involved in research that spans many aspects of spoken language, including knowledge-based recognition systems, language modelling, architectures for spoken language systems, multimodal interaction, the design of speech interfaces and the rapid prototyping of speech-to-speech translation systems. His most recent work has been in spoken dialogue systems, with contributions to dialogue management, language generation and the computation of confidence metrics for recognition and understanding. He is a recipient of the Allen Newell Award for Research Excellence.

Sven Scheible studied communications engineering at the University of Applied Sciences in Ulm, Germany, where he obtained his Diploma in 1999. Since then, he has been working in the research department of Temic, Germany, for three years. During this time he joined the EU research project SENECA where he was responsible for the application development and system integration. Afterwards, he moved to the product development department and is currently responsible for tools supporting the grammar and dialogue implementation process.

Stephen Springer has over 19 years of experience in the design and implementation of intelligent language systems. He managed the Speech Services Technology Group at Bell Atlantic, where he worked with Victor Zue's Spoken Language System Group at MIT. At SpeechWorks International, he has designed enterprise systems that have handled over 10,000,000 calls, with transaction completion rates exceeding 95%. He leads the international User Interface Design team at SpeechWorks.

Janienke Sturm is a Researcher at the Department of Language and Speech of the University of Nijmegen. She graduated as computational linguist at the University of Utrecht, The Netherlands, in 1997. Since then her research focussed mainly on design and evaluation of spoken dialogue systems for information services.

Satoshi Tamura is a PhD candidate at Tokyo Institute of Technology (TIT), Japan. He received the ME degree in Information Science and Engineering from TIT in 2002. His research interests are speech information processing, especially multimodal audio-visual speech recognition.

Jacques Terken has a background in experimental psychology and received a PhD in 1985. He has conducted research on the production and perception of prosody and on the modelling of prosody for speech synthesis. Currently, his research interests include the application of speech for human-computer interaction, mainly in the context of multimodal interfaces.

Marilyn Walker is a Royal Society Wolfson Professor of Computer Science and Director of the Cognition and Interaction Lab at the University of Sheffield in England. Her research interests include the design and evaluation of dialogue systems and methods for automatically adapting such systems through experience with users. She received her PhD in Computer and Information Science from the University of Pennsylvania in 1993 and an MSc in Computer Science from Stanford University in 1988. Before coming to Sheffield, she was a Principal Research Scientist at AT&T Shannon Labs.

Matt Wesson is a Research Programmer at the Center for Human-Computer Communication (CHCC) in the Department of Computer Science at the Oregon Health & Science University (OHSU). He holds a BA in English and an MA in Computer Science.

Steve Whittaker is the Chair of the Information Retrieval Department at the University of Sheffield, United Kingdom. His main interests are in computer-mediated communication and human-computer interaction. He has designed and evaluated videoconferencing, email, voicemail, instant messaging, shared workspace and various other types of collaborative tools to support computer-mediated communication. He has also conducted extensive research into systems to support multimodal interaction, including speech browsing and multimodal mobile information access.

Eric Woudenberg began work in speech recognition at ATR, Kyoto, Japan, in 1993. He joined Bell Laboratories, Murray Hill, New Jersey, USA, in 1998, and SpeechWorks International, New York, in 2000. Since 2002 he has been a senior developer at LOBBY7, Boston, working on commercially deployable multimodal systems.

Hirobumi Yamada received the BE degree in 1993 and the PhD degree in 2002 from Shinshu University, Japan. He joined Toyohashi University of Technology as a Research Associate in 1996. His current interests are in multimodal interaction, E-learning systems and pattern recognition.

Introduction

Spoken multimodal human-computer interfaces constitute an emerging topic of interest not only to academia but also to industry. The ongoing migration of computing and information access from the desktop and telephone to mobile computing devices such as Personal Digital Assistants (PDAs), tablet PCs, and next generation mobile phones poses critical challenges for natural human-computer interaction. Spoken dialogue is a key factor in ensuring natural and user-friendly interaction with such devices which are meant for everybody. Speech is well-known to all of us and supports hands-free and eyes-free interaction, which is crucial, e.g. in cars where driver distraction by manually operated devices may be a significant problem. Being a key issue, non-intrusive and user-friendly human-computer interaction in mobile environments is discussed by several chapters in this book.

Many and increasingly sophisticated over-the-phone spoken dialogue systems providing various kinds of information are already commercially available. On the research side interest is progressively turning to the integration of spoken dialogue with other modalities such as gesture input and graphics output. This process is ongoing both regarding applications running on stationary computers and those meant for mobile devices. The latter is witnessed by many of the included chapters.

In mobile environments where the situation and context of use is likely to vary, speech-only interaction may sometimes be the optimal solution while in other situations the possibility of using other modalities possibly in combination with speech, such as graphics output and gesture input, may be preferable.

Users who interact with multimodal devices may benefit from the availability of different modalities in several ways. For instance, modalities may supplement each other and compensate for each others' weaknesses, a certain modality may be inappropriate in some situations but the device and its applications can then still be used via another modality, and users' different preferences as to which modalities they use can be accommodated by offering different modalities for interaction. Issues like these are also discussed in several of the included chapters in particular in those dealing with usability and evaluation issues.

We have found it appropriate to divide the book into three parts each being introduced by an overview chapter. Each chapter in a part has a main emphasis on issues within the area covered by that part. Part one covers issues in multimodal spoken dialogue systems and components, part two concerns system architecture and example implementations, and part three addresses evaluation and usability. The division is not a sharp one, however. Several chapters include a discussion of issues that would make them fit almost equally well under another part. In the remainder of this introduction, we provide an overview of the three parts of the book and their respective chapters.

Issues in Multimodal Dialogue Systems and Components. The first part of the book provides an overview of multimodal dialogue systems and discusses aspects of speech recognition, dialogue management including domain reasoning and inference, and multimodal output generation. By a *multimodal* dialogue system we understand a system where the user may use more than one modality for input representation and/or the system may use more than one modality for output representation, e.g. input speech and gesture or output speech and graphics.

In his overview chapter Rudnicky discusses multimodal dialogue systems and gives a bird's-eye view of the other chapters in this part. He discerns a number of issues that represent challenges across individual systems and thus are important points on the agenda of today's research in multimodal dialogue systems. These issues include the detection of intentional user input, the appropriate use of interaction modalities, the management of dialogue history and context, the incorporation of intelligence into the system in the form of domain reasoning, and finally, the problem of appropriate output planning.

On the input side speech recognition represents a key technique for interaction, not least in ubiquitous and wearable computing environments. For the use of speech recognition to be successful in such environments, interaction must be smooth, unobtrusive, and effortless to the user. Among other things this requires robust recognition also when the user is in a noisy environment.

Two chapters in this part deal with the robustness issue of speech recognition systems. Furui provides an overview of the state-of-the-art in speech recognition. Moreover, he addresses two major application areas of speech recognition technology. One application area is that of dialogue systems. The user speaks to a system e.g. to access information. A second major area using speech technology is that of systems for transcription, understanding, and summarisation of speech documents, e.g. meeting minute transcription systems. Furui discusses the very important issue of how to enhance the robustness of speech recognisers facing acoustic and linguistic variation in spontaneous speech. To this end he proposes a paradigm shift from speech recognition to speech understanding so that the recognition process rather delivers the meaning of the user's input than a word to word transcription.

Tamura et al. discuss audio-visual speech recognition, a method that draws not only on the speech signal but also takes visual information, such as lip movements, into account. This approach seems promising in improving speech recognition accuracy not least in noisy environments. The authors propose a multimodal speech recognition method using optical flow analysis to extract visual information. The robustness of the method to acoustic and visual noises has been evaluated in two experiments. In the first experiment white noise was added to the speech wave form. In the second experiment data from a car was used. The data was distorted acoustically as well as visually. In both experiments significantly better results were achieved using audio-visual speech recognition compared to using only audio recognition.

The next two chapters in this part by Macherey and Ney and Bühler and Minker focus on aspects of dialogue management. Ideally dialogue managers should be application-independent. To achieve this, one must, according to Macherey and Ney, distill the steps which many domains have in common leading to parameterisable data structures. Macherey and Ney propose trees as an appropriate way in which to represent such data structures. Using a tree-based structure the focus of the chapter is on dialogue course management, dialogue cost features, and the selection of dialogue actions. Based on proposed cost functions the dialogue manager should in each state be able to choose those actions which are likely to lead as directly as possible through the tree to the user's goal. Encouraging results are presented from evaluating an implemented tree-based dialogue manager in a telephone directory assistance setting.

Bühler and Minker present a logic-based problem assistant, i.e. a reasoning component which interacts with and supports dialogue management. The problem assistant constantly draws on various contextual information and constraints. In case of conflicts between new constraints provided by the user and information already in the system, the problem assistent informs the dialogue manager about its inferences. Thereby it enables the dialogue manager to explain the problem to the user and possibly propose solutions to it. The functionality of the problem assistant is illustrated on calendar planning using a scenario in which a user plans a series of meeting appointments in various locations.

The last chapter in part one concerns multimodal output generation. Beskow et al. present a formalism for GEneric System Output Markup (GESOM) of verbal and non-verbal output. The idea is that the dialogue manager will use the markup formalism to annotate the output to be produced to the user next.

The markup provides information about the communicative functions of output but it does not contain details on how these are to be realised. The details of rendering are encapsulated in a generation component, allowing the dialogue manager to generate fairly abstract requests for output which are then rendered using the relevant and available output devices. This is valuable both for applications that operate over a variety of output devices and also for developers who no longer need to spend time coding details of generation. The markup formalism has been used in an animated talking head in the Swedish real-estate AdApt system. The use of GESOM in this system is also discussed in the chapter.

System Architecture and Example Implementations. The second part of the book discusses architectural issues in system design and example implementations. Most existing implementations of multimodal and unimodal dialogue systems are based on architectural infrastructures that allow for a distribution of computation between host computers, operating systems, and programming languages. With multimodal dialogue systems evolving from speech-only server-based systems, such as call centre automation systems, to personal multimodal and mobile interaction partners, such as PDAs and mobile phones, a new dimension of requirements is being placed on the underlying architectures.

The overview chapter by Kellner presents an analysis of these requirements and applies it to two particular system architectures, the Galaxy Communicator infrastructure used by the US American DARPA (Defence Research Project Agency) Community and the SmartKom testbed that served as a basis for a German national research project where partners from university and industry were involved. The common goal of both of these frameworks is to integrate several independently developed modules into one coherent system. Multimodality and cooperative behaviour are key factors, requiring the base architectures to provide a more sophisticated handling of streams of information than those used for implementing traditional telephone-based systems. Related to this comparison, an overview of existing and emerging standards for speech-enabled applications, such as VoiceXML and SALT, is given. Kellner also pays attention to a second emerging requirement, namely, the need to enable the user to access and combine different applications through a coherent user interface (e.g., using an assistant metaphor impersonated as an avatar.)

As claimed by Katsurada et al. in their chapter multimodal dialogue systems, in particular those being used in different environments or on hardware as distinct as PCs, PDAs, and mobile phones, require abstractions from traditional presentation management techniques, such as hypertext (HTML). These abstractions should enable a developer to describe modalities more flexibly, so that it becomes possible to add or modify modalities as needed when porting an application to new devices supporting new types of modalities. Ideally, application logic that is not modality-dependent should be reusable on all devices. To this end, a modality-independent Man-Machine Interface (MMI) description language called XISL (eXtensible Interaction Scenario Language) is proposed. The authors describe the implementation of three execution environments for XISL: a PC terminal, a mobile phone terminal, and a PDA terminal. The PC and the PDA feature multimodal interaction via touch screen, keyboard, and audio device, while the phone uses speech and Dual Tone Multi-Frequency (DTMF).

Mobile terminal capabilities seem especially relevant since appealing applications and services are necessary to convince industrial developers and device manufacturers of the possibilities for the commercial exploitation of multimodal interfaces. As described in the chapter by Niklfeld et al., these interfaces must be tailored to the specific capabilities and limitations of the *end* device, which is particularly important for mobile phones that may be based on different standards such as GPRS, UMTS, or WLAN. It is shown that multimodality can indeed bring about usability advantages for specific applications, such as a map service.

Pieraccini et al. also discuss the various issues related particularly to the design and implementation of multimodal dialogue systems with wireless handheld devices. Focus is on the design of a usable interface that exploits the complementary features of the audio and visual channels to enhance usability. One aspect arising from the mobility of the user is the fact that the handheld devices could potentially be used in a variety of different situations in which certain channels are or are not preferred. Pieraccini et al. present two implementations of client-server architectures demonstrated by map and navigation applications.

Also dealing with map interaction and navigation as an application of multimodal interaction, the chapter by Bühler and Minker presents the mobile scenario of the SmartKom project. Like Pieraccini et al. the authors focus on a specific issue in mobile multimodal dialogue systems, namely the required ability of the system to dynamically adapt itself or be adaptable by the user to the current environment of use in terms of the modalities used for interaction. The authors present situations in SmartKom's integrated driver and pedestrian scenario in which the user might want to change the modalities used by the system, or in which the system might decide to enable or disable certain channels. From a developer's point of view this is also related to the modality-independent MMI description language presented in the chapter by Katsurada et al., but the focus is on different mobile situations of use of one device rather than on the use of a single application on different devices.

Finally, the required adaptations of a dialogue system when porting it to a new application domain and environment of use is also investigated in the chapter by Bohus and Rudnicky. The intended use of a dialogue system as an aircraft maintenance and repair assistant requires major adaptations and adjustments of existing dialogue technologies, originally developed for telephone-based problem solving. Multimodality constitutes an important factor in this development process. Results from two field evaluations of the maintenance and repair system are reported.

Evaluation and Usability. The chapters in the third and last part of the book have a main focus on evaluation and usability issues. Evaluation and usability of dialogue systems, unimodal as well as multimodal, are as crucial as ever, and the importance is likely to increase along with the technical advances and market growth in the field. The chapters included here give an impression of some of the research challenges being addressed today and some which will soon need our attention.

Dybkjær et al. provide an overview of the state-of-the-art in evaluation and usability and review a number of initiatives with a main focus on evaluation and/or usability. In addition they point to a number of challenges ahead. Clearly there has been significant progress on unimodal dialogue systems evaluation and usability. However, the emergence of, among others, multimodal, mobile, and non-task-oriented systems pose entirely new challenges. For instance we need to address issues such as online user modelling, emotions, non-task-oriented dialogue, mobile environments, and user preferences and priorities in interaction. These issues are important to the usability of many future and emerging systems and must of course also be evaluated. A major challenge is in realising these issues in appropriate ways in systems and in finding adequate ways in which to evaluate them.

Some of the challenges mentioned by Dybkjær et al. are addressed in more detail by other chapters in this part of the book. User models are addressed both by Whittaker and Walker and by Bernsen and Dybkjær. Mobile environments are mentioned by all chapters but are central to the applications in Bernsen and Dybkjær, Minker et al., Geldof and Dale, Sturm et al., and Jameson and Klöckner. The ability to take into account user preferences and priorities is of course central to user models but aspects of the issue are also discussed in the chapters by Sturm et al. and Jameson and Klöckner and to some extent by Geldof and Dale. An important issue is that of adaptability. To which extent will users naturally adapt to the system and in which ways must the system be able to adapt to users in order to be accepted? This question is touched upon by most chapters in this part but most clearly in Sturm et al., Jameson and Klöckner, and Oviatt et al.

The chapter by Whittaker and Walker addresses the problem of how to select the most relevant options to mention and what to say about them when the task domain is complex as in restaurant information. The hypothesis is that a user model may be an adequate solution to the problem. Results from a Wizard-of-Oz experiment showed that interaction strategies tailored to user requirements and which reduce dialogue length are preferable. In a subsequent experiment subjects overheard dialogues about restaurant selection and provided information quality judgements for each dialogue. Dialogues with individual user models scored higher than those with a default user model.

Bernsen and Dybkjær discuss four user-oriented design analysis problems in the context of a research prototype of an in-car system. The prototype is multimodal and accepts input via speech and via a push-to-activate button which will activate speech recognition. Output is provided in terms of speech and on the in-car display. The prototype enables navigation assistance to addresses and to points of interest and hotel reservation. The problems addressed concern when the system should (not) listen, how to optimise use of the display, driver identification, and online adaptive user modelling. Possible solutions to these four problems are proposed and discussed regarding their pros and cons.

Like Bernsen and Dybkjær, Minker et al. address in-vehicle applications. They describe a spoken command-based user interface for telephone and navigation applications. The system can be operated via speech or manually either via input from a remote control (for navigation) or by using the keypad on the phone. Among the topics addressed in the chapter is the evaluation of the system with users who were driving while carrying out various tasks given to them. The evaluation showed that speech input was faster, driving skills were in general less affected by speech input, and users preferred speech input due to e.g., better safety and comfort and less distraction. However, task completion rate was considerably lower with speech input compared to manual input the main reason being forgotten command words and use of out-of-vocabulary words.

Geldof and Dale also address navigation though not as an in-car application. They focus on route descriptions via mobile devices and how to present the descriptions in an adequate way. The descriptions must be recognisable and rememberable and the small screen size of mobile devices must be taken into account. The approach proposed is to summarise the route description. This description can then be expanded in a tree-like way to provide more detail if desired by the user. The approach has been evaluated and compared to a route description representation in terms of a flat numbered list of instructions. The evaluation was performed in a car. Three teams on half of the route used the tree representation while for the other half of the route the list representation was used. Two teams preferred the tree structure while one team preferred the list structure.

Sturm et al. present experience from a study on users' development of interaction patterns over time. The system used in the study is a train timetable information system designed for small portable devices. The system accepts spoken and pointing input and provides spoken and graphics output. After an introduction subjects completed six scenarios as a pre-test. Then they practised for a couple of hours in total divided on different days. In a post-test the first six scenarios were carried out again. Evaluation showed that while effectiveness (measured as dialogue success rate) was not really affected, efficiency (measured as task completion time) clearly improved over time and interaction patterns changed. For instance, the users learned how to speak to the system, how to use pointing for more reliable data entry and error correction, and how to speed up interaction in various ways.

Jameson and Klöckner discuss the implications of user multitasking for the design of mobile multimodal systems. They address the tasks of using a mobile phone while walking. Eye-based dialling and ear-based dialling are analysed theoretically, and possible resource conflicts are pointed out when adding the task of walking. In an experiment subjects were asked to walk around in a room with several obstacles while calling different phone numbers and talking to those who answered the call. Half of them used eye-based dialling, one used ear-based dialling, while two used a hybrid approach. Several different subjective factors seemed to influence their preferences, such as habits from other tasks, dislikes related to design, and ideas of what is socially acceptable. A conclusion of the chapter is that the observed factors may be hard to be aware of and design for but nevertheless need attention since they seem crucial to user acceptance.

In the final chapter of this part, Oviatt et al. investigate to which extent the basic acoustic-prosodic features of users' speech are influenced by text-to-speech (TTS). Young children interacted for an hour each with animated marine animals. In addition to spoken input and output the system enabled pen-based input and graphics output. The output voices were tailored to represent opposite ends of the introvert-extrovert personality spectrum. Amplitude, duration, and dialogue response latencies were measured. Good convergence with the TTS voice was found: When exposed to an extrovert voice, the children increased their amplitude and decreased utterance duration and dialogue response latencies, and contrarily, when interacting with an introvert voice. The hope is that future systems may be able to guide users' speech to fall within a range that is easily processed by the recogniser without any explicit instructions to users.

I

ISSUES IN MULTIMODAL SPOKEN DIALOGUE SYSTEMS AND COMPONENTS

Chapter 1

MULTIMODAL DIALOGUE SYSTEMS

Alexander I. Rudnicky
Carnegie Mellon University, Pittsburgh, Pennsylvania, USA
air@cs.cmu.edu

Abstract Multimodal systems are moving to the centre-stage of dialogue research, reflecting the maturing of component technologies and the recognition that "interface" per se may not be the best way to describe the functionality of such systems. Rather they are emerging as full communications systems, with a corresponding rich set of expressive capabilities.

Keywords: Modes and modalities; Context; Intention learning and adaptation.

1. Introduction

Multimodal interfaces allow humans to create inputs for a machine in a natural and concise form using the mode or mixture of modes that most precisely convey the intended meaning and to adjust this mix to reflect communication needs. For example, specifying a travel destination is most easily done by voice, but describing the shape of an object, especially an irregular one, is more easily done by gesture. Embedding such inputs in a consistent sequence of interactions, a dialogue, produces a rich conversation that might otherwise be difficult to carry out with the same degree of efficiency using any single mode. One could even say that true communication is only possible when human (and machine) expression is allowed to range over multiple modes, optimally matching the needs of the communication to the modes available.

Having made this observation, we are still left with the problem of understanding what principles might govern multimodal communication and how these principles might be reduced to practice. The papers in this section present a cross-section of work in the area of multimodal dialogue systems that attempt to address this question. While each application area presents the researcher with its own unique set of challenges we can nevertheless discern a number of common themes that cut across individual system building efforts. These com-

W. Minker, D. Bühler and L. Dybkjær (eds), Spoken Multimodal Human-Computer Dialogue in Mobile Environments, 3-11

monalities could be understood to define the agenda for contemporary research in multimodal dialogue.

2. Varieties of Multimodal Dialogue

The term "multimodal" can have several meanings. It is useful to keep these distinct. The papers in this section mostly understand multimodal to refer to interfaces that provide the human with the opportunity to produce multiple separate input streams; for example voice and gesture. As implemented in such systems the streams are under the voluntary control of the user, in the sense that the human, in the process of composing an input, will have the option of consciously deciding to use one or the other or a combination of modes to formulate an input that is appropriate for a particular situation.

But the term multimodal can also be used to describe other types of inputs that humans naturally produce in the process of communication. For example, we can also understand multimodal in terms of recognition that takes in *multiple coordinate streams* of information generated by the user, not necessarily by conscious choice. For example, in addition to voice, lip movement can be tracked and used to improve the accuracy of interpretation since information in each stream is generated by the same underlying process and each contributes coordinated evidence about the operation of that process. (Tamura et al., 2004) describe a system that integrates speech and image processing to improve recognition under difficult conditions. We might also think of *virtual streams* of information that can be derived from the same physical signal through additional processing but are not usually thought of by the user as independently manipulable components of the input. For example a voice can include, in addition to its conscious linguistic content, prosodic or emotional information which if extracted allows more precise interpretation of the speaker's intent. We might furthermore consider *independent streams* of information that are only loosely related to an ongoing communication act, but that provide information useful for interpreting the user's intended communication. An example of this might be a user location in a room, say in front of a particular device, or their movements within a space, each of which can be used to more precisely interpret the meaning of an input.

The papers in this section focus primarily on the first sense of multimodal, the conscious choice on the part of the user to generate a communication using one or more available input modes, in either a coordinate or complementary relationship.

All implementations of multimodal dialogue systems need to address similar issues, but the needs of each particular application place stress on unique issues. It is useful to consider the chapters in this section in terms of which aspects of multimodal dialogue that the authors have chosen to focus on. Figure 1 shows an abstract model of a multimodal system and notes which aspects are addressed in the papers (see caption for key). The components should be familiar to most practitioners in the field, yet reviewing the diagram is a useful exercise, as it helps us understand which aspects currently attract the greatest research interest. The first thing to note is that, with the exception of the first one, the current papers do not focus on the details of the recognition and rendering technologies (recognition and synthesis) that provide the surface of the interface. It is notable that these technologies, although not perfected, are for the most part sufficiently mature so that they can be treated as black boxes in the design of multimodal systems. The internal operation of these components may still be of interest, but they do not need to be created anew for a particular application, allowing researchers to concentrate on other components and on system architecture.

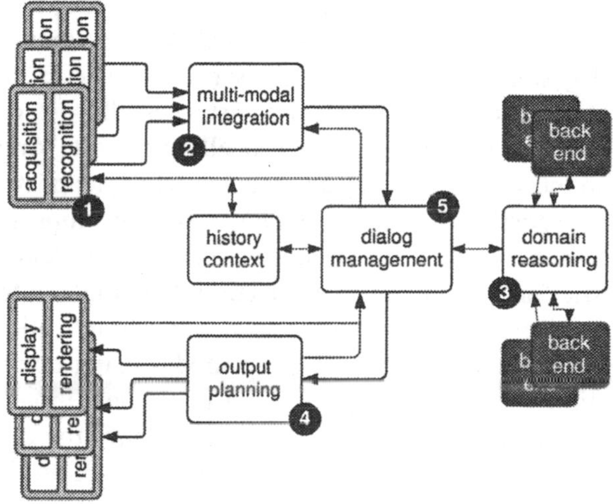

Figure 1. An abstract multimodal dialogue system. Solid lines indicate major data paths; dotted lines indicate feedback paths. The round numerals locate the work described in the papers in this section. These are as follows: 1) (Furui, 2004), 2) (Tamura et al., 2004), 3) (Bühler and Minker, 2004), 4) (Beskow et al., 2004), 5) (Macherey and Ney, 2004). The locations refer to the thrust of the paper in the present volume, though in fact all authors work with complete systems.

While the papers in this section represent work addressing problems in diverse application domains, we nevertheless can see several common themes emerging. The following sections discuss these in greater detail.

3. Detecting Intentional User Inputs

Voice, and to some extent gesture, inputs can be produced without any actual physical contact between the user and a device. Moreover a particular behaviour on the part of the user (such as a vocalisation) may or may not be intended as a conscious input to the system, as the user's intention in this respect is not directly observable by the system. This is unlike the case where a deliberate physical contact (with a keyboard, touch panel) unambiguously signals the intent to input. In some sense, there is no complete solution to this problem that does not presuppose that the system has complete awareness of the context of interaction and of the user's intention. Such a rich capability is likely far off in the future if at all achievable. Nevertheless researchers are currently starting to explore the use of certain physical cues, such as gaze, as evidence for the user's intent.

In practice most systems solve the problem of identifying intentional input by implementing some form of push-to-talk activation or require some comparable physical gesture on the part of the user to indicate to the system that a speech input is about to occur. If the circumstances allow it, continuous listening can be used. For example, a noise cancelling close-talking microphone can minimise the intrusion of extraneous sounds, while adaptive modelling of user speech characteristics can further minimise spurious inputs. But the user him or herself can also generate extraneous vocalisations and therefore microphone properties and adaptive voice detection do not guarantee robustness. Additional mechanisms might be implemented, for example allowing the user to explicitly toggle between listen and sleep modes using commands, or requiring an attention word prefix for signalling intentional input. While these are practical solutions to the problem at hand, they have the disadvantage of requiring additional conscious acts by the user. These add to the complexity of the interface and to the cognitive load imposed on the user. Humans on the other hand appear to deal with such problems with relative ease by what appears to be a superior grasp (relative to machines) of the broader context of interaction and also by their superior ability to detect and recover from errors of interpretation. Some of these themes are further discussed in the chapter by (Furui, 2004).

Effective communication requires the active participation of two (or more) skilled actors who take joint responsibility for maintaining the integrity of the channel. Current systems mostly shift this responsibility to the human. The challenge is to have machines assume increasing responsibility and to be able to do so robustly.

4. Modes and Modalities

Equipping an application with multiple input modes does not automatically define how these modes will be used in practice. Depending on circumstances and the nature of the user's activity, different modalities of use can be observed (or, alternately, seem desirable for systems to enforce). For example, in noisy environments speech is not always the best input mode and so gesture becomes preferred because of the robustness it affords. The structure of a user's task can dictate a particularly efficient mapping of mode to task component: voice may be preferable for entering constraints for searching in a database while gesture may be preferable for selecting among the retrieved items.

While it is extremely useful to understand the role that different modalities play in the interface, it is not immediately clear whether current systems need to explicitly keep track of different modalities, or explicitly model modality-specific interaction. It may be sufficient and probably desirable for systems to support different redundant modes and allow the user to select input modes and combinations depending on their needs and on the circumstances in which the application is being used (neither of which is easy for the developer to predict with sufficient accuracy). Certainly we can presume that the user has a much fuller grasp of the context that the system is being used in and can make decisions that are more optimal than those of an automatic process. In the longer term the challenge is for machines to become aware of modality affordances and to use this knowledge to provide a better interface. Adaptation or learning-based solutions seem most likely to succeed.

5. History and Context

Underlying all dialogue systems is some notion of context, for "dialogue" implies a sequence of related inputs and outputs that build shared meaning between human and computer and individually reference this shared meaning. In some systems, the context is implicit in the current state, for example in graph-based (directed dialogue) systems. In other systems, separate data structures are used. We can also define context in terms that go beyond the sequence of inputs and outputs of the dialogue itself and take into consideration dynamic properties of the environment in which the system is being used. The personal history of the individual is yet another important element. This is particularly true for a device that is owned (such as a speech system in a car) as opposed to one that is public (such as a telephone- or kiosk-based service). An individual's history of interaction with a device can be an extremely valuable source of information and can be used to improve different aspects of system performance: information about an individual voice can be used to adapt acoustic models to produce better recognition, information about the pattern of language use can be used to tune grammars and increase understanding, information about common tasks sequences and parameter-setting preferences can be used to anticipate user requests and produce more efficient execution.

A particular challenge for research in multimodal interfaces is the development of platforms and environments that allow realistic investigation of history mechanisms since often research systems are built in prototype form only. Implementing and studying history mechanisms implies having systems that people use repeatedly over time as part of their routine activities. This in turn implies robust prototypes that, even at baseline, provide sufficient value to a user to motivate extended use. Such applications have proven surprisingly difficult to identify.

6. Domain Reasoning

Language-based interfaces, including multimodal interfaces, implicitly mediate between user goals and system actions. Doing so correctly implies the existence of two processes. First the user's input must be correctly understood (that is: the speech must be recognised, the gestures interpreted, and information from different modes, as well as context, fused into a unified understanding of the input). Second this understanding must be correctly related to entities in the domain and the appropriate action taken. The papers in this section do not directly address the former problem, although it is key to creating a working system. However (Bühler and Minker, 2004), address the latter problem and find that they need to introduce mechanisms, such as a planning component and an explicit ontology, that allow a system to represent the information in a domain (its objects and relationships) and to compute over this information. Doing so gives his system the ability to dynamically react to user requests that propose novel (or at least not otherwise anticipated by the developer) behaviour sequences. The ability to do so means that developers are not obligated to code these behaviours individually. This decreases the cost of implementation both for domain-specific behaviours and for dialogue structure. From the user's perspective this permits systems to react appropriately to domain complexity, increasing the system's value.

We could consider an alternative approach in which the system learns by observation of user behaviour and through instruction by the user. While potentially burdensome for the user such an approach does exhibit the virtue of creating domain knowledge that is tailored to the needs of a particular user. There may be additional value in such a process: We might imagine a situation where devices of a particular class, owned by different individuals, "share" information about users and their activities and collectively improve the quality of the interface while reducing the training burden on any one user.

7. Output Planning

Effective communication supposes that the system is capable of generating output that advances the conversation and brings both the system and the user closer to their respective goals. This is an issue in all dialogue systems: having the system produce responses that are appropriate to the current context and that give the user the right information for moving the dialogue forward. The problem becomes more complex when the system has available to it several equivalent ways of producing an output, or when the exact generation options are not known beforehand. A dialogue system that simply reads the contents of a display screen to the user is not of much use—the user can more rapidly read the display on their own or better yet search for and focus on those portions that contain information most relevant to the purpose at hand. In these cases, the role of speech output should probably be that of a second parallel channel that provides additional information. For example it can be used to draw attention to critical information, to summarise the contents of an extensive display or to provide alerts. Minimally the user needs to be given control of the channel since there will be situations (such as eyes-busy) in which the user would request a reading of the display. Better yet would be a system that can model the user and the context so as to proactively select the output style of greatest predicted utility for a particular situation.

(Beskow et al., 2004) address this problem on a general level and consider situations in which multiple output channels may be available to the system and where the system developer may not have control of which of these channels are actually available at run-time. The details of rendering are encapsulated in a generation component, allowing the dialogue manager to generate fairly abstract requests for output which are then rendered using the available output devices. This is valuable both for applications that operate over a variety of output devices and also for developers who no longer need to spend time coding details of generation. Learning and adaptation could also be of use here: the system could monitor the success of its presentation strategy and adjust it as necessary to improve communication.

8. Dialogue Management

A dialogue manager accepts a stream of semanticised inputs from the user, computes over them, and formulates actions and replies. Computation may involve interaction with a back-end component (the "application" proper) or the use of information about the user or about the task that can be found in the history of the interaction. Dialogue management may also involve more direct interaction with lower-level processes in the system. For example, biasing the speech recogniser's language model to reflect dialogue state, or accepting information about what portions of spoken output were actually heard by the user (in the case of barge-ins). Dialogue management plays a central role in these systems since this component critically influences overall system behaviour.

But dialogue managers are difficult to implement. One solution has been to emphasise dialogue manager architectures that enforce a clear separation between an execution engine, specifications for discourse behaviour and specifications for domain-specific behaviour. Ideally only the domain-specific behaviour should have to be specified during implementation of an application. The execution engine then acts as an interpreter for this information and as well provides a set of general procedures (such as confirmation dialogues) that together generate final system behaviour. (Macherey and Ney, 2004) provide an example of such a scheme that uses a uniform domain representation in the form of trees and provides a heuristic that drives a dialogue to resolution solely on the basis of tree properties. (Bühler and Minker, 2004) focuses on the problem of dynamically computing the anticipated structure of a dialogue based on the state of the back-end. Dynamic computation is particularly crucial in domains whose state changes over time (or as a result of a previous input) or for systems that can generate, either autonomously or in collaboration with the user, a rich variety of plans. Broadly speaking, different approaches have tried either to introduce an explicit reasoning component that automatically generates successive steps of a dialogue or have attempted to design task and dialogue representations that by virtue of their structure produce the desired sequence of interactions. It is not clear as yet which approach will in the long run be the most successful one; one suspects that the latter solution would be preferable, as it subsumes explicit reasoning.

9. Conclusion

If a single overall theme emerges from the papers in this section it is the need to find techniques that allow us to automatically create application-specific knowledge, including detailed dialogue structure, domain reasoning components and adaptation to the characteristics of individual users. Automatic learning techniques are needed because there is simply too much knowledge to manually encode for applications of even moderate complexity, and human effort and expertise are hard to come by. Multimodal systems that learn and adapt remain the grand challenge for the field.

Acknowledgements

I would like to thank the anonymous reviewers of an earlier draft of this chapter for their insightful comments.

References

Beskow, J., Edlund, J., and Nordstrand, M. (2004). A model for multimodal dialogue system output applied to an animated talking head. In Minker, W., Bühler, D., and Dybkjær, L., editors, *Spoken Multimodal Human-Computer Dialogue in Mobile Environments*. Kluwer Academic Publishers, Dordrecht, The Netherlands. (this volume).

Bühler, D. and Minker, W. (2004). A reasoning component for information-seeking and planning dialogues. In Minker, W., Bühler, D., and Dybkjær, L., editors, *Spoken Multimodal Human-Computer Dialogue in Mobile Environments*. Kluwer Academic Publishers, Dordrecht, The Netherlands. (this volume).

Furui, S. (2004). Speech recognition technology in multimodal/ubiquitous computing environments. In Minker, W., Bühler, D., and Dybkjær, L., editors, *Spoken Multimodal Human-Computer Dialogue in Mobile Environments*. Kluwer Academic Publishers, Dordrecht, The Netherlands. (this volume).

Macherey, K. and Ney, H. (2004). Feature functions for tree-based dialogue course management. In Minker, W., Bühler, D., and Dybkjær, L., editors, *Spoken Multimodal Human-Computer Dialogue in Mobile Environments*. Kluwer Academic Publishers, Dordrecht, The Netherlands. (this volume).

Tamura, S., Iwano, K., and Furui, S. (2004). A robust multimodal speech recognition method using optical flow analysis. In Minker, W., Bühler, D., and Dybkjær, L., editors, *Spoken Multimodal Human-Computer Dialogue in Mobile Environments*. Kluwer Academic Publishers, Dordrecht, The Netherlands. (this volume).

Chapter 2

SPEECH RECOGNITION TECHNOLOGY IN MULTIMODAL/UBIQUITOUS COMPUTING ENVIRONMENTS

Sadaoki Furui
Tokyo Institute of Technology, Department of Computer Science, Tokyo, Japan
furui@cs.titech.ac.jp

Abstract In the ubiquitous (pervasive) computing era, it is expected that everybody will access information services anytime anywhere, and these services are expected to augment various human intelligent activities. Speech recognition technology can play an important role in this era by providing: (a) conversational systems for accessing information services and (b) systems for transcribing, understanding and summarising ubiquitous speech documents such as meetings, lectures, presentations and voicemails. In the former systems, robust conversation using wireless handheld/hands-free devices in the real mobile computing environment will be crucial, as will multimodal speech recognition technology. To create the latter systems, the ability to understand and summarise speech documents is one of the key requirements. This chapter presents technological perspectives and introduces several research activities being conducted from these standpoints.

Keywords: Speech understanding; Speech summarisation; Human-computer interaction; Robustness; Adaptation; Spontaneous speech.

1. Ubiquitous/Wearable Computing Environment

The continuing progress in hardware and software development technologies have lead to the augmentation of computer performance at such a rapid pace that it improves several hundred times in every 10-year period. Resultingly, computers are getting smaller, more powerful and cheaper. Regardless of whether and to what degree they are noticed by users, computers will proliferate into every facet of our daily lives. People will actually walk through their day-to-day lives wearing several computers at a time. Thus, making com-

W. Minker, D. Bühler and L. Dybkjær (eds), Spoken Multimodal Human-Computer Dialogue in Mobile Environments, 13-36

puters mobile and portable, exemplified by the present PDA (personal digital assistant) technology, is considered to be the transition phase to wearable computing (Pentland, 1998). Making computers more functional and smaller will generate not only quantitative changes but also qualitative changes in the way we use computers. In the near future, various computers including portable equipment existing everywhere will work together in autonomous collaboration (Weiser, 1991). Indeed, the new characteristics of computing will greatly change the focus and approach of human-computer interaction.

The transmission channel capacity of portable terminals will be easily expanded to the level of several Mbps, taking advantage of the technological progress available through, for example, MMAC (Multimedia Mobile Access Communication) systems. The exchange of dynamic information will be possible in addition to that of simple characters and voice information. In turn, this will give rise to sophisticated collaboration and coordination of human-machine systems based on autonomous protocol and information exchange between computers distributed everywhere.

2. State-of-the-Art Speech Recognition Technology

Speech is the primary, and the most convenient means of communication between people (Juang and Furui, 2000). Therefore, speech recognition systems are expected to play important roles in the ubiquitous/wearable computing environment (Furui, 2000b). The field of automatic speech recognition has witnessed a number of significant advances in the past 5-10 years, spurred on by advances in signal processing, algorithms, computational architectures, and hardware. These advances include the widespread adoption of a statistical pattern recognition paradigm, a data-driven approach which makes use of a rich set of speech utterances from a large population of speakers, the use of stochastic-based acoustic and language modelling, and the use of dynamic programming-based search methods (Juang and Furui, 2000; Rabiner and Juang, 1993; Furui, 2001; Furui, 2000a). Major applications of speech recognition technology can be classified into (a) conversational systems for accessing information services and (b) systems for transcribing, understanding and summarising ubiquitous speech documents such as meetings, lectures, presentations and voicemails.

Figure 1 shows a mechanism of state-of-the-art speech recognisers (Ney, 1997). Common features of these systems are the use of cepstral parameters and their regression coefficients as speech features, triphone HMMs as acoustic models, vocabularies of several thousand or several tens of thousand entries, and stochastic language models such as bigrams and trigrams. A word sequence, $w_1, \cdots, w_k$, which maximises the a posteriori probability is selected as a recognition result. Such methods have been applied not only to English but also to French, German, Italian, Japanese and many other languages. Although there are several language-specific characteristics, similar recognition results have been obtained.

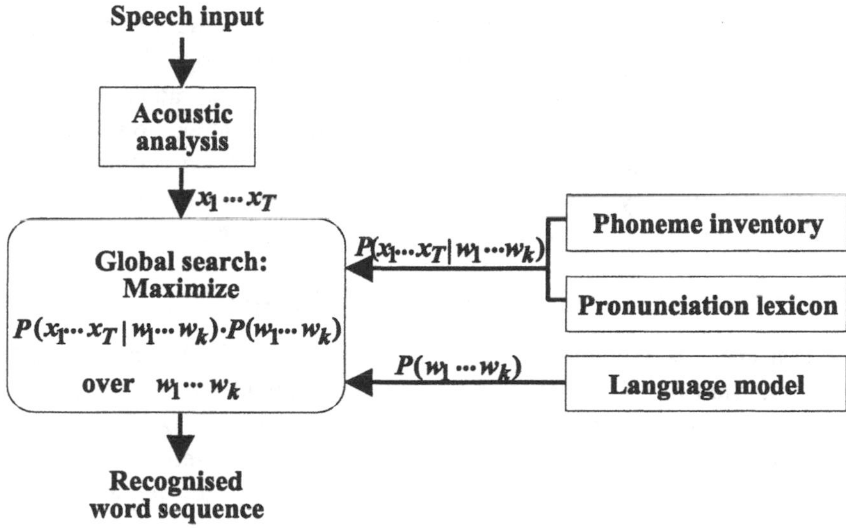

Figure 1. Mechanism of state-of-the-art speech recognisers.

Ultimately, speech recognition systems should be capable of robust, speaker-independent or speaker-adaptive, continuous speech recognition. It is crucial to establish methods that are robust against voice variation due to individuality, the physical and psychological condition of the speaker, telephone sets, microphones, network characteristics, additive background noise, speaking styles, and other aspects. Also important is for the systems to impose few restrictions on tasks and vocabulary. Developing automatic adaptation techniques is essential to resolve these problems (Furui, 1997).

Another important issue for speech recognition is how to create language models (rules) for spontaneous speech. When recognising spontaneous speech both in dialogues or monologues, it is necessary to deal with variations that are not encountered when recognising speech that is read from texts. These variations include extraneous words, out-of-vocabulary words, ungrammatical sentences, disfluency, partial words, repairs, hesitations, and repetitions. It is crucial to develop robust and flexible parsing algorithms that match the characteristics of spontaneous speech. A paradigm shift from the present transcription-based approach to a detection-based approach will be important to resolve such problems (Juang and Furui, 2000). How to extract contextual information, predict users' responses, and focus on keywords are very important issues.

Stochastic language modelling, such as bigrams and trigrams, has been a very powerful tool, so it would be very effective to extend its utility by incorporating semantic knowledge. It would also be useful to integrate unification grammars and context-free grammars for efficient word prediction. Style shifting is also an important problem in spontaneous speech recognition. In typical laboratory experiments, speakers are reading lists of words rather than trying to accomplish a real task. Users actually try to do the latter, however, use a different linguistic style. Adaptation of linguistic models according to tasks, topics and speaking styles is a very important issue since collecting a large linguistic database for every new task is difficult and costly.

3. Ubiquitous Speech Recognition

The conventional human-computer interface such as GUI, which assumes a keyboard, mouse, and bit-map display, is insufficient for the ubiquitous/-wearable computing environment, especially for wearables. Although handwritten character recognisers and keyboards that can be used with one hand have been developed as input devices for computers, speech recognition has recently received more interest. The main reason for this is that it permits both hands and eyes to be kept free and therefore is less restricted in its use and can achieve quicker communication. In addition, speech can convey not only linguistic information but also the emotion and identity of speakers.

In the history of speech recognition research, most speech recognisers and systems have been developed separately for each particular place and application, and each system has been shared by many people who come to the system or access it over the telephone. In speech transcription, common equipment has been adapted to each user's voice, but has never been considered as something to be carried around or controlled collaboratively with various other computers. In the ubiquitous/wearable computing environment, speech recognition will be, in most cases, performed using a microphone and a networked computer worn and tailored to each person (Furui, 2000b). Accordingly, future speech recognition systems will comprise very different structures than present systems. It is therefore important to investigate how to construct and use speech recognition systems in the new ubiquitous/wearable computing environment. Such an investigation will significantly change the foci of speech recognition research.

As described above, one of the important problems of state-of-the-art speech recognition technology is its robustness, i.e., the stability of its performance for the change of speakers, additive noise and distortions (Furui, 2000c). Some of the robustness problems can be easily solved if speech recognition by wearable computers is achieved. If everybody wears a device that recognises his/her own voice, for example, the problem of speaker-to-speaker variability of voice can be eliminated. Models on the device can be incrementally adapted to the user using his/her daily utterances. Although it is possible to measure continuously the acoustic environmental conditions, such as noise, using the wearable itself, the process can be eliminated if computers are located everywhere and used to regularly measure the noise level and spectrum. By transmitting the noise information to the wearable recogniser, noise-adapted recognition can be easily performed.

If task-dependent information can be transmitted by radio to the wearable speech recogniser from the station of each service, such as train ticket machines, the recogniser can easily be adapted to the change of vocabulary and grammar according to the services as shown in Figure 2. Take the case of speech recognition for car navigation as an example. Here, the vocabulary and grammar for car navigation are quickly transmitted to the wearable recogniser as soon as the user gets in the car, and input speech is recognised by the recogniser adapted to the user. In general, by storing general vocabulary and grammar in the speaker-adapted wearable speech recognisers and quickly transmitting only a task-dependent part, task-adapted speech recognition can easily be performed.

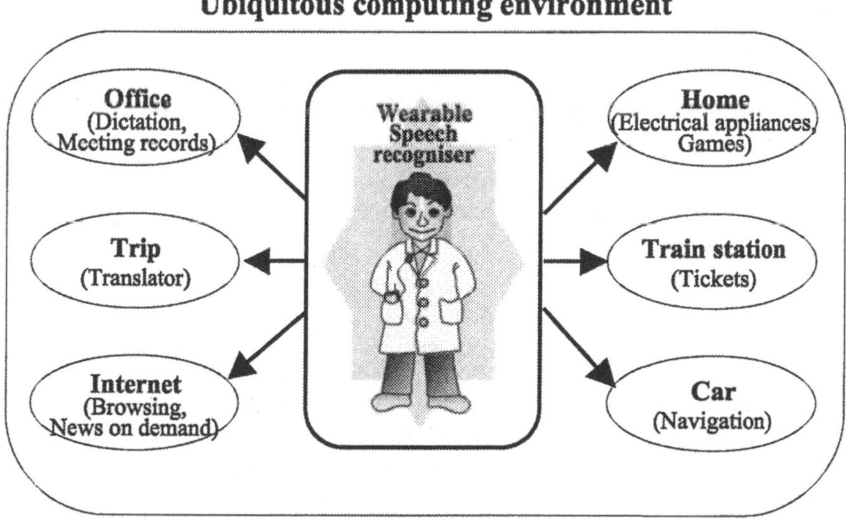

Figure 2. Speech recognition in the ubiquitous/wearable computing environment.

4. Robust Speech Recognition

4.1 Maximum Likelihood-Based Model Adaptation

Mismatches between the model and testing data are the main factor causing speech recognition errors. Decreasing these mismatches should reduce the recognition error rate (Sankar and Lee, 1996). As described in Section 2, speech recognition is the process of decoding an observation sequence X by using the model λ and the MAP (maximum a posteriori probability) decoder:

$$W' = \arg\max_{W} P(X|W,\lambda)P(W). \tag{2.1}$$

where W is a specified word sequence, W' is the recognition result. Let's consider a transformation with parameter η that maps λ into a transformed model. One approach to decreasing the mismatch is to find the η and the word sequence W that maximise the likelihood of X in Equation (2.1), given the model λ. Trying every possible combination of hypothesis W and η is very costly. In a simple way which is widely used for adaptation (unsupervised adaptation), the word sequence W used for adaptation is given by using the model λ. By keeping W fixed, maximisation is thus performed only for η, with the expectation that the transformed model λ will decrease the mismatch between the test data and the model. Then Equation (2.1) can be written as a likelihood maximisation problem:

$$\eta' = \arg\max_{\eta} P(X|W,\eta,\lambda). \tag{2.2}$$

The transformed model λ is then used to decode the input speech again using Equation (2.1). This process can be repeated until the recognition result converges.

4.2 Speaker Adaptation

Extraction and adaptation to voice individuality is one of the most important issues in robust speech recognition. A small percentage of people occasionally cause systems to produce exceptionally low recognition rates. This is an example of the "sheep and goats" phenomenon. Speaker adaptation (normalisation) methods can usually be classified into supervised and unsupervised methods. Unsupervised, online, instantaneous/incremental adaptation is ideal, since the system works as if it were a speaker-independent system, and it performs increasingly better as it is used. However, since we have to adapt many phonemes using a limited amount of adaptation data including only a limited number of phonemes, it is crucial to use reasonable modelling of speaker-to-speaker variability or constraints.

In many applications of speech recognition, speakers change frequently, new speakers appear, and each of them utters a series of several sentences. In such a situation, an unsupervised and online adaptation method, which uses the unknown utterance itself for adaptation, is expected to be effective. The adaptation should also work incrementally within a segment in which one speaker utters several sentences. To create such a system, we must ensure that speaker change is detected automatically and correctly.

We have proposed an online, unsupervised, instantaneous and incremental speaker adaptation method combined with automatic detection of speaker changes for broadcast news transcription (Zhang and Furui, 2000). The MLLR (Leggetter and Woodland, 1995), MAP (Gauvain and Lee, 1994) and VFS (vector-field smoothing) (Ohkura et al., 1992) methods were instantaneously and incrementally carried out for each utterance. The speaker change is detected by comparing likelihoods using speaker-independent and speaker-adaptive GMMs (Gaussian mixture models). A single-state speaker-independent GMM with 64 Gaussian distributions is constructed at the training stage using the same utterances that were used to construct the speaker-independent phone HMM.

For the first input utterance, the speaker-independent model is used for both recognition and adaptation, and the first speaker-adapted HMM and GMM are created. For the second input utterance, the likelihood value of the utterance given the speaker-independent GMM and the one given the speaker-adapted GMM are calculated and compared. If the former value is larger, the utterance is considered to be the beginning of a new speaker, and another speaker-adapted HMM as well as GMM are created. Otherwise, the existing speaker-adapted HMM and GMM are incrementally adapted. For the succeeding input utterances, speaker changes are detected in the same way by comparing the acoustic likelihood values of each utterance obtained from the speaker-independent GMM and speaker-adapted GMMs. If the speaker-independent GMM yields a larger likelihood than any of the speaker-adapted GMMs, a new speaker is detected and new speaker-adapted HMM and GMM are constructed. Since GMM has only one state, it is adapted using a transformation matrix obtained by a single-cluster MLLR adaptation procedure applied to the phone HMM although HMM is actually adapted using multiple phonemic clusters.

Experimental results show that the adaptation reduces word error rates by 10.0% relative to the speaker-independent models. If multiple initial HMMs modelled by speaker clustering instead of a single speaker-independent HMM are used, further word error rate reduction can be achieved (piecewise-linear transformation) (Zhang et al., 2002).

Adapting the speech recognition engine to changing speaker traits, such as emotion and stress, has also been investigated. While this is a hard task, it has been considered in some speech recognition tasks (Hansen, 1996).

4.3 Noise Adaptation

Increasing the robustness of speech HMMs to additive noise is also a very important issue. HMMs with Gaussian mixtures are usually used to model speech represented by cepstral coefficients, meaning that speech is modelled in the logarithmic spectral domain. However, noise is often additive to speech in the waveform or in the linear spectral domain, so the incorporation of additive noise into HMMs is not straightforward. Parallel model combination (PMC, also called HMM composition) (Varga and Moore, 1990; Gales and Young, 1992; Martin et al., 1993) is one of the most practically useful methods used to handle additive noise.

The PMC can derive noisy speech HMMs by combining clean speech HMMs, a noise HMM and a signal-to-noise ratio (SNR). Observation probabilities (means and covariances) for a noisy HMM are estimated by convoluting the observation probabilities in the linear spectral domain. This method requires numerical conversion of the distribution parameters between cepstral and linear spectral domains. Even though several papers addressed speed issues in PMC and showed a speed-up factor by more than two times normal PMC (Sarikaya and Hansen, 2000), it still needs a large amount of computation. In addition it is difficult to combine PMC with other generally used and effective mismatch compensation techniques such as CMS (cepstral mean subtraction).

To solve these problems, a method using neural network mapping functions to learn the effects of additive noise on HMMs has been proposed (Furui and Itoh, 2001). The neural network is trained using an input consisting of a clean speech HMM, noise HMM and the speech and noise energy. The output of the neural network is a noisy speech HMM which, during training, is obtained by a combination of the MLLR, MAP and VFS adaptation techniques. The neural network learns the mapping between the input and output. During testing, the mapping is used to obtain the noisy speech HMM from the inputs. Once the network is trained under various conditions of speech, noise and SNR, the network produces noise-added speech HMMs under new speech, noise and SNR conditions within the bounds of generalisation capabilities of neural networks. In the present framework only the mean vectors of Gaussian mixtures are adapted, and covariance values are preserved unchanged for simplicity.

Noisy broadcast-news speech was recognised in speaker-dependent and speaker-independent network training conditions, and the trained networks were confirmed to be effective in the recognition of new speakers and under new noise and SNR conditions. It was found that the neural-network-based method was more effective than the PMC.

However, the neural network-based method still requires a large amount of computation, which is especially serious when noise varies over time and the noise effect needs to be estimated and compensated online. Another serious problem with both the PMC and the neural network-based method is that noise-only period needs to be automatically extracted for estimating the noise model and level at every time the noise is changed, which is often very difficult under real environments, especially when SNR is low.

From these viewpoints, a new noise adaptation method, which does not require the noise/speech segmentation, has been proposed (Zhang and Furui, 2001). Figure 3 shows the principal structure of the proposed method. This method is based on the online speaker adaptation method (piecewise-linear transformation method) described in the previous subsection. In the proposed method, a wide variety of noise data are collected and clustered according to their spectral property, and noisy speech HMMs corresponding to various clustered noises and various SNR conditions are constructed using noisy utterances created by adding the clustered noise signals to clean speech in the training phase. In the recognition phase, a noisy speech HMM which best matches the input noisy speech is selected based on the likelihood maximisation criterion and further converted to reduce mismatches with the input speech by the MLLR technique. In order to reduce the amount of computation for selecting the noisy speech HMM, GMMs corresponding to the HMMs respectively are created and used instead of HMMs.

The proposed method has been evaluated by its ability to recognise noisy broadcast-news speech. It has been confirmed that the proposed method is effective in recognising noisy speech under various noise conditions. Results show that the proposed method performed significantly better than the PMC and the neural network-based adaptation methods. The proposed method minimises mismatches between noisy input speech and the HMMs, sentence by sentence, without requiring explicit noise spectrum/model estimation. The proposed method is therefore easily applicable to real world conditions with frequently changing noise.

5. Conversational Systems for Information Access

5.1 Multimodal Human-Computer Interface

Human beings favour the sensory dimensions of sight, sound, and touch as primary channels of communication. Machines that can accommodate these modes promise flexibilities and functionalities that transcend the traditional mouse and keyboard. Therefore, integration of multiple modalities in human-computer interfaces has long been viewed as a means for increasing ease of use. Recent examples include integration of modalities such as speech, gesture, gaze tracking and lip reading. Figure 4 shows the architecture of a multimodal task-oriented human-computer interaction system (Marsic et al., 2000). Each

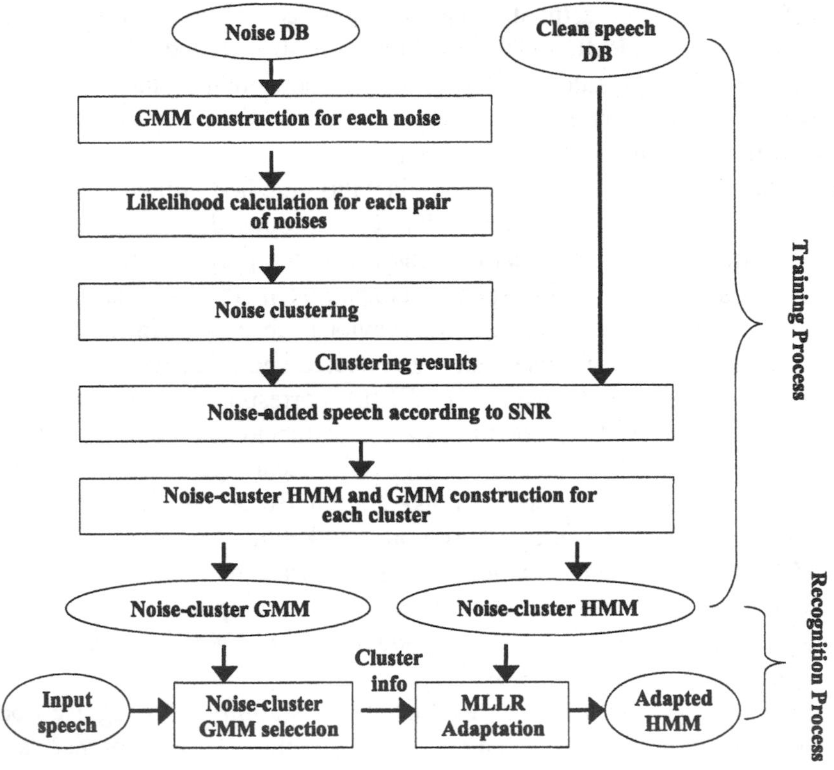

Figure 3. Piecewise-linear transformation for HMM noise adaptation.

application defines a set of application programming interfaces (APIs) that can be invoked to cause different actions. The APIs determine the user's command vocabulary and grammar for both speech and gesture.

Automatic lip reading has been investigated by many researchers as a complementary means to speech recognition, e.g., (Basu et al., 1999). However it is still difficult to establish a robust and accurate approach for tracking the lip movements and extracting important features. In most of the systems, the shape of the lips is measured based on pattern recognition techniques. Since the shape is sometimes difficult to measure correctly due to intensity and colour variations, alternative techniques are being considered that use statistical features based on optical flow analysis for lip images (Tamura et al., 2004). Optical flow is defined as the distribution of apparent velocities in the movement of brightness patterns in an image (Barron et al., 1994; Mase and Pentland, 1991). Since the optical flow is computed without extracting the speaker's lip contours and location, robust visual features can be obtained for lip movements. In order to increase the robustness, a grey-scale image covering the

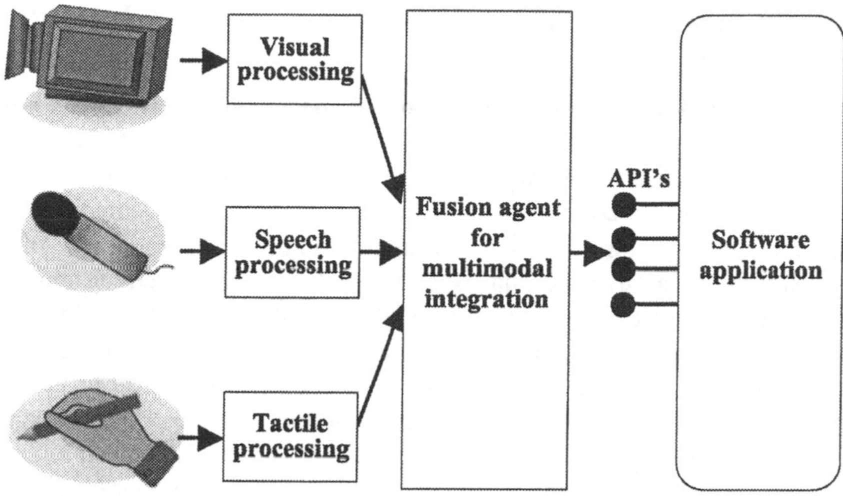

Figure 4. Architecture of a multimodal human-computer interface.

mouth area is passed through a smoothing process, and random noise is added before calculating the optical flow.

Our method calculates two kinds of visual feature sets in each frame. The first feature set consists of variances of vertical and horizontal components of optical flow vectors. These are useful for estimating silence (pause) periods in noisy conditions since they represent movement of the speaker's mouth. The second feature set consists of maximum and minimum values of the integral of the optical flow. The second set is more effective than the first one since this feature set has not only silence (pause) information but also opening/closing information of the mouth. Each feature set is combined with an acoustic feature set using the feature-fusion method in the framework of HMM-based recognition. Triphone HMMs are trained using the combined parameter sets extracted from clean speech data. Noise-corrupted speech recognition experiments have been carried out using audio-visual data from 11 male speakers uttering connected digits. The following improvements of digit recognition accuracy over the audio-only recognition scheme have been achieved when the second set of features was used only for silence HMM: 4% at SNR=5 dB and 13% at SNR=10 dB. The visual features are significantly useful for detecting silence periods and reducing digit insertion errors in silence (pause) periods. This method has also been confirmed to be effective in real environments, such as a car navigation environment in a driving automobile.

5.2 Mixed-Initiative Human-Computer Interface

Numerous commercial spoken dialogue systems are currently being deployed, primarily for access to information over the telephone. There are, however, major open research issues that challenge the deployment of completely natural and unconstrained spoken language interactions even for limited task domains. Most of the conventional dialogue systems are implemented by a system-initiative structure imposing constraints on the range and scope of allowed user inputs at any point during an interaction. Since such systems are very troublesome for the users, mixed-initiative systems have also been investigated, in which the course of the dialogue can be changed by both the user and the system at any point, e.g., (Levin et al., 2000). These systems need to be able to accept and understand unrestricted utterances at any dialogue state. Such expansion automatically degrades not only the processing speed but also the performance of the system. To alleviate these problems, implementation of mixed-initiative systems on a parallel computing architecture, in which multiple recognition systems separately designed according to dialogue contents (subtasks) are run in parallel, has been proposed (Taguma et al., 2002). Dialogue content of the user is automatically detected based on likelihood scores given by the multiple recognisers. Transitional probabilities from one dialogue state to other states uttering various content are incorporated into the likelihood score. A flexible dialogue structure that gives users the initiative to control the dialogue is implemented by this structure. Real-time dialogue systems for retrieving information about restaurants and food shops, such as bakeries, have been built and evaluated in terms of dialogue content identification rate and keyword accuracy. The proposed architecture has the advantage that the dialogue system can be easily modified without remaking the whole language model.

6. Systems for Transcribing, Understanding and Summarising Ubiquitous Speech Documents

6.1 Projects on Spontaneous Speech Corpus and Processing Technology

As described in Section 2, one of the most difficult issues for speech recognition is how to build language models for spontaneous speech. For this purpose, we need to have large spontaneous speech corpora. In the United States, the "Switchboard" and "Call Home" spontaneous speech corpora have been constructed in recent years[1]. In Japan, a Science and Technology Agency Priority Programme entitled "Spontaneous Speech: Corpus and Processing Technology" started in 1999 (Furui et al., 2000). The project will be conducted over a 5-year period under the following three major themes as shown in Figure 5.

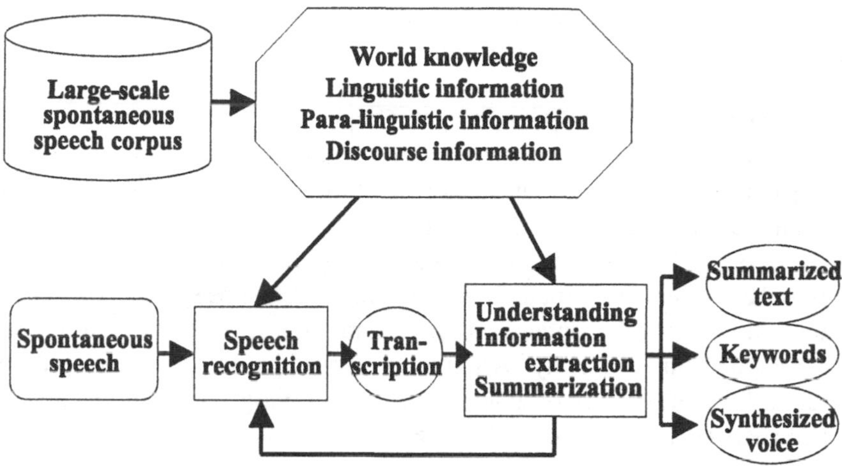

Figure 5. Overview of the Japanese national project on spontaneous speech corpus and processing technology.

1. Building a large-scale spontaneous speech corpus, Corpus of Spontaneous Japanese (CSJ), consisting of roughly 7M words with the total speech length of 700 hours. The recordings will focus primarily on monologues such as lectures, presentations and news commentaries. The recordings will be manually given orthographic and phonetic transcription. One-tenth of the utterances, hereafter referred to as the Core, will be tagged manually and used for training a morphological analysis and part-of-speech (POS) tagging programme for automatically analysing all of the 700-hour utterances. The Core will also be tagged with para-linguistic information including intonation.

2. Acoustic and linguistic modelling will be considered for spontaneous speech understanding using linguistic as well as para-linguistic information in speech.

3. The final theme will consider investigating spontaneous speech summarisation technology.

The technology created in this project is expected to be applicable to wide areas such as indexing of speech data (broadcast news, etc.) for information extraction and retrieval, transcription of lectures, preparing minutes of meetings, closed captioning, and aids for the handicapped.

A survey on activities in spontaneous speech recognition in Europe over the last 10 years, including various research projects, can be found in (Rigoll, 2003). A brief historical review on the development of this topic in Europe is presented, and various technical issues are addressed, distinguishing research projects on spontaneous speech recognition from other research activities in speech.

In the Netherlands, the Spoken Dutch Corpus (in Dutch: Corpus Gesproken Nederlands, or CGN) project started in 1998 (Boves and Oostdijk, 2003). The project aims at the compilation and annotation of a corpus of 1,000 hours of spoken Dutch. Upon completion, the corpus is expected to constitute a valuable resource for research in the field of language and speech technology. Although the corpus will contain a fair amount of read speech, a major part of the data will consist of spontaneous speech, ranging from lectures to conversations recorded unobtrusively. All speech recordings will be made available together with several levels of annotations, from orthographic transcription to syntactic analyses and prosodic labelling, similar to the CSJ.

6.2 Transcription of Presentations

6.2.1 Language and acoustic modelling. Using the CSJ corpus, a preliminary recognition experiment has been conducted. In this experiment, 4.4 hours of presentation speech uttered by 10 male speakers is used as a test set of speech recognition (Shinozaki et al., 2001). The following two corpora are used for training the language and acoustic models.

CSJ: A part of the CSJ corpus, consisting of 610 presentations (approximately 1.5M words of transcriptions), is used. The speakers have no overlap with those of the test set.

Web: Transcribed presentations consisting of approximately 76k sentences with 2M words have been collected from the World Wide Web. Since all the filled pauses have been removed before creating this corpus, an effort is thus made to add filled pauses based on the statistical characteristics. The topics of the presentations cover wide domains including social issues and memoirs.

Two language models, denoted as **SpnL** and **WebL**, have been constructed using **CSJ** and **Web**, respectively. The following two tied-state triphone HMMs have been made, both having 2k states and 16 Gaussian mixtures in each state; **SpnA**: using 338 presentations in the CSJ uttered by male speakers (approximately 59 hours) and **RdA**: using approximately 40-hours of read speech uttered by many speakers.

6.2.2 Experimental results. **SpnL** and **WebL** were compared in terms of the test-set perplexity of trigrams and the out-of-vocabulary (OOV) rate. It was found that these values for **WebL** were almost twice as large as those for **SpnL**. Figure 6 shows recognition results for combinations of the two language models, **SpnL** and **WebL**, and the two acoustic models, **SpnA** and **RdA**. Fillers are counted as words and included in calculating the accuracy. It is clearly shown that **SpnL** achieves much better results than **WebL**, and **SpnA** gives much better results than **RdA**. These results indicate that it is crucial to generate language models from a spontaneous speech corpus to adequately recognise spontaneous speech. It is also suggested that acoustic models made from CSJ have better coverage of triphones and better matching of acoustic characteristics corresponding to the speaking style and also have a better match with recording conditions of the test set. The mean accuracy for the combination of **SpnL** and **SpnA** is 65.3%.

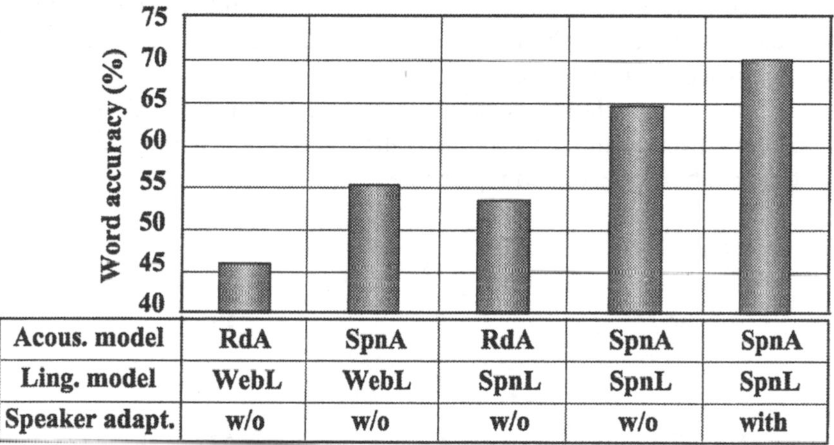

Acous. model	RdA	SpnA	RdA	SpnA	SpnA
Ling. model	WebL	WebL	SpnL	SpnL	SpnL
Speaker adapt.	w/o	w/o	w/o	w/o	with

Figure 6. Word accuracy for each combination of models; RdA: read-speech-based acoustic model, SpnA: CSJ-based acoustic model, WebL: Web-based language model, and SpnL: CSJ-based language model.

The word accuracy largely varies from speaker to speaker. There exist many factors that affect the accuracy of spontaneous speech recognition. They include individual voice characteristics, speaking manners and noise like coughs. Although all utterances were recorded using the same close-talking microphones, acoustic conditions still varied according to the recording environment. A batch-type unsupervised adaptation method has been incorporated to cope with the speech variation. The MLLR method using a binary regression class tree to transform Gaussian mean vectors is employed. The regression class tree is generated using a centroid-splitting algorithm. The actual classes used for transformation are determined on run time according to the amount of data assigned to each class. By applying the adaptation, the error rate is reduced by 15% relative to the speaker-independent case, and the accuracy is raised to 70.5% as shown in Figure 6.

6.2.3 Analysis of the structure of individual differences.

The individual differences in speech recognition performance for spontaneous presentations have been analysed using 10 minutes from each presentation given by 51 male speakers, for a total of 510 minutes (Shinozaki and Furui, 2002). Seven kinds of speaker attributes have been considered in the analysis. They are word accuracy (Acc), averaged acoustic frame likelihood (AL), speaking rate (SR), word perplexity (PP), out of vocabulary rate (OR), filled pause rate (FR) and repair rate (RR). The speaking rate defined as the number of phonemes per second and the averaged acoustic frame likelihood are calculated using the result of forced alignment of the reference triphone labels after removing pause periods. The word perplexity is calculated using trigrams, in which prediction of out of vocabulary words is not included. The filled pause rate and the repair rate are the number of filled pauses and repairs divided by the number of words, respectively.

Figure 7 shows correlation between the seven attributes. This result indicates that the attributes having real correlation with the accuracy are speaking rate, out of vocabulary rate, and repair rate.

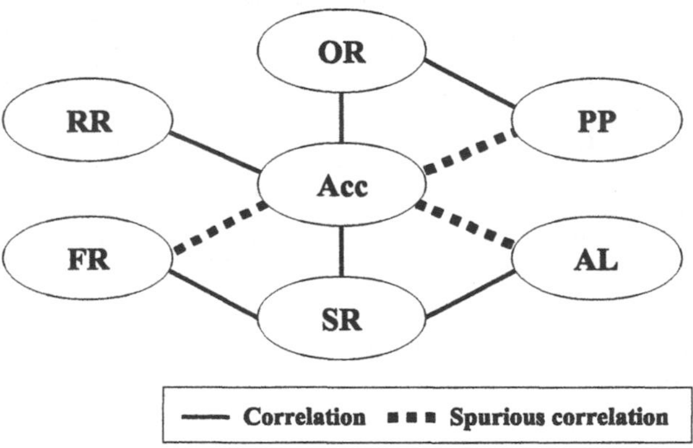

Figure 7. Correlation between various attributes; Acc:word accuracy, OR:out of vocabulary rate, RR:repair rate, FR:filled pause rate, SR: speaking rate, AL:averaged acoustic frame likelihood, and PP:word perplexity.

The following equation has been obtained as a result of a linear regression model of the word accuracy with the six presentation attributes.

$$Acc = 0.12[AL] - 0.88[SR] - 0.020[PP] - 2.2[OR] + 0.32[FR] - 3.0[RR] + 95 \quad (2.3)$$

In the equation, the regression coefficient for the repair rate is -3.0 and the coefficient for the out of vocabulary rate is -2.2. This means that a 1% increase of the repair rate or the out of vocabulary rate respectively corresponds to a

3.0% or 2.2% decrease of the word accuracy. This is probably because a single recognition error caused by a repair or an out of vocabulary word triggers secondary errors due to the linguistic constraints. The determination coefficients of the multiple linear regression is 0.48, which is significant at a 1% level. This means that roughly half of the variance of the word accuracy can be explained by the model.

6.3 Transcription of Discussions

Another recognition experiment has been performed using discussion speech in a broadcast TV programme (Shinozaki et al., 2000). The following language models were built; LM1: constructed using broadcast news text over a 34-month period comprising 380k sentences, LM2: constructed using transcribed speech having 800k words collected from 159 days of the same programme as the test set, and LM3: constructed by adding new words extracted automatically from broadcast news articles with topics similar to the test set to LM2 using part-of-speech class N-gram language models.

Since cross-talk (double talk) frequently occurs during discussion and causes recognition errors, acoustic backing-off was applied to these periods, assuming that these periods can be automatically detected with some method. For these periods, acoustic scores were replaced by acoustic likelihood averaged over other periods and recognition was therefore performed merely based on linguistic scores. Experimental results showed that test-set perplexity and OOV rate were both significantly reduced by using the transcription of the utterances in the same TV programme, and that the OOV rate was largely reduced by automatically adding new words. It was also found that the acoustic backing-off was effective in coping with the cross-talk problem.

6.4 Making Minutes of Meetings

We proposed a system for making minutes of meetings as one of the applications of speech recognition technology in the ubiquitous/wearable computing environment (Furui, 2000b). In this system, each attendant carries or wears a personalised computer to recognise his/her own utterances, and another computer connected by cable or radio to all the personalised computers is used as a meeting manager as shown in Figure 8. Each recogniser is adapted to the attendant's voice, ways of speaking, and vocabulary using his/her utterances under various conditions. Therefore, relatively high recognition accuracy is expected even though speakers take turns during the meeting. The meeting manager computer collects structural information of the meeting, such as transition of topics and content and the speaker of each utterance, and transmits such information to each personalised recogniser. Thus, recognition accuracy can be improved and meanings of even fragmental utterances can be understood. Minutes of the meeting will be automatically made by collecting recognition results by each recogniser and other information, such as speaker change and the transition of topics, to the meeting manager. The minutes can also be summarised if necessary. In the future, if these results are displayed to all the participants in real time, a computer-supported efficient meeting, a.k.a. CSCW (computer-supported cooperative work), will be realisable.

Figure 8. Meeting synopsising system using collaborative speech recognisers.

Since recognition accuracy using present speech recognition technology is inadequate, we are now building an interactive system for making minutes (Shinozaki et al., 2000). The system first recognises utterances and presents sentence hypotheses. When a user indicates recognition errors and provides corrections, the system modifies the acoustic and linguistic models and re-recognises the input utterances. By iterating the process, minutes can be made with less labour than making them by hand. In order to speed up the iterative process, intermediate recognition results including speaker information are stored using a word graph.

6.5 Speech Summarisation

Transcribed speech usually includes not only redundant information such as disfluencies, filled pauses, repetitions, repairs and word fragments, but also irrelevant information caused by recognition errors. Therefore, especially for spontaneous speech, practical applications using speech recognition require a process of speech summarisation which removes redundant and irrelevant information and extracts relatively important information corresponding to the users' requirements. Speech summarisation producing understandable and compact sentences from original utterances can be considered as one form of speech understanding.

A method for automatically summarising speech based on sentence compaction has been investigated (Hori and Furui, 2000; Hori et al., 2002). The method can be applied to the summarisation of each sentence/utterance and also to a set of multiple sentences. The basic idea of this method is to extract a set of words maximising a summarisation score from an automatically transcribed sentence according to a target compression ratio (Figure 9). This method aims at effectively reducing the number of words by removing redundant and irrelevant information without losing relatively important information. The summarisation score indicating the appropriateness of a summarised sentence consists of a word significance score I as well as a confidence score C for each word of the original sentence, a linguistic score L for the word string in the summarised sentence, and a word concatenation score T_r. The word significance score is measured by the amount of information conveyed by each word. The confidence score is given by the posterior probability of each transcribed word. The linguistic score measured by bigrams or trigrams indicates the appropriateness of word strings in a summarised sentence. The word concatenation score indicates a word concatenation probability determined by a dependency structure in the original sentence given by a Stochastic Dependency Context Free Grammar (SDCFG). The total score is maximised using a dynamic programming (DP) technique.

Given a transcription result consisting of N words, $W = w_1, w_2, \cdots, w_N$, the summarisation is performed by extracting a set of $M(M < N)$ words, $V = v_1, v_2, \cdots, v_M$, which maximises the summarisation score given by Equation (2.4).

$$S(V) = \sum_{m=1}^{M} \{L(v_m|\cdots v_{m-1}) + \lambda_I I(v_m) + \lambda_C C(v_m) + \lambda_T T_r(v_{m-1}, v_m)\} \tag{2.4}$$

where λ_I, λ_C and λ_T are weighting factors for balancing among L, I, C and T_r.

To automatically evaluate summarised sentences, correctly transcribed speech utterances are manually summarised by human subjects and used as correct targets. The manual summarisation results are merged into a word network which approximately expresses all possible correct summarisation including subjective variations. A summarisation accuracy of automatic summarisation is calculated using the word network. A word string extracted from the word network that is most similar to the automatic summarisation result is consid-

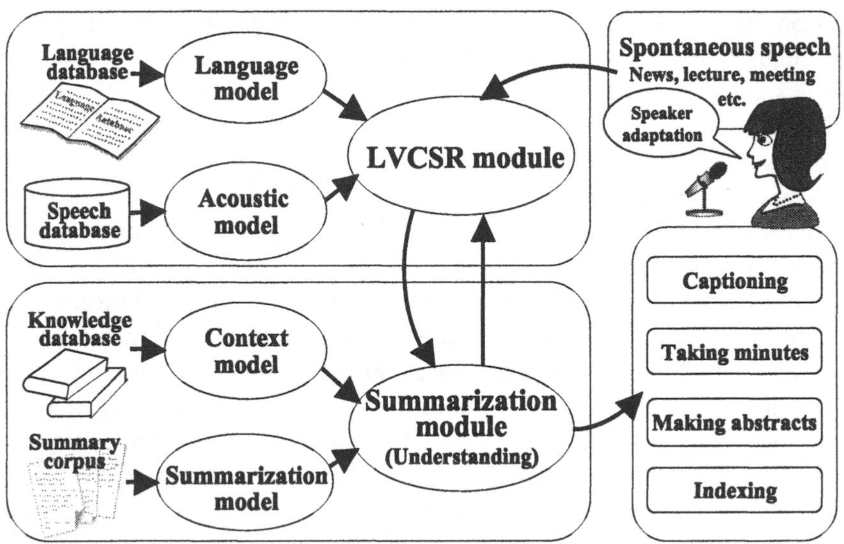

Figure 9. Automatic speech summarisation system.

ered as a correct word string corresponding to the automatic summarisation. The accuracy, comparing the summarised sentence with the word string extracted from the network, is used as an indicator of the "summarisation accuracy", measuring the linguistic correctness and maintenance of the original meanings of the utterance. Experimental results of summarising English CNN news and Japanese NHK news utterances show that the proposed method can effectively extract relatively important information and remove redundant and irrelevant information.

7. Conclusion

Speech recognition technology has made remarkable progress in the past 5-10 years. This progress has enabled various application systems to be developed using transcription and spoken dialogue technology. While we are still far from having a machine that converses with a human like a human, many important scientific advances have taken place, bringing us closer to the "Holy Grail" of automatic speech recognition and understanding by machine (Juang and Furui, 2000). Speech recognition and understanding will become one of the key techniques for human-computer interaction in the multimodal/ubiquitous/wearable computing environment. To successfully use speech recognition in such an environment, every process such as start-stop control of recognition, and adaptation to individuals and the surrounding environment, must be performed without being noticed. Speech recognition should not be as it is in popular science fiction; instead it should be used unobtrusively, unconsciously and effortlessly (Furui, 2000b). It is also necessary to operate in a consistent manner no matter where the user goes.

The most important issue is how to make the speech recognition systems robust against acoustic and linguistic variation in spontaneous speech. In this context, a paradigm shift from speech recognition to understanding, where underlying messages of the speaker, that is, meaning/context that the speaker intended to convey, are extracted, instead of transcribing all the spoken words, will be indispensable. To reach such a goal, we need to have an efficient way of representing, storing, retrieving, and utilising "world knowledge".

Notes

1. `http://www.ldc.upenn.edu/`

References

Barron, J. L., Fleet, D. J., and Beauchemin, S. S. (1994). Performance of optical flow techniques. *International Journal of Computer Vision*, 12(1):43–77.

Basu, S., Neti, C., Rajput, N., Senior, A., Subramaniam, L., and Verma, A. (1999). Audio-visual large vocabulary continuous speech recognition in the broadcast domain. In *Proceedings of International Workshop on Multimedia Signal Processing (MMSP)*, pages 475–481, Copenhagen, Denmark.

Boves, L. and Oostdijk, N. (2003). Spontaneous speech in the spoken Dutch corpus. In *Proceedings of IEEE International Workshop on Spontaneous Speech Processing and Recognition*, pages 171–174, Tokyo, Japan.

Furui, S. (1997). Recent advances in robust speech recognition. In *Proceedings of ESCA-NATO Workshop on Robust Speech Recognition for Unknown Communication Channels*, pages 11–20, Pont-a-Mousson, France.

Furui, S. (2000a). *Digital Speech Processing, Synthesis, and Recognition*. Marcel Dekker, New York, New York, USA, 2nd edition.

Furui, S. (2000b). Speech recognition technology in the ubiquitous/wearable computing environment. In *Proceedings of International Conference on Acoustics, Speech and Signal Processing (ICASSP)*, pages 3735–3738, Istanbul, Turkey.

Furui, S. (2000c). Steps toward natural human-machine communication in the 21st century. In *Proceedings of COST249 Workshop on Voice Operated Telecom Services*, pages 17–24, Gent, Belgium.

Furui, S. (2001). Toward flexible speech recognition - recent progress at Tokyo Institute of Technology. In *Proceedings of Canadian Conference on Electrical and Computer Engineering (CCECE)*, Toronto, Canada.

Furui, S. and Itoh, D. (2001). Neural networks-based HMM adaptation for noisy speech. In *Proceedings of International Conference on Acoustics, Spe-*

ech and Signal Processing (ICASSP), pages 365–368, Salt Lake City, Utah, USA.

Furui, S., Maekawa, K., Isahara, H., Shinozaki, T., and Ohdaira, T. (2000). Toward the realization of spontaneous speech recognition - Introduction of a Japanese priority program and preliminary results. In *Proceedings of International Conference on Spoken Language Processing (ICSLP)*, pages 518–521, Beijing, China.

Gales, M. J. F. and Young, S. J. (1992). An improved approach to the hidden Markov model decomposition of speech and noise. In *Proceedings of International Conference on Acoustics, Speech and Signal Processing (ICASSP)*, pages 233–236, San Francisco, California, USA.

Gauvain, J.-L. and Lee, C.-H. (1994). Maximum a posteriori estimation for multivariate Gaussian mixture observations of Markov chains. *IEEE Transactions on Speech and Audio Processing*, 2(2):291–298.

Hansen, J. H. L. (1996). Analysis and compensation of speech under stress and noise for environmental robustness in speech recognition. *Speech Communication, Special issue on speech under stress*, 20(1–2):151–173.

Hori, C. and Furui, S. (2000). Automatic speech summarization based on word significance and linguistic likelihood. In *Proceedings of International Conference on Acoustics, Speech and Signal Processing (ICASSP)*, pages 1579–1582, Instanbul, Turkey.

Hori, C., Furui, S., Malkin, R., Yu, H., and Waibel, A. (2002). Automatic speech summarization applied to english broadcast news speech. In *Proceedings of International Conference on Acoustics, Speech and Signal Processing (ICASSP)*, pages 9–12, Orlando, Florida, USA.

Juang, B.-H. and Furui, S. (2000). Automatic recognition and understanding of spoken language - A first step to wards natural human-machine communication. *Proceedings of IEEE*, 88(8):1142–1165.

Leggetter, C. J. and Woodland, P. C. (1995). Maximum likelihood linear regression for speaker adaptation of continuous density Hidden Markov Models. *Computer Speech and Language*, 9:171–185.

Levin, E., Narayanan, S., Pieraccini, R., Biatov, K., Bocchieri, E., Fabbrizio, G. D., Eckert, W., Lee, S., Pokrovsky, A., Rahim, M., Ruscitti, P., and Walker, M. (2000). The AT&T-DARPA Communicator mixed-initiative spoken dialogue system. In *Proceedings of International Conference on Spoken Language Processing (ICSLP)*, pages 122–125, Beijing, China.

Marsic, I., Medl, A., and Flanagan, J. (2000). Natural communication with information systems. *Proceedings of IEEE*, 88(8):1354–1366.

Martin, F., Shikano, K., and Minami, Y. (1993). Recognition of noisy speech by composition of hidden Markov models. In *Proceedings of European Conference on Speech Communication and Technology (EUROSPEECH)*, pages 1031–1034, Berlin, Germany.

Mase, K. and Pentland, A. (1991). Automatic lipreading by optical-flow analysis. *Transactions Systems and Computers in Japan*, 22(6):67–76.

Ney, H. (1997). Corpus-based statistical methods in speech and language processing. In Young, S. and Bloothooft, G., editors, *Corpus-based Methods in Language and Speech Processing*, pages 1–26. Kluwer Academic Publishers, Dordrecht, The Netherlands.

Ohkura, K., Sugiyama, M., and Sagayama, S. (1992). Speaker adaptation based on transfer vector field smoothing with continuous mixture density hmms. In *Proceedings of International Conference on Spoken Language Processing (ICSLP)*, pages 369–372, Banff, Canada.

Pentland, A. (1998). Wearable intelligence. *Scientific American*, 276(11).

Rabiner, L. R. and Juang, B. H. (1993). *Fundamentals of Speech Recognition*. Prentice-Hall, Inc., New Jersey, USA.

Rigoll, G. (2003). An overview on European projects related to spontaneous speech recognition. In *Proceedings of IEEE International Workshop on Spontaneous Speech Processing and Recognition*, pages 131–134, Tokyo, Japan.

Sankar, A. and Lee, C.-H. (1996). A maximum-likelihood approach to stochastic matching for robust speech recognition. *IEEE Transactions on Acoustics, Speech and Signal Processing*, 4(3):190–202.

Sarikaya, R. and Hansen, J. H. L. (2000). PCA-PMC: A novel use of a priori knowledge for fast parallel model combination. In *Proceedings of International Conference on Acoustics, Speech and Signal Processing (ICASSP)*, pages 1113–1116, Instanbul, Turkey.

Shinozaki, T. and Furui, S. (2002). Analysis on individual differences in automatic transcription of spontaneous presentations. In *Proceedings of International Conference on Acoustics, Speech and Signal Processing (ICASSP)*, pages 729–732, Orlando, Florida, USA.

Shinozaki, T., Hori, C., and Furui, S. (2001). Towards automatic transcription of spontaneous presentations. In *Proceedings of European Conference on Speech Communication and Technology (EUROSPEECH)*, pages 491–494, Aalborg, Denmark.

Shinozaki, T., Saito, Y., Hori, C., and Furui, S. (2000). Toward spontaneous speech recognition. IEICE/ASJ Technical Report, SP2000-96.

Taguma, R., Moriyama, T., Iwano, K., and Furui, S. (2002). Parallel computing-based architecture for mixed-initiative spoken dialogue. In *Proceedings of IEEE International Conference on Multimodal Interfaces*, pages 53–58, Pittsburgh, Pennsylvania, USA.

Tamura, S., Iwano, K., and Furui, S. (2004). A robust multimodal speech recognition method using optical flow analysis. In Minker, W., Bühler, D., and Dybkjær, L., editors, *Spoken Multimodal Human-Computer Dialogue in*

Mobile Environments. Kluwer Academic Publishers, Dordrecht, The Netherlands. (this volume).

Varga, A. P. and Moore, R. K. (1990). Hidden Markov Model decomposition of speech and noise. In *Proceedings of International Conference on Acoustics, Speech and Signal Processing (ICASSP)*, pages 845–848, Albuquerque, New Mexico, USA.

Weiser, M. (1991). The computer for the twenty-first century. *Scientific American*, 265(3):94–104.

Zhang, Z.-P. and Furui, S. (2000). On-line incremental speaker adaptation with automatic speaker change detection. In *Proceedings of International Conference on Acoustics, Speech and Signal Processing (ICASSP)*, pages 961–964, Instanbul, Turkey.

Zhang, Z.-P. and Furui, S. (2001). Piecewise-linear transformation-based HMM adaptation for noisy speech. In *Proceedings of IEEE Automatic Speech Recognition and Understanding Workshop (ASRU)*, pages 43–58, Madonna di Campiglio, Italy.

Zhang, Z.-P., Furui, S., and Ohtsuki, K. (2002). On-line incremental speaker adaptation for broadcast news transcription. *Speech Communication*, 37(3–4):271–281.

Chapter 3

A ROBUST MULTIMODAL SPEECH RECOGNITION METHOD USING OPTICAL FLOW ANALYSIS

Satoshi Tamura, Koji Iwano, Sadaoki Furui
Department of Computer Science, Tokyo Institute of Technology, Tokyo, Japan
{ tamura,iwano,furui } @furui.cs.titech.ac.jp

Abstract We propose a new multimodal speech recognition method using optical flow analysis and evaluate its robustness to acoustic and visual noises. Optical flow is defined as the distribution of apparent velocities in the movement of brightness patterns in an image. Since the optical flow is computed without extracting speaker's lip contours and location, robust visual features can be obtained for lip movements. Our method calculates a visual feature set in each frame consisting of maximum and minimum values of the integral of the optical flow. This feature set has not only silence information but also open/close status of the speaker's mouth. The visual feature set is combined with an acoustic feature set in the framework of HMM-based recognition. Triphone HMMs are trained using the combined parameter set extracted from clean speech data. Two multimodal speech recognition experiments have been carried out. First, acoustic white noise was added to speech waveforms, and a speech recognition experiment was conducted using audio-visual data from 11 male speakers uttering connected Japanese digits. The following improvements of relative reduction of digit error rate over the audio-only recognition scheme were achieved when the visual information was incorporated into the silence HMM: 32% at SNR=10dB and 47% at SNR=15dB. Second, real-world data distorted both acoustically and visually was recorded in a driving car from six male speakers and recognised. We achieved approximately 17% and 11% relative error reduction compared with audio-only results on batch and incremental MLLR-based adaptation, respectively.

Keywords: Audio-visual speech recognition; Lip movement; Robustness to noise; Real-world data; Speaker independence.

W. Minker, D. Bühler and L. Dybkjær (eds), Spoken Multimodal Human-Computer Dialogue in Mobile Environments, 37-53

1. Introduction

Automatic Speech Recognition (ASR) systems are expected to play important roles in an advanced multi-media society with user-friendly human-machine interfaces, such as ubiquitous computing environments (Furui et al., 2001). High recognition accuracy can be obtained for clean speech using the current state-of-the-art technology even if the vocabulary size is large, however, the accuracy largely decreases in noisy conditions. Therefore, increasing the robustness in noisy environments is one of the most important present challenge of ASR.

Multimodal speech recognition, in which acoustic features and other information are used jointly, has been investigated and found to increase robustness and thus improve the accuracy of ASR. Multimodal speech recognition methods mostly use visual features, typically lip information, in addition to acoustic features (Nakamura et al., 2000; Miyajima et al., 2000; Potamianos et al., 1997; Bregler and Konig, 1994). By using visual information, acoustically similar sounds, such as nasal sounds /n/, /m/, and /ng/, become easier to recognise (Basu et al., 1999; Mase and Pentland, 1991). In most of the studies, a lip is located in an image by mouth tracking, subsequently the lip contour is extracted, and visual features are obtained by pattern matching techniques or signal processing methods such as Fast Fourier Transform (FFT). Since it is not easy to determine a mouth location and extract a lip shape, lip marking is often needed to ensure robust extraction of visual features in these schemes.

Mase and Pentland reported their lip reading system for recognising connected English digits using an optical flow analysis (Mase and Pentland, 1991). Optical flow is defined as the distribution of apparent velocities in the movement of brightness patterns in an image (Horn and Schunck, 1981). The following advantages exist when using the optical flow for audio-visual multimodal speech recognition. First, the visual features can be detected robustly without extracting lip locations and contours. Second, it is more reasonable to use lip motion for lip reading rather than using a lip shape. Third, the visual features are independent from the speaker's mouth shape or beard.

We have proposed a multimodal speech recognition scheme using the optical flow analysis for extracting visual information (Iwano et al., 2001). We have used variances of horizontal and vertical elements of optical flow vectors as a visual feature set, and found that they are especially useful for estimating pause/silence periods. We achieved about a 30% relative error reduction compared with audio-only results when recognising white-noise-added speech at a 10dB SNR level condition. However, robustness of the proposed method to visual noise using an audio-visual data in real environments has not yet been evaluated. Increasing the visual robustness is crucial to make the method applicable to mobile environments.

We have conducted recognition experiments for not only artificially noise-added speech but also real-world speech using a new visual feature extraction method. In the following, we describe recognition results compared with results with the audio-only recognition scheme, and evaluate both the acoustic and visual robustness of our method. This chapter is organised as follows: in Section 2, the principle of the optical flow method is explained. Our audio-visual multimodal speech recognition system is described in Section 3. Experimental setup and results for acoustic noise-added data are shown in Section 4, and those for real-world data are in Section 5. Finally we conclude our research and describe our future works in Section 6.

2. Optical Flow Analysis

Optical flow is the distribution of apparent velocities in the movement of brightness patterns in an image. We use the Horn-Schunck algorithm (Horn and Schunck, 1981). This algorithm has the advantages that it needs no characteristic point in contrast to pattern-matching-based algorithms, and that it requires only two images in processing. In this method, brightness at each point is assumed to be constant during a movement $(\Delta x, \Delta y)$ for a short time Δt:

$$I(x, y, t) = I(x + \Delta x, y + \Delta y, t + \Delta t) \tag{3.1}$$

where $I(x, y, t)$ is a brightness of a point (x, y) in an image at time t. Expanding the right side of the equation around the point, the Equation (3.1) can be modified to:

$$I(x, y, t) \simeq I(x, y, t) + \Delta x \frac{\partial I}{\partial x} + \Delta y \frac{\partial I}{\partial y} + \Delta t \frac{\partial I}{\partial t} \tag{3.2}$$

Subtracting $I(x, y, t)$ and dividing by Δt, the following equation is obtained at the limit, $\Delta t \to 0$:

$$I_x \cdot u + I_y \cdot v + I_t = 0 \tag{3.3}$$

where I_x, I_y, I_t, u and v are:

$$I_x = \frac{\partial I}{\partial x} \ , \ I_y = \frac{\partial I}{\partial y} \ , \ I_t = \frac{\partial I}{\partial t} \ , \ u = \frac{dx}{dt} \ , \ v = \frac{dy}{dt} \tag{3.4}$$

$u(x, y)$ and $v(x, y)$ correspond to horizontal and vertical elements of the optical flow at a point (x, y). Since we cannot determine $u(x, y)$ and $v(x, y)$ using only the Equation (3.3), we incorporate another restraint called the "smoothness constraint":

$$\iint \{({u_x}^2 + {u_y}^2) + ({v_x}^2 + {v_y}^2)\}\, dx\, dy \to \min \tag{3.5}$$

where u_x, u_y, v_x and v_y denote partial derivatives of u and v with respect to x and y, respectively. This constraint means that the square of the magnitude of the gradient of $u(x, y)$ and $v(x, y)$ at each point must be minimised. In other words, the optical flow velocity changes smoothly between every neighbouring two pixels in an image. The optical flow vectors $u(x, y)$ and $v(x, y)$ are computed under these two constraints (3.3) and (3.5):

$$\iint \{(u_x{}^2 + u_y{}^2) + (v_x{}^2 + v_y{}^2) + \mu(I_x u + I_y v + I_t)^2\}\, dx\, dy \rightarrow \min \quad (3.6)$$

where μ is a weighting factor, which is set at 0.01 throughout our experiments. This minimisation can be accomplished by a variational approach with iterations:

$$u_{x,y}^{k+1} = \bar{u}_{x,y}^{k} - \mu \frac{I_x \bar{u}_{x,y}^{k} + I_y \bar{v}_{x,y}^{k} + I_t}{1 + \mu(I_x{}^2 + I_y{}^2)} I_x \quad (3.7)$$

$$v_{x,y}^{k+1} = \bar{v}_{x,y}^{k} - \mu \frac{I_x \bar{u}_{x,y}^{k} + I_y \bar{v}_{x,y}^{k} + I_t}{1 + \mu(I_x{}^2 + I_y{}^2)} I_y \quad (3.8)$$

where $u_{x,y}^k$ is the k-th estimated horizontal optical flow vector at (x, y), and $\bar{u}_{x,y}^k$ is the k-th estimated average of $u_{x,y}^k$ at the neighbouring pixels. $v_{x,y}^k$ and $\bar{v}_{x,y}^k$ are the corresponding vertical components. An example of the optical flow analysis is shown in Figure 1. The left image (a) is extracted from a video sequence at a certain time, and the right image (b) is the next picture. Computed optical flow velocities are shown at every 8 pixels in (c). The horizontal axis indicates the x coordinate in an image, and the vertical axis indicates the y coordinate. Each line or dot in this figure illustrates the amount and direction of optical flow velocity at the corresponding position in the images (a) and (b).

3. A Multimodal Speech Recognition System

3.1 Feature Extraction and Fusion

Figure 2 shows the structure of our audio-visual multimodal speech recognition system. Speech signals are recorded at a 16kHz sampling rate, and a speech frame with the length of 25ms is extracted at every 10ms. Each frame is converted into a 39-dimensional acoustic vector consisting of 12-dimensional mel-frequency cepstral coefficients, normalised log energy, and their first and second order derivatives. A video stream is captured with the frame rate of 15 frames/sec and the resolution size of 360×240. Before computing the optical flow, the resolution is reduced to 180×120 keeping the aspect ratio so that computation complexity should be reduced, and the image is transformed into grey-scale. Low-pass filtering (smoothing) and low-level noise addition are

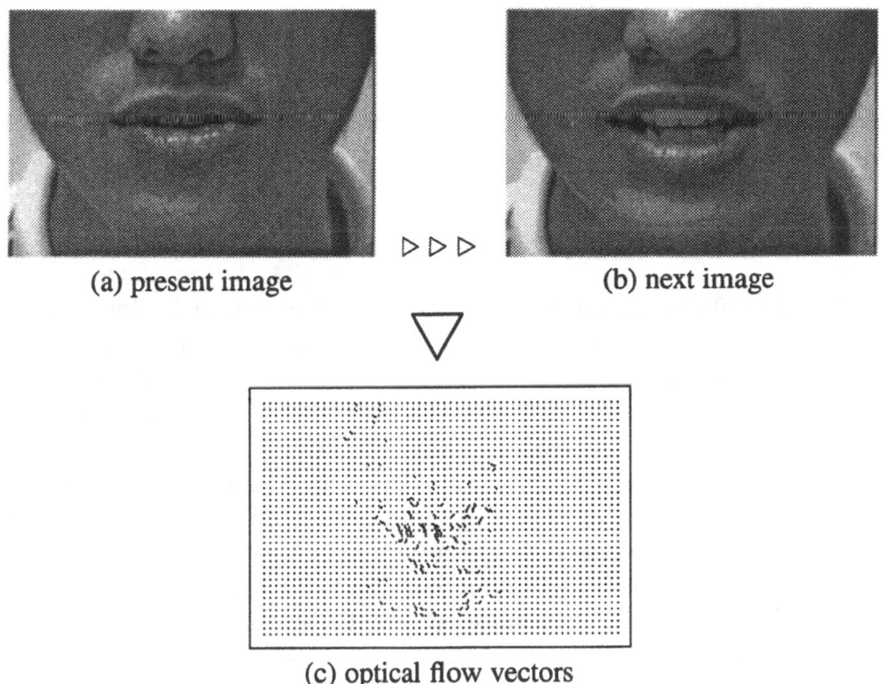

Figure 1. An example of optical flow analysis.

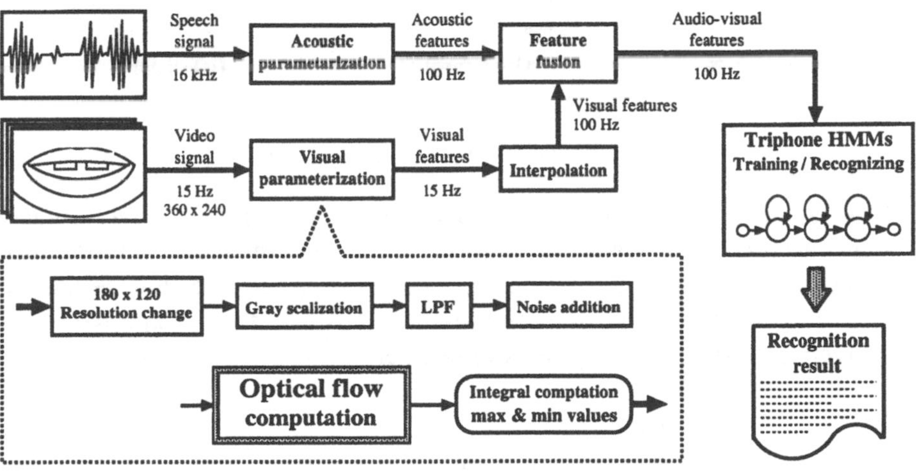

Figure 2. Our multimodal speech recognition system.

applied in order to increase the precision of the optical flow. Then the optical flow is computed from a pair of consecutive images with five iterations.

We extract a visual feature set from the optical flow analysis. It consists of maximum and minimum values of the integral of the optical flow vectors. The 3-D images of integral results are shown in Figure 3. The horizontal and vertical axes indicate the x and y coordinates in an image, respectively. By denoting the integral by $f(x, y)$,

$$\frac{\partial}{\partial x} f(x, y) = u(x, y) \ , \ \frac{\partial}{\partial y} f(x, y) = v(x, y) \tag{3.9}$$

are obtained. When a speaker is not speaking, the surface is almost flat as shown in the left image (a). When the speaker's mouth is opening, optical flow vectors point to diffusing directions around the mouth shape. As a result, a mountain-like surface is created as shown in the centre image (b), and it produces the maximum value. When the mouth is closing, converging vectors of optical flow occur around the lip contour. Then the integral operation produces a dip in the mouth area, as shown in the right image (c), and the minimum value is observed. Therefore, this feature set contains not only moving information but also open/close information of the mouth. The 39-dimensional acoustic features and the 2-dimensional visual features are combined into a 41-dimensional audio-visual vector, after synchronising the visual frame rate with the audio frame rate using a 3-degree spline function.

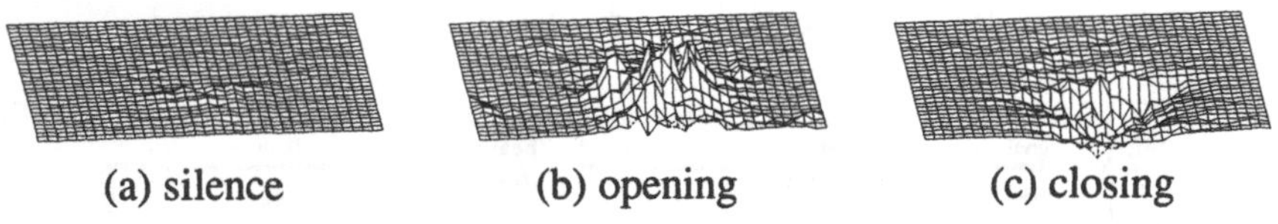

(a) silence (b) opening (c) closing

Figure 3. Examples of optical flow integral results.

The visual features based on the optical flow analysis have the advantage in that they are independent of the lip location in the image. Therefore, this method does not need the lip contour extraction nor lip location detection. This is different from many conventional methods, and this is expected to be effective for making robust systems in real fields.

3.2 Modelling

A set of triphone Hidden Markov Models (HMMs) having three states and two mixtures in each state is used in our system. HMM parameters are trained using 41-dimensional features with the EM algorithm in the same way as the traditional audio-only method. The 41-dimensional audio-visual triphone HMM is divided into a 39-dimensional audio HMM and a 2-dimensional visual HMM for recognition. The observation probability $b_j(O_{AV})$ of generating an audio-visual feature O_{AV} is given by the following equation:

$$b_j(O_{AV}) = b_{A_j}(O_A)^{\lambda_A} \times b_{V_j}(O_V)^{\lambda_V} \tag{3.10}$$

where $b_{A_j}(O_A)$ and $b_{V_j}(O_V)$ are probabilities of generating an acoustic vector O_A and a visual vector O_V in a state j respectively, and λ_A and λ_V are weighting factors for the audio and visual streams. By properly controlling these weighting factors according to the noise condition, improvements of the recognition accuracy compared with the audio-only ASR is expected.

4. Experiments for Noise-Added Data

4.1 Database

An audio-visual speech database was collected in a clean/quiet condition from 11 male speakers, each uttering 250 sequences of connected digits in Japanese. Each sequence consisted of 2–6 digits, such as "3029 (*san-zero-nī-kyū*)" and "187546 (*ichi-hachi-nana-gō-yon-roku*)", with an average of four digits. The total duration of our database is approximately 2.5 hours.

A microphone and a DV camera were located in front of a speaker roughly one meter away and the speaker's face was illuminated by ceiling lights. We recorded images around the speaker's mouth as shown in (a) and (b) in Figure 1. The zooming and positioning of the images were set manually before recording, and they were not changed throughout the recording for each subject. Since the features used in our method are independent of the lip location in the image, no detection technique was used. Several speakers had a beard or moustache, but no speaker had lip marking. The audio and visual signals were recorded simultaneously in the DV tape.

4.2 Training and Recognition

Experiments were conducted using the leave-one-out method: data from one speaker were used for testing while data from the other 10 speakers were used for training. This process was rotated for all possible combinations. Since visual features are considered to be effective especially to detect silence, we controlled the stream weight factors, λ_A and λ_V, only for the silence HMM under the following constraint:

$$\lambda_A + \lambda_V = 1 \ , \ \lambda_A \geq 0 \ , \ \lambda_V \geq 0 \tag{3.11}$$

For any other triphone HMM, we fixed λ_A and λ_V at 1.0 and 0.0 respectively. This means that our visual feature set was used only for silence detection in this study. All the phonemes except silence were recognised using acoustic information only. It is extremely important to separate speech and non-speech (silence) periods in speech recognition under noisy environments. Although many methods have been proposed for silence detection, it is still very difficult to correctly detect silence periods, especially when the noise level is high. Therefore, we decided to first use visual features to detect silence and investigate how much the recognition performance could be improved. Research on using audio-visual features for recognising phonemes will be reported in the future.

4.3 Results

Figures 4 and 5 show the digit recognition results at (a) 5dB, (b) 10dB, (c) 15dB and (d) 20dB SNR level conditions with white noise, and (e) in the clean condition. The horizontal axis indicates the audio stream weight λ_A, and the vertical axis indicates the percentage of digit recognition accuracy. The dotted line indicates the accuracy of the audio-only recognition scheme as the baseline, while the solid line indicates the performance of our multimodal automatic speech recognition method. Table 1 shows the best multimodal recognition results and corresponding audio stream weights in comparison with the audio-only results. These results show that our multimodal automatic speech recognition system achieves better performance than the audio-only ASR in all environments. Especially, approximately 47% and 32% of relative reduction in the digit error rate, compared with the audio-only recognition scheme, have been achieved in a 15dB and 10dB SNR level condition, respectively.

Table 1. The best recognition results for noise-added audio-visual data.

SNR	Audio-only	Audio-visual (λ_A)
5dB	39.50%	43.22% (0.78)
10dB	58.55%	71.89% (0.82)
15dB	78.25%	88.21% (0.90)
20dB	94.66%	94.74% (0.86)
clean	97.59%	97.94% (0.88)

We conducted a supplementary experiment for comparing the precision of silence detection by the audio-visual and audio-only HMMs. Noise-added and clean utterances were segmented by either of these models using the forced-alignment technique. Detected onset boundaries, that is, the boundaries between silence and the beginning of a digit sequence, were compared with manually detected boundaries to evaluate the performance. The amount of error (ms) was averaged over noise-added utterances and clean utterances, respectively. Table 2 shows the detection errors under various SNR conditions. The audio and visual stream weights in the audio-visual HMMs were optimised at each condition. The mean onset detection error rate was reduced to approximately 1/10 in average by using the audio-visual HMMs. We attribute the

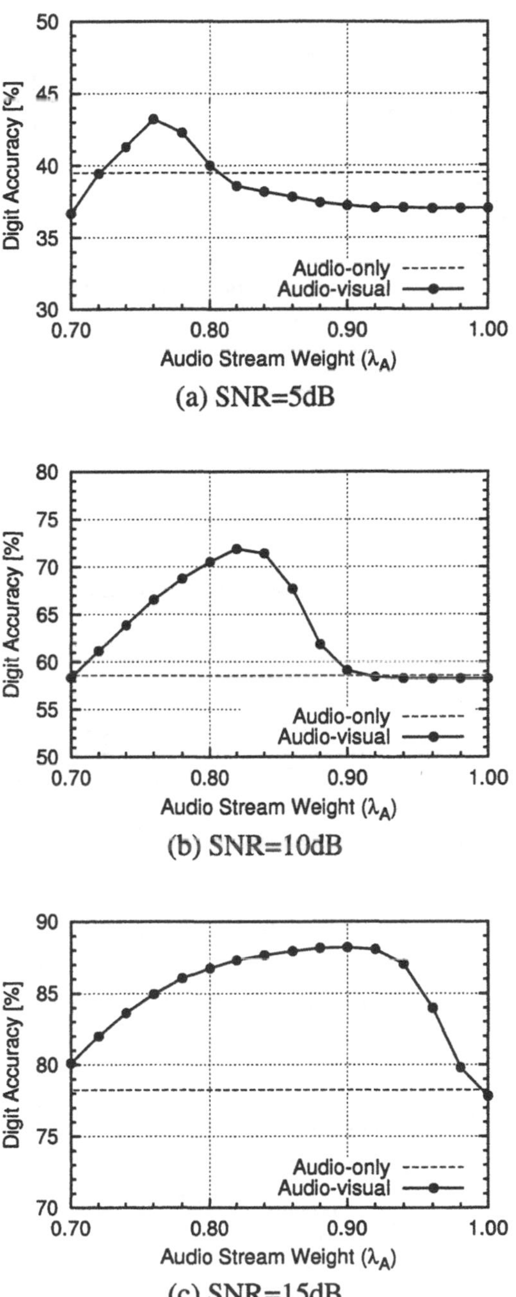

(a) SNR=5dB

(b) SNR=10dB

(c) SNR=15dB

Figure 4. Recognition results for white noise-added speech at SNR=5, 10 and 15dB.

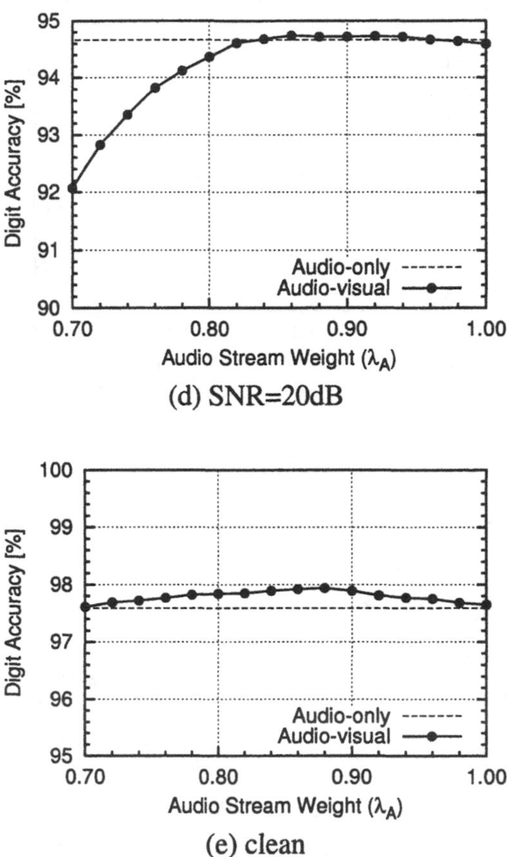

Figure 5. Recognition results for white noise-added speech at SNR=20dB and clean speech.

better recognition performance by the proposed method mainly to the precise boundary detection.

Table 2. Comparison of the onset detection errors (ms) of speaking periods in various SNR conditions.

SNR	Audio-only	Audio-visual
5dB	2443.1	397.4
10dB	1375.7	36.1
15dB	288.6	15.4
20dB	11.4	13.1
Ave.	1029.7	115.5

4.4 Discussions

We consider that one of the reasons why the recognition performance was improved is that digit insertion and silence deletion errors were restrained by audio-visual features. In real applications, it is important that digits must not be inserted in pause/silence periods and silences should not be inserted within digit sequences. Since the above evaluation did not account for silence deletion, substitution and insertion errors, we needed to conduct another evaluation in which silence insertion within speech periods and substitution of silences by digits as well as digit insertion within silences are counted as errors. Table 3 shows the comparison between results of evaluations "with silence" and "without silence" for both audio-only and audio-visual methods at the best stream weight factor $\lambda_A = 0.82$ when SNR=10dB. The table shows the number of errors within 100 utterances per speaker. The difference between the results with/without silence is obvious for substitution and insertion errors in the audio-only condition, whereas there are few differences in the audio-visual condition. This means that silence periods are more correctly detected by the audio-visual method than the audio-only method.

Table 3. The error analysis results (the number of errors) with/without silence evaluations for noise-added audio-visual data consisting of 100 utterances per speaker.

			Del	Sub	Ins
Audio-only	(with	silence)	14.36	25.01	4.12
	(without	silence)	9.64	18.90	12.91
Audio-visual	(with	silence)	14.47	9.52	2.35
	(without	silence)	14.01	11.83	2.27

(Del: deletion error, Sub: substitution error, Ins: insertion error)

The visual feature set used in this work is effective mainly to detect silences and is not powerful enough to recognize digits by itself. Therefore, if SNR is very low and the audio signal is severely distorted, the improvement by combining the visual feature set is limited. This is probably the reason why the improvement shown in Figure 4 by combining the visual features at SNR=5dB is smaller than that at SNR=10dB.

Note that the digit accuracy of an audio-only scheme is different from the performance of the multimodal method at $\lambda_A = 1$. This is because the audio-visual HMM was trained using 41-dimensional audio-visual features with the EM algorithm while the audio-only HMM was trained using 39-dimensional audio-only features. In addition, the stream weights were determined independent of the EM algorithm. The audio-only HMM was therefore not the same as the audio-visual HMM even using $\lambda_A = 1$, and consequently the performances were different.

In Figure 4, it is shown that the lower the SNR level becomes, the smaller the optimum audio stream weight becomes. This means that it is very important to optimise the stream weights according to the audio conditions.

5. Experiments for Real-World Data

5.1 Database

We collected another audio-visual database in a real environment to evaluate both audio and visual robustness of our multimodal automatic speech recognition system. Six male speakers different from those in the clean database respectively uttered 115 sequences of connected digits in a driving car on the expressway. The total duration of this database is about an hour.

Each speaker sat in the passenger seat. A portable DV camera was located in front of the speaker approximately half a meter away, without any special light. A lapel microphone was used for recording audio data. Other conditions were the same as the experiments for noise-added data described in Section 4.

There were several kinds of acoustic noises in our database, such as engine sounds, wind noises, and non-stationary blinker sounds. The acoustic SNR level of this database is approximately 10–15dB. As for visual noise, extreme brightness changing when going through shadows of viaducts and signs, head shaking on bumpy roads, and slow car-frame shadow movements on the face when driving on a curve were observed. An example of visual data in our database is shown in Figure 6.

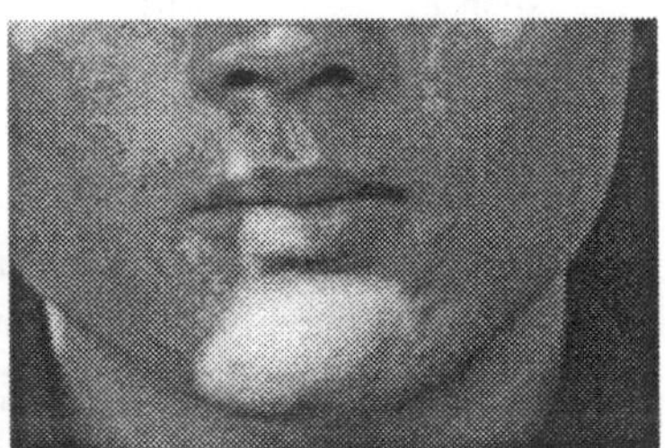

Figure 6. An example of an image in our real-world database (sunlight and car-frame shadow are observed).

5.2 Training and Recognition

In this experiment, the clean audio-visual database was used for training, while the real-world database was used for testing. The stream weight parameters were restricted by the Equation (3.11). In order to increase the robustness of ASR, Cepstral Mean Normalisation (CMN) and unsupervised adaptation using the Maximum Likelihood Linear Regression (MLLR) (Leggetter and Woodland, 1995) technique were applied. The log-energy coefficient was removed from the feature set since there was a large mismatch between the recording conditions for training and testing. The audio-visual feature therefore consisted of 38-dimensional acoustic and 2-dimensional visual features.

5.3 Results

Figure 7 shows the recognition results for the real-world audio-visual data recorded in the driving car, under the condition of (a) no adaptation, (b) unsupervised batch MLLR adaptation and (c) unsupervised incremental MLLR adaptation. The batch MLLR adaptation is the method in which all test data were used for adaptation before recognition. In the incremental MLLR adaptation, the test set was incrementally used for adaptation; every time an utterance is recognised, it is then used to update the HMMs. In both methods, not only mean but also variance values of every HMM were adapted, and the number of transformation matrices was three. In the results shown in Figure 7, our system achieved about 17% and 11% relative error reduction compared with the audio-only results on batch and incremental MLLR adaptation, respectively, while about 13% relative error reduction was achieved when no adaptation was applied.

5.4 Discussion

We conducted the evaluation in the same way as in Section 4. Table 4 shows the error analysis results on unsupervised batch MLLR adaptation comparing the audio-only method with our multimodal automatic speech recognition system ($\lambda_A = 0.78$). We evaluated only three speakers' speech data since others often uttered isolated digits, which are inadequate utterances for this analysis. This result is almost the same as the one shown in Table 3. Therefore, it is concluded that the improvement on recognition accuracy is due to the better performance in silence detection by visual features.

Although there is a difference between visual conditions of the clean data for training and the real-world data for testing due to visual distortion and noise in real environments, our proposed system still achieved a significant improvement. The performance of multimodal automatic speech recognition is higher than the audio-only scheme irrespective of using the MLLR adaptation. Thus, we can conclude our visual feature works efficiently in real environments.

6. Conclusion and Future Work

We have proposed a robust visual feature extraction technique for audio-visual multimodal automatic speech recognition, and evaluated the robustness

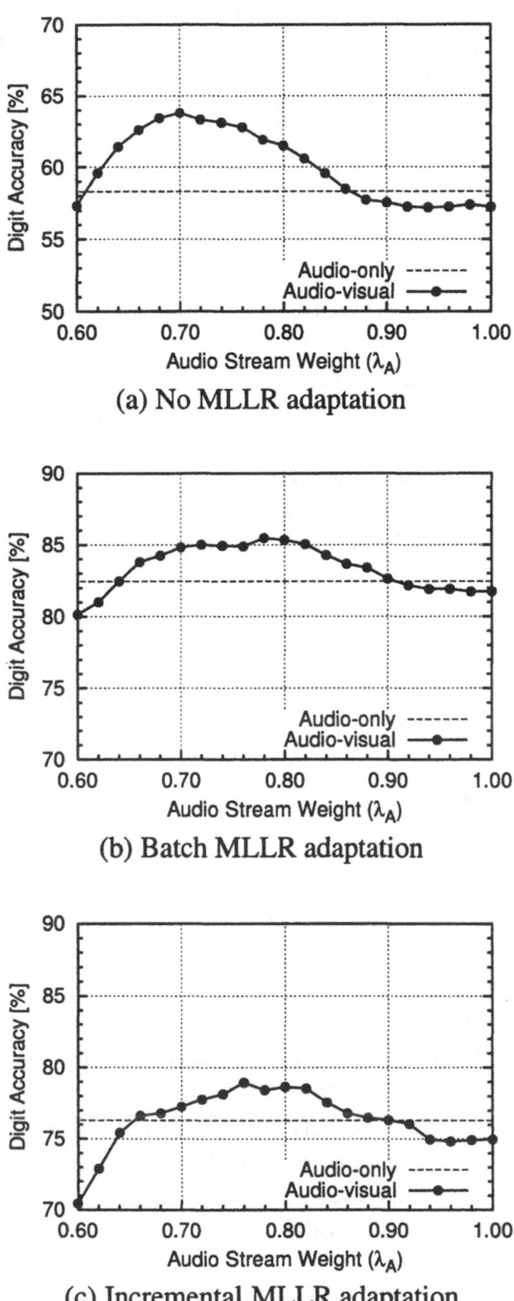

Figure 7. The recognition results on various MLLR adaptations for real-world data.

Table 4. The error analysis results (the number of errors) with/without silence evaluations for real-world audio-visual data consisting of 100 utterances per speaker.

			Del	Sub	Ins
Audio-only	(with	silence)	16.75	8.73	0.94
	(without	silence)	2.68	7.83	4.12
Audio-visual	(with	silence)	1.46	6.33	4.63
	(without	silence)	1.74	7.68	3.19

(Del: deletion error, Sub: substitution error, Ins: insertion error)

of our method against both acoustic and visual noises using real-world data. Our method has achieved the following digit error rate reduction compared with the audio-only schemes: 46% reduction in the white noise condition at 15dB SNR level, and 17% in the real environment on unsupervised batch MLLR adaptation. These experimental results show that our multimodal automatic speech recognition system performs well even in noisy conditions such as mobile environments. The visual features are significantly useful for detecting silence and reducing digit insertion errors in silence periods. Since these experiments have been conducted in a speaker-independent condition, it has also been confirmed that our method is effective for speaker-independent tasks.

Our future works include: (1) investigation of more robust and informative visual parameters, such as features including the direction and amount of lip movements, (2) optimisation of the stream weight for each triphone HMM to improve the performance by applying the maximum likelihood method or other algorithms, (3) investigation of fusion algorithm and audio-visual synchronisation methods in order to invent robust and high-performance multimodal automatic speech recognition techniques, (4) testing of the proposed techniques on larger data sets, (5) comparing the performance of the proposed method with other methods under real environments, and (6) investigation for optimising the robustness of multimodal systems, in order to increase the recognition ability to distinguish not only silence periods but also all phonemes.

Concerning the stream weight optimisation, several approaches have been investigated, e.g., (Hernando, 1997; Miyajima et al., 2001). In most of these schemes, stream weight factors are determined in the training stage or by using a development set. Although it is difficult to develop an effective real-time stream weight optimisation method, we are currently trying several approaches along this line.

Acknowledgements

This research has been conducted in cooperation with NTT DoCoMo. The authors wish to express thanks for their support.

References

Basu, S., Neti, C., Rajput, N., Senior, A., Subramaniam, L., and Verma, A. (1999). Audio-visual large vocabulary continuous speech recognition in the broadcast domain. In *Proceedings of International Workshop on Multimedia Signal Processing (MMSP)*, pages 475–481, Copenhagen, Denmark.

Bregler, C. and Konig, Y. (1994). "Eigenlips" for robust speech recognition. In *Proceedings of International Conference on Acoustics, Speech and Signal Processing (ICASSP)*, pages 669–672, Adelaide, Australia.

Furui, S., Iwano, K., Hori, C., Shinozaki, T., Saito, Y., and Tamura, S. (2001). Ubiquitous speech processing. In *Proceedings of International Conference on Acoustics, Speech and Signal Processing (ICASSP)*, pages 13–16, Salt Lake City, Utah, USA.

Hernando, J. (1997). Maximum likelihood weighting of dynamic speech features for CDHMM speech recognition. In *Proceedings of International Conference on Acoustics, Speech and Signal Processing (ICASSP)*, pages 1267–1270, Munich, Germany.

Horn, B. K. and Schunck, B. G. (1981). Determining optical flow. *Artificial Intelligence*, 17(1-3):185–203.

Iwano, K., Tamura, S., and Furui, S. (2001). Bimodal speech recognition using lip movement measured by optical-flow analysis. In *Proceedings of International Workshop on Hands-free Speech Communication (HSC)*, pages 187–190, Kyoto, Japan.

Leggetter, C. J. and Woodland, P. C. (1995). Maximum likelihood linear regression for speaker adaptation of continuous density Hidden Markov Models. *Computer Speech and Language*, 9(2):171–185.

Mase, K. and Pentland, A. (1991). Automatic lipreading by optical-flow analysis. *Transactions on Systems and Computers in Japan*, 22(6):67–76.

Miyajima, C., Tokuda, K., and Kitamura, T. (2000). Audio-visual speech recognition using MCE-based HMMs and model-dependent stream weights. In *Proceedings of International Conference on Spoken Language Processing (ICSLP)*, pages 1023–1026, Denver, Colorado, USA.

Miyajima, C., Tokuda, K., and Kitamura, T. (2001). Minimum classification error training for speaker identification using Gaussian mixture models based on multi-space probability distribution. In *Proceedings of European Conference on Speech Communication and Technology (EUROSPEECH)*, pages 2837–2840, Aalborg, Denmark.

Nakamura, S., Ito, H., and Shikano, K. (2000). Stream weight optimization of speech and lip image sequence for audio-visual speech recognition. In *Proceedings of International Conference on Spoken Language Processing (ICSLP)*, pages 20–24, Beijing, China.

Potamianos, G., Cosatto, E., Gref, H. P., and Roe, D. B. (1997). Speaker independent audio-visual database for bimodal ASR. In *Proceedings of European Tutorial Workshop on Audio-visual Speech Processing (AVSP)*, pages 65–68, Rhodes, Greece.

Chapter 4

FEATURE FUNCTIONS FOR TREE-BASED DIALOGUE COURSE MANAGEMENT

Klaus Macherey, Hermann Ney
Lehrstuhl für Informatik VI, Computer Science Department, RWTH Aachen - University of Technology
{ k.macherey,ney } @informatik.rwth-aachen.de

Abstract We propose a set of feature functions for dialogue course management and investigate their effect on the system's behaviour for choosing the subsequent dialogue action during a dialogue session. Especially, we investigate whether the system is able to detect and resolve ambiguities, and if it always chooses that state which leads as quickly as possible to a final state that is likely to meet the user's request. The criteria and data structures used are independent of the underlying domain and can therefore be employed for different applications of spoken dialogue systems. Experiments were performed on a German in-house corpus that covers the domain of a German telephone directory assistance.

Keywords: Domain independence; Dialogue costs; Dialogue strategy; Confidence measures; XML.

1. Introduction

Nowadays, there are numerous spoken dialogue systems for a variety of applications like inquiry systems for hotel reservations and travel information, restaurant guides, train timetable information systems, etc. (Constantinides et al., 1998; Seneff and Polifroni, 1996; Aust et al., 1995). If several tasks and domains are to be treated by a single dialogue system without replacing or rewriting parts of the system, the need for an application-independent dialogue manager arises. In order to develop an application-independent dialogue manager one has to identify those steps that are common to all of the domains. These steps include:

W. Minker, D. Bühler and L. Dybkjær (eds), Spoken Multimodal Human-Computer Dialogue in Mobile Environments, 55-76

- *information request,*
- *information collection and evaluation,*
- *ambiguity resolution, and*
- *information retrieval.*

Therefore, parameterisable data structures must be derived from the knowledge of each domain, and all other operations like storing and managing concept/attribute pairs describing the semantics of input data, ambiguity detection and resolution as well as dialogue course management should be based on this structure. Appropriate data structures for this purpose are trees which are constructed from the knowledge of a given domain. The tree nodes encode concepts, and the edges of a tree represent relations between these concepts. The tree is an over-specification of the given domain (Ammicht et al., 2001). Using trees rather than directed acyclic graphs, we can identify different dialogue goals with different paths. Paths that have common nodes share some common information. In the context of spoken dialogue systems, trees have been used by Potamianos et al. (2000) and Ammicht et al. (2001) for the purpose of domain-independent dialogue management and ambiguity resolution. In (Abella and Gorin, 1999), the task knowledge is encoded as a hierarchy of constructs represented as tree structures. The dialogue manager is based on a so-called Construct Algebra defining a set of elementary relations and operations on a set of constructs.

In this work, we also use tree-based data structures in order to obtain domain-independent representations. Here, the analysis of different features for dialogue course management and investigations on the system's behaviour for choosing the subsequent dialogue action based on a foregoing assessment are the main focus of attention. Especially, we investigate whether the proposed features are able to determine the best path that leads as quickly as possible to a final state which is likely to meet the user's request.

2. Basic Dialogue Framework

The basic framework of the dialogue system is depicted in Figure 1. The XML-based dialogue description consists of different dialogue states, subdividing a dialogue into smaller sections. Each dialogue state may again be subdivided into several action states. During a dialogue session, the dialogue manager incorporates the knowledge from user input into the knowledge tree. If the subsequent dialogue state is not explicitly given by the dialogue description, the manager will determine the next state/action pair by analysing the tree's information content. Depending on the chosen state/action pair, the dialogue manager will execute only those dialogue commands that are specified in the dialogue description for this chosen pair.

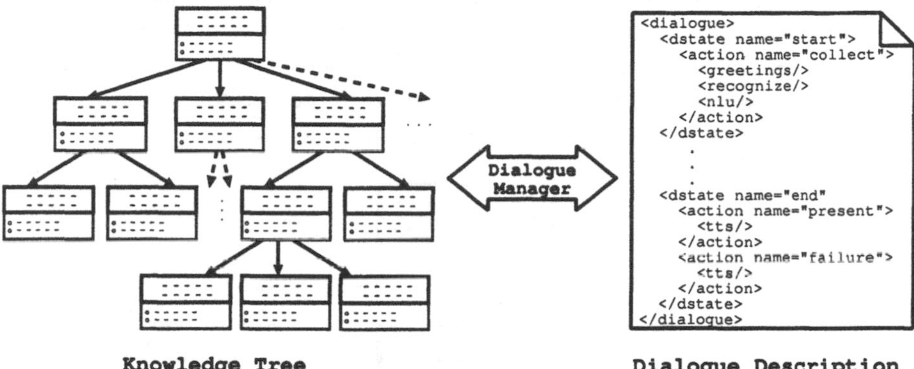
Dialogue Manager
<dialogue>
<dstate name="start">
<action name="collect">
<greetings/>
<recognize/>
<nlu/>
</action>
</dstate>
<dstate name="end">
<action name="present">
<tts/>
</action>
<action name="failure">
<tts/>
</action>
</dstate>
</dialogue>
Knowledge Tree
Dialogue Description

Figure 1. Basic structure of the dialogue system: the dialogue manager incorporates knowledge from the user input into the knowledge tree and determines the next dialogue action by analysing the tree's information content.

2.1 Tree-Based Representations

In order to obtain domain-independent representations, we use trees as the fundamental data structure. An example is depicted in Figure 2. The tree is a knowledge representation for the specific task of a telephone directory assistance. Users can ask for information about telephone numbers, email addresses, and fax numbers of persons and companies. The upper half of each tree node describes the part of the dialogue that is processed by the corresponding subtree. The lower half of each node consists of a list of concepts that are associated with that specific node (for presentation reasons, only the concept names and the attribute values are included in the figure). Each path of the tree describes a separate dialogue goal. As depicted in the figure, the root node's name is 'telephone inquiries' and the associated list consists of concepts which are related to different kinds of request verbalisations. The successor nodes are specifications of the corresponding parent node. For the given example, the specifications are requests for email addresses, fax numbers, and phone numbers, respectively. For a given utterance, the sequence of concepts is produced using methods derived from statistical machine translation (Macherey et al., 2001). In this framework, the transcription of an utterance is considered to be a source language sentence and the corresponding sequence of concepts is considered to be the unknown target language sentence. The machine translation approach translates the source sentence into the sequence of concepts and provides an alignment between source and target words. In the example, the word sequence 'I would like' is aligned to the concept @want_question, the word sequence 'to speak with' is aligned to the concept @connect, etc. These alignments are used in order to extract the attributes for each concept out of the aligned words. Each concept together with its attributes is then incorporated into all nodes of the tree, in which the concept's name occurs. In Figure 2, the concept @person{Mr. Miller} is incorporated into two nodes. Since the concepts of the tree are instantiated with the attribute values derived from user input, we call the resulting tree an *instance tree*.

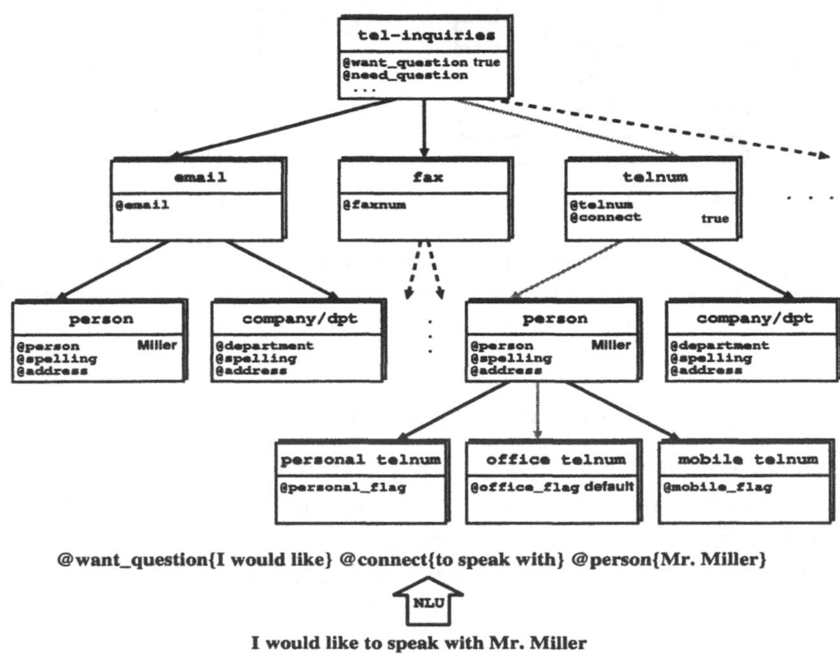

Figure 2. Tree-based knowledge representation for a telephone directory assistance task. The sentence 'I would like to speak with Mr. Miller' is transformed into a concept representation via natural language understanding. After that, each concept/ attribute pair is inserted into the corresponding tree nodes.

2.2 Dialogue Course Management

During a dialogue session, instance trees are built from the original knowledge tree. Concept/attribute pairs which have been retrieved from the user input are incorporated in such an instance tree. If there is only one path from the root to a leaf in such that all necessary concept/attribute pairs of the nodes along the path are filled, the user's request will be answered by the dialogue system. If more than one path exists, the data retrieved from the user is ambiguous and the user is required to constrain his request[1]. If there is no path from the root to a leaf, some of the nodes are still empty. In this case the system must ask for additional information in order to fill the remaining nodes. In general, there are several possibilities to continue a dialogue. Therefore, a cost function is introduced that computes a score for all nodes depending on several features which are described in the following section. Starting from the root node, the dialogue system chooses that node, whose corresponding subtree has minimal cost. Besides choosing the subsequent dialogue state, the dialogue system also has the possibility of verifying information within a node (e.g., in case of low confidence of the recognised words), to resolve ambiguities, or to answer the user's request. The subsequent action of the dialogue system is determined by the proposed cost function.

3. Feature Functions

For the cost function, different features and knowledge sources can be taken into account. We have chosen the following node-specific features.

3.1 Word Confidence Measures

In speech recognition, confidence measures can be employed for detecting possible recognition errors. Thus, word confidence measures can provide a score for the reliability of the concepts that have been produced by these words. Among several approaches to confidence measures, word posterior probabilities have proven to be effective in detecting misrecognised words (Wessel et al., 1998). Given a sequence of acoustic feature vectors x_1^T and a word hypothesis w with starting and ending time t_a and t_e respectively, the posterior probability $p([w, t_a, t_e]|x_1^T)$ is computed in the framework of a forward-backward algorithm by summing over all incoming partial paths W_a starting at the graph's source and ending at time $t_a - 1$, and all partial paths W_e starting at time $t_e + 1$ and ending in the graph's sink. That is, we sum up the posterior probabilities of all those word hypothesis sequences that contain the word hypothesis w with the same starting and ending time. The word confidence $\widetilde{p}(\cdot)$ is then computed by summing over all word hypothesis probabilities $p(\cdot)$ that share the same word label and that have at least one common time frame t:

$$\widetilde{p}([w, t_a, t_e]|x_1^T) = \max_{t:t_a \le t \le t_e} \sum_{(t_i,t_j):t_i \le t \le t_j} p([w, t_i, t_j]|x_1^T) \qquad (4.1)$$

The basic principle is depicted in Figure 3. The maximisation over t is motivated by the following property. For each time frame t, all word hypothesis probabilities that are contained in the word graph and that intersect this time frame must sum to unity. For a word hypothesis $[w, t_a, t_e]$ of the recognised word sequence, the word graph may contain several word hypotheses sharing the same word label but having slightly different time boundaries. Thus, the probability mass is distributed over several edges. Although word hypotheses sharing the same word label may indicate the correctness of the word hypothesis under consideration, they belong to different paths and compete with each other. To mitigate this effect, we maximise over the time frame t, for which the sum of the word hypothesis probabilities with the same word label and approximately the same time boundaries is maximal and use this value as word confidence. For details, see (Wessel et al., 1998; Wessel et al., 2001). This confidence measure is probabilistic and exploits only information which is contained in the output word graph of the speech recognition system. After computing the confidence, each recognised word is tagged as either correct or wrong, depending on whether its confidence exceeds a given threshold τ. Let $\mathcal{W}(c)$ be the set of words that are assigned to a concept c. Then the first feature for node n is defined as follows:

$$v_1(n) := \min_{c \in \mathcal{C}(n)} \left\{ \left(\prod_{w \in \mathcal{W}(c)} \widetilde{p}(w) \right)^{\frac{1}{|\mathcal{W}(c)|}} \right\} \tag{4.2}$$

where $\mathcal{C}(n)$ is the set of concepts of node n and $\mathcal{W}(c)$ is the multiset of words that are aligned to concept c. The feature function $v_1(n)$ computes the minimal geometric mean of the word confidence values for concepts c of node n.

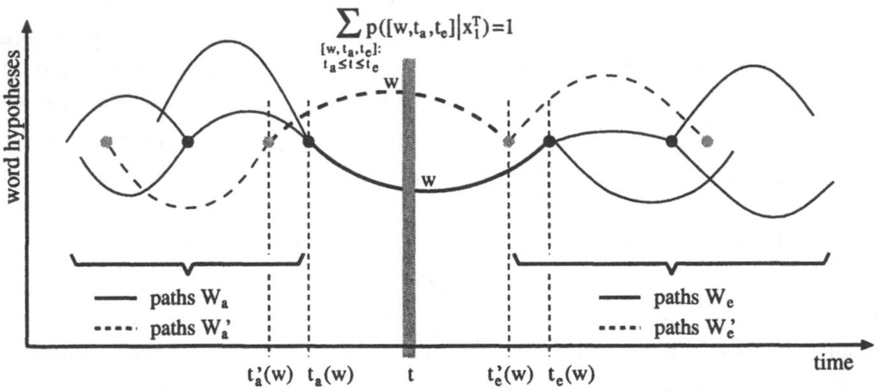

Figure 3. Basic principle of the word graph-based confidence computation. The word posterior probabilities are computed within the framework of a forward backward algorithm with the constraint that for each time frame t, all word hypothesis probabilities that intersect this time frame must sum to unity.

3.2 Importance and Degree of Concept Instances

The importance of a concept c and of an attribute a depends on the given domain. For the telephone directory example, the last name of a person is more important than its first name. Therefore, we introduce a ranking r describing the relevance of concepts and attributes. Consequently, a person's last name is *mandatory* ($r(a) = 1$) whereas the first name is *supplementary* ($r(a) = 0$). The ranking of concepts and attributes is taken into account by summing over all concepts and attributes respectively, for which the associated attribute value is required but has not yet been instantiated by user input. For an attribute a of a concept c, we compute:

$$
\begin{aligned}
f(a) &\longmapsto \begin{cases} 1 & \text{if attribute } a \text{ is assigned a value} \\ 0 & \text{otherwise.} \end{cases} \\
v_2(n) &:= \sum_{c \in \mathcal{C}(n)} \sum_{a \in \mathcal{A}(c)} \delta(r(a), 1) \cdot \delta(f(a), 0) \qquad (4.3)
\end{aligned}
$$

where $\mathcal{C}(n)$ is the set of concepts of a node n and $\mathcal{A}(c)$ is the set of attributes belonging to a concept c. $v_2(n)$ counts the number of mandatory attributes for node n that still have no value. Here, $\delta(\cdot,\cdot)$ denotes the Kronecker function. The importance $r(c)$ of a concept c can be derived from the maximum ranking of its related attributes. However, for some nodes, it is more convenient to fix a concept's rating independently of the related attributes. Therefore, we compute the second feature for node n as follows:

$$
\begin{aligned}
g(c) &\longmapsto \begin{cases} 1 & \text{if concept } c \text{ is sufficiently instantiated} \\ 0 & \text{otherwise.} \end{cases} \\
v_3(n) &:= \sum_{c \in \mathcal{C}(n)} \delta(r(c), 1) \cdot \delta(g(c), 0) \qquad (4.4)
\end{aligned}
$$

Again, $\delta(\cdot,\cdot)$ denotes the Kronecker function. A concept c is sufficiently instantiated if all its related attributes with ranking $r(a) = 1$ have already been assigned values, i.e., $|\{a \in \mathcal{A}(c) | r(a) = 1, f(a) = 1\}| = \sum_{a \in \mathcal{A}(c)} r(a)$. The feature function $v_3(n)$ counts the number of concepts for node n that are not sufficiently instantiated.

3.3 Degree of Ambiguity

Ambiguities can result from several sources: misrecognised utterances, errors during the natural language understanding step, or ambiguous user language (Ammicht et al., 2001). In the context of a telephone directory assistance, ambiguities may also occur from proper names that can be used as both first names and last names. Another source of ambiguities are homophones, that is, proper names that have the same pronunciation but different spellings can result in additional ambiguities that must be detected and resolved by the dialogue system. In the latter case, the speech recognition system simply constructs a list of all possible sentences with different homophone names and leaves it to the dialogue manager to resolve this kind of ambiguity. The dialogue manager constructs an instance tree for every sentence hypothesis that is delivered by the recognition system. If an ambiguity has been detected in node n, this is annotated in the cost vector:

$$\begin{aligned} \text{amb}(n) &\longmapsto \begin{cases} 1 & \text{if node } n \text{ has ambiguous information} \\ 0 & \text{otherwise.} \end{cases} \\ v_4(n) &:= \text{amb}(n) \end{aligned} \tag{4.5}$$

The feature function $v_4(n)$ keeps a record of detected ambiguities for node n. If the ambiguity is resolved by the dialogue system, the $\text{amb}(n)$ flag is reset to 0.

3.4 Contradictory Information

A node n contains contradictory information if an already instantiated attribute is overwritten by a new value that is inconsistent with the old one. In this case, the following feature is set to 1:

$$\begin{aligned} \text{cnt}(n) &\longmapsto \begin{cases} 1 & \text{if node } n \text{ has contradictory information} \\ 0 & \text{otherwise.} \end{cases} \\ v_5(n) &:= \text{cnt}(n) \end{aligned} \tag{4.6}$$

The feature function $v_5(n)$ keeps a record of nodes that contain contradictory information. Note that the number of SQL results for a database query of a node containing contradictory information is always 0.

3.5 Number of SQL Results

If the number of database entries returned from a database query is too large, the user should restrict the request. If no database entry has been returned, the answer to the user's request is either not covered by the database or the request should be less restrictive. The number of SQL results is taken as an additional feature for the cost vector. Let $t(q)$ be a table returned by a database query q. Then, the feature $v_6(n)$ is defined as follows:

$$v_6(n) := |t(q_n)| \tag{4.7}$$

Here, $|\cdot|$ describes the number of table entries. Thus, the feature function $v_6(n)$ simply counts the number of returned table entries.

3.6 Verification of Information

Since automatic speech recognition is error-prone, it seems reasonable to authorise verification questions in order to verify the attribute values of some concepts, particularly, if the confidence of the aligned words is low. Verification of node information is taken as an additional feature for the cost vector:

$$\begin{aligned} \text{verf}(n) &\longmapsto \begin{cases} 1 & \text{if information in } n \text{ has been verified} \\ 0 & \text{otherwise.} \end{cases} \\ v_7(n) &:= \text{verf}(n) \end{aligned} \tag{4.8}$$

The feature function $v_7(n)$ keeps a record of whether the information stored in node n has been verified by the system.

4. Computing Dialogue Costs

For each input sentence, a semantic analysis is performed. The concept/attribute pairs are extracted and inserted into temporary arrays for all tree nodes that are associated with these pairs. Temporary arrays are used in order to detect contradictory information. The dialogue costs are then computed on different levels: the local node costs, the path costs, and the tree costs.

4.1 Node Costs

For a node n, the computation of the node costs is done by applying the feature functions described in Section 3. For a tree t, this yields a node-specific cost vector $v_t(n)$ consisting of the feature values derived from the feature functions:

$$v_t(n) = \begin{pmatrix} v_1(n) \\ v_2(n) \\ \vdots \\ v_7(n) \end{pmatrix}, \quad n \in \text{nodes}(t) \tag{4.9}$$

where $\text{nodes}(t)$ is the set of nodes of the instance tree t. The node costs are local costs and are computed independently from each other. Although not expressed in the formulae, some of the cost functions' values depend on the chosen input modality. For example, when using text input via keyboard in contrast to speech input, the confidence is always set to 1.0, and the verification function is set to 1, accordingly.

4.2 Path Costs

For many applications, a knowledge tree has only a moderate number of leaves. Since a tree has as many paths as leaves, there is no need to combine the costs of different paths within all parent nodes. Instead, all paths of a tree are treated separately. For computing the costs of a path π for an instance tree

t, we simply add the node costs for all nodes along this path π.

$$v_t(\pi) = \bigoplus_{n \in \pi(t)} v_t(n) \tag{4.10}$$

The combination function $\oplus$ for combining node-specific cost vectors is defined as follows: most of the feature values are added componentwise, except the confidence feature and the feature that computes the number of SQL results. Here, the confidence of a path is defined as the minimum of the confidence values of all its nodes. For the SQL feature, we internally expand the SQL query by additional 'where' constraints that are given by the information stored in the nodes along the path. At the end of the computation, each path is assigned a cost vector corresponding to the costs that arise for continuing the dialogue along that path.

4.3 Tree Costs

At the end of the path costs computation, each path is assigned a cost vector corresponding to the costs that arise for continuing the dialogue along that path. If there are different possible paths that may conclude the dialogue, the dialogue manager will choose the path with the best score in order to proceed the dialogue. This requires a comparison function, for which we use a decision tree. The decision tree determines the best scored path of a tree. By equating the best scored path vector with the tree costs, the decision tree is also used for determining the best scored tree.

5. Selection of Dialogue State/Action Pairs

There are different dialogue actions that can be chosen by the dialogue manager in order to continue the dialogue. Typical dialogue actions are the collection of information and the presentation of database query results to the user. The choice of the subsequent dialogue action depends on the costs that have been computed for each path of a tree. Since the best-scored path as well as the subsequent dialogue action are determined by decision trees, the structure of the decision trees has an immediate influence on the dialogue strategy. A partial decision tree for choosing the subsequent dialogue action is shown in Figure 4. If the confidence of some information is lower than a given threshold, the information stored in the node with the lowest confidence is explicitly verified by further requests. If the best-scored path includes ambiguous information (which is marked by the ambiguity function, cf. Equation 4.4) that cannot be resolved by the system, the user is queried by the system in order to resolve this ambiguity. If the best-scored path is incomplete because at least one node is empty, the system asks for additional information in order to complete this path. If there is a complete path with a moderate number of SQL answers, the system replies to the user's request.

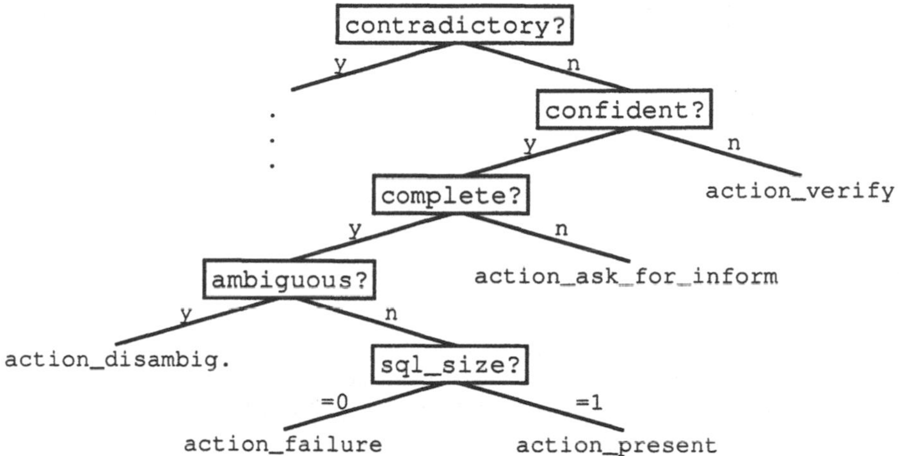

Figure 4. Partial decision tree for determining the subsequent dialogue action.

6. XML-based Data Structures

The feature functions and selection criterion described in the previous sections do not use any task-specific knowledge and can therefore be used for different applications of spoken dialogue systems. For a concrete task, however, some domain-specific knowledge must be defined that is provided by three XML files. These files are the concept/attribute table defining the concepts and attributes for the natural language understanding part, the knowledge tree collecting and storing information provided by the natural language understanding module, and the dialogue description specifying concrete dialogue actions.

6.1 Concept/Attribute Tables

To represent the meaning of an utterance, a set of domain-specific concepts is used. A concept is defined as the smallest unit of meaning that is relevant to a specific task (Levin and Pieraccini, 1995). Each concept may have several values which are called attributes. In order to derive the values from the concepts, we assume that the attributes only depend on their associated concept and its aligned words. Each concept may have two rules: one for deriving the attribute values and one for converting the values into a more formal SQL constraint. Figure 5 shows part of the XML-based concept/attribute table for the telephone directory assistance task.

```
<?xml version="1.0" encoding="ISO-8859-1"?>
<!DOCTYPE concept_attribute_table SYSTEM "ca_table.dtd">

<concept_attribute_table>
 <concept name="@person">
   <attrib name="surname"    type="str" value="" nlu=".." sql=".." rating="man"/>
   <attrib name="forename"   type="str" value="" nlu=".." sql=".." rating="sup"/>
   <attrib name="gender"     type="str" value="" nlu=".." sql=".." rating="sup"/>
   <attrib name="occupation" type="str" value="" nlu=".." sql=".." rating="sup"/>
 </concept>
      :
      :
</concept_attribute_table>
```

Figure 5. Part of an XML-based concept/attribute table. Each concept may consist of several attributes. An attribute is a tuple consisting of the attribute's name, the type and its value. The `rating` specifies the importance of the attribute and can be either mandatory or supplementary (default).

6.2 Knowledge Tree

This XML file specifies the structure of the knowledge tree. A knowledge tree stores the information that is extracted from user utterances during a dialogue. Each node of a knowledge tree consists of a list of concepts that are associated with this specific node. Additionally, each tree node has a link to a dialogue state (as specified in the dialogue description file, see Section 6.3). For the dialogue manager, this link acts as a mediator between the knowledge representation and the dialogue description. While the determination of the subsequent dialogue action only depends on the analysis of the tree's information content, the concrete realisation and execution of this action is not a part of the tree specification but of the dialogue description. If, for example, the dialogue manager has determined the best scored path and decides for a subsequent dialogue action, it will switch to the next dialogue state as given by the node's dialogue state name and executes the dialogue commands of this dialogue state/action pair. A part of the knowledge tree specification for the telephone directory assistance task is listed in Figure 6.

6.3 Dialogue Description

The XML-based dialogue description consists of different dialogue states, subdividing a dialogue into smaller sections. In addition to dialogue states for ordinary tasks like greeting the user or presenting some introductory information, there are more specialised dialogue states corresponding to the nodes of the knowledge tree. These dialogue states will be chosen by the dialogue manager if the subsequent dialogue state is not explicitly determined by the dia-

```
<?xml version="1.0" encoding="ISO-8859-1"?>
<!DOCTYPE knowledge_tree SYSTEM "knowledge_tree.dtd">

<knowledge_tree name="telephone directory assistance" root="0">
  <!-- node definitions -->
  <node name="0" alias="Telephone Inquiries" dstate="0">
    <concept name="@can_question"/>
    <concept name="@want_question"/>
    <concept name="@need_question"/>
  </node>

  <node name="0.1"     alias="email" dstate="0.1">
    <concept name="@email"/>
  </node>

  <node name="0.2"     alias="fax" dstate="0.2">
    <concept name="@faxnum"/>
  </node>

  <node name="0.3"     alias="telephone number" dstate="0.3">
    <concept name="@number"/>
  </node>
      :
  <node name="0.1.1"   alias="person" dstate="0.1.1">
    <concept name="@person"/>
    <concept name="@spelling"/>
    <concept name="@location"/>
  </node>

  <node name="0.1.2"   alias="company/institute" dstate="0.1.2">
    <concept name="@organisation"/>
    <concept name="@spelling"/>
    <concept name="@location"/>
  </node>

  <!-- edge definitions -->
  <edge> 0,0.1 </edge>
  <edge> 0,0.2 </edge>
  <edge> 0,0.3 </edge>
  <edge> 0,0.4 </edge>
      :
</knowledge_tree>
```

Figure 6. Part of an XML-based knowledge tree representation. Each node of the tree has a unique name, an alias name, and a dstate referring to a dialogue state in the dialogue description. A node's child tags describe the list of concepts that are associated with the node. The edges between the nodes are defined within the 'edge definitions' section. The attribute `root` of the tag `knowledge_tree` defines the name of the tree's root node.

logue description itself. In the dialogue state `START` of Figure 7, for example, the subsequent dialogue state is explicitly determined by the `next_state` command, whereas for dialogue state `0` the following dialogue state must be determined by the dialogue manager. Since the actions that are performed during a dialogue act depend on the tree's information content, the dialogue states

```
<?xml version="1.0" encoding="ISO-8859-1"?>
<!DOCTYPE dialog_description SYSTEM "dialog_description.dtd">

<dialogue>
  <dialogue_state name="START">
    <action_state name="arbitrary">
      <set variable="TTS_DIR" type="str" value="..." />
      <next_state name="GREETINGS"/>
    </action_state>
  </dialogue_state>

  <dialogue_state name="GREETINGS">
    <action_state name="arbitrary">
      <greetings time="0-17"  text="Good morning."  barge_in="0"/>
      <greetings time="18-23" text="Good evening."  barge_in="0"/>
      <tts barge_in="1"> How may I help you? <tts/>
      <nlu/>
    </action_state>
  </dialogue_state>

  <dialogue_state name="0">
    <action_state name="guidance">
      <tts> Do you need a phone number, fax number, or email address? <tts/>
      <nlu/>
    </action_state>
  </dialogue_state>
        :
        :
</dialogue>
```

Figure 7. Part of an XML-based dialogue description. A dialogue description consists of several dialogue states where each dialogue state is subdivided into different action states. Only those dialogue commands occurring in an action state that corresponds to the dialogue action as chosen by the dialogue manager are being executed.

are further subdivided into different action states. Beside others, these action states include the collection and presentation of information, and disambiguation and verification of information. Only those dialogue commands, which occur within those action states that correspond to the dialogue action as chosen by the manager, are being executed. All other action states state "arbitrary" which can always be executed when occurring within a dialogue state, regardless of the current dialogue action chosen by the dialogue manager. Figure 7 shows part of the dialogue description for the telephone directory assistance task.

7. Usability in Mobile Environments

An important research area in human-machine interfaces is the use of spoken dialogue systems in mobile environments. Essentially, there are two extreme cases. In the first case, the dialogue system is completely embedded within a mobile computer, e.g., a hand-held device. Dialogue systems in hand-held devices have special demands concerning their computational resources. If the hand-held device shall be independent from external resources, all components of a spoken dialogue system (i.e., the speech recogniser, the text-to-speech system, the dialogue manager, etc.) and the application data (e.g., the application database) must be stored within a small memory. In the second case, the dialogue system runs on an external server so that the mobile system simply connects via a wireless network to the server. Here, the mobile device only needs to transmit the user's input data and to communicate the server's response.

The system described in this chapter belongs to the latter case. This has the advantage that it is easier for the system developer to administrate the dialogue system, e.g., to change the database or to add new components to the speech recogniser without taking into account the limited computational resources of hand-held devices. The disadvantage is that the user needs to establish a connection with costs to the server. Additionally, the performance of speech recognition systems receiving speech that has been transmitted over mobile channels can be significantly degraded when compared to using an unmodified signal. The degradations are a result of both the low bit rate speech coding and channel transmission errors. A solution to this is the use of Distributed Speech Recognition (DSR) where an error protected data channel is used to send a parameterised representation of the speech signal, that is the signal analysis is computed on a hand-held device or a mobile phone and the signal representation is transmitted to the external dialogue server. The definition of appropriate standards and protocols for this is the objective of the Aurora Working Group (Hirsch and Pearce, 2000; Pearce, 2000).

Although the dialogue manager described in this chapter was running on a single server it is possible to separate this part from the complete dialogue system and implement it on a mobile computer. The domain knowledge and the dialogue description can also be provided by the mobile computer, thus allowing for different applications on different mobile devices. Since the basic knowledge tree and the dialogue description only require a small amount of memory, both data files could be downloaded from a server. This would give the user the flexibility to easily change the application's domain.

8. Results

Experiments were performed for a German in-house telephone directory assistance corpus. The objective was to answer naturally spoken requests for telephone numbers, fax numbers, and email addresses of persons, companies, and organisations. The data for training the speech recognition system and the natural language understanding component were recorded over several months from fixed telephones as well as wireless and mobile phones under different conditions. The conditions cover clean speech, office noise, and traffic noise. The corpus allocation is summarised in Table 1.

Table 1. Corpus allocation for the German telephone directory assistance task. Here, train describes the training corpus, dev and eva describe the development and evaluation corpus, respectively.

corpus	# sessions	# speakers	dur. [min]	# sentences	# words
train	131		101	1164	7310
dev	44	151	30	344	2039
eva	21		15	168	1013

For the speech recognition part we used an online speech recogniser based on the RWTH *Verbmobil* recogniser (Kanthak et al., 2000). The recogniser uses a time-synchronous beam search algorithm based on the concept of word-dependent tree copies and integrates the trigram language model constraints in a single pass. No speaker-adaptive or normalisation methods were applied. According to telephone bandwidth, the signal analysis generated feature vectors with 25 dimensions, i.e., 12 cepstral coefficients with 12 first derivatives and the second derivative of the energy.

Table 2 shows recognition results for the development and evaluation test set of the collected data. Since there was only a small subset of proper names covered by the collected data, a class-based trigram was used for recognition purposes. The recogniser vocabulary has a size of 1343 words, including pronunciation variants.

Table 2. Recognition results using a class-based trigram language model and confidence error rates for the development and the evaluation corpus. The confidence measure's free parameters were optimised on the development test set beforehand.

corpus	WER [%]	baseline CER [%]	CER [%]
dev	15.7	14.3	10.5
eva	16.4	14.1	9.4

We used word posterior probabilities as confidence measures. Although the recogniser performs an integrated trigram recognition, the forward/backward probabilities on the generated word lattices were computed in bigram mode for reasons of real-time performance. All free parameters of the confidence measure, i.e., the acoustic scaling factor, the language model scaling factor, and the tagging threshold, were optimised on the separate cross-validation development test set beforehand.

We evaluated the quality of the confidence measure using two criteria: the detection error trade-off curve, DET (Lleida and Rose, 1996), and the confidence error rate, CER (Weintraub et al., 1997). For the DET criterion, two types of errors were taken into account: erroneously recognised words that have been falsely accepted and correctly recognised words that have been falsely rejected. In general, both error types depend on each other. This dependency can be visualised by plotting both error types for different tagging thresholds, resulting in a DET curve. The CER is defined as the ratio between the number of false tags and the number of all recognised words. In contrast to the DET criterion, there is no further distinction concerning the error type. The baseline CER is received by labelling each word as being recognised correctly. Results for the CER are given in Table 2. A DET-curve is depicted in Figure 8.

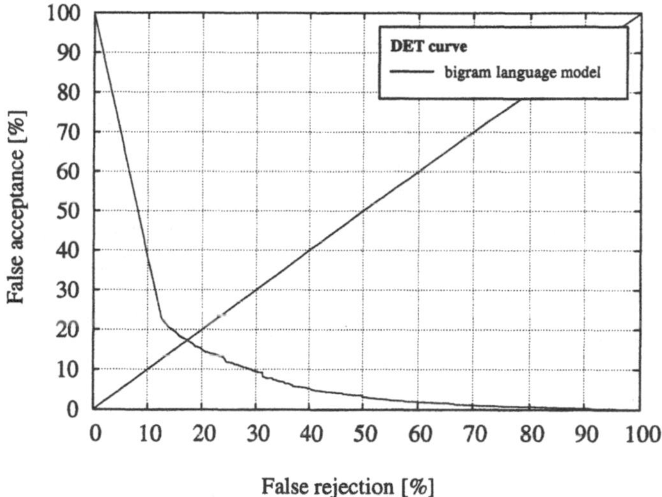

Figure 8. Detection error trade-off curve for the test corpus. The point of intersection between the diagonal and the DET curve corresponds to the equal-error rate.

The natural language understanding component was trained using a method derived from statistical machine translation (Macherey et al., 2001). The collected data were transcribed and semantically annotated. A set of 21 concepts has been used as target language.

The underlying database includes approximately 500 German and foreign proper names as well as personal related data, e.g., the office phone number, the home number, position of a person in a company, etc. For evaluating the dialogue course manager, we recorded and analysed 40 new dialogue sessions. These dialogue sessions were annotated by a human judger who decided whether the dialogue manager chose the correct or wrong action depending on the user's query. In 88% of all cases, the dialogue manager was able to choose the correct subsequent action and finished the dialogue successfully. For text input, the attribute error rate (AER) was lower than 5%. Therefore, the more interesting input modality is speech. Despite the high word error rate, the concept translation proved to be very robust against recognition errors. Table 3 summarises some results for the 40 speech-based dialogue sessions. In case of poor recognition performance, the low confidence measure often causes the dialogue manager to verify erroneous data explicitly.

Table 3. Dialogue evaluation using speech as input modality. As evaluation criteria, the attribute error rate (AER), the percentage of correct chosen successor states, and the percentage of successfully finished dialogue sessions are used.

# dialogues	AER [%]	choice of best state [%]	successful sessions [%]
40	18.4	88.4	90.0

The following two examples describe typical dialogue sessions as they occurred during the recordings of the 40 dialogues that were evaluated. Recognised words that were rejected by the confidence measure are underlined. The output of the natural language understanding component is given as a sequence of concepts for each input sentence. The tree's state and the chosen dialogue action are described verbally. The first example is a dialogue where no recognition errors occurred. The second dialogue covers the case, where the confidence measure causes the dialogue manager to verify some information explicitly. For understanding purposes, the dialogue sessions are translated into English.

Example 1 for the telephone directory assistance task.

System: Hello. This is the RWTH telephone directory assistance. You can ask questions about telephone numbers, fax numbers, and email addresses of persons as well as companies. How may I help you?

User: Uhm, what shall I do now?

rec: [hesitation] what shall I do now

nlu: @FILLER{what shall I do now}

tree: all tree nodes empty → select action `ask_for_information`

System: Do you need a telephone number, a fax number, or an email address?

User: Can you give me the number of Mr. Macherey?

rec: can you give me the number of [pause] Mr. Macherey

nlu: @can_question{can you give me} @telnum{the number of} @person{Mr. Macherey}

tree: found path with completely filled nodes, SQL-size > 1 → select action `disambiguation`

System: I have more than one entry of persons with name Macherey in my database. Please constrain your request.

User: Mr. Wolfgang Macherey

rec: Mr. Wolfgang Macherey

nlu: @person{Mr. Wolfgang Macherey}

tree: found path with completely filled nodes, SQL-size = 1 → select action `present`

System: The telephone number of Mr. Wolfgang Macherey is 80 21613. Shall I repeat the number?

...

Example 2 for the telephone directory assistance task.

System: Hello. This is the RWTH telephone directory assistance. You can ask questions about telephone numbers, fax numbers, and email addresses of persons as well as companies. How may I help you?

User: I need the number of Mrs. Hummel

rec: [noise] need the number of Mrs. Mail

nlu: @need_question{need the} @telnum{number of} @person{Mrs.} @UNKNOWN{Mail}

tree: last name required, confidence low → select action `verification`

System: Excuse me but I did not understand the last name. Please repeat.

User: Hummel

rec: Hummel

nlu: @person{Hummel}

tree: found path with completely filled nodes, SQL-size = 1 → select action `present`

System: The telephone number of Mrs. Hummel is ...

9. Summary and Outlook

We have proposed a set of feature functions for spoken dialogue course management. We have investigated whether the proposed cost functions are able to select those dialogue states during a dialogue session which lead as quickly as possible to a final state that is likely to meet the user's request. In 88% of all cases, the dialogue manager was able to choose the best successor state during a dialogue session. Although the word error rate was relatively high, the statistical natural language understanding component proved to be robust against recognition errors.

One of the advantages of this approach is that the features do not depend on the given domain. For a concrete task, the domain-specific knowledge is provided by three XML-based descriptions. Thus, the dialogue management module can be used for different domains and applications in the field of spoken dialogue systems without rewriting parts of the system.

The framework allows for incorporating additional features for the cost vectors, for example the length of a path within a tree, or one can use a-priori probabilities for different paths and nodes. Also, there are a lot of possibilities to combine feature functions for selecting subsequent dialogue actions. For future work, it would be interesting to use a maximum entropy framework in order to select the subsequent dialogue action since the described feature functions can be directly used within this framework.

Acknowledgements

This work was partially funded by Ericsson Eurolab Deutschland GmbH. The authors wish to thank Drs. S. Dobler, K. Reinhard, and J. Junkawitsch for their support.

Notes

1. Of course, this simple strategy is not able to detect all kinds of ambiguities that may occur during a dialogue session. For example, ambiguities caused by homophones are not covered by this strategy. Additional methods for handling ambiguities are described in Section 3.

References

Abella, A. and Gorin, A. L. (1999). Construct Algebra: Analytical dialog management. In *Proceedings of Annual Meeting of the Association for Computational Linguistics (ACL)*, pages 191–199, University of Maryland, USA.

Ammicht, E., Potamianos, A., and Fosler-Lussier, E. (2001). Ambiguity representation and resolution in spoken dialogue systems. In *Proceedings of European Conference on Speech Communication and Technology (EUROSPEECH)*, pages 2217–2220, Aalborg, Denmark.

Aust, H., Oerder, M., Seide, F., and Steinbiss, V. (1995). The Philips automatic train timetable information system. *Speech Communication*, 17:249–262.

Constantinides, P., Hansma, S., Tchou, C., and Rudnicky, A. (1998). A schema based approach to dialog control. In *Proceedings of International Conference on Spoken Language Processing (ICSLP)*, pages 409–412, Sidney, Australia.

Hirsch, H.-G. and Pearce, D. (2000). The aurora experimental framework for the performance evaluation of speech recognition systems under noisy conditions. In *Proceedings of International Workshop on Automatic Speech Recognition: Challenges for the new Millenium*, pages 181–188, Paris, France.

Kanthak, S., Sixtus, A., Molau, S., Schlüter, R., and Ney, H. (2000). Fast search for large vocabulary speech recognition. *Verbmobil: Foundations of Speech-to-Speech Translation*, pages 63–78.

Levin, E. and Pieraccini, R. (1995). Concept-based spontaneous speech understanding system. In *Proceedings of European Conference on Speech Communication and Technology (EUROSPEECH)*, pages 555–558, Madrid, Spain.

Lleida, E. and Rose, R. C. (1996). Efficient decoding and training procedures for utterance verification in continuous speech recognition. In *Proceedings of International Conference on Acoustics, Speech and Signal Processing (ICASSP)*, pages 507–510, Atlanta, Georgia, USA.

Macherey, K., Och, F. J., and Ney, H. (2001). Natural language understanding using statistical machine translation. In *Proceedings of European Conference on Speech Communication and Technology (EUROSPEECH)*, pages 2205–2208, Aalborg, Denmark.

Pearce, D. (2000). Enabling new speech driven services for mobile devices: An overview of the ETSI standards activities for distributed speech recognition front-ends. In *Proceedings of Applied Voice Input/Output Society Conference*, San Jose, California, USA.

Potamianos, A., Ammicht, E., and Kuo, H.-K. J. (2000). Dialogue management in the Bell Labs Communicator system. In *Proceedings of International Conference on Spoken Language Processing (ICSLP)*, pages 603–606, Beijing, China.

Seneff, S. and Polifroni, J. (1996). A new restaurant guide conversational system: Issues in rapid prototyping for specialized domains. In *Proceedings of International Conference on Spoken Language Processing (ICSLP)*, pages 665–668, Philadelphia, Pennsylvania, USA.

Weintraub, M., Beaufays, F., Rivlin, Z., Konig, Y., and Stolcke, A. (1997). Neural-network based measures of confidence for word recognition. In *Proceedings of International Conference on Acoustics, Speech and Signal Processing (ICASSP)*, pages 887–890, Munich, Germany.

Wessel, F., Macherey, K., and Schlüter, R. (1998). Using word probabilities as confidence measures. In *Proceedings of International Conference on Acoustics, Speech and Signal Processing (ICASSP)*, pages 225–228, Seattle, Washington, USA.

Wessel, F., Schlüter, R., Macherey, K., and Ney, H. (2001). Confidence measures for large vocabulary continuous speech recognition. *IEEE Transactions on Speech and Audio Processing*, 9(3):288–298.

Chapter 5

A REASONING COMPONENT FOR INFORMATION-SEEKING AND PLANNING DIALOGUES

Dirk Bühler, Wolfgang Minker
University of Ulm, Department of Information Technology, Ulm/Donau, Germany
{ dirk.buehler,wolfgang.minker } @e-technik.uni-ulm.de

Abstract Motivated by the need to make the human-machine information-seeking dialogue as efficient and user-friendly as possible we propose a logic-based reasoning component for a Spoken Language Dialogue Systems architecture. This component, called Problem Assistant, is responsible for processing constraints on a possible solution obtained from various sources, namely the user and the system's domain-specific information. The core processing is finite model generation. This inference technique tries to find solutions that fit both the user's constraints and that are consistent with the Problem Assistant's rule base. Since the assistant interactively generates transparent information about its inference process, our approach provides the basis for incremental explanation dialogues and collaborative conflict resolution.

Keywords: User assistance; First order logic; Problem solving.

1. Introduction

Many existing Spoken Language Dialogue Systems (SLDS) are either very limited in the scope of domain functionality or require a rather cumbersome interaction (Minker and Bennacef, 2000). With more and more application domains becoming available, ranging from unified messaging to trip planning and appointment scheduling, it is obvious that the current interfaces need to be rendered more efficient. In particular, the possibility to construct and to manage complex tasks and interdependencies with these applications requires a high cognitive burden from the user, which may be dangerous in certain environments (e.g., driver distraction). However, rather than prevent the use of such applications, it seems preferable to relieve the user as much as possible from

W. Minker, D. Bühler and L. Dybkjær (eds), Spoken Multimodal Human-Computer Dialogue in Mobile Environments, 77-91

the need to manage the complexities involved alone in his mind. In our proposed solution the SLDS serves as an integrated assistant to the user, i.e., it is able to collaborate with the user to find a solution that fits his/her requirements and constraints and that is consistent with the system's world knowledge. In particular, the system's world model is a *cross-domain model*, i.e., it includes knowledge about dependencies between concurrent tasks in different domains: In a travelling sales person scenario, for instance, the system may automatically calculate route durations and check for parking space depending on the user's itinerary (calendar).

In order to substantiate our claim we have developed a domain reasoning component, called *Problem Assistant* (PA), that supports the Dialogue Manager (DM) in a SLDS (cf. Figure 1). Specifically, the PA aims at

- providing a common knowledge representation for integrating information from the user as well as from various domain-specific information sources in terms of *constraints* (assertions in a logical language). This enables a rule-based **reasoning** service to combine these constraints in order to produce inferences (in particular, conflicts) that may initiate negotiation (sub-) dialogues between the user and the system;
- providing sufficient information for the DM to engage in **explanation** and conflict resolution dialogues and enabling hypothetical reasoning by maintaining concurrent partial solutions (possible worlds) for these dialogues.

Constraint-based information-seeking dialogue is becoming a more and more popular approach. Such systems overcome the "two-phase approach" of prior query construction, subsequent database retrieval and result presentation (Qu and Green, 2002).

They aim at an efficient constraint tightening and relaxation which is *interactive* in the sense that both the system and the user may tighten and relax constraints at any time instead of two pre-defined phases.

Although many conventional systems provide some form of automatic constraint relaxation, they often require the user to specify a certain minimal number of constraints – sometimes due to a rigid dialogue flow. This may result in a *delayed detection* of a conflict, i.e., a situation where additional constraints are queried from the user, although the existing constraints are already conflicting.

Our approach extends and generalises the information management for information-seeking dialogues.

Typically, in a system based on database retrieval

- there is only one domain *task* at a time (often represented as a *frame* of a certain type), i.e., the user may not switch back and forth between topics,

- consequently, there is only one domain involved, corresponding to the frame;
- the information obtained from the user essentially consists of value assignments for the *slots* of the frame that are required for accessing the database;
- no explanations for *conflicts* (situations where the user's goals cannot be satisfied) are given, i.e., the user has to find out himself which constraints cause the result set to be empty.

In contrast to conventional systems, we allow multiple simultaneous tasks in different domains. These may share (sub-) domains, such as common temporal and spatial concepts. Thus, cross-domain interdependencies become expressible. E.g., it is possible to state rules like "Travels and calendar appointments may not overlap" (where travels and calendar appointments are entities in distinct domains). Domain-specific information sources, such as time tables and calendar entries, are integrated in this reasoning process.

In this chapter, we use the term *domain services* for the specific routines in the system back-end for accessing these information sources. The services' duty is to implement certain information processing procedures that are atomic in the sense that the internals are hidden from the user and the reasoning system (e.g., for route calculation).

Compared to conventional systems, we employ a more general form of constraints based on first order logic (FOL). A constraint is a ground FOL expression (cf. Section 3.1). Conventional value assignments (slot values in forms) may be embedded as equality constraints. Using FOL expressions we also want to allow the user to specify negations or disjunctions of values, which is not directly possible with simple slot-value assignments. The meaning of a constraint is defined in terms of a logical rule base, the PA's domain theory.

Our approach is based on the notion of consistency (i.e., satisfiability) of the constraints with the domain theory. Thus, we enable the system to explain possible sources of conflicts between the user and system constraints (Chu-Carroll and Carberry, 2000) by indicating those constraints and rules that result in a conflict. Explanation is the basis for an efficient interactive conflict resolution, as the user may retract those constraints that are part of the conflict.

The remainder of the chapter is organised in the following way: Section 2 presents related approaches to problem solving dialogues. Section 3 presents the Problem Assistant and its relation to the Dialogue Manager and the domain services layer. In Section 4 an example application is provided for the illustration of these concepts. Finally, we conclude by reviewing our approach in Section 5.

2. State-of-the-Art in Problem Solving Dialogues

In the following we review some of the related work in the field of cooperative human-machine interface technology.

One of the pioneer systems investigating the role of task and domain knowledge in spoken human machine dialogue is the Smith's "Circuit Fix-It Shop" (Smith, 1992; Smith et al., 1992), an electric circuit repair assistant. The problem domain of circuit repair was carefully chosen in order to make collaboration between a human user and the computer system necessary: the system has the expert detail knowledge about how to solve the task, but lacks the user's sensory and physical capabilities necessary to interact with the external world. Task completion is modelled as the construction of a theorem (a PROLOG goal). Subtasks are represented as subgoals. There is always one current subgoal while more than one other subgoal may be *open*. The role of language is to allow the user to supply *missing axioms* that are needed to complete the proof process. A missing axiom may, for instance, be the current state of a circuit display that is only visible to the user.

AMICA (Pieraccini et al., 1997) is an architecture for a mixed-initiative conversational system for database queries, such as the Air Travel Information Services (ATIS) task. For handling domain information provided by both the user and the system it provides the dialogue functions *Constraint Consistency Verification*, *Data Retrieval*, *Constraining* and *Relaxation*. Consistency verification is the process of detecting inconsistencies in the constraints specified by the user, such as an invalid day and month for a departure date. The use of so-called constraint networks which may be mapped to a relational database overcomes the ad-hoc fashion of data retrieval implemented in many comparable systems. Data Retrieval results in a list of variable bindings that each represent a solution found in the data base. Constraining and relaxation are functions that implement the process of adding or replacing constraints in the constraint network, respectively, in order to achieve a non-empty but manageable result set. The mechanisms for implementing these functions would perhaps benefit from and be simplified by the domain reasoning approach we advocate in this chapter.

Rich and Sidner (1997) have implemented an application-independent Collaboration Manager called COLLAGEN based on the *SharedPlan* theory of discourse (Grosz and Sidner, 1986). According to the authors, a key benefit of the domain-independent collaboration manager is the automatic construction of a interaction history that is hierarchically structured depending on the user's and agent's goals and intentions. The collaboration manager maintains and updates a plan structure that is derived from the recognised user goals based on a library of domain-specific *recipes* (plan templates). This plan serves as a basis for the generation of suggestions and questions to be presented to the user.

The Rochester Interactive Planning System TRIPS (Ferguson and Allen, 1998) is a multimodal prototype for a collaborative planning assistant in the logistics domain. The usage scenario consists of a domain (logistics) expert working with the computer assistant in order to plan out the details of some operations, e.g., evacuating an island in the face of an approaching hurricane. The task involves a high-level goal and plan as well as a detailed schedule of the associated primitive actions. TRIPS features a complex logistics domain including a variety of vehicle types and capabilities. Its planning involves multiple agents and temporally extended actions. Conflicts may arise when a plan's actions violate the deadline, but the conflict resolution seems to rely mainly on the user's ability to determine and resolve the causes of the conflict.

A more recent approach is Qu et al's work on constraint-based approaches to mixed-initiative information-Seeking dialogues (Qu, 2001; Qu and Green, 2002). They present a dialogue generation model that uses a constraint-based problem solver (CBPS) to support cooperative mixed-initiative information-seeking dialogue. According to the authors, this approach is able to

1 incrementally interleave query construction with solution construction;

2 immediately detect under-constrained and over-constrained information requests;

3 provide cooperative responses when these types of problems are detected.

The underlying CBPS provides functions of *Solution Construction*, *Solution Evaluation*, and *Solution Modification* based on graphs that represent subsets of user constraints and matching database tuples. As in the case of AMICA, these functions correspond to the domain reasoning approach proposed in this chapter.

3. Reasoning Architecture

This section presents the Problem Assistant and its relations to the DM and the Domain Services layer. In general terms, the PA acts as a mediator between the user and the Domain Services. Therefore, it is responsible for combining the knowledge it receives from both sides, i.e., the "goals" and requirements from the user and the relevant application constraints from the services. This is shown in Figure 1. The boxes labelled *NL Input* and *NL Output* represent the modules that translate between natural language utterances and DM acts, i.e., speech recognition and understanding, and speech generation, respectively. The knowledge exchanged between DM and PA is represented as logical constraints and processed with the PA's rule base in order to produce inferences.

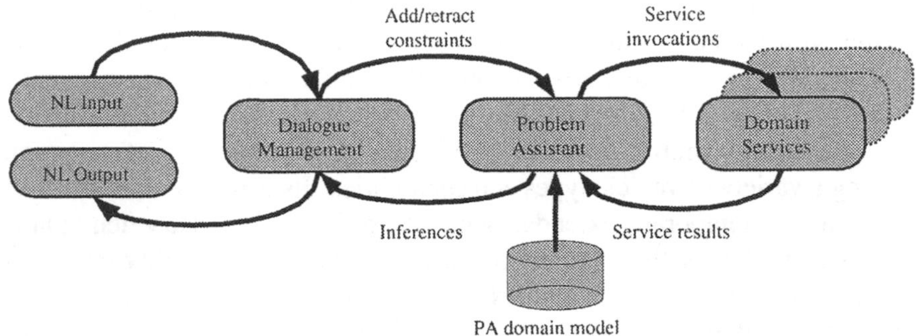

Figure 1. The modules of the proposed reasoning architecture. The PA acts as a mediator between the DM and the Domain Services.

Our focus is on the interface between an abstract Dialogue Manager and the reasoning component (PA) of the system. We deliberately leave out some issues that are not relevant to this interface. The types of dialogues we envision are information-seeking and planning interactions. The ultimate goal of the human-machine interaction is to integrate different sources of constraints in a cooperative way.

The contribution of a dedicated domain reasoning component provides the basis for a generic negotiation dialogue about the user's goals and constraints, as it enables the system to engage in explanation dialogues, notably in the case of conflicting constraints.

3.1 Problem Assistance and Domain Reasoning

The PA is a domain-independent processing module that integrates the information from the DM and from the specific services into a coherent reasoning process. In order to infer new domain constraints, the PA operates on a domain-specific rule base, its *domain theory*. It is a library of general logical rules (axioms) that are valid for all entities in a certain domain. Typically, such a rule base contain an ontology of domain concepts as a core.

In addition, during an interaction the PA maintains a current set of constraints to be combined with the domain theory (comparable to an A-Box[1] for each situation, we use the term *context* in this chapter). This set of constraints represents the currently assumed and inferred constraints that a solution has to satisfy. It is updated whenever the user asserts or retracts a constraint, or when the PA contributes an inference.

Knowledge representation. The domain theory is represented as a set of range-restricted clauses of first order logic. In this logic, a *term* t is a variable X, a constant c, or a function $f(t_1, ..., t_n)$ applied to a list of terms. An *atom* $p(t_1, ..., t_n)$ consists of a predicate symbol and a list of terms. A *literal* is an atom or a negated atom. A *clause* is a disjunction of literals. The set of negated atoms is referred to as the clause's *body*, the rest is referred to as its *head*. Clauses can be written as $b_1, ..., b_n \rightarrow h_1, ..., h_m$. The empty clause denotes inconsistency. A *range-restricted* clause is a clause in which all variables that appear in the head also appear in the body. All variables in a clause are implicitly universally quantified. An atom or a clause is *ground* if it does not contain variables.[2]

Model generation. The PA uses a finite model generation algorithm as its basic inference procedure. Throughout the inference process a positive unit hyper resolution (PUHR) (Bry and Yahya, 1996; Bry and Torge, 1998) tableau structure is built up. At the beginning of the dialogue, the set of constraints obtained through the DM from the user is used as the starting point for inference. We use the term *constraint* for referring to a disjunction of ground atoms (facts).

The basic model generation algorithm works in the following way: The reasoner maintains an *agenda*, a collection of constraints that it has yet to consider, and the set of leaf nodes of the tableau (called *contexts* here). The agenda is initialised with the given constraints. The initial set of leaf nodes is a singleton, containing an empty context. Given a context and an agenda:

1. Report the context as success, if the agenda is empty. Otherwise, remove one constraint from the agenda. Depending on the constraint, proceed with the first of the following alternatives that matches and resume recursively with step 1.

2a. Fail: If the constraint is an empty disjunction, signal failure for this context.

2b. Apply the PUHR rule, if the constraint is a single atom: Use this atom to generate new constraints by combining it with all applicable rules and the other facts in the context. The range-restriction condition ensure that the results are disjunctions of ground atoms. Add the results to the agenda.

2c. Split: For each atom in the disjunction, fork one thread and put the atom on the respective agenda.

In our implementation, the basic algorithm is extended in several ways. For using equality, each context has to maintain a set of reductions of terms: For each term there exists a *normal form*. Furthermore, the processing has to be adapted for equality constraints: When an equality $t_1 = t_2$ is taken from the agenda, all the occurrences of term t_2 have to be replaced by t_1 in all the existing facts in the context. All new facts have to be added to the agenda.

In addition, for each inference a *proof* (trace) is recorded. It describes the constraints that were used in order to infer a particular consequence. An additional feature is the use of *no-goods*: A no-good is a set of constraints already proven to be inconsistent. No-goods are generated as the set of assumptions of a context when this context becomes inconsistent. No-goods enable a proof-by-contradiction mechanism: Consider a situation when a disjunction of atoms $\rightarrow a, b, c$ was derived. At some point of time, the algorithm will branch contexts for each alternative. If two alternatives can be proven not to hold, the remaining one is proven to hold.

3.2 Interface to Dialogue Management

The DM manages the interaction with the user. It includes facilities for interpreting user utterances and generating appropriate system responses depending on the context and situation in which the system is used. In this section we describe the requirements for the DM to interact with the PA reasoning component.

In our approach the DM attempts to "synchronise" the user's and the system's knowledge states relative to a certain domain problem in order to determine a mutually accepted solution. The dialogue may be modelled as a collaborative negotiation about a set of *domain constraints* on a set of *domain objects*. A domain object is any entity in the domain of discourse, i.e., any entity that can be talked about and referred to in the dialogue. Domain objects embody the domain problem (such as a travel plan) that is the subject of the dialogue. Domain objects may be either primitives such as integer values or complex structures, such as complete travel plans. A domain constraint is a general relational assertion that has to hold among a certain set of domain objects.

Initially, both the user and the system may have their individual sets of required constraints. The goal of the dialogue is to find a solution for the domain problem. The dialogue attempts to achieve a situation in which the user's and the system's sets of constraints

- are *consistently satisfiable*, i.e., they are not over-constrained with respect to the domain theory;
- have a *unique model*, i.e., they are not under-constrained with respect to the domain theory;

- are *identical*, i.e., the constraints are mutually accepted.

3.3 Interface to Domain Services

Services execute the atomic system operations that are invoked by the PA's reasoning process during the dialogue. Two basic types of domain services exist: *read-only* (information generating) and *read/write* services.

A read-only service is a computation that returns a result solely depending on the arguments of the call, i.e., there are no side-effects. In the read-only case the service may be conceived as a special forward inference rule. A route calculator, for instance, may be formalised as an inference rule that adds an equality constraint for term d when a fact $route(from, to, d)$ becomes known (with $from$ and to bound to literals). One advantage of handling service queries as inference steps with explicit antecedents relies in the fact that it enables pre-fetching and caching of queries.

The read/write case is conceptually different the from read-only. An example of a read/write service is an appointment database. In contrast to the route calculation, the contents of the database may change, e.g., when a new appointment is scheduled. We treat database updates implicitly: Certain relations are *mirrored* in the database, i.e., should the user require a certain instance of the relation, it is inserted into the database. Conversely, if the user rejects an instance it is removed from the database.

4. Application to Calendar Planning

In the following we discuss the application of our architecture to a simple calendar planning domain. In the proposed scenario a user plans several appointments in different locations. Using our logic-based approach, a basic calendar domain is combined with a route planning domain that contributes additional concepts and rules that a global solution has to satisfy. For instance, travels from one appointment to another and the appointments themselves may not overlap. The rules ensure that there is enough time between appointments to travel from one appointment location to another. The calendar and route planning domains share basic concepts such as locations and temporal durations.

The domain theory for the enriched calendar domain defines the following major classes of objects: time points, time intervals, and locations from the base ontology, appointments and travels from respective specialised domain models.

Time intervals are represented as pairs of time points, where the beginning of the interval has to precede the end:[3]

$$timeinterval(I) \rightarrow timepoint(start(I)). \tag{5.1}$$
$$timeinterval(I) \rightarrow timepoint(end(I)). \tag{5.2}$$
$$timeinterval(I) \rightarrow start(I) \leq end(I). \tag{5.3}$$

Attributes are relations that act as functions:

$$start(I,T), start(I,S) \rightarrow T = S. \tag{5.4}$$

Locations are abstract geographical positions. Appointments have a location attribute as well as a time interval:

$$appointment(A) \rightarrow location(location(A)). \tag{5.5}$$
$$appointment(A) \rightarrow timeinterval(time(A)). \tag{5.6}$$

Travels have origin and destination attributes of type location, as well as a time attribute denoting the time interval occupied by travelling.

The following two rules 5.7 and 5.8 realise the connection of the basic calendar and basic route planning domains: Two appointments are either in the same location or there is a travel from the location of the preceding appointment to the location of the succeeding one:

$$\begin{array}{l} appointment(A_1), appointment(A_2) \rightarrow \\ A_1 = A_2, travel(A_1, A_2), travel(A_2, A_1). \end{array} \tag{5.7}$$

Travelling takes time depending on the origin and destination locations:

$$\begin{array}{l} travel(A_1, A_2), location(A_1, L_1), location(A_2, L_2), \\ route\_duration(L_1, L_2, D) \rightarrow \\ end(time(A_1)) + D \leq start(time(A_2)). \end{array} \tag{5.8}$$

The aim of the following example is to clarify the reasoning behaviour of the PA on the basis of the constraints it receives from the DM and the applications. A fairly general mechanism for utterance interpretation and generation within the DM is taken for granted.

We assume that the user has already fixed an appointment a_1 in Heidelberg at a certain time. This situation is represented by the following set of constraints:

$$\{appointment(a_1), time(a_1, i_1), start(i_1, 9.30am), end(i_1, 11.00am)\}$$

We further assume it is now 7.15am and the user is driving on the highway from the city of Ulm to Heidelberg. This (current) information is also coded as a placeholder appointment, where l_0 represents the current position known to the system (e.g., through a global positioning system).

$$\{appointment(a_0), time(a_0, i_0), end(i_0, 7.15am), location(a_0, l_0)\}$$

Applying rule (5.7) the PA infers that a_0 precedes a_1 and not vice versa:

$$\{travel(a_0, a_1)\}$$

In the next step, the user may wish to arrange a new appointment. The constraint $appointment(a_2)$ for a newly created constant a_2 as well as the implied assumptions $\{a_1 \neq a_0, a_1 \neq a_2, start(time(a_2)) \leq 7.15am\}$ (supplied by the utterance interpretation) are received from the DM and added to the constraint set. According to the domain theory, the PA generates terms for the start time, end time, and the location attributes of a_2.

$$\{time(a_2, i_2), start(i_2, t_1), end(i_2, t_2), location(a_2, l_2)\}$$

Furthermore, the PA infers

$$\{travel(a_0, a_2), route\_duration(l_0, l_2, u_0), 7.15am + u_0 \leq t_1\}$$

from (5.7) and (5.8). Again, since the appointments a_1 and a_2 may not overlap, the PA infers a disjunction which, given $a_1 \neq a_2$ from above, simplifies to:

$$travel(a_1, a_2) \vee travel(a_2, a_1).$$

Since the disjunction above is the only one unresolved at the moment, it is selected for splitting in the model generation algorithm (cf. Section 3.1). The PA branches concurrent contexts for both elements of the disjunction. In both cases the complete solutions depend on the unknown location l_2, which is involved in a $route\_duration(l_1, l_2, u_1)$ or $route\_duration(l_2, l_1, u_2)$ constraint, respectively. The navigation service generates hypotheses about l_2 that trigger the DM to ask the user for the value of l_2.

SYSTEM: Where is your appointment?

The user provides the requested information: $location(a_2, Stuttgart)$. With this information, the PA is able to infer:

$$\{u_0 = 1.05h, 7.15am + 1.05h \leq t_1\}$$

As both alternatives are satisfiable the DM generates a dialogue task in order to present the choices to the user:[4]

We already have an appointment in Heidelberg today.
Where do you want to go first, Stuttgart or Heidelberg?

The user reacts by evaluating the first alternative as a hypothetical scenario:

USER: How much time would we have in Stuttgart if we went there first?

The PA has already inferred the following constraints, based on the hypothesis $travel(a_2, a_1)$:

$$\{route\_duration(Stuttgart, Heidelberg, 1.00h), t_2 + 1.00h \leq 9.30am\}$$

The DM is now able to provide the requested information:

SYSTEM: We would have at most 10 minutes there.

At this stage of the dialogue the user may ask the system to explain its reasoning by means of *why* questions. From the PA the DM has obtained the relevant proof traces (which rules have been applied to which assumptions) in order to provide an explanation. Alternatively, the user may add other constraints, e.g., $t_1 + 0.30h \leq t_2$ meaning that he needs at least half an hour for the appointment a_2: This would lead to a conflict and the alternative $travel(a_2, a_1)$ would be ruled out. Instead, the system would propose the remaining alternative $travel(a_1, a_2)$:

SYSTEM: So we go to Heidelberg first, right?

Again, the user may ask the system to explain the inference:

SYSTEM: We cannot go to Stuttgart first, since we would only have at most 10 minutes there.

If the user accepts, the system may go on to provide further inferences (based on the duration of the route from Heidelberg to Stuttgart):

SYSTEM: We will arrive in Stuttgart at 12:00pm at the earliest.

To summarise, the example interaction has illustrated how the constraint processing done by the PA provides the basis for an interactive solution construction in which both user and system contribute some requirements. In particular, the inference process generates information that may be used by a DM to engage in an explanation dialogue. In the conventional approach using database access, usually such a direct explanation for conflicts is not possible, since there is no information about what caused the result set to be empty. Also, non-conflict inferences that interconnect different tasks and domains as illustrated in the last system utterance are more difficult to realise.

5. Conclusion

We have presented a logic-based reasoning approach to be used for efficient and user-friendly human-machine dialogues. User-friendliness may be achieved by supporting the Dialogue Manager with a module for problem solving assistance, the Problem Assistant. In particular, this reasoning component aims at enabling the DM to engage in explanation dialogues on the basis of the PA's inferences.

The Dialogue Manager is viewed as the central interface component between the user and the system. Its strategy consists of constructing a shared set of constraints in a mixed initiative interaction with the user. The PA supports the DM by providing a common knowledge representation based on logical constraints. On this basis, it combines the user's and the system's constraints with the its cross-domain rule base. Finally, the PA provides proof traces for its inferences in order to enable the Dialogue Manager to engage in explanation and conflict resolution dialogues.

Our approach is similar to the Circuit-Fix-It-Shoppe (Smith, 1992; Smith et al., 1992) in that the dialogue is driven by an underlying domain reasoner that cooperates with a (sub-)dialogue controller. In particular, the concept of *axioms* (user assumptions) is used in both approaches. However, there also exist a number of important differences. First, in CFS the interaction is modelled as the construction of a theorem. In our approach saturated models are constructed based on reasoning about consistency. One of our aims is to make alternative solutions explicit, allowing the user to choose from them. It is unclear how this might be handled in CFS. It seems the system always chooses one solution and tries to apply it to the current situation.

In contrast to AMICA (Pieraccini et al., 1997), we consider constraint verification and retrieval as a specialisation of the more general approach of rule-based domain inference. Our approach features a more expressive form of constraints than the equality constraints considered in their paper. In addition, the rule-based inference provides additional features for an explanation facility.

In our approach the goal of assisting the user in a specialised application domain is also similar to COLLAGEN (Rich and Sidner, 1997). There are also a number of differences. COLLAGEN aims at providing assistance to existing full-scale applications. In some sense, it is similar to a tutoring system. The representation of the domain knowledge as recipes is different. One question arises whether the representation is suitable for reasoning about the consistency of the user's goals and actions.

Our approach is similar in spirit to TRIPS (Ferguson and Allen, 1998) in that we basically deal with a *planning problem*. In particular, satisfiability seems to be important. In contrast to our approach, however, the user is not informed about possible alternatives in the course of action. The system chooses one alternative instead. Should more than one solution exist, the planning module makes an arbitrary choice. The user is (by default) not informed about alternative options (the user has to infer that himself or propose alternatives). Finally, the system applies a rather simple paradigm to resolve conflicts arising in the plan. The user in fact is only notified that some specific action in the plan may "need to be revised". However, neither explanations nor possible solutions to the problem are suggested.

Compared to Qu's work on constraint-based approaches to mixed-initiative information-seeking dialogues (Qu, 2001; Qu and Green, 2002), our approach features a more expressive logical language for formulating constraints. In addition, over-constraintness and under-constraintness are treated with respect to a domain-specific rule base. Qu et al. consider only a table of database tuples. In addition, we aim at being able to explain on the basis of the domain rules why certain inferences (of which a conflict is a special case) are drawn. This efficiently enables the user to modify his constraints in order to resolve a conflict. Finally, our rule-based approach aims at integrating multiple application domains.

We have illustrated the functionality of the reasoning component with an example interaction in the calendar application domain. For an end-to-end integration into a spoken language dialogue system a range of questions need to be discussed further. The mapping between dialogue acts and problem solving actions (e.g., asserting and retracting constraints) is not yet fully understood. Also, how to present highly detailed computer-generated proofs most efficiently to the user is a topic for further research.

Notes

1. In the theory of description logics (DL), an A-Box is a set of assertions about entities. The domain theory corresponds to the terminological T-Box in DL, although we try to employ a more expressive logical language.

2. We adopt the PROLOG convention of writing variables with a upper-case initial letter and regular terms with lower-case initials.

3. We often use numbers to represent time points. In this case the $\leq$ relation may be used for ordering time points.

4. Of course, the DM might also just ask for the time of the appointment, assuming that the user knows his schedule by heart. However, the user may also indicate that he does not know the exact schedule yet and he wants to find a time for the appointment depending on the other appointments. This is the scenario we assume here, since we want to show that the reasoner *could* provide assistance when needed.

References

Bry, F. and Torge, S. (1998). A deduction method complete for refutation and finite satisfiability. *Lecture Notes in Computer Science*, 1489:122–138.

Bry, F. and Yahya, A. (1996). Minimal model generation with positive unit hyper-resolution tableaux. In *Proceedings of International Workshop on Theorem Proving with Analytic Tableaux and Related Methods*, pages 143–159, Terrasini, Palermo, Italy. Springer-Verlag, Berlin/Heidelberg, Germany.

Chu-Carroll, J. and Carberry, S. (2000). Conflict resolution in collaborative planning dialogues. *International Journal of Human-Computer Studies*, 53(6):969–1015.

Ferguson, G. and Allen, J. F. (1998). TRIPS: An integrated intelligent problem-solving assistant. In *Proceedings of National Conference on Artificial Intelligence (AAAI)*, pages 567–572, Madison, Wisconsin, USA.

Grosz, B. and Sidner, C. (1986). Attention, intentions, and the structure of discourse. *Computational Linguistics*, 12(3):175–204.

Minker, W. and Bennacef, S. (2000). *Parole et Dialogue Homme-Machine*. CNRS Editions & Editions Eyrolles, Paris, France.

Pieraccini, R., Levin, E., and Eckert, W. (1997). AMICA: The AT&T mixed initiative conversational architecture. In *Proceedings of European Conference on Speech Communication and Technology (EUROSPEECH)*, pages 1875–1878, Rhodes, Greece.

Qu, Y. (2001). *A Constraint-Based Model of Mixed-Initiative Dialogue in Information-Seeking Interactions*. PhD thesis, School of Computer Science, Carnegie Mellon University.

Qu, Y. and Green, N. (2002). A constraint-based approach for cooperative information-seeking dialogues. In *Proceedings of International Conference on Natural Language Generation (INLG)*, pages 136–143, New York, New York, USA.

Rich, C. and Sidner, C. L. (1997). COLLAGEN: When agents collaborate with people. In Johnson, W. L. and Hayes-Roth, B., editors, *Proceedings of International Conference on Autonomous Agents*, pages 284–291, Marina del Rey, California, USA. ACM Press, New York, NY, USA.

Smith, R. (1992). Integration of domain problem solving with natural language dialog: The Missing Axiom Theory. In *Proceedings of Applications of Artificial Intelligence X: Knowledge-Based Systems*, pages 270–278, Orlando, Florida, USA.

Smith, R., Hipp, D., and Biermann, A. (1992). A dialog control algorithm and its performance. In *Proceedings of Conference on Applied Natural Language Processing (ANLP)*, pages 9–16, Trento, Italy.

Chapter 6

A MODEL FOR MULTIMODAL DIALOGUE SYSTEM OUTPUT APPLIED TO AN ANIMATED TALKING HEAD

Jonas Beskow, Jens Edlund, Magnus Nordstrand*

KTH, CTT - Centre for Speech Technology, Stockholm, Sweden

{ beskow,edlund,magnusn } @speech.kth.se

Abstract We present a formalism for specifying verbal and non-verbal output from a multimodal dialogue system. The output specification is XML-based and provides information about communicative functions of the output, without detailing the realisation of these functions. The aim is to let dialogue systems generate the same output for a wide variety of output devices and modalities. The formalism was developed and implemented in the multimodal spoken dialogue system AdApt. We also describe how facial gestures in the 3D-animated talking head used within this system are controlled through the formalism.

Keywords: GESOM; AdApt; Standards; XML; 3D-animation; Gesture; Turn-taking; Lip synchronisation.

1. Introduction

In the context of mobile devices, where a keyboard, for example, is not available, speech is a useful modality. Using other modalities together with speech may alleviate some of the problems associated with spoken human-computer dialogue. Spoken dialogue systems incorporating some form of animated characters are increasingly common in the research community. There are many compelling reasons to include an animated agent in the interface. Since people have life-long experience at interpreting facial expressions and gestures (McNeill, 1992), it is potentially a most intuitive and non-intrusive interface. Using gestures, an agent can continuously provide the user with feedback about the

*Names in alphabetical order

W. Minker, D. Bühler and L. Dybkjær (eds), Spoken Multimodal Human-Computer Dialogue in Mobile Environments, 93-113

progress of the dialogue. This is an elegant way to handle problems with turn-taking, potentially resulting in a smoother dialogue flow, while at the same time making the system appear more responsive. Given proper speech-synchronised articulatory movements and emphatic gestures, the agent will boost the intelligibility of the spoken output (Agelfors et al., 1998).

When considering dialogue systems in mobile environments, the task of coding output separately for each conceivable output device and modality is clearly complicated and time-consuming. If the problem is modularised in such a way that each output device is responsible for presenting the output in a manner suitable for its capacity, the task gets more manageable. Text, for example, may be presented as written text or speech, and emphasis signalled with either boldface, prosody and/or facial gestures. This chapter presents an abstraction layer between the dialogue manager and the output device(s) developed in the AdApt spoken dialogue system (Gustafson et al., 2000). The abstraction layer, GESOM (GEneric System Output Markup), frees the dialogue system's output generation from the need to know details about the capabilities of the output device (see Figure 1). The aim is to allow the dialogue system to work with a variety of output devices and modalities with a minimum of adaptation.

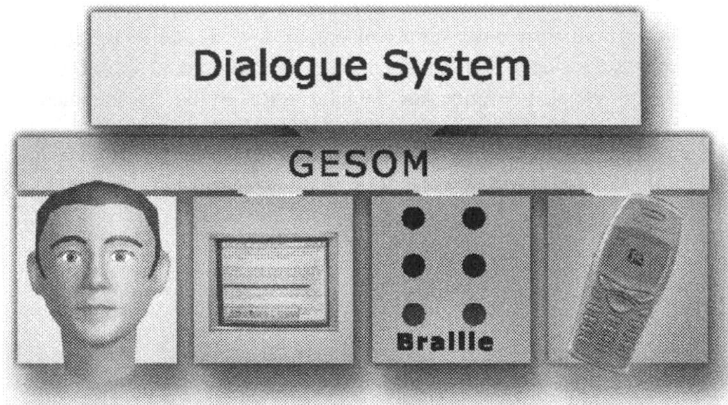

Figure 1. GESOM - a layer between the dialogue system and an output device.

1.1 Related Work

Several models for automatic generation of gestures for animated characters in conversational systems have been proposed. Nagao and Takeuchi (1994) present static facial displays for signalling communicative functions in a dialogue system. Pelachaud and Prevost (1994) present a model for generating facial expressions and intonation from a common representation. Poggi and Pelachaud (2000) present an agent capable of signalling its communicative goal, e.g., by showing emotions in the face. Thórisson (1999) and Cassell et al. (2001) both describe complete frameworks for conversational dialogue systems that incorporate animated agents capable of generating deictic gestures, turn-taking signals, and emblematic gestures, relying on input from several sources. In contrast, our more limited model aims at separating the dialogue system from the realisation of output in order to facilitate rapid development and portability, which is a goal perhaps more closely related to that of proposed markup languages such as the Virtual Human Markup Language (VHML) (Gustavsson et al., 2001) and the Speech Synthesis Markup Language (SSML) (Burnett et al., 2002). Thorough discussions of these markup languages and others are found in (Pirker and Krenn, 2002) and (Gustavsson et al., 2002). In their present state, these languages tend to specify the output on a low level, with considerable detail, which makes them less well suited for our purposes.

The work presented in this chapter also builds on experiences gained from previous efforts at integrating animated characters into dialogue systems developed at CTT (Bertenstam et al., 1995; Beskow et al., 1997; Granström et al., 2002; Gustafson et al., 1999).

1.2 Background

The GESOM specification was created to cope with needs that arose during the development of the AdApt system (see Figures 2a and 2b), which was built at CTT, with Telia Research as an industrial partner (Gustafson et al., 2000). The system allows users to browse the real-estate market in downtown Stockholm, and features multimodal input (speech, mouse clicks) and a 3D-animated talking head producing lip synchronised synthetic speech (Beskow, 1997). It is used as a research platform for development and user testing, e.g., of multimodal input and output. The system is modular (Figure 2b), in order to facilitate rapid implementation and integration of new functionality. When the output side of the AdApt architecture was developed, it was important to allow for rapid testing of different types of non-verbal output in the animated talking head. One of the goals of the system was to implement meaningful facial gestures, inspired by results in for example (Cassell et al., 2001). In this process problems arose with issues such as backward compatibility (the introduction of new entities in the output generated by the dialogue system would cause output modules to malfunction). Inter-modular communication in AdApt is encoded in XML, which is good for backward and forward compatibility, but the original specification for output generation clearly needed some work. In order to make the output robust and general, the following had to be addressed:

- The dialogue system should preferably not have to know too much about the output device and its capabilities.
- Some of the events one would want the dialogue system to signal are of unpredictable length, e.g., listening to or waiting for speech input, processing speech, or waiting for a database search to complete. The dialogue system does not know when these tasks will end until they in fact have. A method for handling this was needed.
- An animated talking head, which uses exactly the same gesture every time a particular event occurs, makes the dialogue system very repetitive. By specifying nothing more than the general pragmatic function to be signalled, the animated talking head could be allowed to choose any means available to realise the signal. This would not work in a dialogue system that generates specific instructions for non-verbal output.

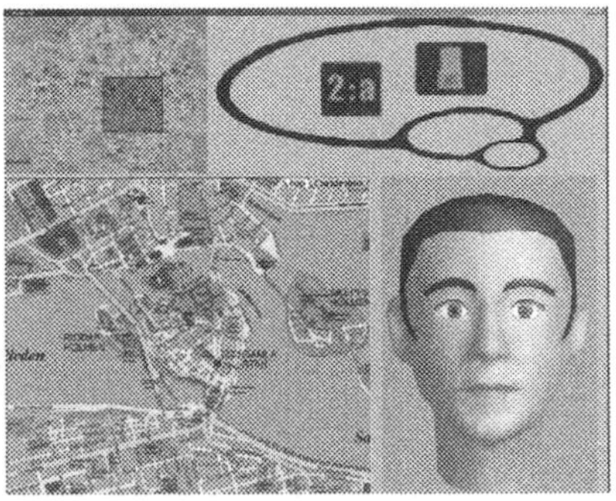

Figure 2a. The AdApt GUI.

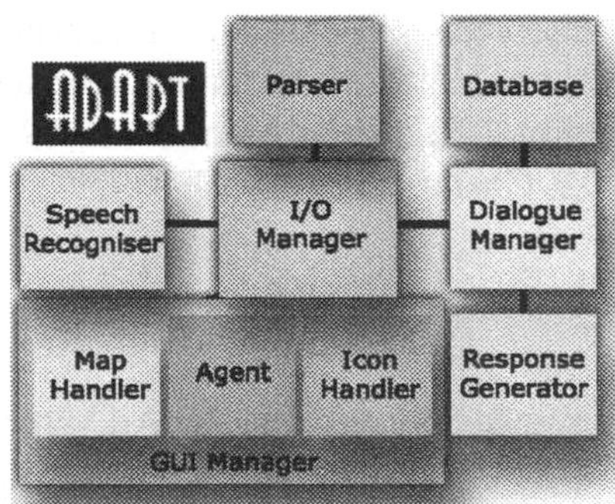

Figure 2b. The AdApt architecture.

Whilst an XML specification that catered to these needs was written and tested for the animated talking head, other user interfaces were used in the development of the other parts of the dialogue system. Text input and output were used for regression tests, and for debugging purposes there were GUIs with coloured indicators signalling what the system was occupied with at any given time. Although the data sent to each of these interfaces was generated separately at the time, it became clear that most of the information could be unobtrusively built into a general XML specification, so that the same dialogue system output could be used as input for a variety of user interfaces. These considerations led to the GESOM specification.

1.3 Overview

In order for a formalism such as GESOM to work, a few requirements must be met. Firstly, the dialogue system must generate system output following the specification, which is proposed and explained next. Secondly, the dialogue system must be able to send the GESOM message to the output device. This is straightforward and can be done through any means available to both modules, e.g., TCP/IP sockets or pipes. Thirdly, the output device must know how to decode, interpret and realise, or render, the markup. Section 3 describes how to interpret the markup using standard XML techniques. Next, some examples of how GESOM messages might be realised in different output devices are given, and finally in Section 4 we give a detailed description of how GESOM is interpreted and realised in the animated talking head used in the AdApt system. A brief summary and a listing pointing to future work concludes the chapter.

2. Specification

GESOM is fully compliant with the Extensible Markup Language (XML) 1.0 specification (Bray et al., 2000). Complying with a standard has the advantage that there are many tools for viewing, editing, and, not least, validating messages. The GESOM 1.0 DTD (Document Type Definition, i.e., XML grammar)[1] is presented in simplified form in Figure 3. The actual DTD defines `<head>` and `<body>` elements, which are forward compatibility considerations, as well as a number of formal XML entity definitions. These have been hidden here, but the semantics of the DTD are virtually identical to Figure 3. Any textual content is sent as CDATA (character data type in XML), and XML elements are used to mark other aspects. All GESOM examples in this chapter have identical elements down to, and including, the `<body>` element, so for space and legibility reasons, the remaining GESOM examples will contain only the `<output>` part of the message. An example of a minimal GESOM message is shown in Figure 4. The remainder of the specification is somewhat more interesting. The next two sections describe the motivation and function of the `<state>` and `<event>` elements, as well as the background attribute.

2.1 Encoding Output Using <state> and <event> Elements

Most dialogue systems, and indeed most interactive systems in general, are based on an event-driven model, i.e., actions that are carried out by the system are triggered by some kind of event. The events occurring in a dialogue system (dialogue system events, or DS-events hereafter) can either be the direct result of a user action (such as speaking) or internally generated during data processing. Any dialogue system has, at the bare minimum, one DS-event, which we can call "input done": the user has finished speaking and the utterance is available to the system. The system will process the utterance and respond in some

```
<!ATTLIST       output
                blocking        (0|1)    "0"
                callback        (0|1)    "0"
                background      CDATA    #IMPLIED       >
<!ELEMENT       state
                EMPTY                                   >
<!ATTLIST       state
                type            CDATA    "default"
                name            CDATA    #REQUIRED
                background      CDATA    #IMPLIED       >
<!ELEMENT       event
                (#PCDATA)                               >
<!ATTLIST       event
                type            CDATA    "default"
                name            CDATA    #REQUIRED
                background      CDATA    #IMPLIED       >
```

Figure 3. GESOM 1.0 DTD.

```
<?xml version="1.0" encoding="iso-8859-1"?>
<!DOCTYPE gesom PUBLIC "-//CTT//DTD GESOM 1.0//EN"
 "http://www.speech.kth.se/gesom/v1/dtd/gesom.dtd">
<gesom xmlns:ges="http://www.speech.kth.se/gesom/">
<head/>
<body>
<output>this is as simple as it gets</output>
</body>
</gesom>
```

Figure 4. GESOM message: nothing but text.

way, after which it will wait for the next "input done". This one-event-per-turn model is sufficient for simple systems, but in more complex systems we may want to give feedback during several stages in a dialogue turn, not just during the system's speech output. In the AdApt system, the following DS-events, at which the system may produce feedback, occur during a dialogue turn (see Figure 5):

1. *Start of speech* - the speech recogniser has detected that the user is speaking.

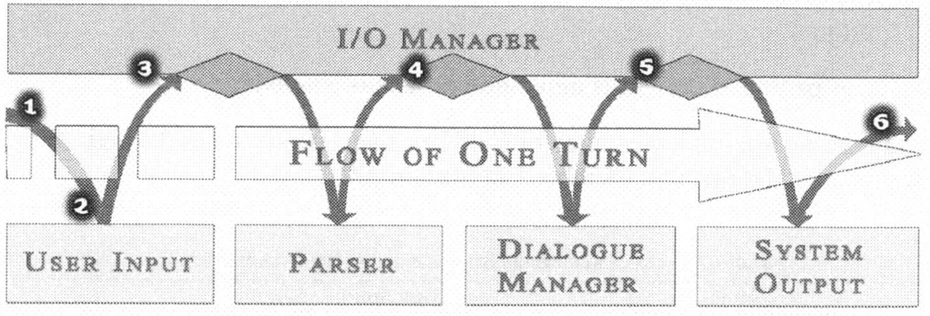

Figure 5. Opportunities to send feedback in an AdApt dialogue turn.

2. *End of speech* - the speech recogniser has detected that the user has stopped speaking.

3. *Recognition done* - the speech recogniser has processed the utterance and passed the result on to the parser.

4. *Semantics done* - the parser has processed the recogniser output. The parser will categorise an utterance as either closing (the utterance can be interpreted in its own right) or non-closing (more input is needed to make sense of the utterance) (Bell et al., 2001). Closing utterances will be passed on to the dialogue manager. Non-closing utterances cause the system to go back to listening.

5. *Planning done* - the dialogue manager has decided what to do next, and a response is generated.

6. *Response done* - the system has presented its response.

Conceptually, the system can be said to be in different conversational states at different times: waiting for speech, listening, thinking and speaking. The DS-events listed above cause transitions from one state to another. Such states are the foundation for GESOM encoding of output. States can be used to encode output of which the duration is not known beforehand. If we want to signal that the agent is performing an action, e.g., is listening, searching a database ("thinking") or just being idle, we need signals that are visible for an arbitrary amount of time, i.e., until the system stops doing whatever it is doing. This type of output is encoded in the `<state>` element. If the system is waiting for a database search to finish or for someone to pick up the phone, it has no way of predicting when this state will end. A state, then, has the following properties:

1. The output device must always be in one and only one state at any given time

2. A particular state lasts until another state is entered

In the AdApt implementation of GESOM, there are six states defined. They are listed in the first part of Table 1 in Section 2.4.

Table 1. States and events implemented in the AdApt system.

	Name	Description
State	idle	system is inactive
	attentive	system is ready for input
	cont_attentive	system has received input that is not sufficient to prepare a response
	busy	the system is busy preparing a response
	text_presentation	the system is presenting a response
	asleep	the system is offline
Event	break	small system should pause the presentation at this event
	emphasis	marked text should be emphasised
Attitude	negative	Relates to type of response
	positive	
	neutral	
	question	

In addition to being in different states, a dialogue system may need to send non-textual transient output at times. By transient we mean that the duration of the output is known in advance. This type of output is encoded in the `<event>` element. Examples from the AdApt system include emphasis and break (see Figure 6 and the second section of Table 1). Note that these events are only for describing output, and should not be confused with the DS-events described above, that govern transitions between states in the dialogue manager.

Figure 7 shows a timeline where we pass through the states `busy`, `presenting-text` and `idle`. During `presenting-text` two transient `emphasis` events are marked. Synthesised text is represented as a speech waveform in the figure.

The categorisation of output into states and events is simple (probably too simple for certain applications), but as our goal was to allow a dialogue system to generate output without much knowledge of the output device, and the output device to realise the output without much knowledge of the dialogue system, a general, high-level abstraction was needed. The specification is largely based on what output a distributed dialogue system can be expected to produce,

```
---
<output>
<event name="emphasis">this</event>
is an emphasised word and this
<event name="break" value="1000"/>
was followed by a 1 second pause
</output>
---
```

Figure 6. GESOM snippet: an `emphasis` and a `break` event.

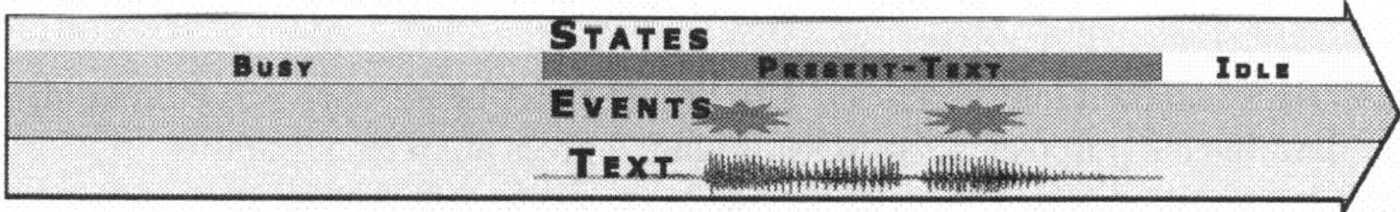

Figure 7. Timeline: a state lasts until another state is entered, whilst events are transient.

which seems necessary in order to keep the specification free from dependencies on the capabilities of dialogue systems and output devices alike.

2.2 The Background Attribute

If the states and events are to be manageable and useful, their number needs to be limited. In some cases, however, the same state or event would best be realised in different ways depending on some other parameter. An example would be emphasis gestures (events) in an animated talking head: a small nod works well in most cases, but not if the sentence with the emphasised word is a negative reply, as in Figure 8. Defining the events negative emphasis, positive emphasis, and neutral emphasis would solve the problem. However, this kind of solution would cause the set of events to grow rapidly, thus defeating the purpose of this specification. Instead, the specification allows the dialogue system to send background attributes, which work much like global variables. Background attributes can affect the realisation of the output. In the AdApt GESOM implementation, four values of the background attribute are defined, listed in the third section of Table 1. For an example of how the background attributes can be used to affect realisation of gestures in a talking head, see Section 4.2.

It should be noted that the background attributes should be used with care, since they permit any kind of content to be sent, and no particular restrictions

```
---
<output background="attitude:negative">
<state type="turn-taking" name="presenting-text"/>
the apartment does
<event name="emphasis" value="5">not</event>
have three rooms
<state type="turn-taking" name="listening"/>
</output>
---
```

Figure 8. GESOM snippet: the `background` attribute.

are placed on their interpretation. They could easily be misused and thoroughly undermine the purpose of GESOM. Figure 9 gives an example of this.

```
---
<output background="call synthesis(gesture(shake), no, I,
shall, not, conform, gesture(smirk))">
</output>
---
```

Figure 9. GESOM abused: some foreign code snuck into a `background` attribute. The message is otherwise empty.

2.3 Tiers and the Type Attribute

The two fundamental properties of states listed above (namely that the output device must always be in one state at a given time and that a particular state lasts until another one is entered) are valid within one state tier. The specification allows for an arbitrary number of tiers. In the present implementations, however, we have only used one tier at a time. The states in one tier are separate from the states in another. Tiers are encoded in the `type` attribute of the `<state>` element. If no type attribute is given, a default, single tier should be assumed. The tier used in the AdApt system is concerned with feedback for improving dialogue flow, and is called `turn-taking`. Figure 10 shows a GESOM message encoding two turn-taking states, `presenting-text` and `idle`, and Figure 11 demonstrates the `busy` and `listening` states. The latter example occurs when the AdApt system does a database search or prepares a reply. The busy state ends when the reply is presented and the `presenting-text` state is triggered.

```
---
<output>
<state type="turn-taking" name="presenting-text"/>
the present text state is used when outputting text, and the
idle state when the system is idle
<state type="turn-taking" name="idle"/>
</output>
---
```

Figure 10. GESOM snippet: the `presenting-text` and `idle` turn-taking states.

```
---
<output>
<state type="turn-taking" name="busy"/>
</output>
[database search completing]
<output>
<state type="turn-taking" name="presenting-text"/>
the apartment has three rooms
<state type="turn-taking" name="listening"/>
</output>
---
```

Figure 11. GESOM snippet: the `busy`, `presenting-text` and `listening` turn-taking states.

2.4 Permissible Attribute Values

The specification does not attempt strict control over the use of states and events. GESOM is designed to give as many output devices as possible a fair chance at doing something useful with any message. Table 1 lists the states, events and background attributes that are used in the AdApt system. Note that all the states are on the tier `turn-taking`. We do not claim that the set of states, events and background attributes used in AdApt are optimal for all dialogue systems. It is a matter of further investigation to find out how well they generalise to other systems.

3. Interpretation

An obvious inspiration in developing GESOM has been the development of the Web protocols: HTML encoding in general, and browser, or user agent, compliancy guidelines in particular. An output device interpreting a GESOM message is analogous to a Web browser interpreting an HTML document.

Thus, the output device should meet the criteria listed in e.g., the XHTML 1.0 recommendation, 3.2 User Agent Conformance[2]. In summary, the output device should

1. be able to parse GESOM messages for XML well-formedness and, preferably, to validate the message against the referenced DTD

2. disregard unrecognised elements, but process their content

3. ignore any unrecognised attributes

4. substitute any unrecognised attribute values for the attribute's default

These criteria serve to safeguard backward and forward compatibility, and make it possible to interpret and render the content for unimodal channels with sparse capabilities, such as telephones or text-only devices (see examples in Figure 1).

3.1 Existing Tools and Standards for XML Rendering

Using XML encoded messages lets one take advantage of many existing tools and standards. The remainder of this section shows how to interpret GESOM messages with very little coding effort. With simple Extensible Style Sheet transformations (XSL, XSLT) (Clark, 1999) and/or Cascading Style Sheets (CSS) (Bos et al., 1998), which can be used with any available XSLT and CSS processors, GESOM messages can be interpreted, transformed and/or realised. Note that the non-transient signals represented by state elements are not likely to be represented well in a static message, which is in itself transient. In the following web browser examples, the state elements are simply ignored. We start with a simple example using CSS to render the message in Figure 8 as a static message in a web browser. The CSS and the result of applying the style sheet on the GESOM message in a CSS compliant web browser are shown in Figure 12. Using a slightly more complex XSL transformation, we can get more interesting results. The essential bits of the XSL and the result in an XSL compliant web browser are shown in Figure 13.

The code in these examples can be changed to produce e.g., plain text, complete and highly formatted HTML messages, instructions for voice browsers, or the equivalent message in some other voice or speech markup language. CSS Mobile Profile (Wugofski et al., 2002) and similar technologies can be used to interpret the messages in PDAs. However, the range of output devices is not limited to XML-based standard user agents. Any output device able to interpret the messages may be used.

```
/* gesom2browser.css */
[background="response-type:negative"]:before
{ color:  red; content:  ":-( "; }
[background="response-type:positive"]:before { color:  green;
content:
":-) "; } event[name="emphasis"] { font-weight:  bold;
font-style:
italic; }
```

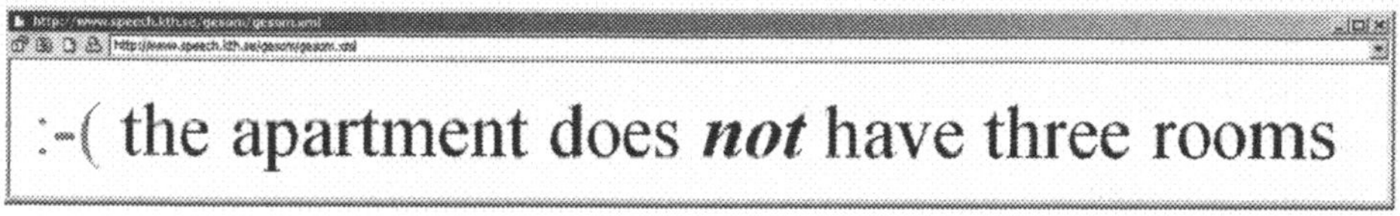

:-(the apartment does ***not*** have three rooms

Figure 12. Example of CSS style sheet.

In the next section we will show how the GESOM messages are interpreted and realised in the animated talking head, which is the AdApt system output module originally targeted by GESOM.

4. Realisation in an Animated Talking Head

The AdApt system uses a 3D parameterised talking head that can be controlled by a TTS system to provide accurate lip synchronised audio-visual synthetic speech (Beskow, 1997). The facial model includes control parameters for articulatory gestures as well as facial expressions. Parameters in the former category include jaw opening, lip closure, labiodental occlusion, tongue tip elevation, lip rounding and lip protrusion while the latter category includes controls for raising and shaping of eyebrows, smile, eyelid opening, gaze and head movement. Gestures can be developed using an interactive parameter editor based on the WaveSurfer platform (Beskow and Sjölander, 2000).

4.1 Gesture Library

The events, states and background attributes provide all the semantic information the animated agent needs in order to produce meaningful gestures, and the set of defined events and states constitute all the information that needs to be encoded both on the agent side and in the dialogue system. How the gestures should actually look like is up to the agent. In our implementation, this information is encoded in a gesture library.

At the lowest level of the library are descriptions of the actual gesture realisations. For most states and events there are multiple realisations with subtle differences. For our parametrically controlled animated agent, the descriptions

```
<!-- gesom2browser.xsl -->
<xsl:template match="text()"> <xsl:value-of select="."/> \
</xsl:template>
<xsl:template match="@background">
<xsl:choose>
<xsl:when test=".='attitude:positive'">
<a href=http://www.speech.kth.se/gesom/img/positive.gif>
</xsl:when>
<xsl:when test=".='attitude:negative'">
<a href=http://www.speech.kth.se/gesom/img/negative.gif>
</xsl:when>
</xsl:choose>
</xsl:template>
<xsl:template match="event">
<xsl:choose>
<xsl:when test="@name='emphasis'">
<span style=''font-weight:bold''><xsl:apply-templates/></span>
</xsl:when>
</xsl:choose>
</xsl:template>
```

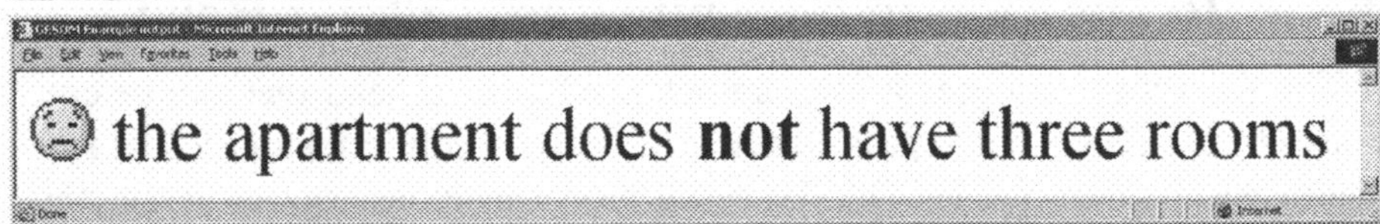

Figure 13. Example of XSL transformation.

are coded in terms of parameter tracks. For other types of agents, they would be coded in other ways, for example as 2D-animation sequences. Our gesture realisation descriptions include the time offset to the stroke phase of the gesture, i.e., the core part that carries the meaning of the gesture. This information is used to synchronise the timing of gestures with other events such as stressed syllables of emphasised words.

The gesture library contains a separate entry for each event and state. For events, a set of alternative gesture realisations is defined. Gestures defined for a particular event will typically have similar semantic meaning - some gestures might only have subtle differences (e.g., in duration) whereas others may differ in style (such as a head nod vs. an eye widening gesture to signal emphasis).

Each gesture has an associated weight that determines how likely it is to occur. By allowing alternative realisations, the agent will be less predictable and more natural in its behaviour.

In order to deal with the arbitrary length of states, they are divided into three phases: enter, sustain and exit. For each of the phases, as of the events, one out of a set of alternative gestures will be chosen. Gestures in the enter and exit phases are performed once per state (on state entrance and exit respectively), while the sustain gestures are executed at random intervals throughout the duration of the sustain phase. Enter and exit gestures are paired in such a way that, if a particular enter gesture is picked, the corresponding exit gesture will be chosen. This makes it possible for the exit gesture to restore the parameters that have been changed by the enter gesture. Figure 14 illustrates the layout of the gesture library.

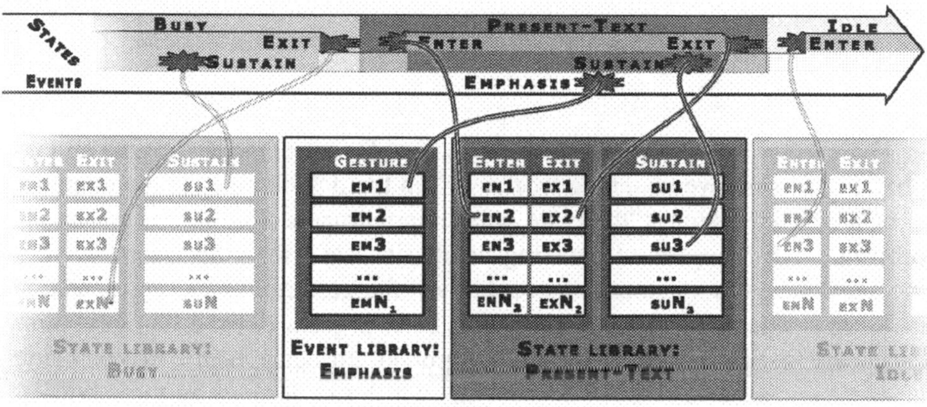

Figure 14. The structure of the gesture library. Gestures are picked from the library (bottom) and scheduled for realisation in the timeline (top).

4.2 Choosing between Multiple Realisations

Selection of a particular gesture is done in a weighted random fashion, based on the weights specified for each entry in the library. Although the gestures in each group are supposed to be semantically equivalent, there might be external factors making a particular gesture more or less appropriate at some given point. To reflect this in the library, the gesture weights could be dynamically updated, based on background attributes, or as a function of time. Table 2 shows how this can be represented. To begin with, each gesture within a category has a weight as seen in column two in the figure. The remaining columns are weight modifiers for different background attributes. The gesture weights are multiplied by the modifiers of the present background attributes. Note that several background attributes can be present at the same time. It is possible to specify a default modifier that will be used if no modifiers match the present background attributes. This is required when certain gestures should not be part of the default behaviour. In this case, the default modifier can be used to mask away the unwanted gestures by multiplying them with zero.

Table 2. Example of how gesture weights can be modified in the presence of `background` attributes.

		Event: emphasis	
Gesture	Weight	Modifier (default) attitude:positive	Modifier attitude: negative
Nod	2.0	1	0
Eyebrow widening	1.0	1	1
Eyebrow lowering	1.0	0	1

For example, when choosing a realisation for an emphasis event, an emphatic nod or an eye widening works well in the default case. If the utterance is of a negative nature ("there are *no* such apartments..."), the nod is less appropriate, but an eyebrow lowering would fit. Let's see what happens when the agent receives an emphasis event, given the gesture library representation in Table 2. The agent computes the probability *p(gesture)* for each of the three candidate gestures. If there are no background attributes, or if `background` is `attitude:positive`, the weights will be multiplied by the modifiers in the default (i.e., `attitude:positive`) column and then normalised, resulting in the probabilities *p(nod)*= $^2/_3$, *p(eye widening)* = $^1/_3$ and *p(eyebrow lowering)* = 0. If background is `attitude:negative`, the result will instead be *p(nod)* = 0, *p(eye widening)* = $^1/_2$ and *p(eyebrow lowering)* = $^1/_2$.

We can even let the weights be functions of time, by specifying them as an expression of t, where t is the time that has passed since the current state was entered. This makes it possible to model a gradual change of the agent's behaviour during the sustain phase of a state, for example to simulate boredom or tiredness by increasing the probability of yawning as time passes. An example if this is shown in Table 3.

4.3 Gesture Co-Articulation

Until now we have considered each gesture realisation as being independent of preceding and following gestures. This is however an oversimplification - just as with speech, there is co-articulation among gestures. If a head nod is followed by a look-right-gesture, it may be unnatural if the agent returned

Table 3. Example of gesture weights that change as a function of time (t).

State: idle, sustain gestures	
Gesture	Weight
Blink	5.0
Blink double	1.0
Yawn	t < 30 ? 0.0 : 1.0

to the neutral pose (straight ahead, which is the ending pose of the nodding gesture) before starting to turn the head sideways to the right. The natural thing would be to go more or less directly from the low point of the nod to the looking-right pose. To achieve this behaviour we have implemented a co-articulation algorithm that merges gestures that are overlapping or adjacent in time. The algorithm will always preserve the area around the stroke of each gesture, but segments before and after this area are subject to reduction. Reduced parts of the track are linearly interpolated.

5. Discussion and Future Work

The GESOM specification has been tested extensively in the real estate browsing domain within the AdApt system, with the animated agent as the output device. The only other output devices used have been computer emulated. Testing the system with real mobile phones, PDAs, Braille displays, as well as in other domains, would surely unearth shortcomings in the specification. Some known shortcomings:

- It would be useful to specify, or rather suggest, a number of fruitful sets of states, especially if states are to be used in more than one tier. Even though the specification in itself would allow any set, coding output with markup that is not implemented in any output devices would be a waste of time.

- The background attributes bear great similarity to the HTML/XHTML style attribute, but are not as well thought through. An elegant solution is to use style sheets of some sort to control varieties in execution of gestures. Work along these lines has started, but could use more exploration.

- Although GESOM was developed within a system that, in addition to the animated talking head, uses a clickable map on which apartments are plotted, and visualises search constraints as icons (Gustafson et al., 2002), the specification does not include this type of output. We would thus like to extend the specification so that it can handle the presentation of objects in a general manner.

- There is no good support for generating deictic non-verbal output. This seems straightforward to solve with respect to some output devices: nods, pointing and arrows could be used. Generalisation of the targets is troublesome, however. In order to point at something, one would need to know not only where the target is, but also where the device doing the pointing is and moreover, what it looks like. This goes against the general goal of GESOM, but deictic output may well be specified in a parallel system working alongside GESOM.

- In most cases, the output device would be the same as the input device. The AdApt system uses the same input format for text whether it is typed, comes from a speech recogniser or from a stored dialogue log file. This format is, however, not particularly generalised or formalised. Extending the specification to cover (at least textual) input as well as output would make it a more useful tool. The representation of objects mentioned above might then extend to mouse clicks.

- Work on testing speech recognition and semantic parsing using resynthesis is being done in the Higgins project at CTT. There are also attempts at recognising speaker emotions and emphasis. If GESOM is used for these recognition results, testing through resynthesis would be greatly simplified.

While the AdApt system and the Higgins systems are presently the only implementations of GESOM, it should be stressed that the GESOM specification was created with generalisation in mind, as indicated by its name. We do not presently claim it to be sufficient for the needs of all dialogue system output tasks, but we do believe that it, perhaps with minor adaptation, can be useful to a large number of dialogue systems. Our experiences from the implementation in the AdApt system indicate that it is successful in its pursuit, namely to form an abstraction layer between the dialogue manager and the output module, so that the dialogue manager does not need to know about the capabilities of the output module. The output module, e.g., an animated talking head, is responsible for suitable realisation of the communicative functions requested by the dialogue manager. Since the output description does not assume anything about the capabilities of the output device, it is fully possible to realise the output in some other way than through the gestures in an animated talking head. An alternative is to use familiar GUI metaphors, such as an hourglass for the busy state or a blinking red lamp for listening (recording) (Edlund and Nordstrand, 2002). This allows output to be generated on hardware incapable of rendering the animated agent, such as present day cell phones or PDAs.

Our current implementation of the animated agent uses a library of handcrafted gesture descriptions, grouped by communicative function. This is a very flexible model, since it allows us to model different attitudes, manners, personalities, moods or the socio-cultural identity of the agent simply by defining a new set of gesture descriptions (at least theoretically, assuming that the communicative functions are invariant). However, creating gesture realisations is a laborious process, and to convincingly model e.g., attitudes and emotions would require extensive studies of real-life subjects. A faster and more accurate way of obtaining the gesture realisations would be to record facial movement of an actor using a motion capture system such as[3]. Work towards this end is in progress at CTT.

Acknowledgements

This research was carried out at the Centre for Speech Technology, a competence centre at KTH, supported by VINNOVA (The Swedish Agency for Innovation Systems), KTH and participating Swedish companies and organisations.

Notes

1. `http://www.speech.kth.se/gesom/`
2. `http://www.w3.org/TR/2002/REC-xhtml1-20020801/`
3. `http:/www.qualisys.se/`

References

Agelfors, E., Beskow, J., Dahlquist, M., Granström, B., Lundeberg, M., Spens, K.-E., and Öhman, T. (1998). Synthetic faces as a lipreading support. In Agelfors et al., E., editor, *Proceedings of International Conference on Spoken Language Processing (ICSLP)*, pages 362–365, Sydney, Australia.

Bell, L., Boye, J., and Gustafson, J. (2001). Real-time handling of fragmented utterances. In *Proceedings of NAACL Workshop on Adaption in Dialogue Systems*, Pittsburgh, Pennsylvania, USA.

Bertenstam, J., Beskow, J., Blomberg, M., Carlsson, R., Elenius, K., Granström, B., Gustafson, J., Hunnicut, S., Högberg, J., Lindell, R., Neovius, L., de Serpa Leitaõ, A., Nord, L., and Ström, N. (1995). The Waxholm System - a progress report. In Bertenstam et al., J., editor, *Proceedings of ESCA Workshop on Spoken Dialogue Systems*, pages 81–84, Vigsø, Denmark.

Beskow, J. (1997). Animation of talking agents. In *Proceedings of European Tutorial Workshop on Audio-visual Speech Processing (AVSP)*, pages 149–152, Rhodes, Greece.

Beskow, J., Elenius, K., and McGlashan, S. (1997). Olga - a dialogue system with an animated talking agent. In *Proceedings of European Conference on Speech Communication and Technology (EUROSPEECH)*, pages 1651–1654, Rhodes, Greece.

Beskow, J. and Sjölander, K. (2000). Wavesurfer - an open source speech tool. In *Proceedings of International Conference on Spoken Language Processing (ICSLP)*, pages 464–467, Beijing, China.

Bos, B., Wium Lie, H., Lillie, C., and Jacobs, I. (1998). CSS2 specification. W3C recommendation. last updated 1998-05-12, accessed 2002-10-15. http://www.w3.org/TR/REC-CSS2/.

Bray, T., Paoli, J. Sperberg-McQueen, C. M., and Maler, E. (2000). Extensible Markup Language (XML) 1.0. W3C Recommendation, last updated 2000-10-06, accessed 2002-10-15. http://www.w3.org/TR/2000/REC-xml-20001006.

Burnett, D. C., Walker, M. R., and Hunt, A. (2002). Speech synthesis markup language specification. W3C Working Draft, updated 2002-04-04, accessed 2002-10-15. http://www.w3.org/TR/2002/WD-speech-synthesis-20020405/.

Cassell et al., J. (2001). Human conversation as a system framework: Designing embodied conversational agents. In Cassell, J., Sullivan, J., Prevost, S., and Churchill, E., editors, *Embodied Conversational Agents*, pages 29–63. MIT Press, Cambridge, Massachusetts, USA.

Clark, J. (1999). XSL Transformations (XSLT) version 1.0. W3C Recommendation. last updated 1999-11-16, accessed 2002-10-15. http://www.w3.org-/TR/xslt.

Edlund, J. and Nordstrand, M. (2002). Turn-taking gestures and hour-glasses in a multi-modal dialogue system. In *Proceedings of ISCA Workshop Multi-Modal Dialogue in Mobile Environments*, Kloster Irsee, Germany.

Granström, B., House, D., and Swerts, M. (2002). Multimodal feedback cues in human-machine interactions. In *Proceedings of Speech Prosody 2002*, pages 347–350, Aix-en-Provence, France.

Gustafson, J., Bell, L., Beskow, J., Boye, J., Carlson, R., Edlund, J., Granström, B., House, D., and Wirén, M. (2000). Adapt - a multimodal conversational dialogue system in an apartment domain. In *Proceedings of International Conference on Spoken Language Processing (ICSLP)*, pages 134–137, Beijing, China.

Gustafson, J., Bell, L., Boye, J., Edlund, J., and Wirén, M. (2002). Constraint manipulation and visualisation in a multimodal dialogue system. In *Proceedings of ISCA Tutorial and Research Workshop Multimodal Dialogue in Mobile Environments (IDS02)*, Kloster Irsee, Germany.

Gustafson, J., Lindberg, N., and Lundeberg, M. (1999). The August spoken dialogue system. In *Proceedings of European Conference on Speech Communication and Technology (EUROSPEECH)*, pages 1151–1154, Budapest, Hungary.

Gustavsson, C., Strindlund, L., and Wiknetrz, E. (2002). Verification, validation and evaluation of the Virtual Human Markup Language (VHML). http://www.ep.liu.se/exjobb/isy/2002/3188/exjobb.pdf.

Gustavsson, C., Strindlund, L., Wiknetrz, E., Beard, S., Huynh, Q., Marriot, A., and Stallo, J. (2001). VHML. W3C Working Draft, updated 2001-10-01, accessed 2002-10-15. http://www.interface.computing.edu.au-/documents/VHML/2001/WD-VHML-20011021/vhml.html.

McNeill, D. (1992). *Hand and Mind: What Gestures Reveal about Thought.* University of Chicago Press, Chicago, Illinois, USA.

Nagao, K. and Takeuchi, A. (1994). Speech dialogue with facial displays: Multimodal human computer conversation. In *Proceedings of Annual Meeting of the Association for Computational Linguistics (ACL)*, pages 102–109, Las Cruces, New Mexico, USA.

Pelachaud, C. and Prevost, S. (1994). Sight and sound: Generating facial expressions and spoken intonation from context. In *Proceedings of 2nd ESCA/AAAI/IEEE Workshop on Speech Synthesis*, pages 216–219, New Paltz, New York, USA.

Pirker, H. and Krenn, B. (2002). D9c: Report on the outcome of the markup assessment task. http://www.ai.univie.ac.at/NECA/publications/publication_docs/d9c.pdf.

Poggi, I. and Pelachaud, C. (2000). Performative facial expressions in animated faces. In Cassell, J., Sullivan, J., Prevost, S., and Churchill, E., editors, *Embodied Conversational Agents*, pages 155–188. MIT Press, Cambridge, Massachusetts, USA.

Thórisson, K. R. (1999). A mind model for multimodal communicative creatures and humanoids. *International Journal of Applied Artificial Intelligence*, 13(4–5):449–486.

Wugofski, T., Dominiak, D., Stark, P., and Roy, T. (2002). CSS mobile profile 1.0. W3C Candidate Recommendation, last updated 2002-07-25, accessed 2002-10-16. http://www.w3.org/TR/2002/CR-css-mobile-20020725.

II

SYSTEM ARCHITECTURE AND EXAMPLE IMPLEMENTATIONS

Chapter 7

OVERVIEW OF SYSTEM ARCHITECTURE

Andreas Kellner
Man-Machine Interfaces Department, Philips Research Laboratories, Aachen, Germany
andreas.kellner@philips.com

Abstract Spoken language dialogue systems are evolving from task-specific systems that run on large servers in the public telephone network into personal multi-purpose interaction partners on handheld devices or in the home environment. This requires more flexible system architectures, which can enable multimodal interaction as well as integrate several independently developed applications into one coherent user interface. Together with a powerful set of widely accepted standards for interfaces and application logic, this is the prerequisite for the success of next-generation conversational user interfaces. In this chapter, we analyse the requirements for a system architecture of a multimodal conversational user interface and describe two existing frameworks, the Galaxy Communicator infrastructure and the SmartKom testbed. We also take a short look on emerging and existing standards for spoken language dialogue systems and their multimodal extensions.

Keywords: System architecture; Multimodality; VoiceXML; SALT; Galaxy; SmartKom.

1. Introduction

Spoken language dialogue systems over the telephone have been used in commercial applications for some years now. In most cases, these systems have been specifically designed for a single narrowly defined application such as train or air-traffic information (Aust et al., 1995; Ward and Issar, 1995), directory assistance (Kellner et al., 1998), home banking (Larsen, 1996), or weather information (Zue et al., 2000). These systems are used to perform specific actions within the system's limited domain. Application portals, which support multiple applications from a single entry point have so far mostly been realised by a number of individual systems with an additional call-routing module (Gorin et al., 1997). This module analyses the user's initial utterance and

W. Minker, D. Bühler and L. Dybkjær (eds), Spoken Multimodal Human-Computer Dialogue in Mobile Environments, 117-132

transfers the caller to the appropriate server or a human operator. In all these telephony-based systems, the interaction between the system and the user is naturally restricted to spoken input and output.

As computing devices become smaller, cheaper, and more powerful, full-fledged spoken language dialogue systems can now be implemented on small personal computers or even handheld devices. In addition, wireless high-bandwidth communication allows for distributed approaches, where the user interface front-end is realised on the user's client device, while the application back-end may reside in the network. Consequently, spoken language dialogue systems are beginning to enter the personal space and are evolving from public network-based information lookup systems into conversational user interfaces for personal companion devices. The interaction between the dialogue system and the user is no longer restricted to speech input and output. Touch-sensitive graphics displays and small cameras that can detect mimics, gestures, and lip movements are only few examples for additional input and output modalities that extend the communication bandwidth between the user and the system.

These trends do not only create new challenges on the robustness and flexibility of the system's core modules such as speech recognition, language interpretation, or output generation. They also require system architectures that can cope with several parallel input and output streams and provide enough flexibility to allow for the integration of various independently developed systems into one coherent user interface. Powerful standards are necessary to allow for the interoperability of distributed systems components and for the seamless integration of multiple applications on a single platform.

In this part of the book, these requirements will be highlighted and sample solutions as well as emerging standards in the fields will be discussed.

2. Towards Personal Multimodal Conversational User Interface

Spoken language dialogue systems are evolving from speech-enabled agents for specific tasks in the public telephone network into multimodal conversational user interfaces that give access to a number of different applications in an intuitive and consistent way. Such systems are being built for various environments such as automotive systems, handheld devices, or the living room. Today's commercial automatic inquiry systems already allow for flexible natural language dialogues in task-oriented applications. Dialogue-based user interfaces for mobile and living-room applications, however, have to go further and provide an even more flexible interaction mechanism. In this chapter, we will take a closer look at some of the additional requirements and their consequences for the system design.

As an example of a multimodal conversational user interface, the SPICE prototype (Kellner and Portele, 2002) will be used. This system realises a conversational interface to an Electronic Programme Guide (EPG), which allows the user to navigate through a TV programme database by means of spoken dialogue in combination with touch-screen input on a tablet PC. The user can select TV shows from the database, mark them for viewing or recording, or retrieve background information on a specific programme. Figure 1 sketches the architecture of the SPICE system.

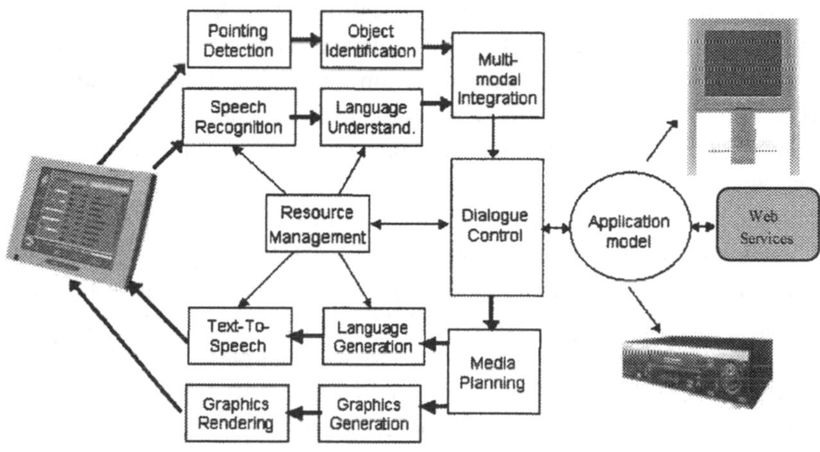

Figure 1. System architecture of SPICE (Kellner and Portele, 2002).

2.1 From Slot-Filling to Information Browsing and Cooperative Problem Solving

The main advantage of a natural language dialogue versus simple command & control interfaces is that the user does not have to remember specific pre-defined keywords or menu hierarchies but uses natural language to express her wishes and intentions. In contrast to the pre-defined menu structure of early Interactive Voice Response (IVR) systems, it is up to the user to decide what information to give and in which order. It is also possible to give multiple commands and/or information items in a single utterance (e.g., 'Are there any sports programmes on BBC1 tonight?').

In many so-called *slot-filling* applications like timetable information, the goal of the user is to retrieve a piece of information (e.g., a train connection) from the system's database. The dialogue system has to collect a number of slot values (e.g., date, time, origin and destination) in order to perform a database query and then presents the result(s) to the user. In these applications the user's dialogue goal is pre-determined by the application and does not change during the interaction. The task of the dialogue manager is to accumulate information from various user turns and to handle corrections and verifications.

Applications like navigating through a TV database or choosing songs from an MP3 database are less goal oriented. The user is often not searching for a single specific programme entity but *browses* through the database without a specific target in mind. The system therefore has to detect, when the user goal changes and has to update its knowledge (i.e., the 'slot history') accordingly.

In conversational user interfaces, the interaction between the user and the system is a two-way communication (Smith and Gordon, 1997). While normally the user is in full control of the dialog, the device takes the initiative in some situations and pro-actively offers some suggestions for content-selection based on the user's preferences, guides the user through a complex task (e.g., programming a VCR), or provides assistance (e.g., a help function) when problems occur.

For this kind of applications, a strictly system-driven interaction as in simple IVR systems is not only inconvenient for the user, but may even be impossible because it can not represent the huge space of potential options in the dialogue flow. In order to perform cooperative dialogues with the user, the system needs to have an abstract representation of the tasks it can perform and a generic set of dialogue strategies that can be used in different situations.

An important feature of personal conversational user interfaces to this end is that they are usually not designed for a single task, but should offer a coherent interface to a number of different applications and services. The number and composition of these services is not static, but changes as additional components (e.g., consumer electronics devices to be controlled or services available in the car environment) are added.

The system should not only be able to integrate new applications 'on the fly' in a plug&play manner, but should also allow for a seamless transition between different applications and possibly even the exchange of information between them.

Therefore the dialogue representation needs to separate the core user interface capabilities and generic dialogue strategies from the specific modelling of the applications and their domain knowledge.

2.2 Access to Unstructured Content

In many applications such as the SPICE EPG system, the user has to navigate through large content spaces such as songs in an MP3 collection or movies in a TV programme guide. Due to the limited 'interaction bandwidth' of conventional living-room interfaces like remote controls or small-vocabulary voice-control systems, current interfaces only allow the user to select individual items by specifying filters like 'genre', 'artist', or 'time' or by navigating up and down a long list of titles. Speech-enabled interfaces, in contrast, allows direct access to the information items the user actually wants by simply speaking the title (e.g., "Record *'Ally McBeal'* tonight").

In some cases, however, the user may not know the exact name of the entity, which is stored in the EPG database. Especially in large databases, the huge variety of possible formulations can no longer be modelled explicitly in the grammar or database. Therefore, the system must be able to handle incomplete and 'fuzzy' input (e.g., 'the new James Bond' instead of 'James Bond 007: Die Another Day').

The SPICE system, for example, uses large-vocabulary speech recognition and stochastic natural language understanding in combination with information-retrieval technology to enable navigation in unstructured information sources such as the programme descriptions. This allows the user to select a programme entry by describing its content (e.g., 'Is there any movie about wildlife in Africa this week?').

Such an approach requires a tight integration of the system's content database and the individual modules of the system. Language resources like speech recognition lexicon and language models have to be updated dynamically as the content of the databases changes.

2.3 Multimodal Interaction

The full potential of human-machine interaction can only be obtained in multimodal systems. Interfaces that provide alternative input modalities like speech and pointing are usually preferred. Humans have a good intuition about when to use different modes and when to switch modalities, which leads to better performance, faster error recovery and less frustration (Cohen et al., 1998). Furthermore, depending on the usage scenario, (e.g., driving a car or listening to music in the living room), some interaction modalities may be more appropriate than others.

The possibility to combine several modalities at once offers an additional benefit to the user. In the SPICE system, pointing input can be used separately or combined with speech input for efficiently selecting information from a list that is currently displayed on the screen (e.g., "Give me more information on THIS ONE", "What else do you have on THAT channel?"). Studies show, that the combination of the two modalities improves the robustness of the recognition due to possible redundancy in the two input modes (Oviatt, 1999).

From an architectural point of view, multimodal interaction increases the complexity of the system. On the input side, several signal streams have to be processed in parallel and information from the different modalities has to be merged. e.g., in a dedicated *multimodal integration* module. On the output side, the multimedia information has to be split and rendered for the different modalities. A multimodal dialogue system must be able to handle sequential use of different modalities as well as simultaneous multimodal input. Synchronisation of different devices in distributed systems, different processing delays for individual modalities, as well as the combination of turn-based (e.g., speech) and asynchronous (e.g., GUI) modalities pose additional challenges on the architectural framework of a multimodal dialogue system.

3. System Architectures for Multimodal Dialogue Systems

A full-fledged multimodal user interface does not only need sophisticated modules for input processing, dialogue management, and output generation, but also requires a powerful architectural framework that hosts these modules and manages the communication between them.

In first-generation mono-modal systems, the modules have often been arranged straightforward in a pipeline architecture as shown in Figure 2. This architecture is sufficient as long as there is only a single information stream in the system and no back-channels or asynchronous modules are required.

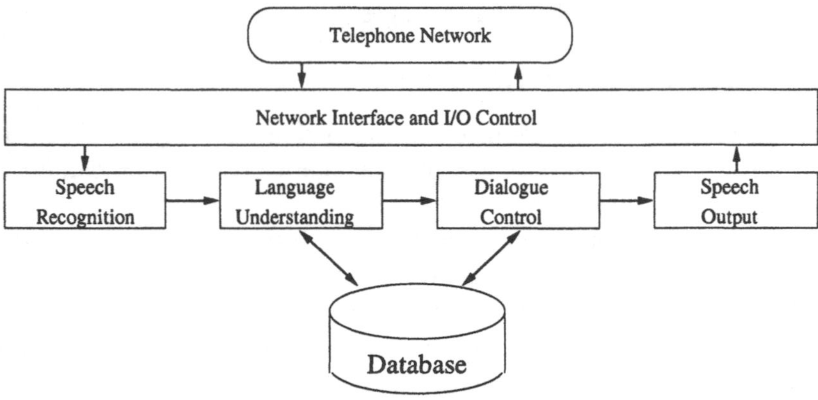

Figure 2. System architecture of PADIS (Kellner et al., 1998).

However, this simple setup is not able to accommodate sophisticated multimodal systems as described in the previous section. The SPICE system overview presented in Figure 1 gives a first indication of the large number of modules and communication links necessary in a multimodal system.

Summarising the requirements from the previous section, the architecture for a multimodal conversational user interface should support:

- a large number of modules with arbitrary connections between them
- distribution of modules across multiple platforms

- merging and splitting of information streams
- handling synchronous as well as asynchronous module behaviour
- dynamic update of system parameters
- debugging of the overall system and individual components

For the interoperability of systems and the re-usability of components for different systems, there are two more pre-requisites: (i) an appropriate decomposition of the overall task in a number of individual modules such as speech recognition, natural language interpretation, dialogue management, output generation and speech synthesis and (ii) the existence of widely accepted interface standards for the data exchange between these modules.

The architectural framework (or testbed) in which a dialogue system is implemented has to provide the infrastructure for module communication, logging, and evaluation. It is responsible for launching and monitoring the individual modules and for establishing the communication between them.

One of the main design issues to be taken in an online system framework is the system's control strategy. Some approaches (Seneff et al., 1999) favour a client-server concept with a central module that controls the information flow between the modules, others favour a distributed architecture. Online architectures without a central control unit are often based on the metaphor of autonomous agents (Russell and Norvig, 1995). Such agents perceive their world through sensors (input streams) and act upon that environment through effectors (output streams). For each possible input sequence, an autonomous agent tries to perform those actions that are expected to maximise a given performance measure. The communication between the agents can either be a peer-to-peer communication e.g., using the agent communication language KQML (Knowledge Query and Manipulation Language) (Finin et al., 1994) or a blackboard style of communication (Engelmore and Morgan, 1988) where the blackboard serves as a shared global database. An important example for an architecture based on the autonomous agent paradigm is the Open Agent Architecture (Cohen et al., 1994). OOA was developed by SRI and is used as a base in several dialogue systems (Cheng and Gupta, 2000; Moran et al., 1997).

As examples of a distributed architecture and a client-server architecture, the SmartKom testbed and the Communicator Galaxy architecture will now be investigated in more detail.

3.1 SmartKom Testbed

The SmartKom architecture (Wahlster et al., 2001) is based on a distributed control strategy as described above. However, instead of one central blackboard a number of different blackboards for different types of information are used. The system's development was motivated by the necessity to provide a flexible environment for a complex speech-to-speech translation system in the German VERBMOBIL project (Wahlster, 2000).

The architecture consists of three components (Klüter et al., 2000):

- a set of independent modules, which provide the expertise needed to solve a problem
- a set of blackboards called *pools*, which serve as a shared global data storage where the modules exchange messages
- a control component, the 'testbed manager', which makes runtime decisions about the resource allocation and the data flow on the blackboards. In contrast to the control module in a client-server architecture, the testbed manager does not control the data flow through the system, but facilitates the infrastructure for the pool communication.

The individual modules in SmartKom can be connected to a number of pools for input and output. They operate autonomously on the information that becomes available on their input pools and generate messages on their output pools. The framework accommodates for synchronous and asynchronous data processing and supports parallel data streams within the system.

The content of each message is described in M3L, an XML dialect. The testbed facilitates validation of messages against their DTDs and provides tools for logging and debugging.

Figure 3 shows the GUI of the SmartKom testbed manager, which gives status information about the modules and allows the configuration of the individual modules at runtime. This testbed is the basis for various demonstrators in the German governmentally funded project SmartKom[1] and was also selected as the basis for the SPICE system described above.

3.2 Galaxy Communicator Infrastructure

The Galaxy Communicator infrastructure (Seneff et al., 1998) is an extension of the MIT Galaxy system (Goddeau et al., 1994) and is being developed and maintained by the MITRE Corporation. It has been selected as the standard software infrastructure for the DARPA Communicator programme[2].

Galaxy is a distributed, message-based architecture which consists of a central *hub* module and a number of processing modules (called *servers*) around it. All communication between the servers is sent through the hub except for high data-rate links (e.g., between the audio server and the speech recognition module), which are not passed directly through the hub, but are brokered by the hub to reduce network load.

Figure 4 shows the architecture of the Galaxy Communicator system.

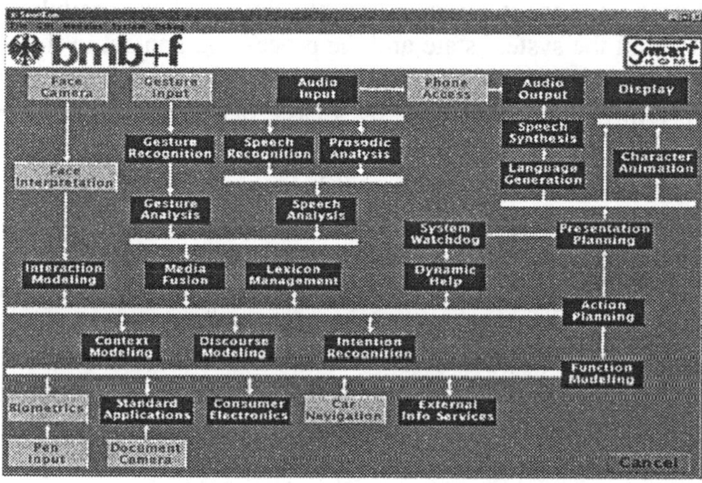

Figure 3. Architecture (and testbed GUI) of the SmartKom System (Wahlster et al., 2001).

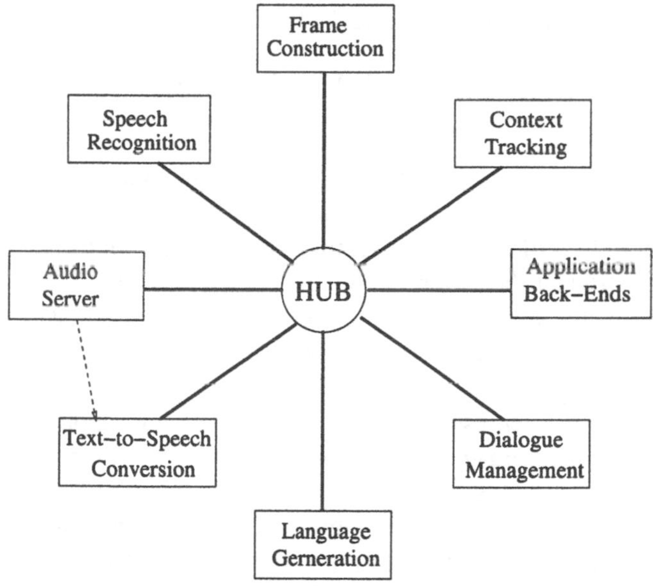

Figure 4. Architecture of GALAXY-II (Seneff et al., 1998).

The hub communicates with the servers via a standardised frame-based protocol. For each user input a token is created and that token is enriched with information frames as it visits different servers. The hub interaction with the servers can be controlled via a scripting language that determines the information flow through the system. Except for user interface modules such as a graphical user interface, the servers are stateless, i.e., the modules store all information about the system state and the processing context in the token. In this way, several inputs can be processed in a single system at the same time.

The Galaxy infrastructure is used by a large number of research institutes around the world. The software is available under an open source license from the Galaxy Communicator download site[1]2.

Even though the SmartKom testbed and the Communicator Galaxy infrastructure are based on different paradigms (central vs. distributed control), both are equally well suited for the realisation of prototypes for multimodal dialogue systems. In the first case, the information flow through the application is pre-determined by the the way the different modules are connected to the different pools, in the second case, it is steered by a hub script. Both architectures share the same approach for module decomposition and distribution and offer tools for evaluation and debugging, which are especially important in a research environment. For actual commercial applications on small-footprint platforms (cell-phones, PDAs, ...) aspects like resource requirement and interaction bandwidth become more important than flexibility and modularity as can be seen in in the chapter by Niklfeld et al.

4. Standardisation of Application Representation

When moving from application-specific system designs to open user interface platforms, which can host a vast number of different applications, it takes a widely accepted set of standards to represent the applications and to describe the interfaces between the different modules in the system. Niklfeld and colleagues highlight the difficulties that arise when trying to create even simple multimodal services with existing standards and interfaces in a real life scenario.

A standard for the representation of spoken dialogue applications should separate the system's built-in interaction capabilities from the actual description of the application. This will finally enable dynamic plug&play of new applications on a generic user interface engine. Another example for the power of a standardised application representation is the notion of the *Voice Web*, which allows the transition from one speech application to another in the same simple way as one HTML page can be linked from another one.

At the moment, there are a number of standards emerging in that area. The two most promising approaches are VoiceXML (Voice eXtensible Markup Language) and SALT (Speech Application Language Tags). Both markup languages describe spoken dialog interfaces, but they follow different strategies, due to their different goals and heritages.

4.1 VoiceXML and its Extensions

VoiceXML – Voice eXtensible Markup Language – was originally developed by the VoiceXML forum[3] consisting of IBM, Motorola, AT&T, and Lucent. Starting with VoiceXML 2.0, the responsibility for development of the markup language has been transferred to the W3C VoiceBrowser Working Group[4].

VoiceXML has been designed for the specification of interactive voice response applications over the telephone network. It is a simple high-level dialog markup language that allows the representation of system driven, as well as mixed initiative speech dialogues. Like any procedural programming language, VoiceXML defines its own execution and data model in addition to the actual user interface description. Therefore, the VoiceXML specification defines a large number of tags for the interaction with the user (e.g., `<prompt>`, `<grammar>`), for procedural programming (e.g., `<if>`, `<then>` `<else>` `<goto>`), and to describe the application's data model (`<form>`, `<field>`). An example of a simple VoiceXML interaction from the W3C specification is shown in Figure 5.

```
<?xml version="1.0"?>
<vxml version="2.0" xmlns="http://www.w3.org/2001/vxml">
  <form>
  <field name="drink">
     <prompt>Would you like coffee,tea, milk,
             or nothing?</prompt>
     <grammar src="drink.grxml" type="application/srgs+xml"/>
  </field>
  <block>
     <submit next="http://www.drink.example.com/drink2.asp"/>
  </block>
 </form>
</vxml>
```

In this example the system prompts the user for input ('Would you like coffee,tea, milk, or nothing?') and activates the grammar 'drink.grxml' to process the user's spoken answer. Once the user has provided a value for the field, the dialogue continues at the specified URL.

Figure 5. Simple VoiceXML example.

The heart of VoiceXML is its Form Interpretation Algorithm (FIA) that automates the control flow to fill the fields within a VoiceXML form. The standard supports different form elements for menus, system-driven interaction, and simple mixed-initiative form filling. This FIA's default behaviour can be manipulated by the application developer with the use of conditional and procedural programming.

VoiceXML is already widely accepted in the telephony speech community and a large number of platforms and tools for this specification are commercially available. However, VoiceXML is primarily designed for speech-only dialogues and currently lacks consistent mechanisms for the integration of different modalities. Therefore, W3C has established a new working group on Multimodal Interaction[5] to extend the Web user interface for multimodal interactions, offering the user the choice of different input and output modalities.

One of the most promising multimodal extensions to VoiceXML is the X+V (XHTML+Voice) specification proposed by IBM, Opera, and Motorola. X+V is a multimodal markup language that mixes XHTML and VoiceXML.

Next to VoiceXML, which describes the dialogue behaviour of a system, the W3C Voice Browser Working Group provides a suite of other specifications necessary for the interoperability of speech applications.

The so called *W3C Speech Interface Framework* currently includes working drafts of:

- SRGS, a speech grammar format
  (see `http://www.w3.org/TR/speech-grammar/`)
- SSML, a speech output format
  (see `http://www.w3.org/TR/speech-synthesis/`)
- NLSML, a format for the semantics of a natural language result
  (see `http://www.w3.org/TR/nl-spec/`)
- CCXML, a telephony call control language
  (see `http://www.w3.org/TR/ccxml/`)

4.2 SALT - Speech Application Language Tags

An alternative proposal is the SALT (Speech Application Language Tags) markup language that was developed by the SaltForum[6] founded by Cisco, Comverse, Intel, Microsoft, Philips, and SpeechWorks. The goal of the SALT specification is to provide a small set of XML elements with associated attributes, events, and methods to extend web pages with speech and multimodal interfaces. Rather than being a standalone dialogue description language like VoiceXML, SALT tags are used within other web standards like HTML or XHTML.

Consequently, SALT does not provide its own data and execution model but leverages the event-based DOM execution model of web pages. Voice-only applications (e.g., for telephony applications) can be realised using XHTML's scripting capabilities.

The three main top-level elements in SALT are:

<listen>: processes spoken input
Configures the speech recogniser (e.g., by specifying a <grammar>), executes the recognition and handles speech events.

<dtmf>: processes and controls DTMF in telephony applications

<prompt>: plays a prompt

Figure 6 presents a simple example of the use of SALT tags within a XHTML page.

```
<input name="txtBoxDestCity" type="text"
       onclick="recoDestCity.Start()" />

<salt:listen id="recoDestCity">
    <salt:grammar src="city.xml" />
    <salt:bind targetElement="txtBoxDestCity"
               value="/result/city" />
</salt:listen>
```

When the user clicks on a button, the grammar 'city.xml' is activated and the recognition result is bound to the specified input field.

Figure 6. Simple SALT example.

The grammar format SRGS as well as the speech output format SSML are recommended by both VoiceXML and SALT. Many experts today believe that even though VoiceXML and SALT were starting from different directions, the two standards might some time converge into one single speech markup standard (Potter and Larson, 2002).

5. Conclusion

Multimodal conversational user interfaces require a more flexible and powerful architectural framework than simple mono-modal systems that host a single application. The architecture must control a potentially very large number of modules that are distributed over multiple platforms and a vast number of parallel communication streams between them. Synchronisation of different devices and modules as well as dynamic parameter update have to be supported. Two research systems that meet these requirements, the SmartKom testbed and the MIT Galaxy platform, that have shortly been presented. While these platforms have been designed to provide a flexible research environment,

Niklfeld et al. describe the requirements and difficulties of porting a multimodal interface to an existing small-footprint platforms.

Standards that describe the interface between individual modules or between individual applications are the other important ingredient for a coherent user interface across devices and applications. In the overview, we have shortly looked at VoiceXML and SALT and the differences and commonalities between them. In the chapter by Katsurada et al., another candidate for a multimodal description language is introduced: XISL (eXtensible Interaction Scenario Language).

Notes

1. `http://www.smartkom.org/`
2. `http://communicator.sourceforge.net/`
3. `http://www.voicexml.org`
4. `http://www.w3.org/Voice`
5. `http://www.w3.org/2002/mmi/`
6. `http://www.saltforum.org/`

References

Aust, H., Oerder, M., Seide, F., and Steinbiss, V. (1995). The Philips automatic train timetable information system. *Speech Communication*, 17(3–4):249–262.

Cheng, Y. and Gupta, A.and Lee, R. (2000). A distributed spoken user interface based on open agent architecture (OOA). In *Proceedings of International Conference on Spoken Language Processing (ICSLP)*, pages 743–746, Beijing, China.

Cohen, P., Johnston, M., McGee, D., Oviatt, S., Clow, J., and Smith, I. (1998). The efficiency of multimodal interaction. In *Proceedings of International Conference on Spoken Language Processing (ICSLP)*, pages 249–252, Sidney, Australia.

Cohen, P. R., Cheyer, A. J., Wang, M., and Baeg, S. C. (1994). An open agent architecture. In *Proceedings of AAAI Spring Symposium*, pages 1–8, Stanford University, Palo Alto, California, USA.

Engelmore, R. and Morgan, A., editors (1988). *Blackboard Systems*. Addison-Wesley.

Finin, T., Fritzson, R., McKay, D., and McEntire, R. (1994). KQML as an agent communication language. In *Proceedings of International Conference on Information and Knowledge Management*, pages 456–463, Gaithersburg, Maryland, USA.

Goddeau, D., Brill, E., Glass, J., Pao, C., Phillips, M., Polifroni, J., Seneff, S., and Zue, V. (1994). GALAXY: A human-language interface to on-line travel information. In *Proceedings of International Conference on Spoken Language Processing (ICSLP)*, pages 707–710, Yokohama, Japan.

Gorin, A. L., Riccardi, G., and Wright, J. H. (1997). How may I help you? *Speech Communication*, 23:113–127.

Katsurada, K., Yamada, H., Nakamura, Y., Kobayashi, S., and Nitta, T. (2004). XISL: A modality-independent MMI description language. In Minker, W., Bühler, D., and Dybkjær, L., editors, *Spoken Multimodal Human-Computer Dialogue in Mobile Environments*. Kluwer Academic Publishers, Dordrecht, The Netherlands. (this volume).

Kellner, A. and Portele, Y. (2002). SPICE – a multimodal conversational user interface to an electronic program guide. In *Proceedings of ISCA Tutorial and Research Workshop Multimodal Dialogue in Mobile Environments (IDS02)*, Kloster Irsee, Germany.

Kellner, A., Rueber, B., and Schramm, H. (1998). Strategies for name recognition in automatic directory assistance systems. In *Proceedings of IEEE Workshop on Interactive Voice Technology for Telecommunications Applications (IVTTA)*, pages 21–26, Torino, Italy.

Klüter, A., Ndiaye, A., and Kirchmann, H. (2000). Verbmobil from a software engineering point of view. In *Verbmobil: Foundations of Speech-to-Speech Translation*, pages 659–670. Springer-Verlag, Berlin/Heidelberg, Germany.

Larsen, L. B. (1996). Voice controlled home banking - objectives and experiences of the Esprit Ovid project. In *Proceedings of IEEE Workshop on Interactive Voice Technology for Telecommunications Applications (IVTTA)*, pages 45–49, Basking Ridge, New Jersey, USA.

Moran, D., Cheyer, A., Julia, L., Martin, D., and Park, S. (1997). Multimodal user interfaces in the open agent architecture. In *Proceedings of International Conference on Intelligent User Interfaces (IUI)*, pages 61–68, Orlando, Florida, USA.

Nikfeld, G., Pucher, M., Finan, R., and Eckhart, W. (2002). Steps towards multi-modal data services. In *Proceedings of ISCA Tutorial and Research Workshop Multimodal Dialogue in Mobile Environments (IDS02)*, Kloster Irsee, Germany.

Niklfeld, G., Pucher, M., Finan, R., and Eckhart, W. (2004). A path to multimodal data services for telecommunications. In Minker, W., Bühler, D., and Dybkjær, L., editors, *Spoken Multimodal Human-Computer Dialogue in Mobile Environments*. Kluwer Academic Publishers, Dordrecht, The Netherlands. (this volume).

Oviatt, S. (1999). Mutual disambiguation of recognition errors in a multimodal architecture. In *Proceedings of Conference on Human Factors in Computing Systems (CHI)*, pages 576–583, Pittsburgh, Pennsylvania, USA.

Potter, S. and Larson, J. (2002). VoiceXML and SALT - how are they different, and why? *SpeechTechnology Magazine May/June 2002*. http://www.-speechtechmag.com/issues/7_3/cover/742-1.html.

Russell, S. and Norvig, P. (1995). *Artificial Intelligence: A Modern Approach*. Prentice Hall.

Seneff, S., Hurley, E., Lau, R., Pao, C., Schmid, P., and Zue, V. (1998). GALAXY-II: A reference architecture for conversational system development. In *Proceedings of International Conference on Spoken Language Processing (ICSLP)*, pages 931–934, Sydney, Australia.

Seneff, S., Lau, R., and Polifroni, J. (1999). Organization, communication, and control in the Galaxy-II conversational system. In *Proceedings of European Conference on Speech Communication and Technology (EUROSPEECH)*, pages 1271–1274, Budapest, Hungary.

Smith, R. and Gordon, S. (1997). Effects of variable initiative on linguistic behaviour in human-computer spoken language dialogue. *Computational Linguistics*, 23:141–168.

Wahlster, W., editor (2000). *Verbmobil: Foundations of Speech-to-Speech Translation*. Springer-Verlag, Berlin/Heidelberg, Germany.

Wahlster, W., Reithinger, N., and Blocher, A. (2001). SmartKom: Multimodal communication with a life-like character. In *Proceedings of European Conference on Speech Communication and Technology (EUROSPEECH)*, pages 1547–1550, Aalborg, Denmark.

Ward, W. and Issar, S. (1995). The CMU ATIS system. In *Proceedings of ARPA Workshop on Spoken Language Technology*, pages 249–251, Pittsburgh, Pennsylvania, USA.

Zue, V., Seneff, S., Glass, J., Polifroni, J., Pao, C., Hazen, T. J., and Hetherington, L. (2000). Jupiter: A telephone-based conversational interface for weather information. *IEEE Transactions on Speech and Audio Processing*, 8(1):85–96.

Chapter 8

XISL: A MODALITY-INDEPENDENT MMI DESCRIPTION LANGUAGE

Kouichi Katsurada, Hirobumi Yamada, Yusaku Nakamura, Satoshi Kobayashi, Tsuneo Nitta
Toyohashi University of Technology, Toyohashi, Japan
{ katurada, nitta } @tutkie.tut.ac.jp, { yamada, nakamura, skoba } @vox.tutkie.tut.ac.jp

Abstract In this chapter we outline a multimodal interaction description language XISL (eXtensible Interaction Scenario Language) that has been developed to describe MMI scenarios. The main feature of XISL is that it allows modalities to be described flexibly, which makes it easy to add new modalities or to modify existing modalities on MMI systems. Moreover, XISL is separately described from XML or HTML contents, thus making both the XISL and XML (HTML) documents more reusable. We constructed three types of XISL execution systems, namely a PC terminal, a PDA terminal, and a mobile phone terminal, and show the descriptive power of XISL by implementing an online shopping application on these terminals.

Keywords: MMI description language; XISL; Modality independence.

1. Introduction

Discussions on multimodal interaction (MMI) have just started. The WWW Consortium organised a multimodal working group[1], and started standardising the MMI description language. Some other organisations have been specifying their own descriptions to deal with multimodalities[2] (Wang, 2002; Beckham et al., 2001). The purpose of these efforts is to provide seamless web services on various types of terminals such as mobile phones, PDAs, and other terminals in addition to ordinary PCs. In the near future, many other types of terminals will be used for accessing the web, and they will provide more advanced web services.

As web access becomes more sophisticated, the newly introduced terminals may support new types of modalities such as gestures, hand-writings, and fa-

W. Minker, D. Bühler and L. Dybkjær (eds), Spoken Multimodal Human-Computer Dialogue in Mobile Environments, 133-148

cial expressions. In order to handle these modalities in MMI applications, the MMI description language should be capable of describing inputs and outputs using these modalities, however, previous languages can only handle graphical user interface (GUI) operations and speech.

With this background, we propose an MMI description language XISL (eXtensible Interaction Scenario Language)[3] (Nitta et al., 2001; Katsurada et al., 2002) that enables input/output modalities to be described flexibly. This flexibility makes it easy to add or modify modalities, and to introduce new types of terminals with different modalities. Moreover XISL is separately described from XML or HTML contents, thus making both the XML(HTML) and XISL documents more reusable. Therefore, developers can easily construct seamless services over networks as shown in Figure 1.

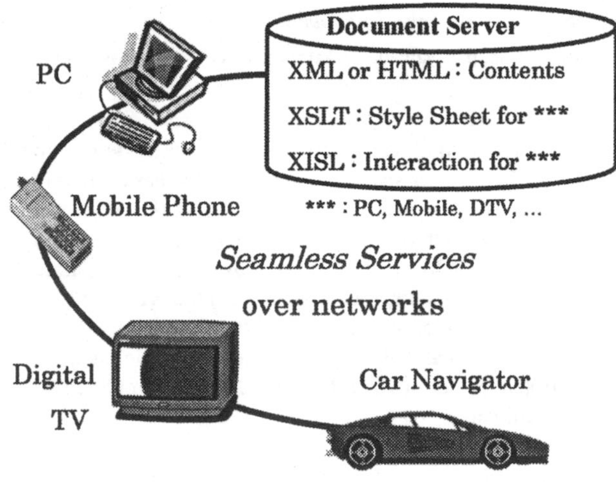

Figure 1. Seamless services over networks.

This chapter is organised as follows. Section 2 outlines an XISL execution system. In Section 3, we describe the latest specifications of XISL. In Section 4, we explain three types of MMI systems implemented on a PC, a PDA, and a mobile phone terminal, and show samples of XISL documents described for these terminals. After comparing XISL with other languages in Section 5, we conclude our work in Section 6.

2. XISL Execution System

Figure 2 shows an outline of an XISL execution system composed of three modules: a front-end module, a dialogue manager module, and a document server module. A document server is a general web server. It holds XISL, XML or HTML contents, and other documents, e.g., speech grammar files,

XSLT documents (style sheets to suit XML or HTML contents for a screen of each terminal), and so on. The document server sends these files to the dialogue manager in response to requests. A dialogue manager interprets XISL documents, manages dialogue flow, and controls inputs and outputs. A front-end is a user interface terminal that handles various modalities.

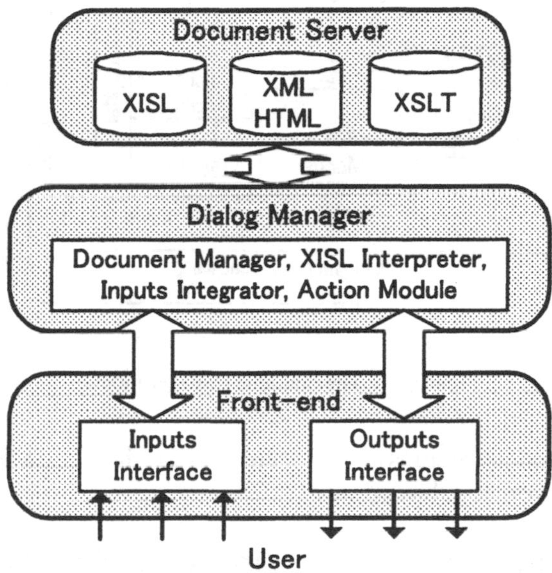

Figure 2. An XISL execution system.

The dialogue manager is constructed as illustrated in Figure 3. When a starting cue from the front-end module is accepted, the XISL interpreter requests the document manager to send an XISL document, then checks its syntax, divides it into descriptions of the user's multimodal operations and that of the system's actions, and sends them to the input integrator and the action module, respectively.

The input integrator extracts the inputs from the descriptions of operations, and sends them to the front-end module. Moreover, the integrator parses the descriptions to prepare for input integration. If a user makes some operations and a set of multimodal inputs is sent from the front-end module, the input integrator matches them with parsed descriptions and informs the result to the action module.

After the input integration, the action module executes some actions that correspond to the operation. There are two types of actions, terminal-dependent actions and terminal-independent ones. The terminal-dependent actions such as outputs to a user are sent to the front-end module, whereas the

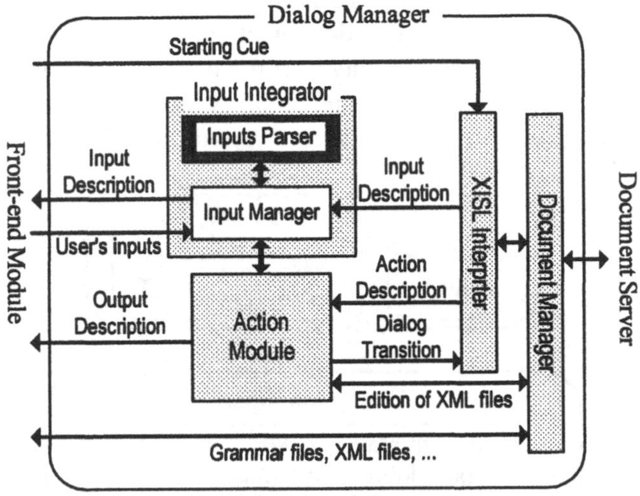

Figure 3. The dialogue manager module.

terminal-independent actions are executed inside the action module by communicating with other sub-modules.

3. Extensible Interaction Scenario Language

3.1 Outline of XISL

XISL is based on XML specification to suit for web access services. It provides basic functions to describe interaction scenarios by the tags shown in Table 1. MMI system developers can describe dialogue transitions, arithmetic operations, conditional branches, and other types of actions in their interaction scenarios by using these tags.

Figure 4 shows an example of an XISL document. The root of the XISL document is an `<xisl>` element (a in Figure 4) that contains at most one `<head>` element and a `<body>` element (b). The `<body>` element is a container of `<dialog>` elements (c). Each `<dialog>` element contains at most one `<begin>` element (d), one or more `<exchange>` elements (f), and at most one `<end>` element, which are used to describe initial processes, a unit of interaction, and terminal processes, respectively.

An `<exchange>` element is composed of at most one `<prompt>` element, an `<operation>` element (g), and an `<action>` element (i). If an `<exchange>` element contains a `<prompt>` element, it is a system initiative interaction. On the other hand, if an `<exchange>` element contains no `<prompt>` element, it is a user initiative interaction. A `<prompt>` element,

Table 1. A part of XISL tags.

Tag name	Function
<action>	Execute actions
<alt_exchange>	<exchange>s in this element are executed alternatively
<alt_input>	<input>s in this element are accepted alternatively
<assign>	Assign a value to a variable
<begin>	Initial processes in a <dialog>
<body>	A container of <dialog>s
<call>	Go to another <dialog> (Return to the original <dialog>)
<dialog>	A set of interactions
<dialog_var>	Declare dialogue level variables (Used together with <var>)
<document_var>	Declare document level variables (Used together with <var>)
<end>	Terminal process in a <dialog>
<exchange>	A turn of interaction
<exchange_var>	Declare exchange level variables (Used together with <var>)
<exit>	Terminate execution of a dialogue, document, and application
<goto>	Go to another <dialog> (Do not return to the original <dialog>)
<head>	Meta information about the XISL document
<if>	Conditional branch used together with <else>, <then>, and <elseif>
<input>	A user input
<operation>	A set of user inputs
<output>	A user output
<par_exchange>	<exchange>s in this element are executed parallel
<par_input>	<input>s in this element are accepted parallel
<par_output>	<output>s in this element are executed parallel
<prompt>	Issue a prompt to the user
<reprompt>	Reprompt to the original <dialog>
<return>	Return to the original <dialog>
<seq_exchange>	<exchange>s in this element are executed sequentially
<seq_input>	<input>s in this element are accepted sequentially
<seq_output>	<output>s in this element are executed sequentially
<submit>	Send some values to the document server via HTTP GET or HTTP POST request, and receive its return value
<switch>	Conditional branch used together with <case>and <other>
<var>	Declare a variable
<value>	Insert the value of an expression in an <output>
<while>	Iterate the process in this element while specified condition is true
<xisl>	The root element of XISL document

an <operation> element, and an <action> element represent a prompt to the user, a user's operation and a system action, respectively.

In a <prompt> element and an <operation> element, the author can describe <output> elements and <input> elements (h), respectively. In

```
<?xml version="1.0" encoding="Shift-JIS"?>
<!DOCTYPE xisl SYSTEM "xisl.dtd">
<xisl version="1.0" application="root.xisl"> ......(a)
   <body> ............................(b)
    <dialog id="Greeting" comb="seq"> ..........(c)
      <begin> .........................(d)
        <output type="browser" event="nabigate"> ....(e)
          <![CDATA[ <param name="id">
             GreetingWindow
           </param>
           <param name="uri"> ./greeting.html </param> ]]>
        </output>
      </begin>
      <exchange> ........................(f)
        <operation comb="alt"> ...............(g)
          <input type="touch" event="click" ........(h)
             match="greeting"/>
          <input type="speech" event="recognize"
             match="greeting.grm#greeting"/>
        </operation>
        <action> ........................(i)
          <output type="tts" event="speech">
            <![CDATA[ <param name="text">
             Hello, nice to meet you.
             </param> ]]>
          </output>
          <call next="NextDialog.xisl"/> .........(j)
        </action>
      </exchange>
           :
    </dialog>
   </body>
</xisl>
```

Figure 4. An example of XISL document.

an <action> element, the author can describe some elements such as <output> elements (e), <call> elements (j), and so on.

3.2 Separation of Contents from XISL Document

An XISL document only contains an interaction scenario between a user and a system. The contents are separately held as some XML or HTML files. This enables system developers to reuse both the XML(HTML) documents and XISL scenarios, and improves the readability of these documents. An XML(HTML) file is displayed on a screen by using <output> elements, and the events raised on the XML(HTML) documents are accepted by `<input>` elements.

For this separation, `<input>` and `<output>` tags have some attributes to specify XML(HTML) contents in addition to attributes for describing modality information. The `<input>` tag has four attributes: `type` (input modality), `event` (input event), `match` (a link to an XML(HTML) element), and `return` (return values). The `<output>` tag has two attributes: `type` (output modality), and `event` (output event) in XISL specifications. An XML(HTML) document for output is specified in a `<param>` element in an `<output>` element. In the example in Figure 4, the `<output>` and `<input>` elements (e, h) specify an HTML document shown in Figure 5. The descriptive details of `<input>` and `<output>` elements for each terminal are explained in Section 4.

```
<html>
    <body>
      <h1> The greeting page </h1>
      <p id="greeting">
        Please push here or speak ''Hello''.
      </p>
    </body>
</html>
```

Figure 5. An HTML document.

Note that strict values of the attributes and contents of `<input>` and `<output>` elements are not specified by XISL to make descriptions of modalities more flexible. The descriptive details of them are specified by the front-end developers, who can therefore expand or modify modalities easily.

3.3 Dialogue Flow Control by XISL

Interactions in an XISL document are executed in document order by default, however, various representations are prepared to control dialogue flow. The `comb` attribute in a `<dialog>` tag specifies how to execute `<exchange>` elements in it. If `comb` is `par` (parallel), all `<exchange>` elements are executed in parallel. If `comb` is `alt` (alternative), one of the `<exchange>` elements is executed alternatively, and if `comb` is `seq` (sequential), all `<exchange>` elements are executed in document order. We can also control the flow by means of the `<par_exchange>`, `<seq_exchange>` and `<alt_exchange>` tags. The `<exchange>` elements bound by one of these tags are executed as if they are bound by the `<dialog>` element whose `comb` attribute is `par`, `alt`, or `seq`. This type of control is also available to `<input>` or `<output>` elements.

4. Three Types of Front-Ends and XISL Descriptions

In order to show the modality independency of XISL, we have developed three types of front-ends in which each terminal has different modalities, namely a PC terminal, a mobile phone terminal, and a PDA terminal. This section outlines these front-ends and XISL descriptions for them.

A PC terminal is developed as an information kiosk put at a station or a convenience store. It accepts user's inputs from a touch-screen display, a keyboard, and a microphone. Outputs are presented to users via a touch-screen or a speaker. The touch-screen displays an anthropomorphic agent as appropriate. Tables 2 and 3 are parts of its <input> and <output> specifications. The match attribute of <input> whose type is "pointing" and event is "click" not only specifies an id attribute of an HTML element, but also specifies substitution of matched id for some variable. This description is introduced for convenience to prevent describing a lot of <input> elements for different ids in an HTML document. An example of this description is shown in (c) of Figure 6. In addition to the modalities shown in these tables, the PC terminal can handle some other touch operations (double-click, drag, etc.), window actions (move, maximise, etc.), and other operations and actions.

Table 2. A part of <input> specification for a PC terminal.

type	event	match	return
"speech"	"recognize"	(grammar file)#(grammar rule)	variables to hold recognition results
"pointing"	"click"	id attribute of an HTML element	abscissa of clicked object ordinate of clicked object
	:	:	:
"key"	"press"	—	pressed key
:	:	:	:

4.1 PC Terminal

We have implemented an OnLine Shopping (OLS) application by XISL. Figure 6 shows an fragment of an XISL document of the application. The OLS application is composed of a dialogue scenario (XISL), data of items and customers (HTML), and a style sheet for HTML files (XSLT). The scenario shown in Figure 6 contains a typical flow of interaction in the OLS application, and which is also a typical flow for most of scenarios executed on a PC terminal.

First, the system displays an HTML page (cf. Figure 6 (a)) by an <output> element, and then the system announces some information about the page by an <output> element (b). A user can usually use touch operation (c) or speech input (d) or both of them. After accepting the inputs, the system

Table 3. A part of `<output>` specification for a PC terminal.

type	event	`<param>`: elements in CDATA section	
		name	*value*
"browser"	"navigate"	"name"	window name
		"uri"	URI of a page
		:	:
	:	:	:
"tts"	"speech"	"text"	speech text
		:	:
"agent"	"speech"	"name"	agent name
		"text"	speech text
	:	:	:
:	:	:	:

makes a response to the inputs (e), and executes some actions. After the actions the system changes a dialogue to another one by using a `<goto>` or a `<call>` element (f).

Since the PC terminal usually has a bigger screen than that of mobile terminals, the `<dialog>` usually contains more than one `<exchange>`s. For example, the screen of the online shopping application shown in Figure 7 contains three fields (a shopping cart, an item list, and a list of item categories) for interaction. So the `<dialog>` in Figure 6 contains some other `<exchange>`s for these fields.

4.2 Mobile Phone Terminal

A telephone-based MMI system composed of a mobile phone terminal and a telephone server has been developed for voice portal services. Users call the terminal from their mobile phones or land-line telephones. When the telephone server receives a telephone call, the server accesses the Internet to download XISL and other files. The mobile phone terminal accepts user's speech or DTMF inputs, and outputs recorded/synthesised speech or tone. Parts of the `<input>` and `<output>` specifications are shown in Tables 4 and 5.

Table 4. A part of `<input>` specification for a telephone server.

type	event	match	return
"speech"	"recognize"	(speech grammar file)#(rule)	variables to hold recognition results
"dtmf"	"push"	(DTMF grammar file)#(rule)	variables to hold pushed numbers
:	:	:	:

```
    :
<dialog id="order" comb="alt" scope="dialog">
 <begin>
  <output type="browser" event="navigate"> ...(a)
   <![CDATA[ <param name="name">
     top-page
    </param>
    <param name="uri"> ./OLS_PC.html </param> ]]>
  </output>
  <output type="tts" event="speech"> .......(b)
   <![CDATA[ <param name="text">
     May I help you?
    </param> ]]>
  </output>
 </begin>
 <exchange>
  <operation comb="alt">
   <input type="touch" event="click"  ......(c)
     match="[item:=@id]"/>
     <!-- substitute a matched id
          into a variable item -->
   <input type="speech" event="recognize" ...(d)
     match="goods.grm#items"
     return="item"/>
  </operation>
  <action>
   <output type="tts" event="speech"> ......(e)
    <![CDATA[ <param name="text">
     You ordered <value expr="item">.
     </param> ]]>
   </output>
   <switch var="item">
    <case value="long coat">
     <assign var="price" expr="300"/>
    </case>
     :
   </switch>
     :
   <goto next="how_many_items.xisl"> .......(f)
  </action>
 </exchange>
     :
</dialog>
    :
```

Figure 6. A fragment of XISL document for the PC terminal.

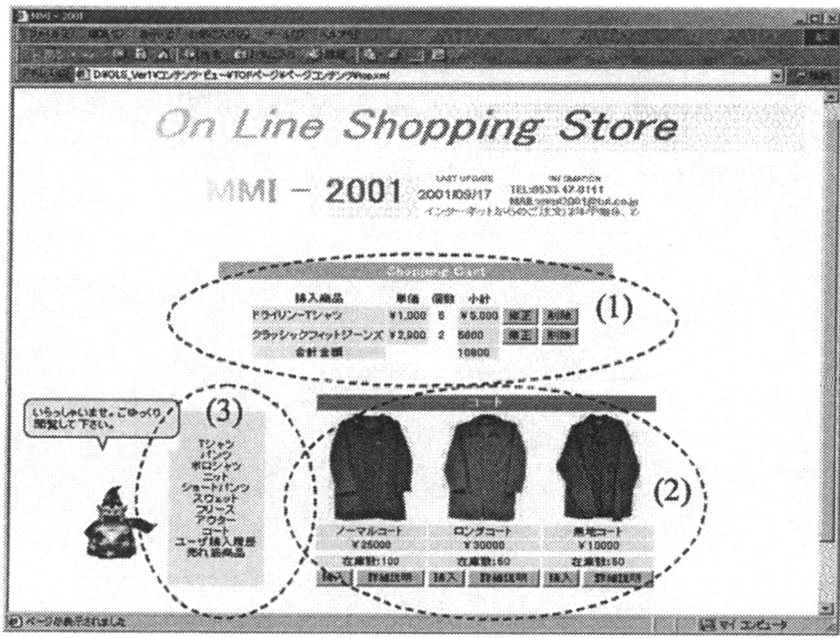

Figure 7. A screen of the online shopping system.

Table 5. A part of <output> specification for a telephone server.

type	event	<param>: elements in CDATA section	
		name	*value*
"speech"	"play"	"speech_text"	speech text
		"mode"	"TTS"
:	:	:	:

Figure 8 shows an fragment of an XISL document for an online shopping application. It shows a typical flow of interaction executed on the mobile phone terminal. A scenario for the mobile phone terminal usually proceeds sequentially because the terminal can not provide much information for its user and needs to provide some information step by step. For example, in Figure 8, after the system announces some information about the OLS application by speech output (a), an <exchange> for category decision (b) is executed sequentially. And then, an item decision <exchange> is executed.

The mobile phone terminal usually uses a <prompt> element (c) for giving some information to its user before accepting inputs. After providing a prompt, the system waits for the user's input from speech device (d), or DTMF (e), and then execute the elements in the following <action>.

```
      :
<dialog id="order" comb="seq" scope="dialog">
  <begin>
    <output type="speech" event="play"> .......(a)
      <![CDATA[ <param name="mode"> TTS </param>
        <param name="speech-text">
         May I help you?
         Which item would you like to buy?
        </param> ]]>
    </output>
  </begin>
  <exchange> ......................(b)
    <!-- Interaction to decide category of items -->
  </exchange>
  <exchange>
    <prompt> ......................(c)
      <output type="speech" event="play">
        <![CDATA[ <param name="mode"> TTS </param>
          <param name="speech-text">
          Please select an item from category sweater.
          </param> ]]>
      </output>
    </prompt>
    <operation comb="alt">
      <input type="speech" event="recognize" ....(d)
         match="goods.grm#sweater" return="item"/>
      <input type="dtmf" event="push" ........(e)
         match="goods_dtmf.grm#sweater_number"
         return="item_number"/>
    </operation>
    <action>
      <output type="speech" event="play">
        <![CDATA[ <param name="mode"> TTS </param>
          <param name="speech-text">
          You ordered <value expr="item">.
          </param> ]]>
      </output>
         :
    </action>
  </exchange>
       :
</dialog>
      :
```

Figure 8. A fragment of XISL document for the mobile phone terminal.

4.3 PDA Terminal

Since a PDA itself does not have sufficient performance as a PC has, we implemented the front-end module on the PDA and the dialogue manager module on the PC. These two modules communicate with each other to execute interactions. A part of the `<input>` and `<output>` specifications are shown in Tables 6 and 7. As same as the specification for the PC terminal, The `match` attribute of `<input>` whose `type` is "touch" and `event` is "tap" not only specifies an `href` attribute of `<a>` tag, but also specifies substitution of matched `href` for some variable. This specification enables to eliminate the use of `return` attribute. The PDA terminal can handle a cursor key, a tap-pen (software keyboard), and speech as inputs, and a www browser and a sound device as outputs. Speech recognition is limited to isolated words, and text-to-speech (TTS) is not implemented.

Table 6. A part of `<input>` specification for a PDA terminal.

type	event	match	return
"touch"	"tap"	`href` attribute of `<a>` tag	—
	"key_up"	—	—
"key"	"key_down"	—	—
	⋮	⋮	⋮
⋮	⋮	⋮	⋮

Table 7. A part of `<output>` specification for a PDA terminal.

type	event	`<param>`: elements in CDATA section	
		name	*value*
	"open_file"	"file_name"	name of a wave file
"sound"	"stop"	—	—
	⋮	⋮	⋮
⋮	⋮	⋮	⋮

However, the PDA terminal displays an HTML page on a screen as PC terminal, the scenario flow is more like the one used on the mobile phone terminal because it cannot provide much information for its user. Figure 9 shows typical flow of interaction executed on the mobile phone terminal. The terminal announces some information by screen and speech output (a), and then execute an `<exchange>` for category decision (b) sequentially. And then, an item decision `<exchange>` is executed. The terminal changes the screen in the `<prompt>` element (c), and system waits for the user's input from stylus pen device (d).

```
      :
  <dialog id="order" comb="seq" scope="dialog">
   <begin> .............................(a)
    <output type="browser" event="navigate">
     <![CDATA[
      <param name="uri"> ./OLS.html </param> ]]>
    </output>
    <output type="sound" event="open_file">
     <![CDATA[
      <param name="file_name"> ./greeting.wav </param> ]]>
    </output>
   </begin>
   <exchange> ...........................(b)
    <!-- Interaction to decide category of items -->
   </exchange>
   <exchange>
    <prompt> ...........................(c)
     <output type="browser" event="navigate">
      <![CDATA[
       <param name="uri"> ./sweater.html </param>]]>
     </output>
    </prompt>
    <operation> .........................(d)
     <input type="touch" event="tap"
       match="[item:=@href]"/>
    </operation>
    <action>
     <output type="speech" event="play">
      <![CDATA[ <param name="mode"> TTS </param>
       <param name="speech-text">
       You ordered <value expr="item">.
       </param> ]]>
     </output>
        :
    </action>
   </exchange>
       :
  </dialog>
      :
```

Figure 9. A fragment of XISL document for the PDA terminal.

5. XISL and Other Languages

Some organisations have specified their own descriptions to deal with multimodalities. In this section we compare XISL with SALT, XHTML+Voice, and a SMIL-based approach.

5.1 Comparison with SALT

SALT[4] (Wang, 2002) defines additional tags for describing speech recognition and TTS that are attached to an HTML document. The most remarkable feature of SALT is that it is highly suitable to HTML documents. SALT speech grammar tags are embedded in an HTML document, and are bound to `<input>` tags in the HTML document. This enables to attach speech interface to current HTML documents by minimal addition. XISL needs much more description than SALT tags. Therefore, SALT is good choice for adding simple speech interaction to an HTML document.

On the other hand, XISL is better suited for describing complex scenario flow using sequential, parallel, or alternative combination of multiple modalities. Since XISL (interaction scenario) is explicitly separated from XML or HTML contents, the application developer can easily read and trace interaction flow. It will increase reusability of XISL in complex multimodal interaction.

5.2 Comparison with XHTML+Voice

XHTML+Voice[5] attempts to add VoiceXML[6] to XHTML pages. A VoiceXML source code is added into a `<head>` element of an XHTML document, and bound to some XHTML tags like SALT. Since some scenario flow are described in VoiceXML code, XHTML+Voice can control more complex scenario than that SALT can control. However, XHTML+Voice assumes only voice interaction as additional modalities to web pages. On the other hand, our approach has more flexibility to add modalities than XHTML+Voice approach.

5.3 Comparison with a SMIL-Based Approach

The SMIL-based[7] approach (Beckham et al., 2001) realises event-based multimodal dialogue control by SMIL and ReX (Reactive XML). In this approach, temporal control of the scenario is described in SMIL, and event control is described in ReX. Since this approach is based on event control, it is easy to extend modalities. However, in this approach, the modality-dependent descriptions are not explicitly separated from the modality-independent descriptions, whereas our approach explicitly separates them. Therefore, XISL is easier to read and reuse than the SMIL-based approach.

6. Discussion

In this chapter, we have described an MMI description language XISL, its elements and document structure. A system designer can develop an MMI system more easily by using XISL, but we consider that a GUI-based prototyping tool is needed for designing such systems quickly (Kamio et al., 1997). The tag set of XISL must also be expanded to apply XISL to various domains. There are many issues concerning the multimodal dialogue manager; in further MMI studies, we will examine dialogue flow control by using dialogue context and task switching in multi-task applications.

Notes

1. http://www.w3.org/2002/mmi/
2. http://www.saltforum.org/
3. http://www.vox.tutkie.tut.ac.jp/XISL/XISL-E.html
4. http://www.saltforum.org/
5. See XHTML+Voice profile specification proposed by IBM, Motorola, and Opera Software.
6. http://www.w3.org/TR/voicexml20/
7. http://www.w3.org/smil20/

References

Beckham, J. L., Fabbrizio, G. D., and Klarlund, N. (2001). Towards SMIL as a foundation for multimodal, multimedia applications. In *Proceedings of European Conference on Speech Communication and Technology (EUROSPEECH)*, pages 1363–1366, Aalborg, Denmark.

Kamio, H., Amamiya, M., Matsu'ura, H., and Nitta, T. (1997). Muse, a rapid prototyping tool. In *Proceedings of International Conference on Human-Computer Interaction*, pages 569–572, San Francisco, California, USA.

Katsurada, K., Ootani, Y., Nakamura, Y., Kobayashi, S., Yamada, H., and Nitta, T. (2002). A modality-independent MMI system architecture. In *Proceedings of International Conference on Spoken Language Processing (ICSLP)*, pages 2549–2552, Denver, Colorado, USA.

Nitta, T., Katsurada, K., Yamada, H., Nakamura, Y., and Kobayashi, S. (2001). XISL: An attempt to separate multimodal interactions from XML contents. In *Proceedings of European Conference on Speech Communication and Technology (EUROSPEECH)*, pages 1197–1200, Aalborg, Denmark.

Wang, K. (2002). SALT: A spoken language interface for web-based multimodal dialog systems. In *Proceedings of International Conference on Spoken Language Processing (ICSLP)*, pages 2241–2244, Denver, Colorado, USA.

Chapter 9

A PATH TO MULTIMODAL DATA SERVICES FOR TELECOMMUNICATIONS

Georg Niklfeld, Michael Pucher
ftw. Forschungszentrum Telekommunikation Wien, Vienna, Austria
{ niklfeld, pucher } @ftw.at

Robert Finan
Mobilkom Austria AG & Co KG, Vienna, Austria
r.finan@mobilkom.at

Wolfgang Eckhart
Sonorys Technology GmbH, Korneuburg, Austria
wolfgang.eckhart@sonorys.at

Abstract This chapter investigates some issues faced in developing multimodal data services for public mobile telecommunications. It discusses applications, standards, mobile devices, and existing R&D efforts. Three demonstrators developed by the authors are presented, including QuickMap, a map finder based on GPRS and WAP-Push. Findings are summarised in the description of a path that will lead to successful multimodal data services in mobile telecommunications.

Keywords: Mobile data services; Multimodality; Telecommunications; Standards; Systems architecture.

1. Introduction

Multimodal interfaces combining speech recognition and keypad/touch-screen input have the potential to alleviate the input bottleneck in mobile data services for 2.5G/GPRS (General Packet Radio Services) and 3G/UMTS (Universal Mobile Telecommunications Service) networks – or equivalently to the

W. Minker, D. Bühler and L. Dybkjær (eds), Spoken Multimodal Human-Computer Dialogue in Mobile Environments, 149-167

latter for 802.11 WLAN (Wireless Local Area Network) environments. Yet there exists so far no easily discernible road-map on how and when this type of interfaces will be ready for real services in public telecommunications networks.

At the same time, due to the recent dramatic changes of the economic environment in telecommunications, many telecom firms are under pressure to search for models to generate new revenues from data services in GPRS and 3G/UMTS networks, which they need to do in order to recuperate the large capital expenditures for GPRS and particularly 3G/UMTS. As they struggle to survive the next three to five years, many firms restrict their financial support to technologies that promise to create revenues in such a short time-frame. They are interested in convincing applications, not mere potential interface capabilities.

In this contribution we introduce three demonstrators that we have built in order to explore various possible building blocks for multimodal data services, and in order to learn what can and what cannot be done in existing infrastructures. The demonstrators are:

- an alternate mode, push-to-talk address entry for a route finder for a UMTS scenario;
- an open-microphone map content navigator for UMTS; and
- a voice/WAP-Push (Wireless Application Protocol) demonstrator for GPRS.

We also discuss the range of applications and interface types that should be implemented first; we give an overview of architectures, standardisation work, and classes of terminals; we then try to position a number of ongoing R&D activities on mobile multimodal interfaces in the resulting conceptual grid, and ultimately propose a road-map for various activities leading up to successful multimodal data services in real-world telecommunications networks.

2. Application Considerations, Technologies and Mobile Terminals

2.1 Applications

In the current difficult economic environment of the telecommunications industry, many companies strongly support innovation in data service technology where the innovations are perceived to translate directly into a value-generation opportunity, whereas nice-to-have innovation that is risky or relies on too many unproven assumptions about user acceptance and device capabilities is often put on hold. For new multimodal data services this means that firstly, every deviation in the user interface from familiar GUI (graphical user interface) paradigms should be justifiable by a significant advantage that is either obvious or can be demonstrated in a usability study; and secondly terminal requirements should be kept low, in particular no capabilities beyond what is already available in a target class of widely used consumer devices should be stipulated. Therefore, in line with the ongoing standardisation efforts, for our work we assume voice I/O capabilities, keypads or touch-screens, and small text or graphics displays for a first generation of network-ready multimodal interfaces. We do not consider video input.

From the point of view of a network operator, interface technologies alone will not generate revenue. Therefore it is necessary to present multimodal interfaces as part of powerful applications. Some applications that are used in multimodality research projects do not scale to telephony-oriented mobile terminals because they rely on rich graphic information that will not fit on most mobile displays - e.g., military resource planning or animated communication agents. During the specification phase for our demonstrators we have learnt that elaborate forms of multimodal input integration (coordinated, concurrent input) can only bring substantial benefits when the visual interface supports information-rich input events, such as gestures that designate arbitrary regions on the display. We expect that a large number of multimodal interfaces to mobile data services will operate without such elaborate input interfaces, but will exploit only the simpler types of multimodal input integration (cf. the three types of multimodal integration in[1]). Applications that seem favourable for multimodal telecommunications services combine visual information such as maps with speech recognition of proper names from a closed set (street names, telephone registers, product catalogues), cf. (Cohen and Oviatt, 1995). An example of a suitable type of application developed at the ftw. research centre is Lol@, a mobile tourist guide for UMTS (Pospischil et al., 2002).

2.2 Architectures

Architectures that have been proposed for multimodal systems, cf. (Maybury, 2002), can be distinguished

- by the way processing (modality-specific recognisers and renderers, modality fusion and fission) is distributed between terminal and server.
- by the layering. In most recognition systems, late (semantic) fusion is applied rather than early feature fusion, cf. (Oviatt et al., 2000). This enables the use of modality-specific recognition modules and implies the existence of at least an additional module for modality integration. More articulated layerings propose up to four layers from multimodal to modality-specific processing, e.g., (Elting and Michelitsch, 2001).

- by the communication model among different system modules. A number of research projects have developed flexible communication models for component interfaces (Galaxy (Seneff et al., 1998), OAA (Cheyer and Martin, 2001), AAA (Kumar et al., 2000)).

2.3 Standards

The VoiceXML standard[2] [3] promotes a development model for spoken language applications that is similar to web programming. Despite its benefits including the availability of development tools and hosting services, VoiceXML is not well suited for implementing interfaces that support coordinated, concurrent multimodal input, due to the lack of a notification model through which an ongoing voice dialogue could be informed about external events. Once a dialogue specified in a VoiceXML document is executing, it operates independent from any events occurring at other modalities such as a GUI.

Nevertheless until now no comparable standard has existed for an easily accessible development model for voice interfaces, and therefore our group chose VoiceXML for building two simple multimodal demonstrators, described below.

Other current standardisation efforts are:

- The W3C consortium has announced plans for a multimodal markup language since 2000, but there is little public documentation of progress[4].
- In July 2002 the SALT initiative for a multimodal markup language [5] released a version 1.0 specification. SALT has substantial support from industry and aims to tie development of multimodal applications closely to visual development using HTML, and to bridge different device characteristics ranging from PC notebooks to smart-phones and even audio-only devices.
- Another standardisation initiative aims at integrating VoiceXML and XTHML, in the X+V language that has been proposed to the W3C and can be tested with plugin extensions in popular web browsers[6].
- The ETSI AURORA initiative[7] for Distributed Speech Recognition (DSR) has also produced proposals for integrating DSR with UMTS for multimodal applications (Pearce and Kopp, 2001).

Finally, it is likely that many early commercial multimodal services will combine proprietary technologies for efficient, but less open services.

2.4 Mobile Terminal Capabilities

In Table 1 we give a classification of some mobile devices according to the wireless connectivity (by rows), and according to the best GUI they offer (by columns). We also mention representative products.

Table 1. Mobile device types for multimodality.

Radio link	GUI SMS	WAP	Smartphone	Quarter-VGA	VGA
GSM	Nokia 8210	most recent GSM phones	Ericsson R380, Nokia Communicator	PDA+GSM - Pocket PC, Handspring Treo	Notebook + GSM/ HSCSD card
GPRS		Ericsson T68	upcoming smartphones	PDA+GPRS - Pocket PC	Notebook + GPRS card
WLAN/ UMTS				PDA + WLAN card	Notebook + WLAN card

Some implications of specific features along both the "Radio link" and the "GUI" axis for multimodal interfaces including speech are:

- Existing terminals to the left of the greyed columns for GUI-type (Quarter-VGA and VGA) provide insufficient computing resources for continuous speech recognition on the device, although some high-end PDAs support isolated-word vocabularies of a few hundred entries. Therefore speech recognition solutions for the devices in the white columns require either server-based speech recognition, or potentially distributed speech recognition.

- Only terminals that support at least GPRS phone connectivity (bottom two rows) provide sufficiently fast switching from voice to data connections to make multimodal interfaces combining voice and data connections feasible. This in turn is a needed capability for all devices that do not provide a software environment that would allow for the transfer of speech over a data link, using VoIP or DSR.

  The darker two shades of gray in the table indicate the device types that are in our opinion the most promising for multimodal service deployments in the short term. We refer to the devices that support GPRS, but not UMTS or WLAN connectivity, as the "stage 1" target group of devices. Some of these devices (e.g., the SonyEricsson T68 phone) are already present in the high-volume mobile phone market.

- Only terminals that support WLAN or UMTS phone connectivity can provide concurrent voice and data connections to enable server-side fusion of coordinated multimodal inputs, and thus advanced forms of multimodality. This group of devices is marked in the darkest cell in the table, we refer to it henceforth as the "stage 2" target group of devices. These devices are not yet used in large numbers.

- Large-size VGA displays (rightmost column) are used on bigger devices that effectively remove the comparative input bottleneck of mobile devices. The improvement potential of multimodality is therefore smaller in this group.

3. Projects and Commercial Developments

In this section, we classify some well-known existing research efforts on multimodal systems, without a claim to completeness, but in order to highlight commonalities and differences that are of interest for our investigation. For such a discussion, one can distinguish:

Basic-research projects: Often focussed on elaborate system architecture for advanced forms of multimodality: DARPA Communicator[8] (Goldschen and Loehr, 1999), which is also used in LARRI (Bohus and Rudnicky, 2004); various projects at Stanford, e.g., WITAS (Doherty et al., 2000; Lemon et al., 2001); projects at Oregon Graduate Institute such as QuickSet (Cohen et al., 1997; Oviatt, 2000); or the German SmartKom project[9] (Wahlster et al., 2001; Bühler et al., 2002).

These large and often multi-year projects are important because they can provide architectural foundations for sophisticated types of multimodal integration. On the other hand, for the resource-handicapped mobile devices in the "stage 1" and even in the "stage 2" classes defined earlier, downward scalability from the often generous resource assumptions in the demo-applications of these basic-research projects is sometimes problematic. There is also sometimes in these projects limited concern for economically viable business models that could carry the applications.

Ambient intelligence projects: Inspired by the ISTAG vision on Ambient Intelligence[10], there will probably be major research projects in the EU's 6th Framework Programme for research that will deal with even more advanced applications of multimodality than the existing basic-research projects mentioned above. Some such projects have already commenced within the 5th Framework Programme, involving special purpose hardware, for example the projects M4[11] and MIAMM[12].

Research along these lines will become important in UMTS/WLAN scenarios over the next five years, but is not implementable for commercial telecom services in the short-term.

Research projects for telecom applications: The SMADA project[13] investigates multimodal interaction for automatic directory assistance (Rössler et al., 2001). The MUST system uses a PDA terminal to implement a multimodal navigation platform suitable for WLAN or UMTS (Almeida et al., 2002).

Consumer-electronics control schemes: These projects often involve special purpose hardware to deliver multimodal interfaces in the home environment. Examples are EMBASSI[14] (Herfet and Kirste, 2001), Speecon[15].

While to some extent the application domains of home environment control devices and of telecommunications services are distinct, we expect both an overlap in future services (WLAN, Bluetooth), and of course some re-use of service architectures and platforms.

Industry-based prototypes and commercial R&D: At the time of writing, a number of US-based private companies are striving to provide products and solutions both for the "stage 1" and the "stage 2" device groups. Kirusa, Inc.[16] is working on technologies that facilitate application development on a number of existing and emerging platforms, starting from GSM+SMS, through WAP-Push based services to UMTS services with video playback. Lobby7, Inc.[17] is providing similar offerings. Microsoft Corporation has developed the MIPAD prototype of a mobile multimodal device (Huang et al., 2000) and will probably soon facilitate SALT-based multimodal solutions on its PocketPC and smartphone platforms. Speechworks International, Inc.[18] is supporting multimodal solutions with its embedded and DSR-based product lines (Pieraccini et al., 2002).

The efforts by Microsoft are obviously influential in setting the conditions for multimodal data service development in the next three years. An open question is how the Microsoft-powered platforms will integrate or compete with the standards provided and supported by telecommunications handset makers. Another question is whether the availability of technology for building simple multimodal interfaces will suffice to set off substantial business activity in this area. Section 4 comments further on this issue.

Consumer products: A number of mobile phones provide voice dialling and some form of voice control, usually based on acoustic pattern matching. High-end PDAs (e.g., iPAQ 3870) offer voice control with up to a few hundred different commands.

4. Three Multimodal Demonstrators

4.1 Push-to-Talk Address Entry for a Route Finder

Map-oriented data services call for visual displays. In one familiar type of service a map-area around a specified address is shown, or a route between two specified addresses (one address may be supplied automatically through handset localisation). In text input of the addresses, relatively long strings of characters occur, while terminal-based predictive typing aids will not work for proper names. Therefore in this first demonstrator we provided push-to-talk buttons next to each of the visual form-fields and blocks of fields for text entry of addresses, see Figure 1. This approach differs slightly from the "Tap and Talk" metaphor in MIPAD (Huang et al., 2000).

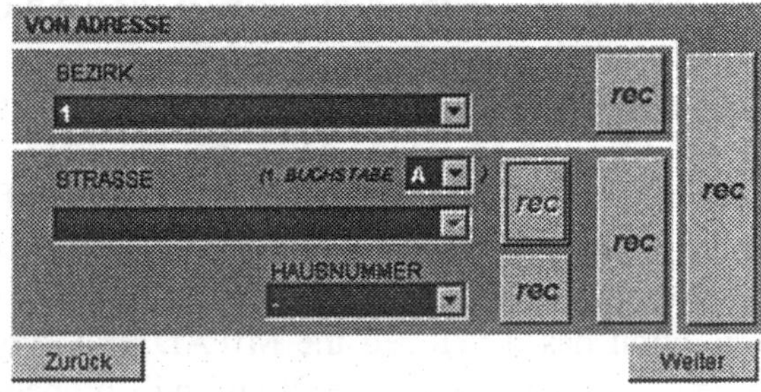

Figure 1. Push-to-talk address entry with simultaneous voice and data connections.

Speech recognition is done on a VoiceXML server. All feedback is given on the display to save time. Users can choose freely among text or speech input for each field depending on preferences or situation. The VoiceXML approach lent itself naturally to a simple re-use of an existing route finder web service by attaching to the CGI-interface. The demonstrator is based on the assumption of a voice call and a parallel data connection for Java applets in a browser on the terminal, as in UMTS, and was implemented for simulation on a PC notebook in a WLAN. See (Niklfeld et al., 2001a) for a more extensive description of this demonstrator, including the architecture that we developed for using the VoiceXML standard in a multimodal interface.

An evaluation study collected video recordings of user sessions with the demonstrator to derive guidelines on evaluation methodology for multimodal data services (Hoellerer, 2002). Empirical results from this study, which are scheduled for later publication, indicate that users give the best satisfaction score to the interface when both speech and GUI are offered as options, followed by a purely GUI-based interaction mode, although there was no advantage in task completion time due to application latencies.

4.2 Open-Microphone Map Content Navigator

The objective in our second demonstrator was to test how far our VoiceXML architecture (see Figure 2) could be taken in terms of more sophisticated multimodal input integration. In particular, it should be possible to perform actions on the GUI at the same time as entering a speech command, and the system should interpret the two input events jointly based on their temporal relationship (concurrent multimodality).

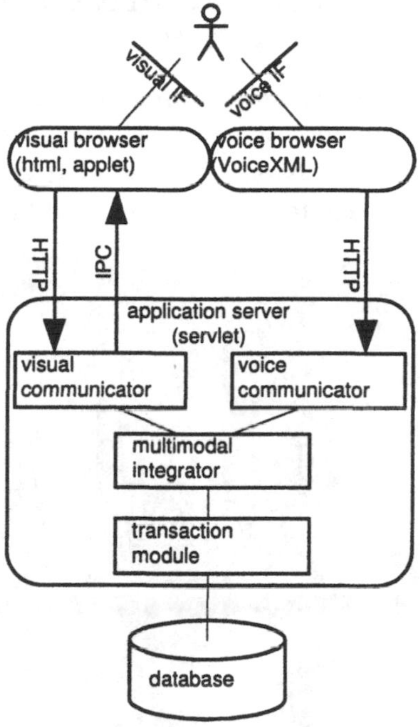

Figure 2. Architecture for multimodal interfaces using VoiceXML.

The user selects a map area, which is presented on the display. He/she can activate location marks on the display using a pointing device such as a pen on a touch-screen. Each mark remains active for a short time, which is indicated by visual cues. At the same time, a speech recognition channel is open permanently. The user can give speech or GUI commands for map navigation such as zooming or centering, or request to display content such as the nearest shops or facilities in a number of categories. Some commands take variable numbers of location marks as arguments. For example "route" will display the shortest route between two active marks, or between the current centre of the display and the active mark if there is only one in the current time window. When a particular type of content has been selected for display, additional commands become available, such as the programme at a cinema, or opening hours of a shop. While this demonstrator implements concurrent multimodality to some extent, it puts more demands on the speech recognition than would be necessary if VoiceXML provided a model for notification about external events that provide context for the dialogue, cf. (Niklfeld et al., 2001b) - without that being the case, we needed to provide at all times a comprehensive VoiceXML grammar for all branches of the dialogue, rather than restricting the speech recogniser by the state information of the application.

4.3 QuickMap - Voice Address Entry and WAP-Push for GPRS

To see what can be implemented in infrastructures now ("stage 1"), this demonstrator puts the voice address entry task for a route finder on a GPRS phone in an Austrian public network. To use GUI entry, users can browse directly to a WAP 1.2.1 [19] page that presents a visual form (see Figure 3).

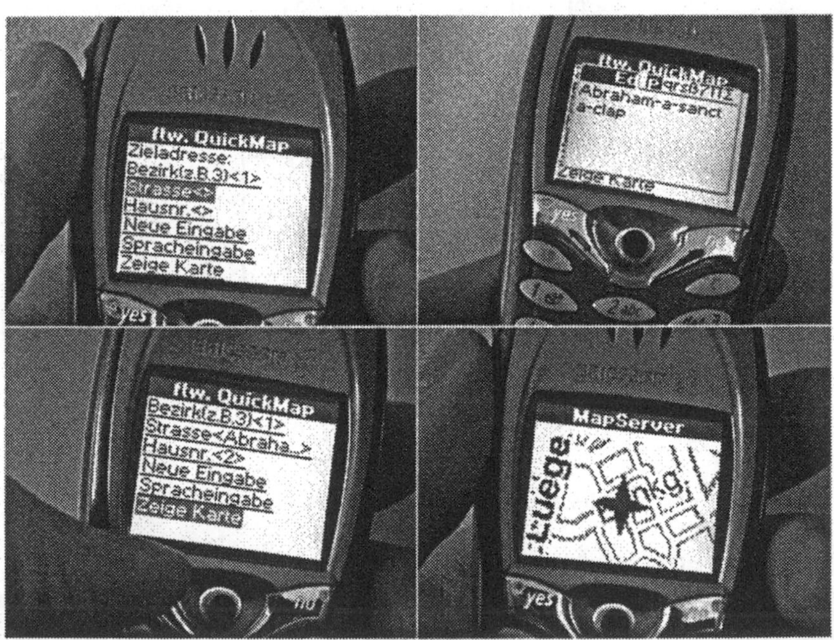

Figure 3. GUI-only map selection in the QuickMap WAP page: in the example, at least 60 key presses are required before the map is displayed, including 44 key presses just for entering the lengthy street name "Abraham-a-Sancta-Clara-G" (cf. Figure 4).

To use voice entry (cf. Figure 4), users call a phone number and get engaged in a voice dialogue (built using VoiceXML) in which they are asked for the required form fields: city district, street name, and street number. DTMF is available as an option during the voice dialog, to enable safe entry of the numeric values for district and street number using the mobile phone keypad.

For most street names however, voice entry is much more convenient than text entry. A long street name such as "Abraham-a-Sancta-Clara-Gasse" is recognised by the speech recogniser with very high confidence, but requires 44 key presses on a typical mobile phone keypad, even though the used map server accepts "G" as an abbreviation for "Gasse" (small street). We have found that users nearly always make a number of mistakes in this typing task, where each correction requires further key presses. On the SonyEricsson T68 device used for our tests, when entering the text-input field the user must also first switch off the T9 predictive-typing aid, which would not work for unknown names. This requires another three key presses (in addition to good command of the mobile phone's features). It should be noted that for some short street names such as "Hegelgasse", speech recognition does not work well and therefore users may prefer text entry. To accommodate this, the demonstrator provides the possibility to switch the entry method in both directions: the WAP page provides a link to "Spracheingabe" (speech input), which triggers the set-up of a voice call to the dialogue system by the phone (using the WTAI-protocol[20] that is part of the WAP 1.2.1 suite of protocols). Conversely, the user can request a "Textformular" (text form) in the voice dialog, which will trigger a WAP-Push Service Indication message [21] being sent to the device with a link to the QuickMap WAP page. If voice-input is used, WAP-Push is also used to send a link to the required map to the user's phone. If a user has activated WAP-Push on his/her device, incoming WAP-Push messages seize control of the display without further user intervention. On the T68 phone, the user then can select to proceed and load the document referenced by the link in the WAP-Push message. We believe that in a commercial implementation, charging for the service invocation (beyond the connection and data transfer fees) should occur when the user follows the link to the map, after he/she has verified that the address was understood correctly by the speech recognition.

A number of unsystematic tests on a live public network have shown some variation in the times various steps of the application take (cf. Table 2).

Table 2. Typical timings for the QuickMap demonstrator.

Action	GUI input	Voice input
GPRS connection setup	3-5s (GSM: 15-20s)	
Voice call setup		5-10s
Address input	typically 60s	typically 30s
WAP-Push delivery		min. 3-5s, typically 15s, max. >300s
GPRS connection setup		3-5s (GSM: 15-20s)
Loading of map		max. 10s

The complete voice dialogs (including confirmation of the recognition results by the user) take about half as long as GUI-only input, for short street street names like "Maderstr(asse)". In our tests, the delivery of a WAP-Push

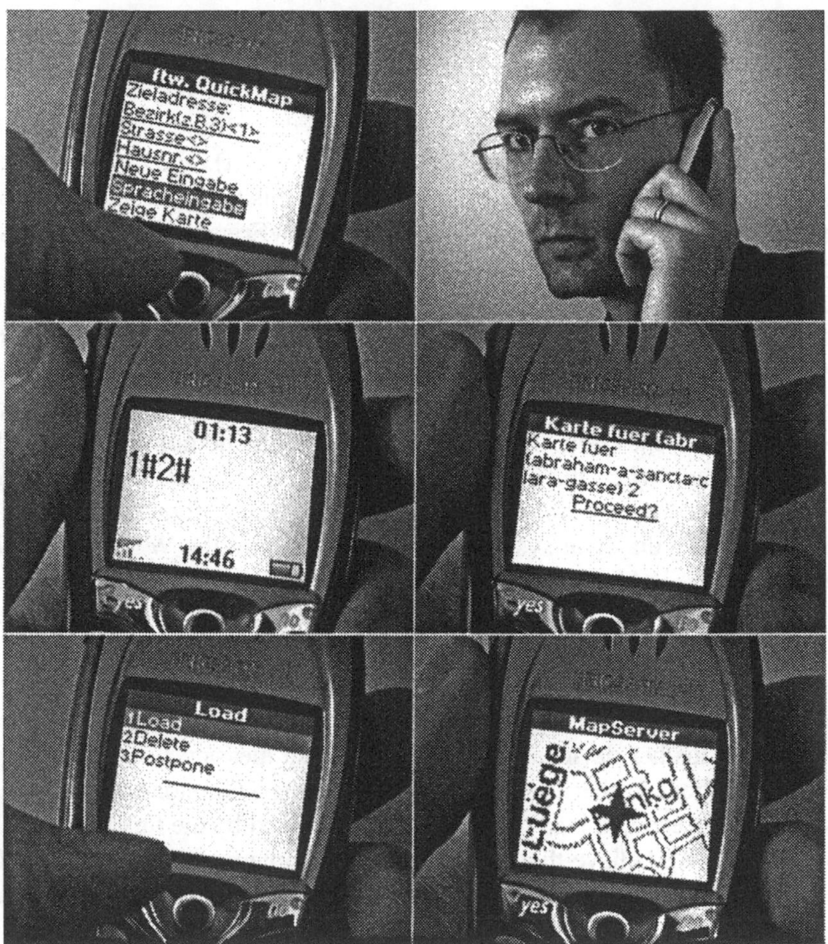

Figure 4. Multimodal or voice-only address entry in the QuickMap demonstrator. The user can initiate the voice-call to the dialogue system either directly or through the WAP page. DTMF can be used during the dialog for safe entry of numeric form-field values (district and street number, third picture). When the voice-form is complete, the application requests the network to send a WAP-Push message to the mobile phone. The WAP-Push message seizes control of the display (fourth picture). After selecting Proceed, the T68 phone asks the user whether to load the document linked in the WAP-Push message through a GPRS connection.

message usually took about 15 seconds, in good cases only around 3-5 seconds. However, there are outliers when delivery of a WAP-Push message takes up to approximately 5 minutes. Setup of a GPRS data connection usually takes 3-5 seconds (compared to 15-20 for setup of a GSM data connection). Loading the WAP-page with the map image over an established GPRS or GSM connection always took less than 10 seconds.

WAP-Push messages are delivered as SMS messages to current mobile phones, therefore there are no timing guarantees. Because of this, applications should be designed to use WAP-Push sparingly and only where timing is not critical. Waiting for a final result, such as the map in our demonstrator, may be an acceptable example. An alternative way to transport the WAP-Push messages would be by IP-Push, which can currently be supported by some PDAs running a special push client software.

4.4 Alternative Way of WAP-Voice Integration

As the timing results with the QuickMap demonstrator show, the WAP-Push implementation for current GPRS phones does not provide a reliable means for smooth switching from voice calls to WAP sessions. Therefore later we re-implemented the application using another way of achieving that integration. This approach is based on URL rewriting and dynamic generation of all WAP and VoiceXML pages, and tight management of user session states at a server that performs multimodal integration. To switch from voice to WAP, users terminate their voice call (during which the server can identify them at least by their calling party information), and re-establish a GPRS connection to their last visited WAP-page (which includes user identification in the dynamically generated link URLs). The server uses centrally stored user state information together with the parameter values transmitted in the HTTP requests to identify the appropriate next content. The time for the switch from voice to WAP is then the sum of GPRS connection setup, user selection of the continuation link, and loading of the successor page, typically totalling around 20 seconds.

5. Roadmap for Successful Versatile Interfaces in Telecommunications

Multimodal interfaces are so far not deployed commercially in telecommunications networks. Here we discuss some of the issues arising in the process that will end with their eventual successful deployment.

One issue is the importance of widely used application development languages. VoiceXML is a successful standard in the area of voice-only applications, so that it would be very attractive to use it also for developing multimodal applications. In addition to our own work described above, we have seen this addressed in a different way independently in (Azzini et al., 2002; Kleindienst et al., 2002). In these works, the approach is to provide extensions to a VoiceXML interpreter that make it possible to achieve synchronisation between a VoiceXML document and a separate HTML or WML document using a dynamic markup representation such as the Document Object Model (DOM). A new round of standardisation and universal software updates would be required to establish such modified interpreter functionality in the installed base of VoiceXML platforms. SALT and X+V are possible alternatives.

One influential class of multimodal prototypes being developed for mobile devices are systems such as SmartKom Mobile (Bühler et al., 2002) and AT&T's MATCH system (Johnston et al., 2002). These are feature-rich applications, which are intended for the "stage 2" devices in our scenario. Both applications address navigation scenarios. Let us briefly consider the business model for such services, once they are ready for commercial deployment. Both systems could probably work as UMTS services, and they could be marketed to enterprises for equipping their mobile work-force, such as field-engineers or executives. As consumer services however, one might speculate that their user interfaces may be too complex, and that their utility beyond existing GUI-only solutions, but also their entertainment value are limited.

The fact that it is not obvious whether users will prefer multimodal interfaces over GUI-only interfaces in all cases has been established in user studies (Sturm et al., 2002a; Sturm et al., 2002b). These studies also show that experience with a multimodal interface will increase both task performance and user satisfaction, which seems to indicate the importance of establishing standardised interaction metaphors, which users will grow accustomed to across independently developed multimodal applications.

Oviatt et al. (2002), Nass (2002) and Ishii (2002) provide evidence for the power of multimodal systems to draw users into a rich conversational situation that exhibits many intriguing features. For example, the speech convergence phenomenon known from human-to-human communication has been observed. These kinds of results may hold the key to successful multimodal applications in telecommunications. While user habits change slowly, and acceptance of a new paradigm in human-computer interaction for mobile telecommunications may come only after a long period of exposure to a range of effective applications, humans seem to be eager to extend presuppositions about human communication partners to artefacts. This includes the readiness to become emotionally attached to the artefact. Apparently such effects become stronger, the more versatile and user-embracing the communicative performance of the artefact is.

To prepare the ground for commercially successful multimodal mobile telecommunications interfaces, consumers should therefore be taken on a path that realistically follows the increasingly more powerful terminal capabilities, where applications are provided at each step that are ever more convincing, entertaining and engaging.

In this chapter, we have presented starting points on this path, involving WAP and WAP-Push technologies, which are now (or will soon be) succeeded in the consumer market for mobile telephony by MMS-based applications, Java midlets, SALT-based browser applications, and finally SIP-based multimedia services in UMTS.

As this scenario unfolds, different roles can be fulfilled by various actors ranging from academically oriented long-term research projects to private software companies. As an application-oriented research project co-financed by the telecommunications industry, we see our own role in putting a focus on innovative forms of multimodality that can be implemented on consumer-market devices in public networks at each development stage. R&D and technology providers will be called to provide APIs, SDKs, demonstrators and usability analyses that inspire the creativity of the application developers and let them concentrate on the content they provide rather than on the technological infrastructure they use.

6. Conclusion

To convince the telecommunications industry of the potential of multimodal data services, appealing applications are required which are tailored to the capabilities and limitations of those mobile devices that are available in high volumes in the market. Map based services that involve entering names from a large set of options are suited to highlight the strengths of multimodal interfaces, although their entertainment value may be limited. Ongoing standardisation efforts such as SALT will make an important contribution to enable independent software developers to create ever more attractive multimodal services, beyond what has been possible on the basis of VoiceXML. Both academically oriented research-projects and commercial technology providers should focus on making the task of these application developers as easy as possible. Concerning our own contributions, the three described demonstrators show that very simple forms of multimodality can bring usability advantages on specific tasks. In particular the final QuickMap demonstrator can be implemented in many existing GSM/GPRS networks, and used with popular mobile phones. It demonstrates the feasibility of mobile multimodal data-services development with the technical means available in the consumer market at the time of this research, when commercial deployments of such services do not yet exist.

Acknowledgements

This work was supported within the Austrian competence centre programme **K***plus*, and by the companies Alcatel, Connect Austria, Kapsch, Mobilkom Austria, Nokia, and Siemens. The authors would also like to thank the many people who have contributed to this work by sharing their experience and opinions with us.

Notes

1. http://www.w3.org/TR/multimodal-reqs/
2. http://www.w3.org/TR/2000/NOTE-voicexml-20000505/
3. http://www.w3.org/TR/voicexml20/
4. http://www.w3.org/2002/mmi/
5. http://www.saltforum.org/
6. http://www.w3.org/TR/xhtml+voice/
7. See RES/STQ-00018 "Speech Processing, Transmission and Quality aspects (STQ); Distributed speech recognition; Front-end feature extraction algorithm; Compression algorithms" (2000) at http://webapp.etsi.org/workprogram/Report_WorkItem.asp?WKI_ID=9948.
8. http://communicator.sourceforge.net/
9. http://www.smartkom.org/
10. ftp://ftp.cordis.lu/pub/ist/docs/istagscenarios2010.pdf
11. http://www.dcs.shef.ac.uk/spandh/projects/m4/
12. http://www.loria.fr/projets/MIAMM/
13. http://smada.research.kpn.com/
14. http://www.embassi.de/
15. http://www.speecon.com/
16. http://www.kirusa.com/
17. http://www.lobby7.com/
18. http://www.speechworks.com/
19. http://www1.wapforum.org/tech/terms.asp?doc=WAP-100-WAPArch-19980430-a.pdf
20. http://www1.wapforum.org/tech/terms.asp?doc=WAP-170-WTAI-20000707-a.pdf
21. http://www1.wapforum.org/tech/terms.asp?doc=WAP-165-PushArchOverview-19991108-a.pdf

References

Almeida, L., Amdal, I., Beires, N., Boualem, M., Boves, L., den Os, E., Filoche, P., Gomes, R., Knudsen, J. E., Kvale, K., Rugelbak, J., Tallec, C., and Warakagoda, N. (2002). The MUST guide to Paris; implementation and expert evaluation of a multimodal tourist guide to Paris. In *Proceedings of ISCA Tutorial and Research Workshop Multimodal Dialogue in Mobile Environments (IDS02)*, Kloster Irsee, Germany.

Azzini, I., Giorgino, T., Nardelli, L., Orlando, M., and Rognoni, C. (2002). An architecture for a multi-modal web browser. In *Proceedings of ISCA Tutorial and Research Workshop Multimodal Dialogue in Mobile Environments (IDS02)*, Kloster Irsee, Germany.

Bohus, D. and Rudnicky, A. (2004). LARRI: A language-based maintenance and repair assistant. In Minker, W., Bühler, D., and Dybkjær, L., editors, *Spoken Multimodal Human-Computer Dialogue in Mobile Environments*. Kluwer Academic Publishers, Dordrecht, The Netherlands. (this volume).

Bühler, D., Minker, W., Häussler, J., and Krüger, S. (2002). The SmartKom Mobile multi-modal dialogue system. In *Proceedings of ISCA Tutorial and*

Research Workshop Multimodal Dialogue in Mobile Environments (IDS02), pages 66–70, Kloster Irsee, Germany.

Cheyer, A. and Martin, D. (2001). The Open Agent Architecture. *Journal of Autonomous Agents and Multi-Agent Systems*, 4(1/2):143–148.

Cohen, P., Johnston, M., McGee, D., Oviatt, S., Pittman, J., Smith, I., Chen, L., and Clow, J. (1997). QuickSet: Multimodal interaction for distributed applications. In *Proceedings of ACM International Conference on Multimedia*, pages 31–40, Seattle, Washington, USA.

Cohen, P. and Oviatt, S. (1995). The role of voice input for human-machine communication. In *Proceedings of National Academy of Sciences*, number 22, pages 9921–9927.

Doherty, P., Granlund, G., Kuchcinski, K., Sandewall, E., Nordberg, K., Skarman, E., and Wiklund, J. (2000). The WITAS unmanned aerial vehicle project. In *Proceedings of 14th European Conference on Artificial Intelligence (ECAI)*, pages 747–755, Berlin, Germany.

Elting, C. and Michelitsch, G. (2001). A multimodal presentation planner for a home entertainment environment. In *Proceedings of Workshop on Perceptive User Interfaces (PUI)*, Lake Buena Vista, Florida, USA.

Goldschen, A. and Loehr, D. (1999). The role of the DARPA communicator architecture as a human computer interface for distributed simulations. In *Proceedings of Spring Simulation Interoperability Workshop*, Orlando, Florida, USA. Simulation Interoperability Standards Organization.

Herfet, T. and Kirste, T. (2001). EMBASSI - multimodal assistance for infotainment & service infrastructures. In *Proceedings of Statustagung der Leitprojekte Mensch-Technik-Interaktion*, pages 35–44, Saarbrücken, Germany.

Hoellerer, S. (2002). Challenges and important aspects in planning and performing evaluation studies for multimodal dialogue systems. In *Proceedings of ELSNET Workshop Towards a Roadmap for Multimodal Language Resources and Evaluation at LREC 2002*, Las Palmas, Gran Canaria, Spain.

Huang, X., Acero, A., Chelba, C., Deng, L., Duchene, D., Goodman, J., Hon, H., Jacoby, D., Jiang, L., Loynd, R., Mahajan, M., Mau, P., Meredith, S., Mughal, S., Neto, S., Plumpe, M., Wang, K., and Wang, Y. (2000). MIPAD: A next generation PDA prototype. In *Proceedings of International Conference on Spoken Language Processing (ICSLP)*, pages 33–36, Beijing, China.

Ishii, H. (2002). Tangible bits: Designing the seamless interface between people, bits and atoms. Keynote speech at Fourth IEEE International Conference on Multimodal Interfaces (ICMI'02). Pittsburgh, Pennsylvania, USA.

Johnston, M., Bangalore, S., Stent, A., Vasireddy, G., and Ehlen, P. (2002). Multimodal language processing for mobile information access. In *Proceedings of International Conference on Spoken Language Processing (ICSLP)*, pages 2237–2241, Denver, Colorado, USA.

Kleindienst, J., Seredi, L., Kapanen, P., and Bergman, J. (2002). CATCH-2004 multi-modal browser: Overview description with usability analysis. In *Proceedings of IEEE International Conference on Multimodal Interfaces (ICMI)*, pages 442–447, Pittsburgh, Pennsylvania, USA.

Kumar, S., Cohen, P., and Levesque, H. (2000). The Adaptive Agent Architecture: Achieving fault-tolerance using persistent broker teams. In *Proceedings of International Conference on Multi-Agent Systems (ICMAS)*, pages 159–166, Boston, Massachusetts, USA.

Lemon, O., Bracy, A., Gruenstein, A., and Peters, S. (2001). The WITAS multi-modal dialogue system I. In *Proceedings of European Conference on Speech Communication and Technology (EUROSPEECH)*, pages 1559–1562, Aalborg, Denmark.

Maybury, M. T. (2002). Multimodal systems, resources, and evaluation. In *Proceedings of International Conference on Language Resources and Evaluation (LREC)*, pages g–n, Las Palmas, Gran Canaria, Spain.

Nass, C. (2002). Integrating multiple modalities: Psychology and design of multimodal interfaces. Keynote speech at Fourth IEEE International Conference on Multimodal Interfaces (ICMI'02). Pittsburgh, Pennsylvania, USA.

Niklfeld, G., Finan, R., and Pucher, M. (2001a). Architecture for adaptive multimodal dialog systems based on VoiceXML. In *Proceedings of European Conference on Speech Communication and Technology (EUROSPEECH)*, pages 2341–2344, Aalborg, Denmark.

Niklfeld, G., Finan, R., and Pucher, M. (2001b). Multimodal interface architecture for mobile data services. In *Proceedings of TCMC Workshop on Wearable Computing*, Graz, Austria.

Oviatt, S. (2000). Multimodal system processing in mobile environments. In *Proceedings of Annual ACM Symposium on User Interface Software and Technology*, pages 21–30, San Diego, California, USA.

Oviatt, S., Cohen, P., Wu, L., Vergo, J., Duncan, L., Suhm, B., Bers, J., Holzman, T., Winograd, T., Landay, J., Larson, J., and Ferro, D. (2000). Designing the user interface for multimodal speech and pen-based gesture applications: State-of-the-art systems and future research directions. *Human Computer Interaction*, 15:263–322.

Oviatt, S., Stevens, C., Coulston, R., Xiao, B., Wesson, M., Girand, C., and Mellander, E. (2002). Towards adaptive conversational interfaces: Modeling speech convergence with animated personas. In *Proceedings of ISCA Tutorial and Research Workshop Multimodal Dialogue in Mobile Environments (IDS02)*, Kloster Irsee, Germany.

Pearce, D. and Kopp, D. (2001). ETSI STQ Aurora presentation to 3GPP. Slide presentation.

Pieraccini, R., Carpenter, B., Woudenberg, E., Caskey, S., Springer, S., Bloom, J., and Phillips, M. (2002). Multi-modal spoken dialog with wireless devices. In *Proceedings of ISCA Tutorial and Research Workshop Multimodal Dialogue in Mobile Environments (IDS02)*, Kloster Irsee, Germany.

Pospischil, G., Umlauft, M., and Michlmayr, E. (2002). Designing Lol@, a mobile tourist guide for UMTS. In *Proceedings of International Symposium on Human Computer Interaction with Mobile Devices (Mobile HCI)*, pages 140–154, Pisa, Italy.

Rössler, H., Sienel, J., Wajda, W., Hoffmann, J., and Kostrzewa, M. (2001). Multimodal interaction for mobile environments. In *Proceedings of International Workshop on Information Presentation and Natural Multimodal Dialogue*, pages 47–51, Verona, Italy.

Seneff, S., Hurley, E., Lau, R., Pao, C., Schmid, P., and Zue, V. (1998). Galaxy-II: a reference architecture for conversational system development. In *Proceedings of International Conference on Spoken Language Processing (ICSLP)*, pages 931–934, Sydney, Australia.

Sturm, J., Bakx, I., Cranen, B., Terken, J., and Wang, F. (2002a). Usability evaluation of a Dutch multimodal system for railway information. In *Proceedings of International Conference on Language Resources and Evaluation (LREC)*, pages 255–261, Las Palmas, Gran Canaria, Spain.

Sturm, J., Cranen, B., Wang, F., Terken, J., and Bakx, I. (2002b). The effect of user experience on interaction with multimodal systems. In *Proceedings of ISCA Tutorial and Research Workshop Multimodal Dialogue in Mobile Environments (IDS02)*, Kloster Irsee, Germany.

Wahlster, W., Reithinger, N., and Blocher, A. (2001). SmartKom: Multimodal communication with a life-like character. In *Proceedings of European Conference on Speech Communication and Technology (EUROSPEECH)*, pages 1547–1550, Aalborg, Denmark.

Chapter 10

MULTIMODAL SPOKEN DIALOGUE WITH WIRELESS DEVICES

Roberto Pieraccini*, Bob Carpenter†, Eric Woudenberg‡,
Sasha Caskey§, Stephen Springer, Jonathan Bloom, Michael Phillips
SpeechWorks International, New York, USA
{ roberto,bob.carpenter,sasha.caskey,stephen.springer,jon.bloom,phillips } @speechworks.com

Abstract We discuss the various issues related to the design and implementation of multimodal spoken dialogue systems[1] with wireless client devices. In particular we discuss the design of a usable interface that exploits the complementary features of the audio and visual channels to enhance usability. We then describe two client-server architectures in which we implemented applications for mapping and navigating to points of interest.

Keywords: Multimodality; Dialogue; User interfaces; Architectures.

1. Introduction

Speech-only dialogue systems are a reality today and are being deployed in telephone-based commercial applications all over the world. As personal communication devices become more and more powerful, the distinction between personal telephones and hand-held computers is becoming fuzzier. In view of this evolution, combined with the convergence of the Internet and telephony, we are observing a growing interest in applications where speech cooperates with other communication modalities, such as visual display, pen, gestures, etc. Hence we are observing a growing interest both in research and industry toward what are generally referred to as multimodal user interfaces.

*Now with IBM, T.J.Watson Research, Yorktown Heights, New York, USA
†Now with Alias-i, Inc., Brooklyn, New York, USA
‡Now with Telleureka, Inc., New York, New York, USA
§Now with IBM, T.J.Watson Research, Yorktown Heights, New York, USA

W. Minker, D. Bühler and L. Dybkjær (eds), Spoken Multimodal Human-Computer Dialogue in Mobile Environments, 169-184

Voice-based user interfaces and graphical user interfaces (GUI) have been successfully employed, independently, as the principal interaction modalities for many applications. However the integration of the two into a multimodal interface still presents many unanswered questions, see (Oviatt, 2003) for a comprehensive review of the issues and the state of the art in multimodal interfaces, and an extensive bibliography. Considering handheld devices, we must be aware that the same multimodal application could be potentially used in a variety of different situations. For instance users may find themselves in situations where both hands are busy but their aural and visual senses are available, even intermittently, as in a car while driving. In other situations the users may not be allowed to freely use spoken input and output, as during a meeting, or the audio channel may be unreliable as in a noisy environment like an airport. Finally there might be situations where both hands and eyes are busy and the device is out of sight, but users can talk to the application through a remote wired or wireless microphone. A well-behaved user interface should be able to function in all of these situations.

Moreover, the design of user interfaces that integrate both audio and visual channels must take into account that the two modalities can be used cooperatively and take advantage of each other's capabilities, especially for coping with limitations that are intrinsic to each independently. Some of the limitations of the voice-only interface derive from the narrow information channel provided by speech. Users cannot absorb and retain large quantities of information such as long lists of items. If it is necessary to present a relatively long list, systems may rely on audio list browsing (e.g., *Say next or previous*), which is not particularly efficient. Information presented only through speech is volatile and systems must rely on the user's short-term memory. Thus it is often very hard to present additional information that could help the user keep the dialogue on course, such as information about what the system knows at a certain point in dialogue, or hints on what to say next. Finally, there is information, such as visual information like maps and pictures that cannot be conveyed through voice.

On the other hand, the limitations of graphical user interfaces on portable devices derive from the absence of convenient text input methods and the small size of the display. Anyone who has used a PDA for input of free form text knows how painfully slow the process is. The need for speech as a text input mechanism is evident. Moreover, as stated before, there are situations, such as in a car, where the user can readily take advantage of the visual output but cannot manually input data. Of course when the two modalities are brought together on the same device, the user interface should take advantage of their complementary capabilities. For instance, the display can include elements that suggest to the user what can be said and indicate how confident the recogniser is with the current interpretation of the utterance. At the same time the system should offer non-speech input modalities, such as buttons and scrollable lists. Finally, spoken prompts and earcons (the audio equivalent of icons) can be used for reinforcing elements of the user interface.

System architecture is another important aspect of multimodal applications. There are several approaches that can be taken within the limitations of today's technology. Those concern the choice of embedded or network-based speech recognition and text-to-speech processing. An interesting hybrid solution is what is known today as distributed speech recognition (DSR), where part of the speech recogniser (typically the front end signal processing) resides on the client device. Of course the choice of architecture depends on the application and on the environment in which the application is used. Other architecture considerations are related to ease of development for multimodal applications. Although good abstractions, generally based on the concept of call-flow, exist today for the design of voice-only dialogue applications we do not have an equivalent abstraction for multimodal applications. This complicates the design of multimodal applications.

2. Why Multimodal Wireless?

Mass adoption of wireless devices truly capable of supporting multimodal applications has not yet occurred, mainly due to limitations in network infrastructure. One of the few exceptions is probably the WAP cellular telephone, which can count a significant number of users[2], especially in Europe. WAP telephones, which are characterised by a small text-based display, typically do not allow simultaneous transmission of voice and data. A multimodal application designed for WAP telephones would require the user to switch between speech and text mode anytime that she needs to change input or output modality. However cumbersome that might seem, a WAP telephone multimodal service would present several advantages over a speech-only or text-only application on the same device, at least for certain applications. For instance, let us consider a voice-only navigation application. The user would call a service's telephone number and be instructed to speak a starting address and a destination address. The system would compute the itinerary as a sequence of steps and recite them one at time, allowing the caller to navigate the list with simple commands such as next, previous, etc. For a long itinerary, a voice-only modality for providing the list of directions would prove quite impractical, since the user would have to keep the call open for the entire journey, or take separate note of the steps, or call back every time the next step was required. Conversely, in a text-only version of the application, while the whole itinerary could be stored in the telephone and easily browsed by the user, entering a street address using the 12 keys of a telephone would prove tedious and impractical. This is certainly a case where even a multimodal interaction that was strongly limited to one modality at a time would be useful. In fact the same navigation application, implemented on a WAP telephone and supported by an infrastructure for switching between voice and text modes, would allow the use of voice for entering an address yet store the resulting directions on the telephone as text. The user could browse them at leisure without any need for keeping the call open.

Besides WAP phones, we are witnessing increasing availability of more sophisticated wireless devices, such as PDAs (e.g., Palm, iPAQ) and smartphones, characterised by powerful processors and displays with higher resolution than those in cell phones. However sophisticated and powerful these devices might be, text and data entry will be constrained by their small size. Mobile devices are becoming smaller and smaller, preventing the use of a keyboard or even a touchpad. Text can be entered, albeit clumsily, with a stylus on a touch sensitive display using handwritten "graffiti" or through taps on a soft keyboard. Speech remains an obvious alternative choice for data entry for these devices. In spite of the fact that the number of owners of PDAs and smartphones is growing rapidly, they are not yet widespread due to their cost and size, and due to the paltry data rates (less than 14kbps), high fees, and spotty coverage of current wireless Internet.

We will probably see increased interest in wireless devices when 3G networks become available. 3G devices, characterised by the simultaneous flow of voice and data, and by being "continuously connected" to the network, will soon be widely available and at a reasonable cost. The continuing evolution of mobile devices toward larger memories, faster processors, and better displays, all in smaller and smaller packages, make the use of speech for data entry increasingly appropriate.

3. Walking Direction Application

The case study described in this chapter refers to the development of an application supplying mapping and directional navigation to points of interest. The development of this application was funded by DARPA within the Communicator project[3] and carried out in collaboration with Compaq[4], Lobby7[5] and MapQuest[6]. The application addresses the scenario of a user walking in an unknown city and trying to find her way to a destination location. The target client device is a HP iPAQ 3765 PocketPC. The application provides functions that include selecting a city, a start and/or an end address, displaying a map, controlling the display of the map (zooming and moving), displaying directions on the map and displaying interactive directions in the form of a list of successive steps. The design of the user interface for this application assumes a mixed style of interaction, where the user will be able to either speak to the device, or enter information through a stylus, or both. We developed this application under two different architectures. The first assumes we have tight control of the widgets displayed on the client device. This would presumably require using a proprietary browser, or a least a browser that is capable of fine grain control of the GUI. The second implementation uses the standard Pocket Internet Explorer browser that comes with the PocketPC OS. Internet connectivity was established with a 802.11b wireless PC card connected to the iPAQ via its PC card sleeve.

4. Speech Technology for Multimodal Wireless

Speech processing for multimodal wireless application centres on two technologies: ASR (automatic speech recognition) for speech input and TTS (text to speech) for speech output. One question that arises when considering a wireless multimodal application accessing network-based content concerns the configuration of ASR and TTS engines. In general there are two possible choices for each engine: a network server or an embedded configuration. In the network server configuration, the engine (either the ASR or the TTS, or both) runs as a server at a remote location with speech being transported to/from the client via wireless connection. In the embedded configuration the engine runs instead on the client. The choice between a network or embedded configuration depends upon several factors. For ASR, it depends on the availability of a small memory footprint speech recogniser that supports the required vocabulary with the speed and accuracy needed for the application. For TTS, the choice depends on the quality requirements for the speech output. Generally small memory-footprint embedded TTS has a lower speech quality than network TTS engines. One can think also of configurations where network and embedded engines are used at different times during an application. An application might use a network speech recogniser for the data entry phase of its operation, for instance to enter the starting and ending address in a mapping application. The same application might sensibly use an embedded recogniser for navigating the downloaded information, such as the list of direction steps (e.g., *next*, *previous*, etc.) or maps (e.g., *zoom in*, *zoom out*, *move left*, etc.). In this case, network connectivity is required only during a limited portion of the transaction, but speech can continue to be used as an input modality even when the network is not available.

Another consideration for the choice between network and embedded speech resources is with respect to the required bandwidth. It is obvious that network-based speech processing requires a larger bandwidth to the device than would embedded processing. For instance, in the case of an embedded speech recogniser, one would need to send to the application server only the transcription (or n-best transcriptions) obtained by the embedded ASR engine. Similarly, in the case of embedded TTS, only the text version of a prompt needs to be sent to the client through the wireless connection. Alternatively, when network resources are used, the whole speech signal (possibly in a compressed format) needs to be exchanged between the wireless client and the application server.

A solution that offers the benefits of network-based speech recognition and the limited bandwidth required by an embedded engine is what is commonly known as distributed speech recognition (DSR). With DSR the speech recognition front end (i.e., the part of the speech recogniser that collects speech and transforms it into a sequence of feature vectors) resides on the client. Only the compressed feature vectors (generally one feature vector for every 10msec of speech) are encoded and transmitted over the wireless digital network. The speech recognition search engine resides on the application server and processes the feature vectors to produce the recognition results. The obvious advantage of DSR is the reduced bandwidth required: recognition performance equivalent to that on telephone quality speech can be achieved at a meager 4.8 to 9.6 kbps data rate (vs. 64kbps for conventional toll quality telephony). Latencies can also be lowered due to the fact that end pointing can be implemented on the client. Moreover, the computational power required on the client for the implementation of DSR is small when compared to the network-based recogniser. We can also envision solutions where the embedded and the network recognisers share the same front end, which remains on the client. ETSI, the European Telecommunication Standards Institute, created the Aurora Working Group[7] with the task of defining the feature extraction algorithms and standardising the DSR protocol.

5. User Interface Issues

One can think of a multimodal interface from two perspectives: a visual-centric or a speech-centric one. In the visual-centric approach the design starting point is an existing graphical user interface (e.g., from a web or a stand-alone application), and the multimodality is achieved by adding the option of speech input, for instance allowing the use of speech for operations such as clicking links, pushing buttons and entering text in fields. Conversely, the speech-centric approach starts with an existing Voice User Interface (VUI) and adds GUI elements in order to enhance and improve the dialogue experience. While we do believe that a multimodal application should be designed as *multimodal* from the beginning, we feel that the speech-centric approach is useful for understanding how the GUI and VUI can complement each other synergistically, rather than simply attempting to *speech enable* an existing GUI application.

For a speech only application, several elements would greatly benefit from the addition of visual information. Many forms of information are not easily and effectively conveyed by speech alone. Certainly images, like maps or pictures, cannot be presented in a speech-only application, but even medium to long lists are difficult without the aid of a display. Speech-only navigation of long lists can be tedious and cumbersome to the user, while this is relatively easy with the help of a scrollable display. Another element that makes the design of speech-only interfaces hard is the difficulty of making the user aware of the state of the dialogue. Users can get lost in a large application, not knowing where they are in the call flow, and not having in front of them the choices they have made during previous turns. Displaying the state of the dialogue, both by showing the previous choices and by persistently identifying the application state would certainly help users. Finally, letting the user know what was understood and what to say next in a visual manner would improve the usability of the application.

5.1 Situationalisation

One of the problems with designing the user interface for an application based on a multimodal mobile client is that there is a wide variety of situations in which the user could be interacting with the system. For instance, a user could potentially be in any of the following situations:

- Sitting at a desk,
- Getting out of a cab, building, subway and preparing to walk somewhere,
- Walking somewhere with hands free,
- Walking somewhere carrying things,
- Driving somewhere in heavy traffic,
- Driving somewhere in light traffic,
- Riding in a car as a passenger, not having to watch traffic,
- Sitting, walking, or standing in a high noise environment such as a station, airport, or restaurant

All of these situations have a different ideal balance of visual and audio interaction. A single invocation of a multimodal application might persist through several situations such as those above as the user moves through the real world. And it is probably unrealistic to assume that the multimodal device could detect when the user is looking or whether their hands are available or not.

One could possibly reduce all the different balances of visual and audio to 4 complementary modalities. Two of them are the single modes (visual only and speech only) and two multi-modes that we can identify as *visual-dominant* and *speech-dominant*. The choice of the modality would affect the design of the prompts and of the GUI. However, from a practical point of view, it is too expensive to consider even four modalities, since this would result in designing four different interfaces. Another problem would be for the user to learn how to select the right modality. A reasonable approach involves designing only one mixed-mode user interface, and allowing for two sets of prompts: short prompts for the mixed-mode or visual-dominant use, and long and more informative prompts for voice-only or voice-dominant use.

5.2 Description of the Application

As in a spoken dialogue system, we can represent an application as a graph (often called a call-flow in spoken dialogue system) where each node represents a distinctive state. The graph shown in Figure 1 is a high-level description of the considered application. For a multimodal application it is convenient to associate each distinct page or form that will appear on the visual display with a node in the graph representation. Thus a node can represent the collection of more than one piece of information. For instance the MAIN MENU node would collect from the user which branch of the application should be activated (i.e., NAVIGATION or POINTS OF INTEREST), but also, for instance, the information about which city/state is the object for the following requests.

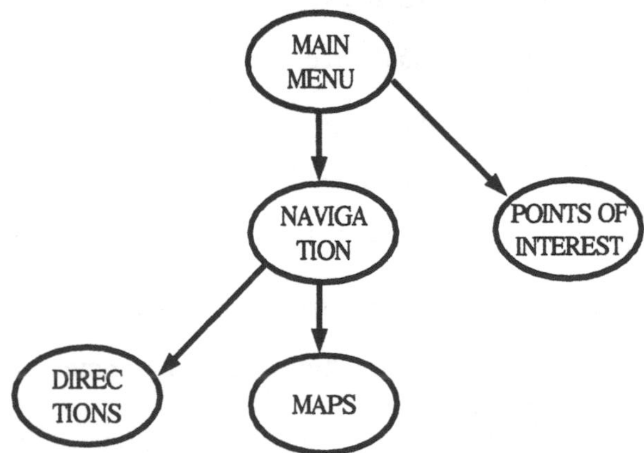

Figure 1. High level description of the application.

Moreover each node would include other universal commands, such as a *main menu* - that would force the application to return to the main menu page, back - that would cause the return to the previously executed node, and a *help* button that would display a help page or play a helpful prompt. Additionally the page might have tabbed panes for moving to other branches and options to change previously selected features. An example of the display layout for a certain node of the application is shown in Figure 2.

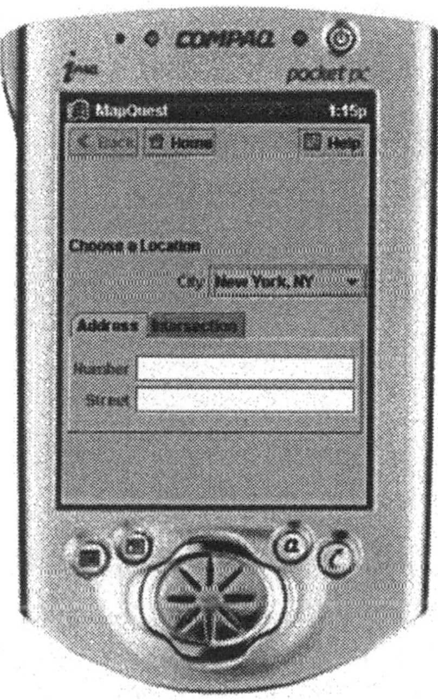

Figure 2. Example of display layout on the multimodal device.

Figure 3 shows an example of the low-level interaction description within one node of the application (commands such as back and help are excluded for simplicity). The transitions are ordered and have conditions. For instance, if a NUMBER is not available (condition !NUMBER), the node called NUMBER is invoked, which would set the focus on the number field and select the ASR grammar for numbers. At the start node an ASR grammar is activated that allows for compound sentences that include all the fields, as for example *twenty three mountain boulevard* or *the number is twenty three and the street is mountain boulevard.*

5.3 Speech Collection Protocol

Unlike telephone-based speech application, in multimodal applications users are not compelled to speak or input visual data within a certain period after the prompt. Moreover, a system based on a handheld client cannot run in an *always listening* mode due to issues of battery consumption and because spurious speech and noise can inadvertently be taken as input. In our imple-

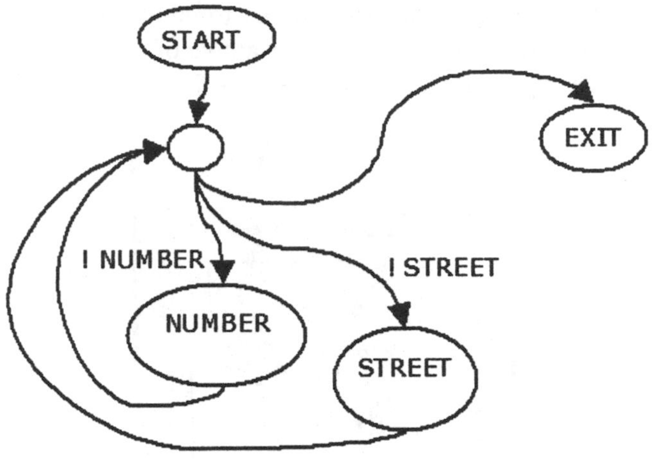

Figure 3. Low level description of the interaction.

mentation we adopted a push-to-talk paradigm, which we believe is appropriate for this kind of application. The recording button, which is located on the left side of the client device, is depressed to start speech collection, and kept depressed until the end of the utterance. This allows the user to operate the application with only one hand. An alternative would be to touch the screen with the stylus to start speech collection. Although this solution would also allow the focus to be set on the displayed page (allowing the appropriate recognition grammar to be simultaneously chosen when a field or text box is selected), we discarded it because it requires the use of both hands, which can be impractical in many situations.

Another issue is that in a push-to-talk paradigm speakers tend to speak simultaneously with, or even slightly before, pushing the collection button. The problem becomes more serious when any delay exists between the time the collection button is depressed and the time recording actually begins. In an informal test we noticed that up to 30% of the utterances collected in a push-to-talk modality were cut at the beginning. We solved this problem by playing a short tone subsequent to the button press as soon as the system actually starts recording speech. The tone helps users learn when to speak. As a result almost none of the utterances that were collected were cut at the beginning after the start-collection tone was introduced, and the users were instructed to wait for it before speaking. An analogous problem is that speakers tend to release the button right at or just before the end of the utterance. However this problem can be corrected by allowing the speech collection to continue for a short time after the button is released.

6. Multimodal Architecture Issues

The state of a multimodal application can be decomposed into two sub-states. The first is the state of the application's internal logic, identified by each node of Figure 1; the second is the state of the application's user interface. Both the visual and the audio interfaces go through different states, and a transition in one, caused by external events originating from the user or the backend, can precipitate a transition in the other. This is shown in the example of Table 1, which describes the state of the audio and visual interfaces during input to a *form* having two input fields (F1 and F2) and a submit button.

Table 1. Visual and audio states of a data input form.

User interaction events	Visual State	Audio State
	Display form	
		Start playing prompt for field F1
		Start recogniser with grammar F1
User selects field F2		
	Set focus on field F2	
		Halt recogniser
		Start recogniser with grammar F2
User speaks item for F2		
		Recogniser returns result for F2
	Result displayed in F2	
	Set focus on field F1	
		Start playing prompt for field F1
		Start recogniser with grammar F1
User speaks item for F1		
		Recogniser returns results for F1
	Result displayed in F1	
	Set focus on submit	

Figure 4 shows an abstract architecture of a multimodal system. The application manager is responsible for the application state while the multimodal manager communicates with the audio and visual resources and is responsible for the interface state. The distinction between the blocks of Figure 4 may not be obvious or they may be connected differently depending on the implementation of the particular multimodal system, although their functionality still remains.

In a multimodal wireless application the visual and the audio resources can be entirely or partially on the client. For instance, in the case of DSR, the speech recogniser is partially on the client (i.e., the front end) while the rest (i.e., the search engine) is on the server. If an embedded solution is adopted, the speech recogniser and the TTS are entirely on the client. The separation of

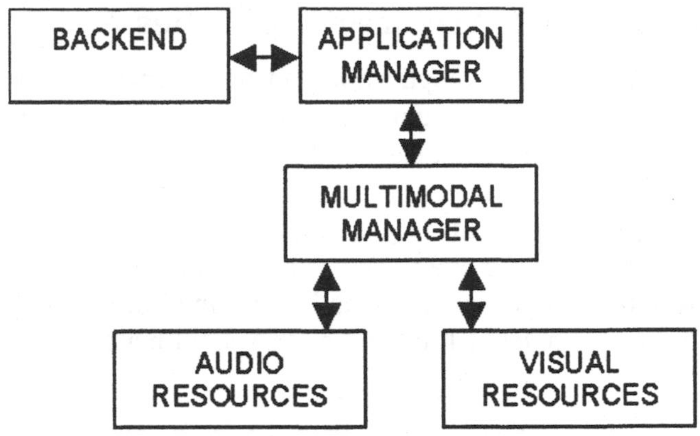

Figure 4. Abstract multimodal architecture.

the audio and visual resources between the client and the server also determines the degree of interaction possible between them.

6.1 Tight Multimodal Control

Figure 5 shows the architecture that we implemented to allow tight multimodal control of the audio and visual resources. The wireless device includes a thin audio client that is able to collect speech and send its digital representation to the server. Similarly the audio client is able to receive prompts and play them. The GUI client was implemented in Java. It receives control frames from the server and is able to create and destroy widgets or modify their properties (e.g., change the colour or shape of a button, or fill a text field). The GUI proxy maintains a symbolic representation of the visual state. Anytime the visual state changes because of a user event (e.g., the user clicking on a button) the GUI proxy is notified. Similarly, anytime the multimodal manager requests a change on the display (e.g., filling a field with the text resulting from recognition of a speaker utterance), the state of the GUI proxy is changed accordingly, and the GUI proxy propagates the state change to the GUI client, which effects the change.

The multimodal manager is implemented as a set of event handlers. Significant events are the return of an ASR result or a change in the visual state. Event handlers act on the ASR process, the prompt output, and the visual state. For instance, when a visual event is detected (e.g., a button is clicked), the ASR process is halted and a playing prompt is interrupted (i.e., a visual barge-in). Similarly when the ASR returns a result, an event handler changes the visual state accordingly.

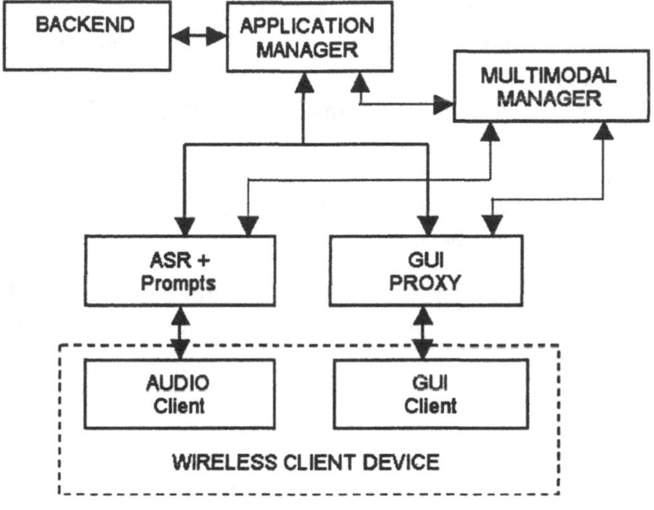

Figure 5. Tight multimodal control architecture.

The application manager is implemented by ETUDE, a dialogue manager based on a recursive transition network representation of dialogue (Pieraccini et al., 2001). The ETUDE engine offers the possibility of describing the dialogue with a graph similar to the ones shown in Figure 1 and Figure 3 where the arcs are ordered and have logical conditions that are verified on the application state. The application state is stored as a frame (i.e., a hierarchical structure of key/value pairs). The ETUDE framework offers, as an additional feature, the possibility of having most of the universal commands (e.g., *backup, main-menu, start-over, go to another branch of the application*) handled directly by the engine. For instance, the designer can specify whether a node is a *backup anchor* and whether a node allows the user to perform a backup action. When the user chooses *backup*, if the current node allows it, the engine will return to the most recently visited backup anchor node and restore the application state (i.e., the engine will perform an undo operation). This set of universal commands is quite useful in multimodal applications, and including support logic for them in the dialogue engine simplifies adding them to any application.

6.2 Loose Multimodal Control

Although the architecture described in the previous section allows for arbitrarily tight control and interaction between the visual and audio state, there are several issues that concern its practical implementation in commercial applications. Among those:

- A proprietary browser that runs on the mobile client has to be implemented for each possible device. Some devices may not support such an implementation. For instance, at the time the demonstrator was built, we could not find a Java virtual machine for PocketPC that implemented Java's Swing graphics package.

- In addition, having to download and configure a proprietary browser results in an additional burden for potential users.

- Depending on how tightly coupled the audio and the visual modalities are, the amount of communication between the server and the client can make the application slow and unusable on a network with low bandwidth or high latency.

- Proprietary communication and presentation protocols, as opposed to standard ones, such as HTML and VoiceXML, can make it difficult to port applications across platforms.

In order to alleviate these problems, multimodal platforms and application makers favour solutions that involve standard markup languages. In the absence, as yet, of a multimodal standard, developers tend to rely on existing standards for voice (i.e., VoiceXML) and visual browsers (i.e., HTML).

We developed a fully functional prototype of the discussed application in collaboration with Lobby7, using Lobby7 technology that leverages the VoiceXML and HTML standards. The prototype follows the architecture described in Figure 6. A thin client collects speech from the device microphone and sends it, through a wireless Internet connection, to a voice browser (SpeechWorks' Open Speech Browser). Additionally, the client plays prompts, monitors barge-in, and navigates *Pocket IE* (the PocketPC HTML browser) to HTML pages generated by the multimodal manager.

The function of the multimodal manager is that of updating the VoiceXML and HTML documents and causing their respective browsers to load them after each user input (input being speech or visual-based). The application manager consists of a set of Java Server Pages managed by the Tomcat servlet container on an Apache web server. The backend data (maps and directions) is provided by the MapQuest enterprise database server (Figure 7).

7. Conclusion

We discussed issues related to the implementation of a multimodal application on a wireless client device. The user interface issues are important since they determine the usability of the application. Exploiting the complementary features of the visual and audio channels we can build applications that will provide usability superior to GUI-only and speech-only interfaces. However,

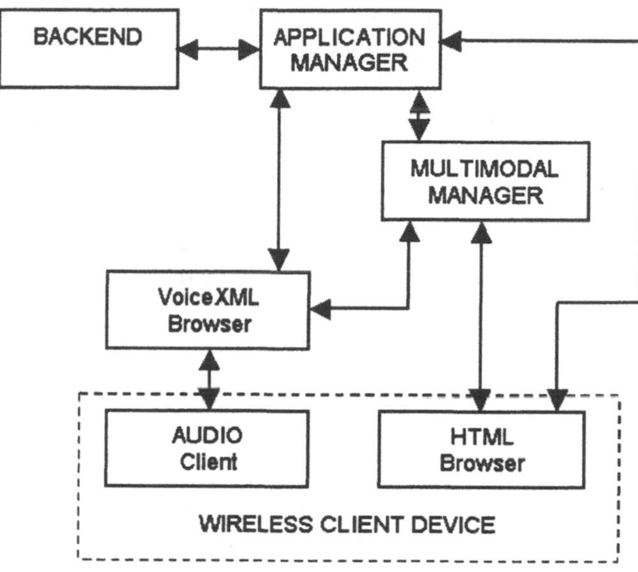

Figure 6. Loose multimodal control architecture.

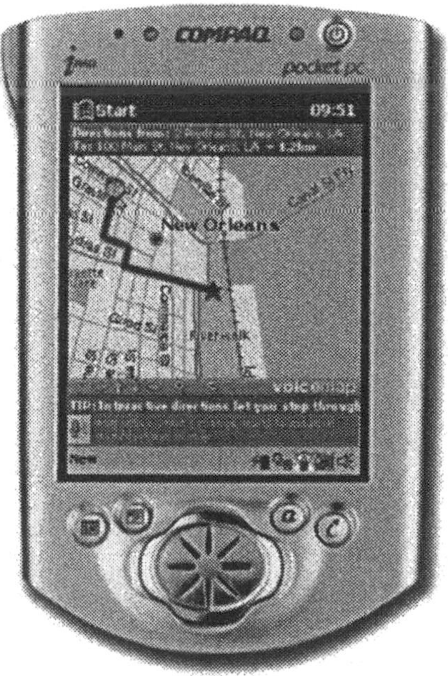

Figure 7. Map and direction rendering.

the adoption of multimodal wireless applications depends not only on the quality and usability of the applications themselves, but also on other elements such as the availability and reliability of wireless digital networks and the existence of standards supporting them.

Acknowledgements

The authors wish to thank the entire Lobby7 team for their support in building the VoiceMap application and Sandeep Sibal from Kirusa[8] for many discussions on multimodal architecture.

Notes

1. The study reported in this chapter was funded by DARPA under contract N66001-00-1-8958 through SPAWAR.
2. However, field studies (`http://www.useit.com/alertbox/20001210.html`) indicate that at least 70% of owners of WAP telephones in UK said that they would not be using WAP in a year.
3. `http://www.darpa.mil/ipto/research/com/`
4. `http://www.compaq.com/`
5. Lobby7 is now part of Scansoft
6. `http://www.mapquest.com/`
7. `http://www.etsi.org/frameset/home.htm?/technicalactiv/DSR/-dsr.htm`
8. `http://www.kirusa.com/`

References

Oviatt, S. L. (2003). Multimodal interfaces. In Jacko, J. and Sears, A., editors, *The Human-Computer Interaction Handbook: Fundamentals, Evolving Technologies and Emerging Applications*, pages 286–304. Lawrence Erlbaum Assoc., Mahwah, New Jersey, USA.

Pieraccini, R., Caskey, S., Dayanidhi, K., Carpenter, B., and Phillips, M. (2001). ETUDE, a recursive dialog manager with embedded user interface patterns. In *Proceedings of IEEE Automatic Speech Recognition and Understanding Workshop (ASRU)*, Madonna di Campiglio, Italy.

Chapter 11

THE SMARTKOM MOBILE CAR PROTOTYPE SYSTEM FOR FLEXIBLE HUMAN-MACHINE COMMUNICATION

Dirk Bühler, Wolfgang Minker

University of Ulm, Department of Information Technology, Ulm/Donau, Germany

{ dirk.buehler,wolfgang.minker } @e-technik.uni-ulm.de

Abstract This chapter presents the SmartKom Mobile prototype. Intended for car drivers as well as pedestrian users, the system provides multimodal human-machine interaction in two substantially different mobile environments. In contrast to state-of-the-art research projects in the field, SmartKom Mobile re-uses architecture as well as the interaction paradigm implemented for other environments, namely SmartKom Home and Public. This paradigm aims at providing an intelligent and intuitive interaction for non-expert users. For demonstration and evaluation purposes, the mobile prototype has been implemented as a PC-based solution in a vehicle which connects to a handheld Personal Digital Assistant (PDA) interface carried by pedestrians. The system needs to account for the different context of use in both environments as well as for the specific hardware constraints.

Keywords: Human-computer interaction; Natural language dialogue; Integrated tasks; Intuitive interfaces; Distributed architectures; Flexible modality control.

1. Introduction

People spend an increasing amount of their time in mobile environments, notably in their cars, but also as pedestrians in urban centres they are not completely familiar with. Naturally, they want to make that time as productive and enjoyable as possible. To this end, technological advances in human-machine interaction open an increasingly realistic perspective.

Since driver distraction, however, runs the risk of becoming a major obstacle to the evolution of these services and technologies, highly efficient though intuitive human-machine interfaces are required. Undeniably, speech dialogue-based interfaces have demonstrated the potential to considerably im-

W. Minker, D. Bühler and L. Dybkjær (eds), Spoken Multimodal Human-Computer Dialogue in Mobile Environments, 185-202

prove the safety and user-friendliness of human-machine interaction (Gärtner et al., 2001; Green, 2000; Minker et al., 2003).

SmartKom (Wahlster et al., 2001) has been a long-term research effort (1999-2003) funded by the German Federal Ministry for Education and Research (BMBF). As the follow-up project to the Verbmobil (1993-2000) speech-to-speech translation project (Wahlster, 2000), SmartKom is a consortium of major industrial and academic research institutions located in Germany. The aim of the SmartKom project is to provide an intelligent and intuitive interaction for non-expert users in different environments, namely Home, Public and Mobile. In this chapter, focus is placed on the SmartKom Mobile scenario and the presentation of a first prototype system.

In the following section, related research projects and initiatives are reviewed. The SmartKom initiative and the SmartKom Mobile application scenario is presented in detail in Sections 3 and 4. The technical realisation of the system as an in-vehicle solution is discussed in Sections 5 and 6. In Section 7, an outlook to a more flexible modality control reflecting the needs of different usage situations is discussed. Section 8 finally concludes the chapter.

2. Related Work

In 1996, Mercedes-Benz introduced the first generation of LINGUATRONIC (Bühler et al., 2003), a commercial spoken language dialogue system that allows entirely hands-free operation of the car's mobile phone, including intelligent number dialling, number storing, user-defined telephone directory entry names, name dialling, and directory editing. LINGUATRONIC has a vocabulary of about 300 words, and also allows for the operation of comfort electronics, such as radio, CD player/changer, air condition, etc. in different languages. As key issues for in-vehicle speech technology, noise reduction and echo cancellation are achieved by an integrated digital signal pre-processing step. Furthermore, the system automatically adapts to the characteristics of the speaker's voice, as well as to the acoustic background in the car. The system has been realised as a compact hardware box that is connected to the in-vehicle data bus system.

The SENECA spoken language dialogue system demonstrator (Minker et al., 2003), resulting from an industrial research cooperation, co-financed by the European Commission, provides speech-based access to a wide range of entertainment, navigation and communication applications. Conceptually the system may be viewed as a speech interface enhancement to the commercially available COMAND device, an advanced in-vehicle electronics system, usually operated manually by a traditional "buttons-and-displays" interface. The SENECA demonstrator has been evaluated by real users. The results showed that with speech input, road safety, especially in the case of manipulating complex tasks, can be significantly improved: the feeling of being distracted from driving is reduced compared to manual input. In terms of error analysis, the most frequent user errors have their origin in spelling problems and a wrong speech command selection. SENECA's success relies on the use of an intelligent dialogue strategy that allows the system to compensate for low speech recognition confidence and word-level ambiguities by engaging in suitable clarification dialogues with the user (Minker et al., 2003).

Other research projects in this domain have also focussed on navigation as the central task for in-vehicle spoken language dialogue systems. Hansen and colleagues, for instance, have developed CU-Move, a research prototype dialogue system in the car environment (Hansen et al., 2003). Technically, the system is based on the MIT Galaxy-II Hub architecture with base system components derived from the CU Communicator (Pellom et al., 2000). Users can enter their origin and destination addresses by voice. The dialogue system then automatically retrieves the driving instructions from the internet using an online route direction provider. During interaction, users inform the system of their current position on the route by providing spoken odometer readings, which are needed since GPS (Global Positioning System) information has not yet been integrated. On that basis, route information such as turn descriptions, distances, and summaries can be queried during travel. Compared to earlier attempts using spoken language dialogue systems in cars that have generally focussed on isolated command words, CU-Move supports natural conversational interaction.

Fundamentally different in terms of technology, but arguably similar in terms of goals, the General Motors OnStar[1] service in the USA is another example of how spoken language dialogue interaction may be a valuable means of driver assistance. Although, voice recognition for simple spoken commands have been added recently, OnStar is in principle a call centre service accessible by a simple mobile phone interface built-in in and available for millions of cars. After pressing an activation button, the driver is connected through the telephone network to a human operator that provides assistive services such as navigation and local information.

More recently, multimodal interaction technology, involving pen and camera-based input, multimedia presentations, and the like, has become a focus of many research projects, with a particular interest in enabling its use in mobile environments. A shift from speech-only to multimodal interaction is particularly useful when the usage scenario is enlarged from a vehicle-only to a scenario which is multimodal in the sense that different forms of travelling (e.g., by car, by air, or as a pedestrian) are involved. The driver and the pedestrian environments, in particular, substantially differ with respect to the modalities that seem preferable for a natural interaction (Bühler et al., 2002).

As an example for the pedestrian domain, Johnston and colleagues (2001, 2002) present the MATCH system, a portable multimodal interface to a restaurant and subway information system for New York City. MATCH allows combined speech and pen (touch screen) input. Pen input may be used for denoting geographical areas and for addressing simple handwritten requests to the system (that could also be spoken, if preferred by the user). The output consists of synthesised speech synchronised with dynamical graphical displays. The system runs on a Fujitsu tablet PC-like PDA, either in a stand-alone or wireless client/server mode.

A similar demonstrator system is the MUST guide to Paris (Almeida et al., 2002). It is the result of a cooperation between three major telecom companies and two research institutions. Realised as a client/server solution with an iPAQ handheld PDA as a display and a mobile phone as an audio client, the system features speech recognition and simple pen-based input, as well as dynamical graphical maps as output. The system serves as a case study about integrating existing technology, rather than an implementation of a particular human-machine interaction paradigm.

In a similar spirit, but with an eye on laying the ground for commercial third-party application development, Pieraccini and colleagues (2002) present two different architectures for multimodal dialogue with wireless handheld devices, such as Pocket PCs. One of them implements *tight* multimodal control where a specialised client written in Java synchronises its visual and audio state with a server running the automatic speech recognition and text-to-speech synthesis. The other architecture (*loose* multimodal control) aims at a solution based on VoiceXML and HTML standards. Both architectures realise a thin client, fat server architecture with wireless communication (between client and server).

Krüger and colleagues (2004) present BPN, the BMW Personal Navigator, a PDA-based solution for an integrated navigation in the car and pedestrian (indoor and outdoor) domains. In their scenario, the user plans a trip using desktop computer access to an Internet navigation service, then transmits the trip data to the PDA. Using the PDA, pedestrian navigation may be executed. The PDA may also be used for programming the on-board navigation system via Bluetooth when entering the car. The system presents an interesting approach to integrated trip execution, whereas it is not aimed at providing a uniform multimodal interface across environments (which seems crucial for non-experts). Speech synthesis and recognition are available on the PDA, however the current vocabulary and grammar size seem to limit the use to small spoken short cuts.

The projects mentioned above allow to conclude that, traditionally, speech is the preferred interaction mode in the automotive area, whereas graphics-based interaction using a handheld PDA (sometimes enhanced with capabilities similar to spoken short cuts) has been mainly used in the pedestrian environment.

However, none of the approaches has so far tried to bridge the gap between these two environments by way of a uniform interaction paradigm.

3. SmartKom - Intuitive Human-Machine Interaction

The main goal of the SmartKom project is to provide an intuitive and intelligent user interface for non-experts to everyday computer-based applications in different usage scenarios (Wahlster et al., 2001). Intuitiveness is achieved by enabling natural conversational interaction with a lifelike virtual character (called *Smartakus*) who embodies the system's functionality (instead of the traditional Windows, Icons, Menus, Pointing (WIMP) paradigm). Within this context, multimodality (i.e., the coordinated use of different code systems, like language, gesture, and mimics) is considered to be one of the central aspects. The most important modalities in SmartKom are speech recognition, enhanced with various types of gestures, for the input, as well as speech synthesis and graphical displays for the output of information. In specific environments additional devices such as a camera for recognising user satisfaction from facial expression are available. Similarly, the system is able to process gesture input through a hand shape tracking camera or by pen-based touch screen input. One of the major scientific goals of SmartKom is to explore new computational methods for the integration and mutual disambiguation of multimodal input and output on a semantic and pragmatic level (Maybury and Wahlster, 1998; Oviatt and Cohen, 2000; Wahlster et al., 2001).

Technically, SmartKom is realised as a set of distributed parallel processing modules based on a common software infrastructure, called MULTIPLATFORM (Herzog et al., 2003). The strength relies in its foundation in proven distributed computing technology and in its innovative XML-based modelling language called M3L (Wahlster et al., 2001) which is consistently used for the communication between the modules. This enables logging and error analysis and even the simulation of individual modules based on logged data.

Figure 1 shows the module layout in the SmartKom system. Each box represents a processing module connected through data channels (white lines). The arrows indicate directed communication channels.

The modules may conceptually be grouped into different processing layers (cf. Table 1). *Devices* represents an abstraction of the hardware managed by the operating system(s). *Recognisers and analysers* provide different levels of unimodal interpretation of the raw device data and generate a meaning representation. The *media fusion* module merges the information originating from different input modalities. *Interaction modelling and planning* modules model the discourse and context, map the user input into a domain-specific action, and decide upon the subsequent step for the system to take. The *presenta-*

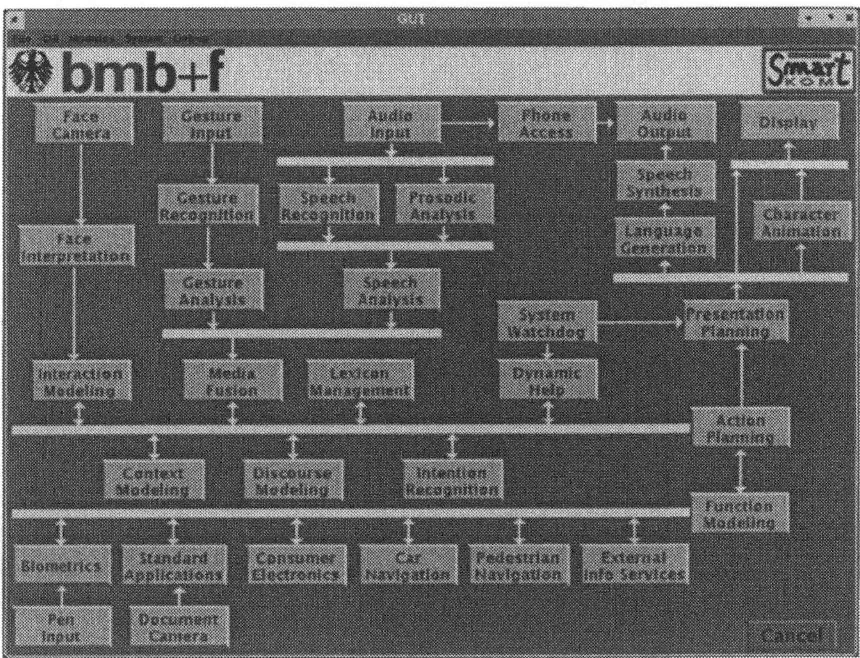

Figure 1. Graphical user interface for tracing the flow of information in SmartKom. The interface reflects the modular software architecture (Wahlster et al., 2001).

tion modules coordinate the output of visual and audio messages. Finally, *services* are back-end functionality providers (e.g., car and pedestrian navigation). Using these generic processing modules, domain-specific applications may be realised using application-specific information in terms of different knowledge bases, such as vocabulary, natural language patterns, and service objects.

The concepts developed for intuitive interfaces have been tested and demonstrated as running systems in three major usage scenarios:

1) *SmartKom Public*: The system will be made available as an advanced multimedia communication centre in central public places such as airports, train stations, or administrative buildings. Here, applications such as video telephony and unified messaging (e.g., scanning a document and sending it as an email or a fax) are targeted. This scenario involves the most sophisticated hardware layout. A face camera is constantly observing the user's facial expression, while an additional camera tracks his hands movements with respect to a projection plane replacing the touch screen.

2) *SmartKom Home/Office*: The system will serve as a personal work and entertainment device comparable to a portable tablet PC, enhanced with multimodal interaction. One of the main application domains is elec-

tronic programme guidance (EPG) and home entertainment electronics control (VCR programming).

3) *SmartKom Mobile*: Realised as a portable device the system acts as a permanent digital companion providing the functionalities and services to the user as a pedestrian or a car driver, i.e., in two different mobile environments. In the following, this scenario will be discussed in detail.

4. Scenarios for Mobile Use

Today's users of mobile devices expect simple and efficient access to data and services in the car. However, the significant differences in the development and life cycles of cars and those of communication devices have so far prevented the establishment of car-specific standards for the majority of mobile devices. Car manufacturers bring up substantial efforts in the design and development of proprietary infotainment systems for in-vehicle use. Nowadays, solutions based on a central display and several operation elements (push buttons) are provided. In-car telephony has pushed the integration of particular audio hardware, like microphones, amplifier and noise cancellation techniques. All these integrated solutions have so far proved superior to external solutions due to a more comfortable operation. However, they are still limited to a small number of services, like navigation, operation of the audio system and the telephone.

Layer	Module names
Devices	Face Camera, **Audio Input**, Phone Access, Audio Output, **Display**
Recognisers and analysers	Face Interpretation, Gesture Recognition, Gesture Interpretation, **Speech Recognition, Prosodic Analysis, Speech Analysis**
Media fusion	**Media Fusion**
Interaction modelling and planning	Interaction Modelling, Context Modelling, Discourse Modelling, Lexicon Management, **Intention Recognition**, System Watchdog, Dynamic Help, **Action Planning**
Presentation	**Presentation Manager**, Language Generation, Speech Synthesis, Character Animation
Services	Function Modelling, Biometrics, Standard Applications, Consumer Electronics, **Car Navigation, Pedestrian Navigation**, External Info Services

Table 1. SmartKom's processing modules may be grouped into several processing layers. The most important modules with respect to SmartKom Mobile are shown in bold face.

The SmartKom Mobile scenario aims at combining the advantages of hardware particularly adapted to the car environment with the flexibility and large variety of services available for mobile devices. The communication system should run on the mobile device, while the car provides suitable periphery hardware for input and output operations. In particular, the driver should benefit from the larger and better placed in-car display and the improved audio functionalities provided by adapted microphone arrays and speakers.

Two usage environments may be distinguished in the SmartKom Mobile scenario:

1) *Pedestrian environment*: The user walks around and carries the SmartKom Mobile device as a permanent and location-aware digital companion. GPS information is provided by a portable sensor connected to it.

2) *Driver environment*: Inside the car the system may be used as a digital assistant that takes advantage of car-specific functionalities, such as real-time information about the car status.

The transition between the two environments takes place when the mobile device is inserted into or removed from its cradle inside the car.

As outlined above, the general goal of the SmartKom project is to make available to the user a common intuitive interaction paradigm in all usage scenarios, whilst flexibly enriching the system with functionality specific to a particular scenario. For SmartKom Mobile, the navigation and location-based information functionality has been chosen as the salient application domain. This functionality includes:

- *Route planning:* A route may consist of multiple segments to be covered either by walking or driving. This requires specifying start and destination locations, as well as optional stops. The user may also wish to specify the route type (e.g., shortest distance versus quickest route). Maps need to be generated that present routes or other related information. For implementing a flexible map interaction involving panning and zooming, the ability to extract more detailed maps is required. Also, in terms of font sizes and level of detail, the style of presentation needs to be adapted according to the output device.

- *Information about points of interest (POI):* This functionality is realised as application data bases which may be accessed any time. For the car environment, parking places are considered to be the most important POIs. For the pedestrian environment, many other types of POIs, such as historical sights, administrative buildings, shops etc. seem to be relevant. The POI data base contains photographs of the respective location, as well as relevant textual information.

- *Route guidance:* This functionality includes *incremental* guidance and monitoring. It involves timed presentation of driving/walking directions as well as the processing of incoming positioning information.

While route planning and POI information may also be useful in other scenarios (e.g., for planning and making reservations at home using SmartKom Home/Office), incremental route guidance is only available within SmartKom Mobile.

Regarding the appropriate applications for SmartKom Mobile, focus has been placed on services that are commonly agreed to be highly relevant for intelligent transportation systems (see, for instance, an initiative by the Canadian Ministry of Transport to establish a common structure for the design of these types of systems[2]) and that are not yet fully commercially available. Route planning and parking place reservation have therefore been implemented as car-specific services. An integrated route planning functionality, involving a combination of the car and pedestrian navigation services has also been realised. For the pedestrian environment, incremental guidance was implemented using a portable GPS sensor.

5. Demonstrator Architecture

Technically, the prototype version of the SmartKom Mobile demonstrator system consists of four computing devices: the car PC, the handheld PDA and two additional portable notebook computers (Bühler et al., 2002). The latter ones are required because the SmartKom research prototype cannot be run on the PDA for a number of reasons, the most important being the resource consumption. Instead, the system's main processing is performed on the two notebook computers, running under Windows XP/2000 and Linux, respectively. However, in the pedestrian environment the interaction is performed through the PDA acting as a periphery client for both voice and graphical data. The term "mobile device" therefore describes the combination of the PDA and the notebook computers. The communication between the computers is realised through a wireless LAN connection (802.11b).

The PDA is a HP iPAQ H3660 running at 206 MHz with 64 megabytes of memory. The operating system is Linux. The screen size is 240 x 320 pixels. For receiving graphical data from the notebook computer through TCP/IP and the screen output, as well as for capturing pen input, standard Virtual Network Computing (VNC) open source software was used. However, for capturing audio data from the PDA's built-in microphone and for reacting to the PDA's short cut buttons, specific software needed to be implemented (Malaka et al., 2004). Similarly to the handheld PDA, the car PC manages all access to the car-specific hardware, i.e., the central display, the car interior audio system, and the push-to-activate (PTA) lever at the steering wheel.

The following information has been taken from the SmartKom demonstration video (Blocher et al., 2003). A high resolution central TFT display (cf. Figure 2, left image) has been integrated in the car. Since the resolution and geometry of the display differs significantly from the handheld device's display, a specialised presentation mode had to be developed: As shown in Figure 3 (a), the display space is partitioned in two presentation zones. In the left area, a presentation of important data is shown in the style that is used for the handheld device. The remaining area is usually used for displaying the virtual character Smartakus. This display is also used for presenting additional detailed information about sights or parking places when appropriate.

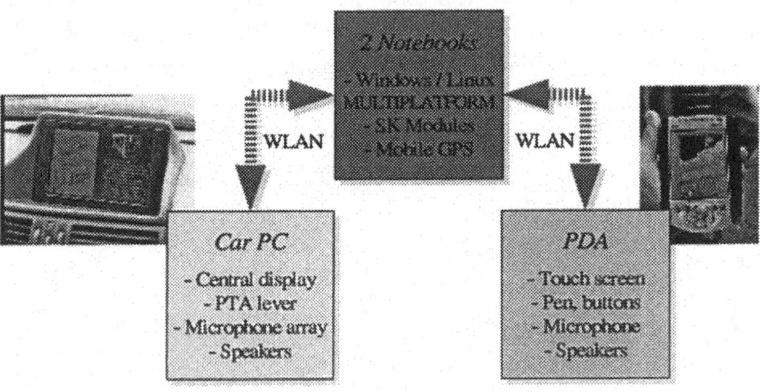

Figure 2. Conceptual outline of the architecture used in the SmartKom Mobile system (left image taken from the SmartKom demonstration video[3], right image taken from (Bühler et al., 2003)).

The audio output was realised by streaming audio data via the mobile car PC to the stereo speakers built in the car. A microphone array is used for acquiring audio input.

The PTA lever on the right of the steering wheel is managed by the car PC. The lever is pulled by the user either to activate the car environment after having used the handheld device or to start speech input when the car environment is already active, e.g., whilst driving.

6. Dialogue Design

When designing multimodal dialogues for mobile environments the context of use and also the specific user requirements need to be taken into account. Some modalities may be reasonable and desired, while others may distract the user, violate privacy or disturb others. The transition between different modalities needs to be modelled accordingly, i.e., the pedestrian user is able

(a)

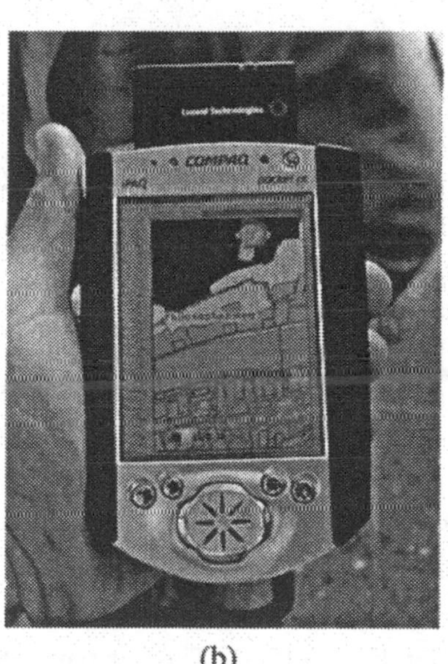

(b)

Figure 3. SmartKom Mobile's display layout in the two environments: (a) car central display shown a city map and information about a selected sight (image taken from the SmartKom demonstration video (Blocher et al., 2003), (b) handheld device showing a pedestrian route (image taken from (Bühler et al., 2003)).

to combine speech and pen input on the PDA, while the car driver has to rely exclusively on speech input due to safety reasons.

Wizard-of-Oz experiments were performed (Türk, 2001; Steininger et al., 2002) in parallel to the development of the first SmartKom Public demonstrator. Even though most relevant for a different scenario, these experiments strongly influenced the design process for SmartKom Mobile. The dialogues were realised as natural as possible using mixed initiative, natural speech, barge-in, and brief prompting. With one aim of the project being to provide the user a high level of control over the interaction, suitable repair mechanisms for potential errors had to ensure that the dialogue strategy appears clear and consistent. Another consideration has been to keep the internal organisation of dialogue structures as simple as possible by breaking complex dialogues into smaller, simpler modules. The following example interaction (translated from German) illustrates the dialogue design for the two mobile environments:

The user is driving:

USR: *I would like to go from here to Heidelberg.*

SmartKom understands the start and destination cities for the car route and presents a street map of Heidelberg (cf. Figure 3 (a)).

SMA: *One moment please ...*
SMA: *Here is the map ...*
SMA: *Where do you want to go in Heidelberg?*
USR: *I would like to know more about the Old Bridge.*

The multimedia tourism database is queried for information about the *Old Bridge*. A slide show is presented by Smartakus, shown in the right portion of Figure 3 (a).

SMA: *Here you have some information about the Old Bridge.*
USR: *I want to go there.*

From the dialogue context, the anaphoric word *there* is resolved as referring to the *Old Bridge*. The parking places closest to *Old Bridge* are queried, all system modules are dynamically updated to handle these new entries and a city map with the parking places is presented.

SMA: *Here is the map. Where do you want to park?*
USR: *At Kisselgasse.*

The route is now completely specified. The car navigation service is queried for the complete car route. Before calculating the route, which may take several seconds, a self-explaining message is generated:

SMA: *The route is being calculated ...*

Then, the screen is filled with a map showing the route to the parking place in the *Kisselgasse*.

SMA: *Here you can see the shortest route from here to Heidelberg.*

Upon arrival at the selected parking place in Heidelberg, the user leaves his car. The handheld device is activated and the car PC switched-off. (Alternatively, the user may activate the handheld manually, by pressing a button.)

SMA: *I can show you the footpath from Kisselgasse to Old Bridge.*
USR: *Yes, please.*

The second part of the complete route, the foot path is calculated in the pedestrian navigation module (cf. Figure 1) and presented in the same way as the car route.

SMA: *The route is being calculated ...*
SMA: *Here you can see the footpath from Kisselgasse to Old Bridge.*

The user issues a simple multimodal request:

USR: *<Pointing to the Castle> Oh actually, I would like to go there instead.*

The underspecified unimodal hypotheses produces by the natural language and gesture understanding modules are combined in the media fusion module (cf. Figure 1). Thus, the anaphoric expression is resolved as referring to the representation of the Castle.

SMA: *The route is being calculated ...*
SMA: *Here you can see the footpath from Kisselgasse to Castle.*

The user may now use the GPS-based pedestrian guidance for detailed instructions how to get to the castle (Malaka et al., 2004).

7. Outlook - Towards Flexible Modality Control

It may be concluded from the experiences gained with the SmartKom Mobile prototype, that a multimodal dialogue system should be flexible enough in terms of the modality or the combination of different modalities (even monomodal) to use.

The situations for a limited multimodal interaction are manifold. For instance, unrestricted multimodal output may lead to privacy problems. Requiring input in a certain modality, such as pointing gestures, from a user who may be occupied in doing something else than interacting with the system may also lead to inconvenience, or, even worse, to safety problems. The latter ones are most apparent in the SmartKom Mobile scenario.

The aim of this section is an attempt to identify the particular requirements for modality control in the SmartKom Mobile scenario. Based on experience in developing and testing speech-based user interfaces in mobile environments (Minker et al., 2004), five characteristic combinations of modalities have been identified, i.e., *interaction modes* (cf. Figure 4). The technical realisation of this framework in the current demonstration system may be viewed as incomplete. However, the analysis may prove useful for future multimodal systems in similar domains.

SmartKom Mobile is based on speech and graphical input and output. The interaction modes range from purely speech interaction to purely graphics-based interaction with the default mode enabling both modalities. For both

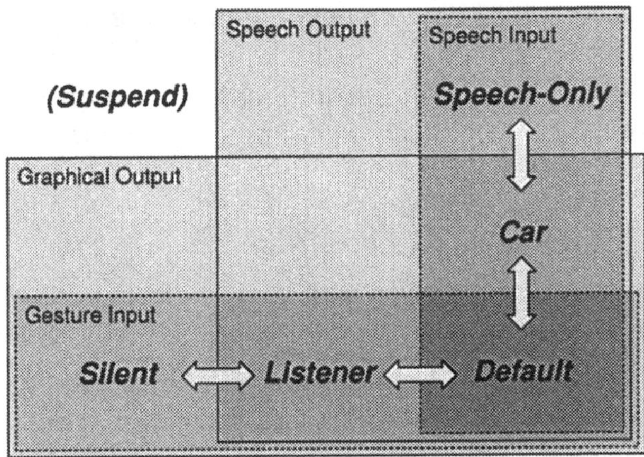

Figure 4. Interaction modes as combinations of communication modalities in SmartKom Mobile. The inter-modal transitions are described in the text (Bühler et al., 2002).

speech and graphics, the input modality is only available if the respective output modality is available as well. However, speech output may complement a mainly graphics-based interaction, as well as graphical displays may enhance spoken messages.

In Figure 4, the *Default* mode is mainly used in the pedestrian environment and when privacy or disturbing others is not an issue. All modalities are enabled. However, this mode is not available in the driver environment since there is not means of gesture input and analysis. When the car is not moving, the user may activate the handheld instead. In the *Listener* mode the user accepts spoken system output but he does not use speech as an input modality (i.e., the user plays the role of a listener). Spoken output is useful for quickly providing concise summaries as well as extended background information to the user. His focus of attention is placed on tasks others than interacting with the system. The user may employ ear phones in order to protect his privacy. In the listener mode, the system should not encourage the user to provide spoken input. It should therefore generate prompts like "Show me ..." rather than "Tell me ...". The *Silent* mode seems particularly useful when speech-based interaction is problematic (e.g., in certain public places or in public transportation). The interface acts similarly to a traditional graphical user interface.

The *Car* mode may be viewed as a restricted version of the *Default* mode for use mainly in the driver environment. Speech is the dominant communication modality, while graphical displays are used only for presenting additional ("non-vital") information, such as maps for presenting a route whilst driving or the locations of parking options. Consequently, the display does not need to be touch-sensitive. The *Speech-Only* mode is mainly used in the driver environment, notably when the car is moving. Any additional safety risk (such as driver distraction from the driving task by gesture input or graphical output) must be avoided. System interaction is restricted to the audio channel, i.e., the use of a speech-only dialogue is mandatory. Technically, suspending the interaction with the system may also be viewed as a transition to a special *(Suspend)* interaction mode. Thus, in this mode the interaction with the system is temporarily frozen, but may be resumed at any time.

8. Conclusion

In this chapter, SmartKom Mobile, the application scenario and demonstration prototype of the SmartKom system in mobile environments have been described. The definition of the Mobile scenario is motivated by analyses of intelligent transport systems architectures and standards indicating the need for new mobile services and forms of human-machine interaction. The services selected for the SmartKom Mobile prototype are route planning and location-based information services such as parking place search and tourist information. The SmartKom system is novel with respect to other research projects in the field in that it is designed for two significantly different mobile environments: a user can walk around interacting with the system on a PDA or plug it into a docking station for using it whilst driving. In particular, the SmartKom Mobile system provides an interaction paradigm which, although adapted to the different situations of use, is uniform in the sense that it employs the same basic design principles as for SmartKom Home and Public, such as its virtual character *Smartakus* enabling natural language interaction. Technically, the architecture of the SmartKom Mobile prototype is based on wireless client/server communication between the "interaction devices" (i.e., handheld and car PC) and conventional PCs, with the main processing being performed in the background.

In an outlook, a framework for a flexible modality control driven by the requirements of the SmartKom Mobile application scenario has been presented. One of the main goal has been to illustrate the necessity of being able to handle situations in which different (combinations of) modalities are preferable. Although open questions concerning an actual implementation of the modality control still remain, such a framework is clearly necessary for making multimodal interaction practical in the every day lives of the general public (considering, for instance, speech or sight-impaired users.)

Acknowledgements

This chapter is based on research carried out within the German Federal Ministry for Education and Research (BMBF) Project SmartKom. The authors have carried out major parts of the described research during their professional activity at DaimlerChrysler - Research and Technology. They want to thank all the partners involved in the project, in particular André Berton, Jochen Häußler and Sven Krüger.

Notes

1. http://www.onstar.com/
2. http://www.its-sti.gc.ca/

References

Almeida, L., Amdal, I., Beires, N., Boualem, M., Boves, L., den Os, E., Filoche, P., Gomes, R., Knudsen, J. E., Kvale, K., Rugelbak, J., Tallec, C., and Warakagoda, N. (2002). The MUST guide to Paris; implementation and expert evaluation of a multimodal tourist guide to Paris. In *Proceedings of ISCA Tutorial and Research Workshop Multimodal Dialogue in Mobile Environments (IDS02)*, Kloster Irsee, Germany.

Blocher, A., Häußler, J., Kaiser, J., and Reithinger, N. (2003). SmartKom video demonstration. http://www.smartkom.org/.

Bühler, D., Minker, W., Häussler, J., and Krüger, S. (2002). The SmartKom Mobile multi-modal dialogue system. In *Proceedings of ISCA Tutorial and Research Workshop Multimodal Dialogue in Mobile Environments (IDS02)*, Kloster Irsee, Germany.

Bühler, D., Vignier, S., Heisterkamp, P., and Minker, W. (2003). Safety and operating issues for mobile human-machine interfaces. In *Proceedings of International Conference on Intelligent User Interfaces (IUI)*, pages 227–229, Miami, Florida, USA.

Gärtner, U., König, W., and Wittig, T. (2001). Evaluation of manual vs. speech input when using a driver information system in real traffic. In *Proceedings of International Driving Symposium on Human Factors in Driver Assessment, Training and Vehicle Design*, pages 7–13, Aspen, Colorado, USA.

Green, P. (2000). Crashes induced by driver information systems and what can be done to reduce them. In *Proceedings of Convergence*, pages 26–36, Warrendale, Pennsylvania, USA. Society of Automotive Engineers.

Hansen, J. H., Zhang, X., Akbacak, M., Yapanel, U., Pellom, B., and Ward, W. (2003). CU-Move: Advances in in-vehicle speech systems for route navigation. In *Proceedings of IEEE Workshop in DSP in Mobile and Vehicular Systems*, pages 1–6, Nagoya, Japan.

Herzog, G., Kirchmann, H., Merten, S., Ndiaye, A., and Poller, P. (2003). MULTIPLATFORM Testbed: An integration platform for multimodal dialog systems. In Cunningham, H. and Patrick, J., editors, *Proceedings of HLT-NAACL Workshop on Software Engineering and Architecture of Language Technology Systems (SEALTS)*, pages 75–82, Edmonton, Canada.

Johnston, M., Bangalore, S., Vasireddy, G., Stent, A., Ehlen, P., Walker, M., Whittaker, S., and Maloor, P. (2002). MATCH: An architecture for multimodal dialogue systems. In *Proceedings of Annual Meeting of the Association for Computational Linguistics (ACL)*, pages 376–383, Philadelphia, Pennsylvania, USA.

Johnston, M. S., Bangalore, S., and Vasireddy, G. (2001). MATCH: Multimodal access to city help. In *Proceedings of IEEE Automatic Speech Recognition and Understanding Workshop (ASRU)*, Madonna di Campiglio, Italy.

Krüger, A., Butz, A., Müller, C., Stahl, C., Wasinger, R., Steinberg, K.-E., and Dirschl, A. (2004). The connected user interface: Realizing a personal situated navigation service. In *Proceedings of International Conference on Intelligent User Interfaces (IUI)*, pages 161–168, Funchal, Madeira, Portugal.

Malaka, R., Häussler, J., and Aras, H. (2004). SmartKom mobile: intelligent ubiquitous user interaction. In *Proceedings of International Conference on Intelligent User Interfaces (IUI)*, pages 310–312, Funchal, Madeira, Portugal.

Maybury, M. and Wahlster, W. (1998). *Readings in Intelligent User Interfaces*. Morgan Kaufmann, San Francisco, California, USA.

Minker, W., Haiber, U., Heisterkamp, P., and Scheible, S. (2003). Intelligent dialog overcomes speech technology limitations: The SENECA example. In *Proceedings of International Conference on Intelligent User Interfaces (IUI)*, pages 267–269, Miami, Florida, USA.

Minker, W., Haiber, U., Heisterkamp, P., and Scheible, S. (2004). Design, implementation and evaluation of the SENECA spoken language dialogue system. In Minker, W., Bühler, D., and Dybkjær, L., editors, *Spoken Multimodal Human-Computer Dialogue in Mobile Environments*. Kluwer Academic Publishers, Dordrecht, The Netherlands. (this volume).

Oviatt, S. and Cohen, P. (2000). Perceptual user interfaces – multimodal interfaces that process what comes naturally. *Communications of the ACM*, 43(3):45–53.

Pellom, B., Ward, W., and Pradhan, S. (2000). The CU Communicator: An architecture for dialogue systems. In *Proceedings of International Conference on Spoken Language Processing (ICSLP)*, pages 723–726, Beijing, China.

Pieraccini, R., Carpenter, B., Woudenberg, E., Caskey, S., Springer, S., Bloom, J., and Phillips, M. (2002). Multi-modal spoken dialog with wireless devices. In *Proceedings of ISCA Tutorial and Research Workshop Multimodal Dialogue in Mobile Environments (IDS02)*, Kloster Irsee, Germany.

Steininger, S., Schiel, F., and Glesner, A. (2002). Labeling procedures for the multi-modal data collection of SmartKom. In *Proceedings of International Conference on Language Resources and Evaluation (LREC)*, pages 371–377, Las Palmas, Gran Canaria, Spain.

Türk, U. (2001). The technical processing in SmartKom data collection: A case study. In *Proceedings of European Conference on Speech Communication and Technology (EUROSPEECH)*, pages 1541–1544, Aalborg, Denmark.

Wahlster, W., editor (2000). *Verbmobil: Foundations of Speech-to-Speech Translation*. Springer-Verlag, Berlin/Heidelberg, Germany.

Wahlster, W., Reithinger, N., and Blocher, A. (2001). SmartKom: Multimodal communication with a life-like character. In *Proceedings of European Conference on Speech Communication and Technology (EUROSPEECH)*, pages 1547–1550, Aalborg, Denmark.

Chapter 12

LARRI: A LANGUAGE-BASED MAINTENANCE AND REPAIR ASSISTANT

Dan Bohus, Alexander I. Rudnicky
Carnegie Mellon University, Pittsburgh, Pennsylvania, USA
{ dbohus,air } @cs.cmu.edu

Abstract LARRI (**L**anguage-based **A**gent for **R**etrieval of **R**epair **I**nformation) is a dialogue-based system for support of maintenance and repair domains, characterised by large amounts of documentation and procedural information. LARRI is based on an architecture developed by Carnegie Mellon University for the DARPA Communicator programme and is integrated with a wearable computer system developed by the Wearable Computing Group at CMU. The system adapts an architecture developed and optimised for a telephone-based problem solving task (travel planning), and applies it to a very different domain - aircraft maintenance. Following two field trials in which LARRI was used by professional aircraft mechanics, we found that our architecture extended readily to a multimodal and multi-media framework. At the same time we found that assumptions that were reasonable in a services domain turn out to be inappropriate for a maintenance domain. Apart from the need to manage integration between input modes and output modalities, we found that the system needed to support multiple categories of tasks and that a different balance between user and system goals was required. A significant problem in the maintenance domain is the need to assimilate and make available for language processing appropriate domain information.

Keywords: Multimodal interactive systems; Maintenance and repair domain; Task representation; Field trials.

1. Introduction

LARRI (**L**anguage-based **A**gent for **R**etrieval of **R**epair **I**nformation) is a dialogue-based system that provides the necessary support and guidance for aircraft mechanics during maintenance and repair activities. LARRI is based

W. Minker, D. Bühler and L. Dybkjær (eds), Spoken Multimodal Human-Computer Dialogue in Mobile Environments, 203-218

on an architecture developed by Carnegie Mellon University for the DARPA Communicator programme and is integrated with a wearable computer system obtained from the Wearable Computing Group at CMU (see, e.g., (Smailagic et al., 2001)).

LARRI is interesting in that it takes an architecture developed and optimised for a telephone-based problem solving task (travel planning), and applies it to a very different domain - aircraft maintenance. On the positive side, we found that our architecture extended readily to a multimodal and multi-media framework. At the same time we found that certain assumptions built into the system that were reasonable in a services domain turn out to be inappropriate for a maintenance domain. For example, the time-scale of activity in the maintenance domain is significantly different. In the travel-planning scenario the primary goal is to help the user rapidly find a satisfactory solution. In the maintenance domain, rapid and accurate solution is no longer the main goal; rather, accurate task execution and easy access to relevant maintenance-related information are the main goals. Moreover the system needs to provide two different usage modes: browsing and guidance. In the former, the user expects to be able to search for information and examine procedures; in the latter, the user and the system need to cooperatively carry out the step sequence associated with a given procedure. In both cases the underlying domain knowledge is the same, but the user's task and hence the structure of the dialogue are different. Our approach to dialogue system design reflects this separation of task and domain.

We continue by describing LARRI's capabilities and functionality, illustrated by a sample interaction with the system. Subsequently, Section 3 presents the architectural and implementational details behind the various system components. In Section 4 we describe a field study with US Navy F/A-18 mechanics, and discuss our current and planned future efforts for improving the system, in light of the feedback obtained during these field trials. Finally, Section 5 concludes the chapter.

2. LARRI - System Description

LARRI is a multimodal system that provides support of maintenance and repair activities for aircraft mechanics. The system implements a Level 4/5 IETM (Interactive Electronic Technical Manual)[1]. Level 4 IETMs are characterised by a hypertext structure, while Level 5 IETMs are intended to incorporate elements of an expert system into the document. We consider the introduction of a language-based interface to be a first step towards Level 5 IETMs. While the use of such documentation is not currently widespread, it represents the next step in the evolution of documentation for complex systems, particularly military ones[2]. LARRI therefore explores the potential integration between language-based interfaces and such materials.

The system integrates a graphical user interface (GUI) for easy visualisation of dense technical information (i.e., instructions, video streams, animations, annotations) with a spoken dialogue system that facilitates information access and offers task guidance and mentoring in the maintenance environment. In the typical field setup, the graphical interface (illustrated in Figure 1) is accessible via a head-worn display connected to a wearable client computer. A rotary mouse (dial) provides direct access to the GUI elements.

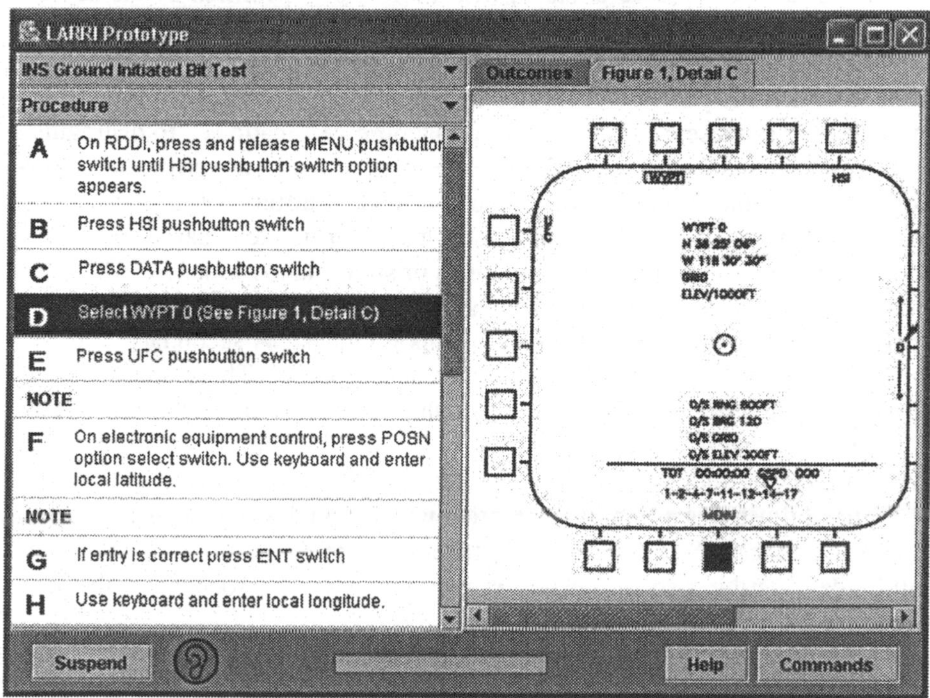

Figure 1. LARRI's graphical user interface.

The natural language spoken-dialogue component enhances GUI functionality (which provides only for simple selection), with support for natural language commands and for direct information access. The preponderance of hands- and eyes-busy situations in this domain makes natural language dialogue a very attractive interaction modality. Communication becomes possible in parallel with manual work, and unwieldy interface devices (such as keyboards) can be eliminated. The use of natural language also provides opportunities for increased efficiency and flexibility: the user can interact with the system both on a simple command level (manipulating the GUI elements or simply stepping through a procedure) and on a goal-oriented level (issuing more complex commands, which are subsequently translated by the system into a corresponding chain of actions). Last but not least, evidence from areas such as intelligent training and tutoring systems indicates that the use of speech and sound to convey information improves learner/user performance (Goodman, 1993).

Next, we present the structure of the typical task in this domain, and then illustrate it based on a sample interaction with LARRI. The typical maintenance task consists of a sequence of steps, which are to be performed by the aircraft maintainer in a certain order. The large majority of the steps (*basic steps*) encapsulate a set of instructions, optionally followed by a set of verification questions in which the possible outcomes of the step are discussed (in the sequel, we will refer to these questions as "step-outcome verifications", to distinguish them from the traditional grounding-related use of the term verification question). The various outcomes of a step can lead to different branches, either within the same task, or into a new (sub-)task. Basic steps can also include additional information, such as animations or short video sequences which are to be displayed to the user, or various step-specific annotations introduced by previous maintainers which are available upon request. A secondary, and less frequent class of steps are *notes*, *warnings* and *cautions*. These are also visually present, and can be read to the user either at the system's own initiative or at the user's request (depending on the severity of the situation), but have no outcomes or any additional information attached.

Figure 2 illustrates a sample interaction with LARRI. Both the user (U:) and system utterances (S:) are presented, together with annotations on the right-hand side describing some specific system behaviours associated with those turns.

An interaction with LARRI consists of a login phase, followed by the aided execution of several tasks and finally a logout phase. Once the user identifies himself to the system, LARRI will retrieve his profile and current schedule from a backend agent (lines 1-2). Subsequently the schedule is displayed and LARRI engages in a multimodal negotiation dialogue to establish the tasks for the current session (lines 3-8). Once a task has been selected and confirmed, the system retrieves the contents of the task from another backend agent, and presents a brief summary of its current state (in case it was left incomplete.)

Lines 10-27 in Figure 2 illustrate LARRI's behaviour in task guidance mode. The system typically reads step instructions aloud (lines 10, 14, 16, 22), and waits for an acknowledgement from the user (lines 11, 15) before moving on to verify the outcomes of that step (lines 12-13). As the maintainers are actually performing a domain task while using with the system, the interaction becomes asynchronous, and the turn-taking behaviour is more complex than

1 S:	Hi, welcome to LARRI. To log in, please state your name	***Login phase***
2 *U:*	*Hi, my name is John Doe*	*Profile retrieval*
3 S:	Hello John Doe. Your schedule for today is displayed on the screen **<displays schedule>**. Task number 1 is urgent and should be completed immediately. To select a task to work on, please say or press the task number.	*Task list negotiation*
4 *U:*	*I'll do task number one*	
5 S:	You have selected the INS BIT test on aircraft 301. Is that correct ?	
6 *U:*	*<clicks Confirm>*	
7 S:	... ...	*System presents*
8 S:	... ...	*task summary*
9 *U:*	*Ready to work*	
10 S:	Okay. Now starting phase 2. Step A: On RDDI press and release the MENU pushbutton switch until HSI pushbutton switch option appears	***Task guidance*** *Step execution*
11 *U:*	*Okay, I've done that*	
12 S:	Does the RDDI menu display the HSI ?	*Step-outcome verification*
13 *U:*	*Affirmative*	
14 S:	Step B: Now press the HSI pushbutton switch	
15 *U:*	*Ok. RDDI displays the HSI. Go to the next one.*	
16 S:	Ok. Step C: Press the DATA pushbutton switch	
17 *U:*	*<long timeout>*	
18 S:	Did you press the DATA pushbutton ?	*State clarification*
19 *U:*	*Yes, I just did*	
20 S:	Does the RDDI display DATA option display with the WYPT option boxed ?	*Step-outcome verification*
21 *U:*	*Yes*	
22 S:	Ok. Step D: Select WYPT 0	
23 *U:*	*Show me the figure*	
24 S:	**<displays figure>** Select WYPT 0	*Speech activated*
25 *U:*	*Show me the outcomes*	*GUI elements*
26 S:	**<displays possible outcomes for step D>**	
27 *U:*	*Okay. WPT is 0 and the latitude is local*	
28 S:	Good. Skipping to step J. On RDDI press and release MENU pushbutton switch until BIT pushbutton switch option appears.	*Branch on outcome*
27 *L:*	... ...	

Figure 2. A sample interaction with LARRI.

in the typical information access domain. To adapt, LARRI uses step-specific timeouts based on the estimated time-to-completion of each step to perform state clarification (lines 18-19). Finally, in lines 24-26, the user issues spoken commands for activating certain graphical user interface elements that provide auxiliary information pertaining to the current step.

Apart from providing guidance, LARRI also supports a browsing mode, in which the maintainer can perform random access to the documentation/task.

This is achieved either by directly accessing the various graphical user interface elements with a pointing device (such as the dial) or by issuing a set of spoken language commands such as "go to step 15", "go to the next phase" etc.

Once a maintenance task has been completed, the system provides again a brief summary of the completed activity, updates the corresponding information on the back-end side, and moves to the next scheduled task. Finally, upon completion of all the scheduled tasks, the user is logged out of the system and the session is concluded.

3. LARRI - Hardware and Software Architecture

LARRI is implemented as a distributed client-server architecture, illustrated in Figure 3. When tested in the field the system runs on three separate computers, one worn by the user and two stand-alone servers (laptop computers). For development purposes, the system runs however on a single desktop computer. The wearable platform hosts clients for audio input and output, and the graphical user interface. Other components (i.e., speech recognition, language understanding, dialogue management, language generation and synthesis, task-specific agents, etc.) run on the server side. Communication between the two sides is accomplished over an 802.11b link, using (TCP/IP) socket connections.

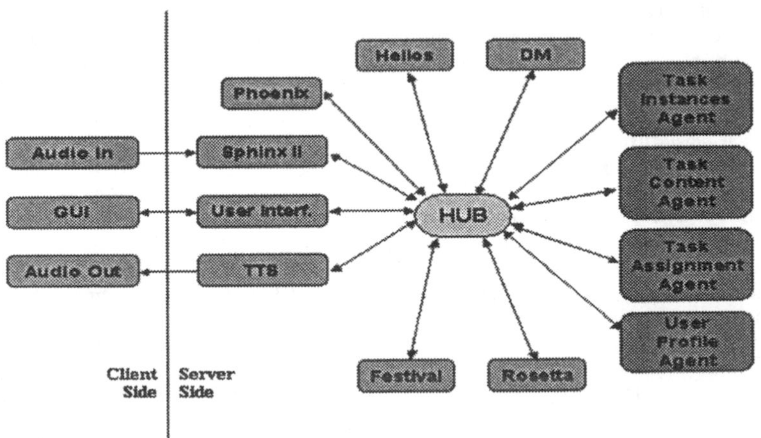

Figure 3. LARRI's Galaxy-based architecture.

To date we have experimented with three different wearable platforms. In the field trials described in Section 4, a prototype IBM wearable device was used. It consisted of a Pentium 233 MMX processor, with 64 MB RAM and a 680 MB hard drive, equivalent to an IBM ThinkPad 560X, but weighing 400 grams and measuring 26 x 80 x 120 mm. In that setup, the device is worn in a belt that enables participants to move the location of the computer to a comfortable area along their torso. The head-worn display, developed at IBM's Watson Research Center, has a small liquid crystal chip with an image transmitted by a prism and redirected to the user's eye. With the magnifying optics contained in this device, it appears to users that they are reading a full-sized desktop computer screen with VGA resolution. LARRI uses a Gentex 100902 noise-cancelling microphone, which is boom-mounted on a cranial (helmet) worn by the mechanic. The Gentex provides a high level of acoustic noise cancellation and allows the system to operate in the hangar environment (where the ambient noise is 85-95 dBA). Speech is acquired using a Telex H-551 USB digitiser and is sampled at 11.025 kHz and 16 bits.

We have also experimented with a Compaq iPAQ 3675 PDA computer. This device is equipped with a StrongArm SA-1110 processor, 64MB of RAM and 32MB of flash-ROM. It has a built-in colour TFT display with a resolution of 240x320 pixels at 64K colours, as well as built-in sound capabilities (Phillips UDA1341TS soundchip). From a laboratory experimentation perspective, this setup is more convenient as it is lighter and benefits from increased mobility. We are currently using it to study performance issues for future mobile systems. For instance, moving more of the server software on the wearable side, can reduce server processing load and overall network traffic.

Finally, a third wearable we are considering is the Fujitsu Stylistic LT P-600 Tablet PC. Performance-wise, this computer is equivalent to a mid-range laptop computer, but has a 24.4x16.0x2.8 cm form factor. It is equipped with a Pentium III 600/300Mhz processor (Intel SpeedStep), 256MB of RAM, 15GB HDD, and has a large 8.4" TFT SVGA display, and SoundBlaster Pro Compatible Audio. This platform is capable of running the entire system.

From a software perspective, LARRI is built upon the Galaxy (Seneff et al., 1998) architecture. On the server side, the system is composed of a series of modules, implemented as parallel processes (i.e., speech recognition, understanding, synthesis, dialogue management, etc.) that interact with each other by passing messages via a central programmable traffic-router—the Galaxy Hub (see Figure 3). Below, we present more details about each of LARRI's components.

Audio in/out. The audio input and output clients are running on the wearable side. Although in the current version they merely relay audio streams over socket connections to and from the server, we are currently investigating the possibility of transferring part of the recognition front-end and a light version of Festival synthesis, Flite (Black and Lenzo, 2001), to the audio clients on the wearable.

Graphical user interface. The Graphical User Interface runs on the wearable side, and its latest version has been written in Java using Swing, to ensure a maximum of portability across different platforms. The interface can be controlled both by events originating from a pointing input device (such as a dial or a stylus), as well as by commands arriving from the dialogue manager. Conversely, the GUI sends notifications to the dialogue management level reflecting the stream of direct manipulation events. Finally, the user interface also interacts with the speech recognition component, providing visual feedback to the users in terms of noise levels, and various recognition status indicators.

Speech recognition. Speech recognition is performed with the SPHINX II (Huang et al., 1993) decoder, using semi-continuous HMMs. Acoustic models were trained using the WSJ-0 corpus of wide-band read speech, and a class-based, trigram language model was constructed and used for recognition. The current vocabulary, covering the INS BIT Test procedure and general system commands, contains 444 words.

Parsing. LARRI uses the Phoenix robust parser (Ward and Issar, 1994) to produce semantic representations of the user's spoken utterances. A semantic grammar, containing 63 top-level concepts, provides coverage for the generic interaction commands, as well as for domain and task-specific objects (i.e., addressing various push-buttons and LED indicators involved in the INS BIT Test, etc.). As discussed later (see Section 4.2.2), given the demands imposed by the vast amounts of technical documentation in this domain, the automatic (or semi-automatic) extraction of domain-specific grammar information from unstructured, mere textual representations of procedures represents one of the major future challenges for building language-enabled interfaces with good scalability characteristics.

HELIOS. This component handles multimodal integration in LARRI. It receives inputs on two separate streams. One stream contains the semantic representations of the user's spoken utterances, as received from parser (Phoenix). The second stream contains the input events captured by the graphical user interface (the GUI sends the events through the **User Interface Module**, which translates them into Phoenix-like parses, and then forwards them to Helios). Helios merges the two streams, augments the inputs with confidence information and forwards them to the Dialogue Management module.

Dialogue management. Initially, LARRI employed a dialogue management component based on the AGENDA architecture (Xu and Rudnicky, 2000). More recently, work at Carnegie Mellon University has led to the development of a new dialogue management framework, dubbed RavenClaw (Bohus and Rudnicky, 2003), and currently employed in LARRI.

RavenClaw draws upon and extends the ideas of the AGENDA architecture, and allows for rapid development of dialogue management components for goal-oriented, multimodal spoken dialogue systems operating in complex domains. The framework provides a clear separation between the domain-dependent dialogue task and domain-independent conversational behaviours. The dialogue task logic is described in terms of a hierarchical decomposition of basic dialogue agents, in which each agent handles the conversation for a particular subpart of the task. The dialogue engine uses this hierarchical decomposition of the task to drive the dialogue, and, at the same time contributes basic conversational strategies, such as timing and turn-taking behaviours, grounding behaviours, support for universal dialogue mechanisms like repeat, suspend, start-over, help etc. One particularly important feature of RavenClaw in this setting is that the dialogue task structure can be dynamically generated/extended at runtime. More specifically, in LARRI, once the maintenance task to be performed has been identified and retrieved from the domain agents, the dialogue agents corresponding to each step, message, image, etc. in the maintenance task are automatically created, and inserted in the corresponding place in the dialogue task hierarchy. For a more detailed account of the RavenClaw dialogue management framework, the reader is referred to (Bohus and Rudnicky, 2003).

Domain agents. On the back-end side, LARRI communicates with 4 separate domain agents that handle user profiles, the maintenance tasks library, as well as task instantiation and assignment information. Currently, the maintenance tasks and procedures are described in terms of a special-purpose declarative language (TML, Task Markup Language). This language is used both for defining *task types* (i.e., the structure of certain tasks, in terms of phases, steps, and the relationships between them), as well as *task instances*, which include additional information pertaining to each specific task instantiation (i.e., the completion status of each phase/step, how much time each step took, various user annotations, etc.). The three task domain agents retrieve this representation from a database, and then provide it to the dialogue manager which uses it to construct the appropriate dialogue agents, as described above. For illustrative purposes, we show in Figure 4 an excerpt from an actual task instance, as represented in this formalism.

Natural language generation. LARRI uses the ROSETTA natural language generation component, employing generic canned expressions, template-based prompts as well as prompts based on material in the task representation (e.g., `instructions` in Figure 4). The language generation com-

```
{
step_id 0003
step_gui_id INS.1.5
step_name c
step_type basic_step
instructions On GND PWR control panel assembly, set and
           hold 1 and 2 switches to B on for 3 seconds
estimated_time 30
default_execute_pointer next_step
outcomes_array :  1
   {
      {
      outcome_nr 1
      outcome_gui_id INS.1.5
      outcome Switches latch and remain on.
      execute_pointer_yes next_step
      execute_pointer_no task 00009
      result 1
      }
   }
start_time 010912-20:13:10
end_time 010912-20:14:02
completed 1
}
```

Figure 4. An excerpt from a task instance representation expressed in TML: the italicised material shows the instance-specific elements added to the basic type when it is instantiated for purposes of guiding the user through a procedure. Note the use of an `estimated_time` parameter that allows the system to trigger reprompts at the appropriate time (when in guidance mode).

ponent receives from the dialogue manager a frame-based semantic representation of the output to be generated. The information in the frame uniquely identifies the prompt and specifies the various parameters and values to be used for filling in the templates when necessary. In our current system, the prompts capturing the task material (e.g., the instructions for the steps, the step-outcome verification questions, the texts for the notes and warnings) were manually prepared starting from the textual instructions available for the INS BIT Test. This situation is therefore similar with the issue of providing grammar coverage for the task: automatic (or semi-automatic) acquisition of this information represents a problem that needs to be addressed before LARRI can be efficiently extended to a large number of tasks in this domain.

Synthesis. Speech synthesis is performed using a Festival-based unit-selection synthesiser (Black and Lenzo, 2000). A limited domain voice was created especially for this task, with a fall-back to a general diphone-unit voice. Limited-domain voices are created from a database of utterances recorded especially for the domain at hand and permit the use of larger units (corresponding to words and phrases) that maximise intelligibility.

4. Experiments and Results

4.1 Field Evaluation

To better understand how the various elements of the system perform under realistic conditions, we evaluated LARRI on two separate occasions, once in July 2001 and once in December 2001. The evaluations took place at the Naval Strike Aircraft Test Squadron, Pautuxent River Naval Air Station, Maryland, with the participation of AE (Aviation Electrical) technicians, all Navy personnel. The evaluation built on previous work with a non-speech version of the system (Siegel et al., 2000), thus task materials as well as a well-defined and tested experimental protocol were available and were incorporated into the current evaluation (with modifications to take into account the use of a speech system). The materials used were modelled on level 4/5 IETMs (Interactive Electronic Technical Manuals) and the task used was the Inertial Navigation System (INS) Built In Test (BIT) for the F/A-18C/D fighter plane. We selected this particular task because of the availability of appropriate IETM material and existing task analysis information. Since this was a heuristic evaluation of a proof-of-concept prototype our primary focus was on understanding the experience of the mechanics. Thus each mechanic performed the task once and was then interviewed about their experience. The testing procedure included a period of instruction, to familiarise the mechanic with the wearable equipment and with the characteristics of the speech system, followed by actual performance of the task (which took place in the cockpit of an F/A-18C aircraft). Five maintainers participated. Three of the five mechanics were able to complete the task but gave the system divergent ratings, either very high or very low (a range of 1 to 4 on a 5-point scale). We attribute this outcome to problems in both interface design and in operational difficulties in the hangar environment, specifically the interaction between the computational requirements of the prototype and the difficulty of operating a wireless network in an environment high in RF noise (involving unpredictable outages in connectivity). Nevertheless both field evaluations provided valuable information that was used for system improvement.

While users commented favourably on the language-based interface, analysis of the sessions and user comments identified several issues. These include: better feedback on system state; a more flexible balance between the spoken and graphical outputs and improvements to the GUI design. In the next subsection, we discuss these issues in more detail, and present our current and future planned efforts addressing them.

4.2 Lessons Learned and Future Plans

4.2.1 Interface design. The initial interface design incorporated graphical elements into the display that conveyed listening status (ready, busy) and input sound level, however the field trials revealed that a more comprehensive and easily assimilated state feedback was needed, both at the signal level (line quality, signal integrity, clipping, etc.), and at the understanding level (recognition success). Specifically, while the user's focus needs to be on the task, he or she requires clear and unobtrusive indication of whether speech input is being processed and understood correctly. This can be achieved through a combination of visual and auditory cues: readily perceptible graphic elements positioned at the periphery of the visual field (i.e., on the edges of the display area) that use colour and spatial cues to communicate speech system status information, and auditory signals (e.g., to signal a mode change or an understanding error).

A second important observation concerns creating an optimal balance between spoken and graphical output. Since a graphic display is available, the role of speech output changes correspondingly: speech is no longer the principal medium for transmitting information to the user. While one solution is to statically assign message types to output medium, we believe that a dynamic assignment would take into account factors like environmental and work conditions (e.g., noise-levels, eyes-busy situations, etc.) as well as the user's history and level of expertise with the task will be more valuable. The current system uses paraphrase and meta-comments to augment screen-based information.

A related, task-level observation is that the most experienced maintainers were actually slowed down by the system taking the time to go through the step-outcome verification questions for each step. This underlined the importance of matching system speech output to the context and to the user's level of expertise. Users familiar with the task will not need to have it read to them step-by-step, while inexperienced mechanics could benefit from this sometimes redundant presentation. As a first solution to this issue, we added a "terse" vs. "verbose" mode for the system. Switching between the modes is achieved at the user's request, with the initial settings (reflecting the user's level of expertise) contained in the user profile. A more sophisticated model could take into account other factors such as the dynamics of the interaction and the user's history with the current task.

Based on the feedback and observations from the field trials, we have designed a new graphical user interface, which provides several improvements over the original one. Changes include: better system state feedback, popup help windows (i.e., on misunderstandings, a list of possible commands acceptable to the system at that point can be popped up on the screen to prime the user), better distinction between steps and step-outcome verification questions, and in general a cleaner design which conveys more clearly the user's current position and focus in the task.

4.2.2 Domain integration. From a practical perspective, a critical issue in the maintenance domain is the problem of preparing source materials for use in a language-based interface. Documentation for the F/A-18 system, on paper, involves many thousands of pages of text, as well as diagrams and other graphical materials. Moreover, this documentation is revised on a regular (weekly) basis. None of this material, understandably, is currently prepared with a view to being accessible through a spoken-language interface. The unresolved problem is how to automatically prepare such materials for (intelligent) spoken-language based access. This is not a problem that is adequately addressed by current "toolkit" approaches to spoken language interface development (which at best simplify the prototyping of small closed-domain applications) but one that necessarily needs to be addressed for large and constantly mutating domains, such as aircraft maintenance.

Currently, we use a declarative language (TML, Task Markup Language) for maintenance tasks, from which dialogue agents in the dialogue manager are generated dynamically, as needed. Nevertheless, both the semantic grammar for the Phoenix parser, and the system's prompts covering the INS BIT Test had to be handcrafted. Given that IETMs for new systems are authored in SGML, which can be translated to XML, we anticipate using an XSLT programme to render the IETM into the corresponding TML; however the process needs to in addition automatically generate a grammar for the parser as well as appropriate prompts for generation. To drive the recognition system we also need to generate a corresponding language model and pronunciation dictionary. Our previous experience with designing such a process (for a movie information service that provided current information (Eskenazi et al., 1999)) indicates that a fully automatic process is difficult to create. Yet such a process would be essential, given the impracticality of manually creating and maintaining the requisite knowledge base.

5. Conclusion

We have described a language-based system for a complex maintenance and repair domain. This domain differs significantly from service-oriented domains such as travel planning in several respects. First, the nature of the activity violates common assumptions made in services domains in that precision and completion are the primary goals, and simple speed of execution is less important. The criterion for success is jointly determined by the system and the user rather than by the user only (who, for example, is the only judge of whether a particular itinerary is satisfactory). The maintenance domain involves multiple categories of interaction such as guidance and browsing, that imply different relationships with essentially the same domain information (thus task and domain representations need to be explicitly differentiated, even when the domain information effectively describes a task). As well, users may be engaged in several comparable maintenance activities, meaning that the system needs to track individual tasks and be able to manage the user's change of focus between them.

Second, the interface is no longer uni-modal and the system must provide for both gestural input and graphic output. In our particular domain, which is hands-busy, gestural input does not play a major role in the interface; voice provides a more appropriate and flexible input for navigation, for data entry and for information access. However, in situations of excess noise, gesture becomes the only viable input. On output, we have found, unsurprisingly, that speech and graphic outputs need to be coordinated and that care must be taken to avoid unnecessary redundancy between the two channels. At the same time the user needs to be given control over the details of how outputs are distributed over modalities, to reflect changing circumstances. For example, in an eyes-busy situation a verbal rendering of screen content is essential.

Finally, the maintenance and repair domain stresses the importance of automating the assimilation of domain information into a form that can be used by a language-based system. In many dialogue systems this knowledge is handcrafted; this is possible because the size or complexity of the domain is manageable. We believe that effective interfaces to maintenance documentation (and indeed many other domains) require the extraction of substantive structure relevant to the tasks performed; the challenge is to extract this information automatically without the aid of complex (and handcrafted) world models.

Acknowledgements

This research was sponsored in part by the Space and Naval Warfare Systems Center, San Diego, under Grant No. N66001-99-1-8905. The content of the information in this publication does not necessarily reflect the position or the policy of the US Government, and no official endorsement should be inferred. We would like to thank the following individuals for their various contributions to this work: Dick Martin, Jane Siegel, Brian Gollum, Jack Moffet and Tom Hawley from the CMU Wearables Group; Yitao Sun, Rong Zhang, Alan Black, Kevin Lenzo, Ananlada Chotimongkol, Tina Bennett, Kayur Patel and Mike Seltzer from the Speech Group.

Notes

1. http://www.dcnicn.com/IETMCentral/
2. A number of resources describe IETMs. For further information please see http://navycals.dt.navy.mil/ietm/ietm.html, http://navycals.dt.navy.mil/ietm/ietm.html, as well as other web-based documents.

References

Black, A. W. and Lenzo, K. (2000). Limited domain synthesis. In *Proceedings of International Conference on Spoken Language Processing (ICSLP)*, pages 411–414, Beijing, China.

Black, A. W. and Lenzo, K. (2001). Flite: a small fast run-time synthesis engine. In *Proceedings of ISCA Workshop on Speech Synthesis*, pages 157–162, Perthshire, United Kingdom.

Bohus, D. and Rudnicky, A. (2003). Ravenclaw: Dialog management using hierarchical task decomposition and an expectation agenda. In *Proceedings of European Conference on Speech Communication and Technology (EUROSPEECH)*, pages 597–600, Geneva, Switzerland.

Eskenazi, M., Rudnicky, A., Gregory, K., Constantinides, P., Brennan, R., Bennett, C., and Allen, J. (1999). Data collection and processing in the Carnegie Mellon Communicator. In *Proceedings of European Conference on Speech Communication and Technology (EUROSPEECH)*, pages 2695–2698, Budapest, Hungary.

Goodman, B. (1993). Multimedia explanations for intelligent training systems. *Intelligent Multimedia Interfaces*, pages 148–171.

Huang, X., Alleva, F., Hon, H.-W., Hwang, M.-Y., Lee, K.-F., and Rosenfeld, R. (1993). The SPHINX-II speech recognition system: an overview. *Computer Speech and Language*, pages 137–148.

Seneff, S., E.Hurley, Lau, R., Pao, C., Schmid, P., and Zue, V. (1998). Galaxy-II: A reference architecture for conversational system development. In *Proceedings of International Conference on Spoken Language Processing (ICSLP)*, pages 931–934, Sidney, Australia.

Siegel, J., Hyder, E., Moffett, J., and Nawrocki, E. (2000). IETM usability: Using empirical studies to improve performance aiding. Technical Report CMU-CS-01-131, Carnegie Mellon University.

Smailagic, A., Siewiorek, D.-P., and Reilly, D. (2001). CMU wearable computers for real-time speech translation. *IEEE Personal Communications*, 8:6–12.

Ward, W. and Issar, S. (1994). Recent improvements in the CMU spoken language understanding system. In *Proceedings of ARPA Human Language Technology Workshop*, pages 213–216, Plainsboro, New Jersey, USA.

Xu, W. and Rudnicky, A. (2000). Task-based dialog management using an agenda. In *ANLP/NAACL Workshop on Conversational Systems*, pages 42–47, Seattle, Washington, USA.

III

EVALUATION AND USABILITY

Chapter 13

OVERVIEW OF EVALUATION AND USABILITY*

Laila Dybkjær, Niels Ole Bernsen
Natural Interactive Systems Laboratory, Odense, Denmark
{laila,nob}@nis.sdu.dk

Wolfgang Minker
University of Ulm, Department of Information Technology, Ulm/Donau, Germany
wolfgang.minker@e-technik.uni-ulm.de

Abstract With the technical advances and market growth in the field, the issues of evaluation and usability of spoken dialogue systems, unimodal as well as multimodal, are as crucial as ever. This chapter discusses those issues by reviewing a series of European and US initiatives which have produced major results on evaluation and usability. Whereas significant progress has been made on unimodal spoken dialogue systems evaluation and usability, the emergence of, among others, multimodal, mobile, and non-task-oriented systems continues to pose entirely new challenges to research in evaluation and usability.

Keywords: Multimodal systems; Spoken dialogue systems; Evaluation; Usability.

1. Introduction

Spoken dialogue systems (SDSs) are proliferating in the market for a large variety of applications and in an increasing number of languages. As a major step forward, commercial SDSs have matured from technology-driven prototypes to business solutions. This means that systems can be copied, ported, localised, maintained, and modified to fit a range of customer and end-user needs

*This chapter is a modified version of the article entitled " Evaluation and Usability of Multimodal Spoken Language Dialogue Systems" published in Speech Communication, Vol. 43/1-2, pp. 33–54, Copyright (2004), reprinted with permission from Elsevier.

W. Minker, D. Bühler and L. Dybkjær (eds), Spoken Multimodal Human-Computer Dialogue in Mobile Environments, 221-246

without fundamental innovation. This is what contributes to creating an emerging industry. At the same time, increasingly advanced SDSs are entering the market, drawing on experience from even more sophisticated research systems and continuous improvements in SDS technologies. Furthermore, in many research laboratories, focus is now on combining speech with other modalities, such as pen-based hand-writing and 2D gesture input, and graphics output, such as images, maps, lip movements, animated agents, or text (Wahlster et al., 2001; Bickmore and Cassell, 2002; Oviatt, 1997; Gustafson et al., 2000; Sturm et al., 2004; Oviatt et al., 2004; Whittaker and Walker, 2004). An additional dimension which influences development is the widening context of use. Mobile devices, in particular, such as mobile phones, in-car devices, PDAs and other small handheld computers open up a range of new application opportunities for unimodal as well as multimodal SDSs as witnessed by several chapters in this book. In this continually expanding field of unimodal and multimodal, mobile and non-mobile SDSs, many research issues still remain to be solved. Two issues of critical importance are evaluation and usability. Systems *evaluation* is crucial to ensure, e.g., system correctness, appropriateness, and adequacy, while *usability* is crucial to user acceptance.

Many results are available from individual development projects regarding evaluation and usability. These issues often receive some amount of attention in SDS projects although only few have their main focus on any of them. By themselves, isolated results and experience are usually neither easily generalisable nor immediately transferable to other projects. However, the results are still important. Generalisations, best practice guidelines, and, eventually, (de facto) standards are typically based on empirical evidence from many different sources and are applicable across projects within their scope. Other important approaches to evaluation and usability that are valid across projects are frameworks and theoretical approaches. A framework may be described as a general toolset with a well-defined scope which reflects some kind of principled approach. A theoretical approach is based on deeper insight into relationships among key concepts or variables. Below, we shall use the distinction between empirical generalisations, frameworks, and theory for the purpose of exposition even though it remains true that theories and frameworks are worthless without empirical evidence and empirical generalisation tends to be couched in theoretically inspired, or even derived, concepts.

This chapter surveys what we have learned and where we are today regarding SDS evaluation and usability. Section 2 presents a brief overview of the state-of-the-art in evaluation and usability. We then discuss empirical generalisations (Section 3), frameworks (Section 4), and theory and generalisations on the usability of multimodal SDSs (Section 5). Section 6 concludes the chapter. Given the fact that, in particular, the state of the art in spoken multimodal and mobile systems usability and evaluation remains uncharted to a large extent, the perspective adopted is necessarily a partial one. Moreover, the reader should be aware that this chapter focuses on spoken input and output while other modalities are only considered to the extent that they are being used together with speech.

2. State-of-the-Art

The first simple, commercial SDS appeared in 1989 (Bossemeyer and Schwab, 1991) based on many years of research, particularly in speech recognition. Increasingly complex and sophisticated technologies were introduced during the 1990s, bringing issues such as barge-in, large-vocabulary recognition in noisy conditions, robust parsing, flexible dialogue management, language generation, and easy portability to the forefront of research. The recent advent of multimodal and of mobile SDSs has compounded the challenges to establishing best practice for the development and evaluation of usable SDSs and their component technologies.

In the USA and Europe, several initiatives have addressed SDSs evaluation and usability since the late 1980s. Several of these are mentioned in (Dybkjær et al., 2004). While the focus in Europe has been on analysing various aspects of evaluation and usability, focus in the USA has been on competitive evaluation among projects addressing the same task(s). Together these initiatives have managed to, at least:

- establish various basic metrics, see examples below;
- vastly increase our knowledge of issues, such as test corpus creation, comparative component and system evaluation, portability to different languages, the need for robust parsing, and, more generally, best practice in the development and evaluation of SDSs and their components;
- introduce a range of new, difficult evaluation topics, such as, how to design informative user questionnaires, when and how to use animated interface agents, how to evaluate education value and entertainment value, how to generalise evaluation results on spoken multimodal systems, how to identify key factors influencing customer satisfaction, and when to use speech interfaces.

Today's SDSs are largely task-oriented but novel, non-task-oriented systems are emerging. Technical sophistication differs dramatically among unimodal as well as multimodal SDSs, which means that the same set of evaluation criteria cannot be applied to all. Rather, some subset of a broader set of evaluation criteria will be relevant to each particular system. As regards usability, system variability includes, e.g., the fact that the skills and preferences of the target users may differ widely. This and other parameters must be taken into account when designing for, and evaluating, usability no matter the technical sophistication of the system.

Broadly, evaluation may be decomposed into (i) technical (including functional) evaluation of systems and their components, (ii) usability evaluation of systems, and (iii) customer evaluation of systems and components. Although (i)-(iii) are interrelated, a technically excellent system may have poor usability whilst a technically inferior system may score highly in user satisfaction questionnaires. Moreover, the customer may prefer yet another system for reasons of, say, cost and platform compatibility which have little to do with technical perfection or end-user satisfaction. Unfortunately, too little is known at present about the important topic of customer evaluation. In the following, we focus on technical evaluation (Section 2.1) and on usability and usability evaluation (Section 2.2).

2.1 Technical Evaluation

Technical evaluation concerns the entire SDS as well as each of its components. In this overview chapter we cannot give a full and detailed account of evaluation criteria for all the individual components of an SDS. This section describes some of the most important evaluation criteria for major SDS components.

Technical evaluation is usually done by developers as objective evaluation, i.e. quantitative and/or qualitative evaluation. Quantitative evaluation consists in measuring something and producing an independently meaningful number, percentage etc. Qualitative evaluation consists in estimating or judging some property by reference to expert standards and rules.

Technical evaluation is well developed for many aspects of SDSs and their components. As a minimum, as many bugs as possible should be found and repaired through diagnostic evaluation. Proper technical evaluation also includes measuring, through performance evaluation, whether the system's or component's functionality is as specified. Finally, technical evaluation may also be done in order to make comparisons with other SDSs.

There is widespread agreement on key evaluation criteria for speech recognisers and speech synthesisers. For speech recognisers, these criteria include word and sentence error rate, vocabulary coverage, perplexity, and real-time performance. Word and sentence error rate are measured by comparing the transcribed input with the recogniser's output. Other examples are metrics for speaker identification and speaker separation. For speech synthesisers, user perception continues to have a central role in evaluation. Some of the basic properties which should be evaluated are speech intelligibility, pleasantness and naturalness (Karlsson, 1999). For natural language understanding, some basic metrics are lexical coverage, grammar coverage, and real-time performance. The particular grammatical properties of spoken language makes grammar coverage metrics a controversial topic. Concept accuracy, or concept error rate, see (Boros et al., 1996; Glass et al., 2000), has become increasingly popular as a measure of the extent to which the natural understanding functionality succeeds in capturing the key concepts in the user's input. It is defined on the basis of substitution, insertion, and deletion of concepts encoded in the meaning representation derived from the input utterance. Dialogue managers remain difficult to evaluate from a purely technical point of view, partly because much of their functionality is closely related with usability and are better regarded as targets for usability evaluation, cf. Section 3. One example of an important target for technical dialogue manager evaluation is reusability of task-independent parts. Like dialogue manager evaluation, response generation evaluation is to a large extent intimately related to usability evaluation. However, evaluation of the grammatical correctness of spoken output may be regarded as technical and quasi-quantitative evaluation.

At system level, several quantitative criteria have been proposed, e.g., real-time performance and robustness measured in terms of number of crashes. Two other metrics quantify how effectively a user can provide new information to a system (Glass et al., 2000): query density measures the mean number of concepts introduced per user query while concept efficiency quantifies the average number of turns for each concept to be understood by the system. In offline batch mode re-processing of user dialogues, comparison can be made between the dialogue state derived from the transcribed user utterance and the one derived from the recogniser outputs. This captures evaluation of understanding, discourse resolution and dialogue modelling as well as recognition. It is also used as a means of regression analysis/testing when system developers have made changes to the dialogue module and want to make sure that nothing has been unintentionally broken as a consequence, see (Polifroni and Seneff, 2000; Glass et al., 2000).

The emergence of spoken multimodal systems poses new challenges for the technical evaluation of SDSs and their components. For instance, at component level, we are beginning to need metrics for evaluating gesture recognisers, facial expression recognisers, gesture interpreters, facial expression and emotion interpreters, gesture and facial expression renderers, and a growing diversity of multimodal input fusion functionality. Sub-component reusability for the more complex dialogue and conversation managers needed will remain an important issue. At system level, new technical evaluation methodologies and metrics will be needed as well.

At this juncture, however, as experience is being gathered on technical solutions for spoken multimodal systems, it seems that the research focus is primarily on how to evaluate the usability of these systems, cf., e.g., the NICE project (Dybkjær et al., 2003) and the chapters in this part of the book. One reason may be that there are more unknown usability factors than technical factors; another, that there is a common pattern involved, i.e. that usability and qualitative evaluation issues tend to become addressed at an earlier stage than do quantitative and technical issues.

2.2 Usability and Usability Evaluation

Usability remains difficult to get right even in unimodal SDSs. In general, a usable SDS must satisfy those user needs which go beyond the need for appropriate functionality, and it must be easy to understand and interact with, especially in the case of walk-up-and-use systems. Interaction should be smooth rather than bumpy and error-prone, and the user should feel in control throughout the dialogue with the system. Moreover, as SDSs begin to serve purposes other than factual information exchange, usability evaluation must be extended to address, e.g., educational value and entertainment value. To develop usable SDSs we need knowledge about issues, such as user reactions to SDSs in the field, users' linguistic, para-linguistic and non-linguistic behaviour, their comprehension of the corresponding system behaviour, and the main factors which determine overall user satisfaction.

Usability evaluation usually concerns the SDS as a whole and is typically done by developers and users. Most usability measures are qualitative or subjective but quantitative criteria also exist, such as transaction success rate, task completion time, turn correction ratio, and number of interaction problems. As a rule, usability should be factored in from the very beginning of the SDS development process. For this reason, it is recommended to have close interaction with representative users from early on. However, this does not in itself guarantee good usability. Additional help can be found in existing knowledge of important factors which affect usability, cf. Section 3.

So far, usability evaluation has been done mainly on task-oriented SDSs. However, usability evaluation is now moving into non-task oriented areas, such as conversational entertainment systems which do not assume that users perform particular tasks. This poses new demands on finding appropriate metrics and methods for usability evaluation.

Evaluation of commercial SDSs is often kept secret. Obviously, however, a crucial parameter for commercial systems is user satisfaction which is related to factors such as call statistics, transaction success, and users' opinion of the system. Contracts often include requirements to the minimum transaction success rate which must be met when users interact with the final system. However, it is well-known that a high transaction success rate does not necessarily imply happy users. It is also known that test subjects, even if representative of the target user group, may behave and judge differently from real users, for instance judging the system more positively than real users in the field. Evaluation metrics which could improve usability prediction would therefore seem highly desirable.

3. Empirical Generalisations

There are many individual projects which have produced, or aim to produce, generalisations based on empirical results. Among those which have had or have a major focus on evaluation and usability and thereby distinguish themselves from most other projects are ATIS (Air Travel Information Systems), Evalda, EAGLES (Expert Advisory Group on Language Engineering Standards), DISC (Spoken Language Dialogue Systems and Components: Best practice in development and evaluation), and the Danish Dialogue Project. Their contributions are presented in the following.

3.1 ATIS

The evaluation methodology for natural language understanding used in the ATIS project (1989-93) is objective response evaluation. The system's ability to understand the spoken input and respond appropriately is measured in terms of the information returned to the user. Thus, only the content of an answer retrieved from the database is assessed. Human annotation is required to identify the correct reference answers and to decide whether the query is ambiguous and/or answerable. This was considered to be easier to agree upon than to specify and evaluate a standard semantic representation.

The evaluation method (Pallett et al., 1995) is to automatically compare an annotated minimal/maximal reference answer pair with the system-generated answer. An answer is considered correct if it contains at least the set of fields in the minimal reference answer to the information explicitly requested by the subject. It should also contain no more than the set of fields described in the corresponding maximal reference answer. The maximal references use supplementary fields that can be reasonably included in an answer to the query. In other words, the system's response must be within a pre-defined range so as to avoid response overgeneration, i.e., the generation of correct answers by including all possible facts, rather than by understanding the requested information. The minimal reference answer was generated using NLPARSE whereas the maximal reference answer had to be defined manually. NLPARSE is a Texas Instruments proprietary system made available to the ARPA research community for the ATIS application. In a Wizard-of-Oz (WOZ) setup, the wizard input, an NL-parse paraphrase, is provided to NLPARSE which then simulates a system response to the user. The *Principles of Interpretation* document accompanying the data provides guidelines for annotators and system developers. Answers may contain scalars, booleans or tables. An automatic *Spoken Language System Answer Comparator* provided by NIST compares the answer generated by the system with the minimal/maximal reference answer pair (Ramshaw and Boisen, 1990). Scalar answers are compared by comparing values. For table-based responses, the comparator explores each possible mapping from the required columns found in the specification to the actual columns found in the answer.

A strong feature of the ATIS evaluation method is that it supports regression analysis, i.e., developers can make changes to, e.g., the dialogue module and ensure that the system still behaves the same way at the dialogue level in responding to a broad range of different user queries. However, there are also several drawbacks of the method, including:

- the dialogue interaction must be entirely user-initiated since the assumption is that context resolution can be performed knowing only the user half of the conversation;
- it requires a static frozen database which is unrealistic for real dialogue systems;
- there is enormous overhead involved in the acquisition of, and adherence to, rigid standards of correctness;
- research in planning and language generation is stifled since the response is only evaluated as a tabular entry.

It follows that there is an additional burden involved in evaluating systems using real databases and mixed-initiative dialogue. If multimodal interaction is added, it becomes difficult to implement mechanisms to assure system reliability, which is a problem for system development. These problems notwithstanding, it may be concluded that the ATIS evaluation methodology succeeded in providing the community some unquestionable benchmarks.

3.2 Evalda

The French Evalda project[1] was launched in 2002 as part of the Technolangue programme (Mariani, 2002) and is coordinated by ELRA (Evaluation and Language Resources Agency)[2]. The goal of the project is within a 3-year period to establish a permanent evaluation infrastructure for the language engineering sector in France and for the French language. A first aim is to collect reusable knowledge and technology in terms of organisation, logistics, language resources, evaluation protocols, methodologies and metrics, as well as major industrial and academic actors in the field. A second aim is to run evaluation campaigns involving linguistic technologies in written and spoken media and covering various aspects of language processing and human-computer interaction. The campaigns are largely based on black-box evaluation protocols and quantitative methods, drawing on and expanding previous evaluation campaigns, such as ARC-AUPELF[3], GRACE[4], and TREC[5]. To enable comparison of performance and benchmarking of language engineering tools, it is considered crucial that the evaluations envisaged are reproducible by third parties, using the resources assembled in the project. Evalda will make available all its evaluation resources by the end of the project in the form of an evaluation package. Eight evaluation campaigns will be run, cf. (Dybkjær et al., 2004). Contrary to the USA, SDS evaluation campaigns are not common in Europe. France is, in fact, the only European country which from early on has conducted larger-scale open evaluation campaigns in language engineering using quantitative black-box evaluation protocols.

3.3 EAGLES

EAGLES[6] (1993-1998) (King et al., 1996) aimed to develop commonly agreed specifications and guidelines for various aspects of language engineering, including evaluation issues. The approach was to collect and unify existing information and provide up-to-date reference documentation for use by researchers and developers as well as in standardisation initiatives. To reach a large audience, the EAGLES evaluation working group used the ISO 9000 norm series and proposed a strongly user-oriented methodology for application in adequacy evaluation and progress evaluation. The idea was to work in terms of classes of typical users, much in the same way that consumer associations target typical users of cars or washing machines when drawing up their product reports. User profiling can help determine the attributes of products which particular classes of users are interested in. Attribute values may then be determined for specific products.

An important point of departure for part of the work was the ISO 9126 (1991) standard on quality characteristics of software. With close contact to ISO, EAGLES looked into the modifications and extensions that would be necessary in order to apply the standard to the evaluation of language engineering systems in general, aiming to produce a formal quality model. ISO 9126 was later revised and split into ISO 9126-1 (1998) and ISO 14598 (2000). ISO 9126-1 (1998) focuses on the quality model which was missing in ISO 9126 (1991), whereas evaluation became the sole topic of the ISO 14598 series.

EAGLES also worked on SDS evaluation recommendations. A problem was that only a few SDSs had been systematically evaluated by the mid-1990s, most of which performed relatively simple tasks. Thus (Gibbon et al., 1997) clearly states that the EAGLES recommendations on SDS evaluation are provisional. EAGLES distinguishes between glass-box evaluation and black-box evaluation, see also (Simpson and Fraser, 1993). Glass-box evaluation is meant for evaluation of sub-components and their contribution to the overall behaviour of the system. The term glass-box is used because the internals of components can be inspected. Black-box evaluation, which is a familiar term from computer science, views a component or entire system as a black box and evaluates some aspect of its overall performance. Both quantitative and qualitative measures are proposed for black-box evaluation. Quantitative measures proposed include: average number of exchanges to obtain relevant responses, task completion rate, transaction success rate, system response time, and terseness of the system's answers. Qualitative measures include user satisfaction, ability to adapt to new users, ability to adapt to the same user, and ability to handle multimodality. Black-box evaluation is also recommended for comparative evaluation of systems. The proposed key comparative evaluation measures include dialogue duration, turn duration, contextual appropriateness, correction rate, and transaction success rate.

The EAGLES recommendations which are documented in the EAGLES handbook (Gibbon et al., 1997) were not only conceived at a time when evaluation experience was sparse. At the time, evaluation was often based on looking at single user-system turn pairs in isolation without regard to context, cf. ATIS. The EAGLES group was aware of the need for evaluating single dialogue turns in the larger discourse context.

EAGLES no doubt contributed to progress in SDS evaluation by articulating its underlying complexity and linking up with standardisation. Many of the proposed metrics are still useful although insufficient for evaluating the full variety of SDSs today. Two main problems with the EAGLES evaluation recommendations probably are that (i) it can be costly and cumbersome to carry out evaluation precisely as prescribed, and (ii) the methodology can be difficult to follow and may not fit equally well into different projects.

3.4 DISC

Based on its academic and industrial partners' broad collective experience in SDSs development, the ESPRIT Long-Term Research project DISC[7] (1997-1998) developed a first dialogue engineering best practice methodology (Dybkjær et al., 1998a). The idea was that, although reference methodologies exist for software engineering in general, no such reference methodology existed for the development and evaluation of SDSs and components in particular. DISC addressed both technical evaluation and usability. Evaluation from the point of view of the end-user was not fully addressed due to data scarcity. For the same reason, DISC did not systematically address the multimodal aspects of the systems analysed.

Work in DISC was grounded in detailed analyses of the properties of, and development processes for, approximately 25 SDS systems and components for different application domains and different languages. Correspondingly, the DISC evaluation methodology is based on a best practice *grid* and *life-cycle*. A grid defines a space of aspect-specific issues which the developer may have to take into account, such as, in dialogue manager development: who should have the initiative, the system and/or the user? For each issue, the available solution *options* are laid out in the grid together with the *pros* and *cons* for choosing a particular option. A life-cycle includes recommendations on how the development process for an aspect and its options should be carried out, such as how to do a requirements analysis in the dialogue manager specification phase. The six SDS *aspects* analysed are: speech recognition, speech generation, natural language understanding and generation, dialogue management, human factors, and systems integration.

DISC produced a comprehensive set of guidelines and heuristics to help determine how a given system or component development task relates to the proposed model. For technical evaluation, DISC proposed for each of its aspects, except human factors, *what* to evaluate, i.e. the full set of properties which should be evaluated, and *how* to evaluate, i.e. the evaluation criteria to apply and how to apply them correctly at the right stages during the development life-cycle. Each evaluation criterion is described using a standard evaluation template (Bernsen and Dybkjær, 2000). As to what to evaluate, DISC defined an aspect-specific notion of evaluation completeness, i.e. that every chosen option from the aspect-specific grid must be evaluated.

The DISC evaluation template supports evaluation correctness. It is a model of what the developer needs to consider when planning to evaluate a particular property of an SDS or component. This knowledge is specified by ten template entries (Bernsen and Dybkjær, 2000): property evaluated, system part evaluated, type of evaluation, methods, symptoms, life-cycle phase(s), importance, difficulty, cost and tools. For each property to be evaluated, i.e. each selected option in the aspect-specific issue space, an empty ten-entry template must be filled by the developer. Filled templates are illustrated at `http://www.disc2.dk/slds/`. If the grid has been used during development, it is easy to generate evaluation criteria for the application by simply including the grid options selected. The harder part is to fill a template per criterion. This requires knowledge of available evaluation methods and metrics, when to apply them, and what to look for in the data. One must also be able to estimate evaluation costs and the risks involved in refraining from evaluating a particular system property.

The DISC approach to complete and correct evaluation would need updating to reflect the issue/option spaces facing today's developers as well as new evaluation metrics. Furthermore, since no developer carries out complete evaluation in practice because of the time and cost involved, developers must be able to carefully judge where to invest their evaluation efforts. How to decide on this important issue was not addressed in DISC nor was comparative system evaluation.

3.5 Usability Guidelines

Building on results from the Danish dialogue project (Dybkjær et al., 1998b) and DISC, Dybkjær and Bernsen (2000) discuss existing knowledge of SDS usability evaluation. They propose that the general design goal of creating usable walk-up-and-use, shared-goal SDSs may be systematically pursued by addressing 13 key usability issues. These issues are aimed at carving up the complex space of SDS usability into intuitively satisfactory and complementary segments. Most issues have implications for the technical development of particular SDS components, such as speech recogniser optimisation or various aspects of interaction optimisation in which the dialogue manager has a central role. The issue of when (not) to use speech in applications highlights the fact that speech is not always the right modality choice for interactive systems, cf. Section 5.

- Input recognition accuracy: good recogniser quality is a key factor in making users confident that the system will successfully get what they say.

- Naturalness of user speech: speaking to an SDS should feel as easy and natural as possible. What is being experienced as natural input speech is also highly relative to the system's output phrasing. Thus, the system's output language should be used to control-through-priming users' input language, so that the latter is manageable for the system whilst still feeling natural to the user.

- Output voice quality: a good SDS output voice quality means that the system's speech is clear and intelligible, does not demand additional listening effort, is not particularly noise-sensitive or distorted by extraneous sounds, has natural intonation and prosody, uses an appropriate speaking rate, and is pleasant to listen to (Karlsson, 1999). Taken together, these requirements still remain difficult to meet today.

- Output phrasing adequacy: the contents of the system's output should be correct, relevant and sufficiently informative without being over informative.

- Feedback adequacy: the user must feel confident that the system has understood the information input in the way it was intended, and the user must be told which actions the system has taken and what the system is currently doing.

- Adequacy of dialogue initiative: to support natural interaction, an SDS needs a reasonable choice of dialogue initiative, depending on factors, such as the nature of the task, users' background knowledge, and frequency of use.

- Naturalness of the dialogue structure: dialogue designers may have to impose some amount of structure onto the dialogue, determining which topics (or sub-tasks) could be addressed when. The structure must be natural to the user, reflecting the user's intuitive expectations.

- Sufficiency of task and domain coverage: even if unfamiliar with SDSs, users often have rather detailed expectations to the information or service obtainable from the system. It is important that the system meets these expectations.

- Sufficiency of reasoning capabilities: contextually adequate reasoning represents a classical problem in the design of natural interaction. SDSs must incorporate both facts and inferences about the task as well as general world knowledge in order to act as adequate interlocutors.

- Sufficiency of interaction guidance: users should feel in control during interaction. Useful help mechanisms may be an implicit part of the dialogue, be available by asking for help, or be automatically enabled if the user is having problems repeatedly, e.g., in being recognised.

- Error handling adequacy: this issue may be decomposed along two dimensions. Either the system or the user initiates error handling meta-communication. When error-handling meta-communication is initiated, it is either because one party has failed to hear or understand the other, because what was heard or understood is false, or because what was heard or understood is somehow in need of clarification.

- Sufficiency of adaptation to user differences: it is useful to distinguish between system expert/domain expert, system expert/domain novice, system novice/domain expert and system novice/domain novice users. An SDS needs not support all four groups.

- Modality appropriateness: the dialogue designers should make sure that spoken input and output, possibly combined with other input/output modalities, is an appropriate modality choice for the planned application. See Section 5 for more detail.

In addition, Dybkjær and Bernsen (2000) discuss user satisfaction measures and metrics for counting the number of interaction problems, both of which provide important information on system and component usability. The work on interaction problem metrics is based on a body of guidelines for cooperative dialogue design (Bernsen et al., 1998) which extends Gricean cooperativity theory (Grice, 1975). These guidelines may be compared with the guidelines for advanced spoken dialogue design developed in a UK project with business exploitation in mind (Gilbert et al., 1999).

This is not an exhaustive list, of course, but it probably covers a good deal of usability basics for task-oriented SDSs. An important problem is that too little is known about the differential effect on general system usability of each of the individual elements on the list. A point missing is that of cultural differences in the perception of SDS usability, such as the degree of system politeness required, which remain poorly understood.

4. Frameworks

In this section we describe the PARADISE (Paradigm for Dialogue System Evaluation) (Walker et al., 1997) framework which addresses usability evaluation of unimodal SDSs. Attempts have been made in the SmartKom project to adapt and extend the PARADISE framework to cope with the evaluation of task-oriented multimodal SDSs (Beringer et al., 2002). However, there does not seem to exist results yet on how well this extended framework works.

4.1 PARADISE

It is a well-recognised fact that too little is known about how to predict overall user satisfaction, i.e., how users will receive a particular SDS. Some would argue that, from a practical standpoint, usability boils down to what users like and prefer although user satisfaction and usability is not one and the same thing. Others would argue that, since they are not identical, the field would do better to keep them separate. One reason why usability and user satisfaction are different quantities is that the latter is very much a function of a constantly changing environment of product availability, cost, and competing technologies, whereas the former is a constant which depends on human nature.

The PARADISE framework views user satisfaction as a measure of system usability and tries to predict user satisfaction from objectively measurable performance parameters. The framework was first applied to SDSs built at AT&T and later adopted as evaluation framework for the DARPA Communicator project (Walker et al., 2002; Sanders et al., 2002). PARADISE has been used in several other projects as well, e.g., (Hjalmarson, 2002). The PARADISE model assumes that the primary objective of an SDS is to maximise user satisfaction (Walker et al., 2000). Task success and various dialogue costs relating to efficiency and quality contribute to user satisfaction. To maximise user satisfaction, one must maximise task success and minimise dialogue costs. Task success is measured as the perceived task completion by users together with the observed task completion. Efficiency is measured through, e.g., elapsed time and number of utterances. Quality is measured via, e.g., recognition score, repair and help (Walker et al., 1997). Users are asked questions on various aspects of their interaction with the system and have to rate the aspects on a five-point multiple choice scale. The response values are summed, resulting in a user satisfaction measure for each dialogue.

The basic claim is that a performance function can be derived by applying multivariate linear regression with user satisfaction as the dependent variable and task success, dialogue quality, and dialogue efficiency measures as independent variables (Walker et al., 2000). Modelling user satisfaction as a function of task success and dialogue cost is intended to lead to a predictive performance model of SDSs, enabling prediction of user satisfaction based on measurable parameters which can be found in log-files, and eventually avoiding costly and hard-to-interpret subjective user evaluation.

It is probably too early for any final assessment of the PARADISE framework. For the moment, there is no better proposal of its kind. Several potential weaknesses may be noted, however:

- The framework may make too tight a coupling between user satisfaction and usability. What users like is significant to usability, but what they like changes depending on what is available, cf. above.

- It is questionable if the model can be concluded to have any reliable predictive power as regards user satisfaction based on log-files alone. Clearly, the independent variables measured are not the only contributors to user satisfaction. An issue which may be difficult to handle quantitatively based on logfiles concerns users actually getting what they want. This may be relatively easy to decide in controlled environments. However, how can we decide from the logfiles from, e.g., a frequently asked questions system whether users actually feel that they got the information they needed or just did not find it in the system? In this case, apparent task completion may be high even if users are dissatisfied because they did not obtain the information they wanted.

- User questionnaires are hard to interpret and there does not seem to exist any strong theoretical foundation for the selection of questions to include. So, how do we know that PARADISE actually correlates objective metrics with “real” user satisfaction? Since the PARADISE questionnaire has not been proven to be reliable and valid for eliciting information about user satisfaction, we cannot be certain that the results obtained with it actually reflect users’ real attitude (Larsen, 2003).

- For the moment, application of PARADISE is restricted to controlled experiments, which makes the framework unsuited for tests with real users having real needs in real environments. Test subjects tend to behave differently from real users. In the Dutch part of the ARISE system, for instance, subjects were very satisfied. However, when the commercial version was launched, user satisfaction dropped dramatically. The drop might be due to in-the-field factors, such as waiting time and price which are not considered in PARADISE, but, ultimately, these factors co-determine user satisfaction.

- User satisfaction is inherently a difficult parameter to deal with. In experiments one can sometimes find dialogues which seem to be inefficient and of low quality. Nevertheless, the user seems happy about the dialogue if the questionnaire or interview data are to be believed. The opposite may also be the case, i.e., the dialogue seems smooth and efficient but the user is not overly satisfied. For some users, task completion may be what really counts while, for others, efficiency or some third parameter is the more important factor. A predictive model might straighten out these differences to some extent but we should be aware that user needs may differ more widely than assumed in the model. In education and entertainment applications, for instance, ultimate educational or entertainment value(s) may be far more important than, for instance, task efficiency, if, indeed, task efficiency is relevant at all.

5. Multimodal SDSs Usability, Generalisations and Theory

Solid empirical generalisations on the usability of multimodal SDSs are emerging. It is well-known, for instance, that system behaviour causes expectations as to what the system can do. Thus, if a human voice and fully natural language is used for spoken output, users may tend to forget that they are interacting with a limited-capability system, expecting human-like capabilities instead. This generalisation seems extensible to multimodal SDSs. For example, Bickmore and Cassell (2002) evaluated the effects on communication of a life-like embodied conversational real-estate agent. They concluded that users tend to compare such animated agent interlocutors with humans rather than machines, judging the system in an unexpected negative fashion as a result. To work with users, life-like animated agents need a high degree of naturalness and personally attractive features communicated non-verbally. This imposes a tall research agenda on spoken and non-verbal output performance, requiring conversational abilities both verbally and non-verbally, cf. also (Cassell et al., 2000). Another empirical generalisation and one supported by modality theory (see below), is that spoken and pointing input, and spoken and graphics output, go well together, see, e.g., (Oviatt, 1997; Roth et al., 1997; Cohen et al., 1997).

So far, we have not gone into much detail with the theoretical underpinnings of the approaches to usability presented, although these certainly exist in many cases. However, when addressing the usability of spoken multimodal systems, in particular, it seems important to point out that, potentially, given their huge scope and the early stage of their investigation, these systems could benefit from the application of a wide range of theoretical approaches. Moreover, several of those approaches definitely do not belong to the standard body of knowledge of the SDS community. Approaches range from film theory and theories of conversation applied to conversational animated agent SDSs for entertainment, through classical psychological theory, such as Gestalt theory, and theories of emotional behaviour, gesture, facial action, etc., to AI planning theory, modality theory, and more. Below, we limit ourselves to briefly presenting a single theoretical approach, i.e. modality theory.

A core question in developing usable spoken multimodal systems is whether or not speech is appropriate for the application to be developed. This is a complex question because the answer depends on many different factors, such as the type and purpose of the application, the application environment (Bühler et al., 2002), bandwidth and transmission channel stability, prioritised performance parameters, such as speed or efficiency versus time to reflect, learning overhead, and the intended users. Clearly, however, a basic factor is the properties of the modalities involved. These are investigated in modality theory based on an exhaustive, hierarchically organised taxonomy of unimodal input/output modalities accessible to human hearing, vision, and touch, see (Bernsen, 1994). Each modality has a number of objective modality properties, such as the property of sound that it is omnidirectional, which implies that speech is omnidirectional as well, or the property of speech in a known language that it has high saliency compared to other acoustic modalities. Modality theory has been applied to the speech functionality problem of when (not) to use speech in unimodal and multimodal applications, see (Bernsen, 2002) for more detail.

Two comprehensive studies of the literature on unimodal and multimodal SDSs written between 1992 and 1998 showed that some 95% of 273 "blind"-selected speech functionality claims made by various authors on when (not) to use speech in unimodal or multimodal contexts could be evaluated as being either true, false, or supported by modality theory. An interesting finding was that the evaluation could be based on only 25 modality properties (Bernsen, 1997; Bernsen and Dybkjær, 1999) of the kind exemplified above. Moreover, the first study looked at 120 early speech functionality claims which mostly concerned unimodal speech input and/or output, whereas the second study looked at 153 claims which were made later in the 1990s and which included a large fraction of claims about speech in multimodal combinations. Nevertheless, it was only necessary to augment the 18 modality properties used for evaluation in the first study by seven, mostly non-speech, modality properties in order to evaluate the new data set. In other words, there is evidence that the theoretical basis needed for evaluating the use of speech in any possible modality combination may be limited and achievable.

6. Discussion and Outlook

With the technical advances and market growth in the SDS field, evaluation and usability of unimodal and multimodal SDSs are becoming crucial issues. We have discussed the state-of-the-art in evaluation and usability and reviewed a number of initiatives which have collected, or built on and contributed to the consolidation of the pool of knowledge we have on SDS evaluation and usability.

There are still important gaps in our knowledge of unimodal, task-oriented SDSs evaluation and usability, and the increasing sophistication even of these systems continues to demand new evaluation metrics. Moreover, the field is moving rapidly beyond the standard task-oriented, speech-only SDS towards multimodal SDSs, mobile systems, situation-aware systems, location-aware systems, internet access systems, educational systems, entertainment systems, etc. In fact, technology development may appear to speed further ahead of the knowledge we already have on evaluation and usability, increasing the proportion of what we do not know compared with what we do know. In the following, we discuss some issues essential to the development of more advanced SDSs.

Online user modelling. By online user modelling we understand the ability of a system to create a model of some property, or properties, of its user at run-time in order to adapt its dialogue behaviour to that property. In generic user modelling, the property is characteristic of a group of users, such as that they are novices in using the system. In individual user modelling, the system builds a model of the property of each individual user, for instance, of the user's hotel reservation preferences, and then uses the model to make it easier for the user to carry out some task. Individual user modelling is, of course, only suitable for frequently used systems. online user modelling for SDSs is receiving increasing attention today for several reasons. Mobile devices (mobile phones, PDAs, note pads, in-car devices, etc.) are usually personal (or quasi-personal) belongings used on a fairly frequent basis. The user of these devices may benefit from functionality which builds knowledge of the individual user. Secondly, many user groups could benefit from generic user modelling functionality. For instance, novice users could receive more extensive interaction guidance; users who repeatedly make particular types of error could be helped by explicit advice or by adaptation of dialogue structure, initiative distribution, and otherwise. Only a few applications of online user modelling in SDSs have been reported in the literature so far. Bernsen and Dybkjær (2004a) describe online individual user modelling for an in-car SDS at a fairly general level while Bernsen (2003) describes an application of individual online user modelling to the hotel reservation task in the same in-car SDS. Komatani et al. (2003) describe an application of generic online user modelling which adapts the system's information level to user experience with a bus information system. Whittaker and Walker (2004) show via a Wizard of Oz experiment the benefit of individual user modelling in a restaurant application. General online user modelling is an active research area. See, for instance, the 9th International Conference on User Modelling in 2003[8] (Brusilovsky et al., 2003). Some key questions to be considered by developers of online user modelling are: (i) is the user modelling functionality feasible and (ii) will it be of benefit rather than a nuisance to the majority of users of the application? For instance, even if the system has enough information on an individual user, the user may experience that adaptation fails because of overly primitive update algorithms or insufficient information about when the user model has been used.

Emotions and personality. Recognition of the emotional states of users followed by appropriate system reactions may contribute to perceived system naturalness. Ongoing research addresses the recognition of facial expressions of emotion, cf. (Ekman and Friesen, 1975; Cohen et al., 2003), and the recognition of prosodic cues to emotion (Batliner et al., 2000; Hirschberg et al., 2001). The ERMIS project[9] on Emotionally Rich Man-Machine Interaction Systems, 2002-2004, analyses speech and face input signals in order to equip systems with the ability to recognise emotions and interact with users in a more natural and user-friendly way. Emotion interpretation could be used to, e.g., change dialogue strategy if the user appears upset. Also, output expression of emotion is an active research topic, see, e.g., (André et al., 2004), and some speech synthesisers are beginning to accept emotion tags. For example, emotion-dependent prosody in synthetic speech is strongly needed in several multimodal entertainment SDSs in current development. System output may among other things be used to communicate certain personality features and thereby influence the user's spoken input, cf. (Oviatt et al., 2004) who investigated the influence of introvert versus extrovert voices on children's vocal behaviour in a spoken multimodal SDS with animated marine animals.

Non-task-oriented dialogue. So far, almost all SDSs have been task-oriented applications. However, research has started in non-task-oriented dialogue, cf., e.g., (Gustafson et al., 1999; Bernsen and Dybkjær, 2004b). In the absence of task constraints, the dialogue may have to follow principles entirely different from task-oriented dialogue. Little is known at this point about the novel usability issues arising in this kind of dialogue. Some of the usability issues discussed in Section 3 will clearly become irrelevant, such as sufficiency of task coverage, and others may suffer the same fate, such as informativeness. Instead, other issues may move into focus, such as conversational naturalness, turn-taking adequacy, and others which will depend on the type of application involved.

Mobile versus static environments. Speech may be a good choice in many mobile environments because of its modality properties of being hands-free and eyes-free. On the other hand, speech is not very private in public spaces because it is omnidirectional, it is potentially disturbing to others because it is highly salient, and speech recognisers remain sensitive to noise. Graphics (including text) output and, e.g., pen-based input may be useful additions because these are not sensitive to noise, do not disturb others, and are usually sufficiently private. Mobile SDSs raise a number of other evaluation issues which have not been fully solved yet, including how (not) to use, and when (not) to use, small and very small screens (Almeida et al., 2002; Sturm et al., 2004), for which purposes (not) to use location awareness and situation awareness, and when and for which purposes it is (not) safe to use displays in, e.g., cars (Bühler et al., 2002; Gärtner et al., 2001; Minker et al., 2004; Bernsen and Dybkjær, 2004).

User preferences and priorities. One thing which can really make life hard for developers are user preferences. For instance, users do not necessarily prefer what is empirically the most efficient modality combination. Thus, some users may prefer pen-based or keypad-based input to spoken input simply because they feel more familiar with GUI-style interfaces, cf. (Sturm et al., 2004) who analysed the behaviour and satisfaction of subjects interacting with a multimodal SDS offering speech input/output, pointing input and graphics output, and (Jameson and Klöckner, 2004) who made an experiment showing different modality preferences in a mobile phone task. The task of calling someone while walking around could be carried out using speech and/or keypad input and acoustic and spoken output and/or display. In other words, depending on the target user group(s), alternative modalities may have to be enabled because it is likely that each of them will be preferred by some users. This is just one reason why user involvement from early on is recommendable and why online user modelling appears attractive.

Another aspect to user preferences is what is perceived as an adequate presentation of information within a given modality, cf. (Geldof and Dale, 2004) who compared two ways of textual presentation of route descriptions.

In fact, one reason why different users may score the same system very differently in terms of usability could be that they have different preferences and priorities. Some preferences we can design for, such as modality preferences and different presentation preferences. Others, however, are hard to cope with. For example, some users may prioritise speed (no queues on the line) or economical benefit (queues but cheap or free calls), while others prioritise human contact which, by definition, cannot be satisfied by a system. The question here is if we can create systems with a usability profile that will make these users change their priorities, and exactly which usability issues must be resolved to do so.

Concluding remarks. The issues discussed in this section are probably just a few of those which should be considered in a systematic approach to evaluation and usability of multimodal, mobile, and domain-oriented SDSs. This approach could lead to a best practice, pre-standard guide for usability and evaluation. EAGLES and DISC took major steps in this direction for unimodal, task-oriented SDSs. Arguably, the expanding SDSs field could benefit from an extension of that work to include multimodal, mobile and domain-oriented SDSs. The foundations for such an approach is just about at hand in the form of a large and growing body of results from very different projects which have built and evaluated next-generation SDSs.

Notes

1. `http://www.elda.fr/rubrique25.html`
2. `http://www.elda.fr/index.html`
3. `http://www.limsi.fr/tlp/aupelf.html`
4. `http://www.limsi.fr/tlp/grace/`
5. `http://trec.nist.gov/`
6. `http://lingue.ilc.pi.cnr.it/EAGLES96/home.html`
7. `http://www.disc2.dk/`
8. `http://www2.sis.pitt.edu/~um2003/`
9. `http://www.image.ntua.gr/ermis/`

References

Almeida, L., Amdal, I., Beires, N., Boualem, M., Boves, L., den Os, L., Filoche, P., Gomes, R., Knudsen, J. E., Kvale, K., Rugelbak, J., Tallec, C., and Warakagoda, N. (2002). Implementing and evaluating a multimodal tourist guide. In *Proceedings of International CLASS Workshop on Natural, Intelligent and Effective Interaction in Multimodal Dialogue Systems*, pages 1–7, Copenhagen, Denmark.

André, E., Dybkjær, L., Minker, W., and Heisterkamp, P., editors (2004). *Affective Dialogue Systems*, volume 3068 of *LNCS/LNAI Lecture Notes*. Springer-Verlag, Berlin/Heidelberg, Germany.

Batliner, A., Fischer, K., Huber, R., Spilker, J., and Nöth, E. (2000). Desperately seeking emotions: Actors, wizards, and human beings. In *Proceedings of ISCA Workshop on Speech and Emotion: A Conceptual Framework for Research*, pages 195–200, Belfast, United Kingdom.

Beringer, N., Kartal, U., Louka, K., Schiel, F., and Türk, U. (2002). Promise - a procedure for multimodal interactive system evaluation. In *Proceedings of LREC Workshop on Multimodal Resources and Multimodal Systems Evaluation*, pages 77–80, Las Palmas, Gran Canaria, Spain.

Bernsen, N. O. (1994). Foundations of multimodal representations. a taxonomy of representational modalities. *Interacting with Computers*, 6(4):347–371.

Bernsen, N. O. (1997). Towards a tool for predicting speech functionality. *Speech Communication*, 23:181–210.

Bernsen, N. O. (2002). Report on user clusters and characteristics. Technical VICO Report D10, NISLab, University of Southern Denmark.

Bernsen, N. O. (2003). On-line user modelling in a mobile spoken dialogue system. In *Proceedings of European Conference on Speech Communication and Technology (EUROSPEECH)*, pages 737–740, Geneva, Switzerland.

Bernsen, N. O., Dybkjær, H., and Dybkjær, L. (1998). *Designing Interactive Speech Systems. From First Ideas to User Testing*. Springer-Verlag, Berlin/-Heidelberg, Germany.

Bernsen, N. O. and Dybkjær, L. (1999). Working paper on speech functionality. Technical Report Esprit Long-Term Research Project DISC Year 2 Deliverable D2.10., NISLab, University of Southern Denmark.

Bernsen, N. O. and Dybkjær, L. (2000). A methodology for evaluating spoken language dialogue systems and their components. In *Proceedings of International Conference on Language Resources and Evaluation (LREC)*, pages 183–188, Athens, Greece.

Bernsen, N. O. and Dybkjær, L. (2004a). Enhancing the usability of multimodal virtual co-drivers. In Minker, W., Bühler, D., and Dybkjær, L., editors, *Spoken Multimodal Human-Computer Dialogue in Mobile Environments*. Kluwer Academic Publishers, Dordrecht, The Netherlands. (this volume).

Bernsen, N. O. and Dybkjær, L. (2004b). Evaluation of spoken multimodal conversation. In *Proceedings of International Conference on Multimodal Interfaces (ICMI)*, Pennsylvania State University, Pennsylvania, USA.

Bickmore, T. and Cassell, J. (2002). Phone vs. face-to-face with virtual persons. In *Proceedings of International CLASS Workshop on Natural, Intelligent and Effective Interaction in Multimodal Dialogue Systems*, pages 15–22, Copenhagen, Denmark.

Boros, M., Eckert, W., Gallwitz, F., Görz, G., Hanrieder, G., and Niemann, H. (1996). Towards understanding spontaneous speech: Word accuracy vs. concept accuracy. In *Proceedings of International Conference on Spoken Language Processing (ICSLP)*, volume 2, pages 1009–1012, Philadelphia, Pennsylvania, USA.

Bossemeyer, R. W. and Schwab, E. C. (1991). Automated alternate billing services at Ameritech: Speech recognition and the human interface. *Speech Technology Magazine*, 5:24–30.

Brusilovsky, P., Corbett, A., and de Rosis, F., editors (2003). *User Modeling 2003*, volume 2702 of *LNCS/LNAI Lecture Notes*. Springer-Verlag, Berlin/-Heidelberg, Germany.

Bühler, D., Minker, W., Häussler, J., and Krüger, S. (2002). Flexible multimodal human-machine interaction in mobile environments. In *ECAI Workshop on Artificial Intelligence in Mobile System (AIMS)*, pages 66–70, Lyon, France.

Cassell, J., Sullivan, J., Prevost, S., and Churchill, E., editors (2000). *Embodied Conversational Agents*. MIT Press, Cambridge, Massachusetts, USA.

Cohen, I., Sebe, N., Chen, L., Garg, A., and Huang, T. (2003). Facial expression recognition from video sequences: Temporal and static modeling. *Computer Vision and Image Understanding, Special Issue on Face Recognition*, 91(1-2):160–187.

Cohen, P., Johnston, M., McGee, D., Oviatt, S., Pittman, J., Smith, I., Chen, L., and Clow, J. (1997). QuickSet: Multimodal interaction for distributed applications. In *Proceedings of ACM International Conference on Multimedia*, pages 31–40, Seattle, Washington, USA.

Dybkjær, L. and Bernsen, N. O. (2000). Usability issues in spoken language dialogue systems. *Natural Language Engineering, Special Issue on Best Practice in Spoken Language Dialogue System Engineering*, 6:243–272.

Dybkjær, L., Bernsen, N. O., Blasig, R., Buisine, S., Fredriksson, M., Gustafson, Martin, J. C., and Wirén, M. (2003). Evaluation criteria and evaluation plan. Technical Report NICE Deliverable D7.1, NISLab, University of Southern Denmark.

Dybkjær, L., Bernsen, N. O., Carlson, R., Chase, L., Dahlbäck, N., Failenschmid, K., Heid, U., Heisterkamp, P., Jönsson, A., Kamp, H., Karlsson, I., v. Kuppevelt, J., Lamel, L., Paroubek, P., D., and Williams (1998a). The DISC approach to spoken language systems development and evaluation. In *Proceedings of International Conference on Language Resources and Evaluation (LREC)*, pages 185–189, Granada, Spain.

Dybkjær, L., Bernsen, N. O., and Dybkjær, H. (1998b). A methodology for diagnostic evaluation of spoken human-machine dialogue. *International Journal of Human Computer Studies (special issue on Miscommunication)*, 48:605–625.

Dybkjær, L., Bernsen, N. O., and Minker, W. (2004). Evaluation and usability of multimodal spoken language dialogue systems. *Speech Communication*, 43(1-2):33–54.

Ekman, P. and Friesen, W. (1975). *Unmasking the Face: A guide to recognize emotions from facial clues*. Prentice Hall Trade.

Gärtner, U., König, W., and Wittig, T. (2001). Evaluation of manual vs. speech input when using a driver information system in real traffic. In *Proceedings of International Driving Symposium on Human Factors in Driver Assessment, Training and Vehicle Design*, pages 7–13, Aspen, Colorado, USA.

Geldof, S. and Dale, R. (2004). Segmenting route directions for mobile devices. In Minker, W., Bühler, D., and Dybkjær, L., editors, *Spoken Multimodal Human-Computer Dialogue in Mobile Environments*. Kluwer Academic Publishers, Dordrecht, The Netherlands. (this volume).

Gibbon, D., Moore, R., and Winski, R. (1997). *Handbook of Standards and Resources for Spoken Language Systems*. Walter de Gruyter.

Gilbert, N., Cheepen, C., Failenschmid, K., and Williams, D. (1999). Guidelines for advanced spoken dialogue design. http://www.soc.surrey.ac.uk/research/guidelines.

Glass, J., Polifroni, J., Seneff, S., and Zue, V. (2000). Data collection and performance evaluation of spoken dialogue systems: The MIT experience. In *Proceedings of International Conference on Spoken Language Processing (ICSLP)*, volume 4, pages 1–4, Beijing, China.

Grice, H. P. (1975). Logic and conversation. In Cole, P. and Morgan, J. L., editors, *Syntax and Semantics, Vol. 3: Speech Acts*, pages 41–58. Academic Press, New York, New York, USA.

Gustafson, J., Bell, L., Beskow, J., Boye, J., Carlson, R., Edlund, J., Granström, B., House, D., and Wirén, M. (2000). AdApt - a multimodal conversational dialogue system in an apartment domain. In *Proceedings of International Conference on Spoken Language Processing (ICSLP)*, pages 134–137, Beijing, China.

Gustafson, J., Lindberg, N., and Lundeberg, M. (1999). The August spoken dialogue system. In *Proceedings of European Conference on Speech Communication and Technology (EUROSPEECH)*, pages 1151–1154, Budapest, Hungary.

Hirschberg, J., Swerts, M., and Litman, D. (2001). Labeling corrections and aware sites in spoken dialogue systems. In *Proceedings of ACL SIGdial Workshop on Discourse and Dialogue*, pages 72–79, Aalborg, Denmark.

Hjalmarson, A. (2002). *Evaluating AdApt, A Multi-modal Conversational Dialogue System using PARADISE*. PhD thesis, KTH.

Jameson, A. and Klöckner, K. (2004). User multitasking with mobile multimodal systems. In Minker, W., Bühler, D., and Dybkjær, L., editors, *Spoken Multimodal Human-Computer Dialogue in Mobile Environments*. Kluwer Academic Publishers, Dordrecht, The Netherlands. (this volume).

Karlsson, I. (1999). A survey of existing methods and tools for development and evaluation of speech synthesis and speech synthesis quality in SLDSs. Technical Report DISC Deliverable D2.3.

King, M., Maegard, B., Schutz, J., and des Tombes, L. (1996). Eagles - Evaluation of natural language processing systems. Technical Report EAG-EWG-PR.2.

Komatani, K., Ueno, S., Kawahara, T., and Okuno, H. (2003). User modeling in spoken dialogue systems for flexible guidance generation. In *Proceedings of European Conference on Speech Communication and Technology (EUROSPEECH)*, pages 745–748, Geneva, Switzerland.

Larsen, L. B. (2003). Assessment of spoken dialogue system usability - What are we really measuring? In *Proceedings of European Conference on Speech Communication and Technology (EUROSPEECH)*, pages 1945–1948, Geneva, Switzerland.

Mariani, J. (2002). Technolangue: Language technology. In *Proceedings of International Conference on Language Resources and Evaluation (LREC)*, Las Palmas, Gran Canaria, Spain.

Minker, W., Haiber, U., Heisterkamp, P., and Scheible, S. (2004). Design, implementation and evaluation of the SENECA spoken language dialogue system. In Minker, W., Bühler, D., and Dybkjær, L., editors, *Spoken Multimodal Human-Computer Dialogue in Mobile Environments*. Kluwer Academic Publishers, Dordrecht, The Netherlands. (this volume).

Oviatt, S., Darves, C., Coulston, R., and Wesson, M. (2004). Speech convergence with animated personas. In Minker, W., Bühler, D., and Dybkjær, L., editors, *Spoken Multimodal Human-Computer Dialogue in Mobile Environments*. Kluwer Academic Publishers, Dordrecht, The Netherlands. (this volume).

Oviatt, S. L. (1997). Multimodal interactive maps: Designing for human performance. *Human-Computer Interaction, special issue on Multimodal interfaces*, 12:93–129.

Pallett, D., Fiscus, J. G., Fisher, W. M., Garofolo, J., Lund, B. A., Martin, A., and Przybocki, M. A. (1995). 1994 benchmark tests for the ARPA spoken language program. In *Proceedings of ARPA Workshop on Spoken Language Technology*, pages 5–36. Morgan Kaufmann, San Francisco, California, USA.

Polifroni, J. and Seneff, S. (2000). Galaxy-ii as an architecture for spoken dialogue evaluation. In *Proceedings of International Conference on Language Resources and Evaluation (LREC)*, pages 725–730, Athens, Greece.

Ramshaw, L. A. and Boisen, S. (1990). An SLS answer comparator. Technical report, BBN Systems and Technologies Corporation. SLS Note 7.

Roth, S. F., Chuah, M. C., Kerpedjiev, S., Kolojejchick, J., and Lucas, P. (1997). Towards an information visualization workspace: Combining multiple means of expression . *Human-Computer Interaction*, 12:131–185.

Sanders, G. A., Le, A. N., and Garofolo, J. S. (2002). Effects of word error rate in the DARPA Communicator data during 2000 and 2001. In *Proceedings of*

International Conference on Spoken Language Processing (ICSLP), pages 277–280, Denver, Colorado, USA.

Simpson, A. and Fraser, N. (1993). Blackbox and glassbox evaluation of the SUNDIAL system. In *Proceedings of European Conference on Speech Communication and Technology (EUROSPEECH)*, pages 1423–1426, Berlin, Germany.

Sturm, J., Cranen, B., Terken, J., and Bakx, I. (2004). Effects of prolonged use on the usability of a multimodal form-filling interface. In Minker, W., Bühler, D., and Dybkjær, L., editors, *Spoken Multimodal Human-Computer Dialogue in Mobile Environments*. Kluwer Academic Publishers, Dordrecht, The Netherlands. (this volume).

Wahlster, W., Reithinger, N., and Blocher, A. (2001). SmartKom: Multimodal communication with a life-like character. In *Proceedings of European Conference on Speech Communication and Technology (EUROSPEECH)*, pages 1547–1550, Aalborg, Denmark.

Walker, M., Rudnicky, A., Prasad, R., Aberdeen, J., Bratt, E., Garofolo, J., Hastie, H., Le, A., Pellom, B., Potamianos, A., Passonneau, R., Roukos, S., Sanders, G., Seneff, S., and Stallard, D. (2002). DARPA Communicator: Cross-system results for the 2001 evaluation. In *Proceedings of International Conference on Spoken Language Processing (ICSLP)*, pages 269–272, Denver, Colorado, USA.

Walker, M. A., Kamm, C. A., and Litman, D. J. (2000). Towards developing general models of usability with PARADISE. *Natural Language Engineering, Special Issues on Spoken Dialogue Systems*, 1(1):1–16.

Walker, M. A., Litman, D., Kamm, C. A., and Abella, A. (1997). PARADISE: A general framework for evaluating spoken dialogue agents. In *Proceedings of Annual Meeting of the Association for Computational Linguistics (ACL-EACL)*, pages 271–280.

Whittaker, S. and Walker, M. (2004). Evaluating dialogue strategies in multimodal dialogue systems. In Minker, W., Bühler, D., and Dybkjær, L., editors, *Spoken Multimodal Human-Computer Dialogue in Mobile Environments*. Kluwer Academic Publishers, Dordrecht, The Netherlands. (this volume).

Chapter 14

EVALUATING DIALOGUE STRATEGIES IN MULTIMODAL DIALOGUE SYSTEMS

Steve Whittaker, Marilyn Walker
University of Sheffield, Sheffield, United Kingdom
{ s.whittaker,m.a.walker } @sheffield.ac.uk

Abstract Previous research suggests that multimodal dialogue systems providing both speech and pen input, and outputting a combination of spoken language and graphics, are more robust than unimodal systems based on speech or graphics alone (André, 2002; Oviatt, 1999). Such systems are complex to build and significant research and evaluation effort must typically be expended to generate well-tuned modules for each system component. This chapter describes experiments utilising two complementary evaluation methods that can expedite the design process: (1) a *Wizard-of-Oz* data collection and evaluation using a novel Wizard tool we developed; and (2) an *Overhearer* evaluation experiment utilising logged interactions with the real system. We discuss the advantages and disadvantages of both methods and summarise how these two experiments have informed our research on dialogue management and response generation for the multimodal dialogue system MATCH.

Keywords: User modelling; Natural language generation; Wizard-of-Oz experiments; Overhearer method; User-adaptive generation; Multiattribute decision theory.

1. Introduction

Multimodal dialogue systems promise users mobile access to a complex and constantly changing body of information. However, mobile information access devices such as PDAs, tablet PCs, and next-generation phones offer limited screen real-estate and no keyboard or mouse. Previous research suggests that spoken language interaction is highly desirable for such systems, and that systems that provide *both* speech and pen input, and that output a combination of spoken language and graphics, are more robust than unimodal systems (André, 2002; Oviatt, 1999). However, such systems are complex to build and typically significant research and evaluation effort must be expended

W. Minker, D. Bühler and L. Dybkjær (eds), Spoken Multimodal Human-Computer Dialogue in Mobile Environments, 247-268

to generate well-tuned modules for each system component. Furthermore, during the development process, it is necessary to evaluate individual components to inform the design process before the whole system is robust enough for data collection with real users. This chapter describes experiments utilising two complementary evaluation methods that can be applied to collect information useful for design during the design process itself. We summarise how we have used these methods to inform our research on improved algorithms for (a) dialogue management and (b) generation for information presentation in multimodal dialogue.

Our testbed application is MATCH (Multimodal Access To City Help), a dialogue system providing information for New York City (Johnston and Bangalore, 2000; Bangalore and Johnston, 2000; Johnston and Bangalore, 2001; Johnston et al., 2002). MATCH runs standalone on a Fujitsu PDA, as shown in Figure 1, yet can also run in client-server mode across a wireless network. MATCH provides users with mobile access to restaurant, entertainment and transportation information for New York City (NYC). Figure 2 depicts the multimodal architecture supporting MATCH, which consists of a series of agents which communicate through a facilitator MCUBE. Figure 2 shows modules that support users in specifying inputs via speech, gesture, handwriting or by a combination of these. Other modules support output generated in speech, using a graphical display, or a combination of both these modes. Automatic Speech Recognition (ASR) is provided by AT&T's Watson engine (Sharp et al., 1997), and the Text-To-Speech (TTS) is based on AT&T's Natural Voices (Beutnagel et al., 1999). MATCH uses a finite-state approach (MMFST) to parse, integrate, and understand multimodal and unimodal inputs (Johnston and Bangalore, 2000). See (Johnston et al., 2002) for more architectural detail.

Our primary research focus has been to provide MATCH with improved capabilities for dialogue management and generation during the information presentation portion of the dialogue, i.e., research on the Multimodal Dialogue Manager (MDM), Text Planner and Multimodal Generator in Figure 2. During this dialogue phase, the system retrieves from its database a set of options that match the user's constraints. The user must then evaluate the various options before selecting one. Even in a multimodal system such as MATCH, that displays some information graphically, this is a complex and time-consuming process: the user must browse a list or graphical representation of the options and access information about each one.

For example, consider a user's request to *Show Italian Restaurants in the West Village*. Figure 3 shows the large number of highlighted options generated as a graphical response. To make an informed choice, the user has to access more detailed information about each individual restaurant either with speech or by graphical browsing. In addition to the tedium of sequentially

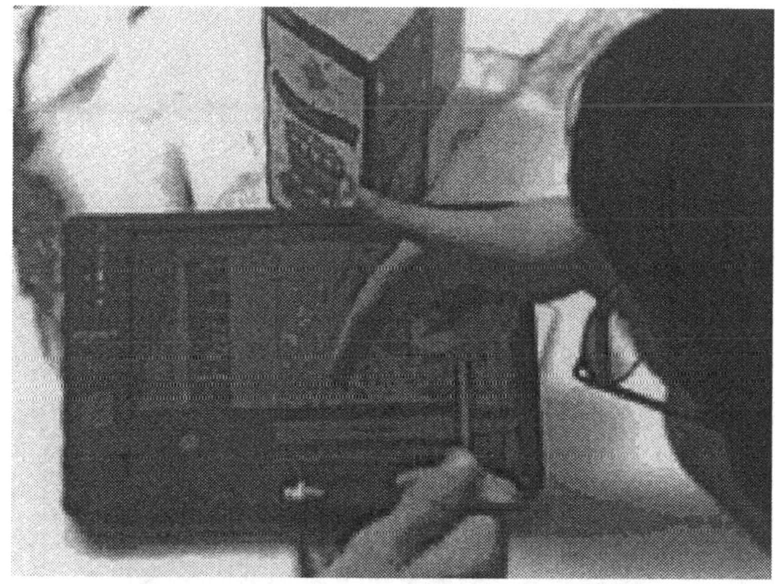

Figure 1. MATCH running on a Fujitsu PDA.

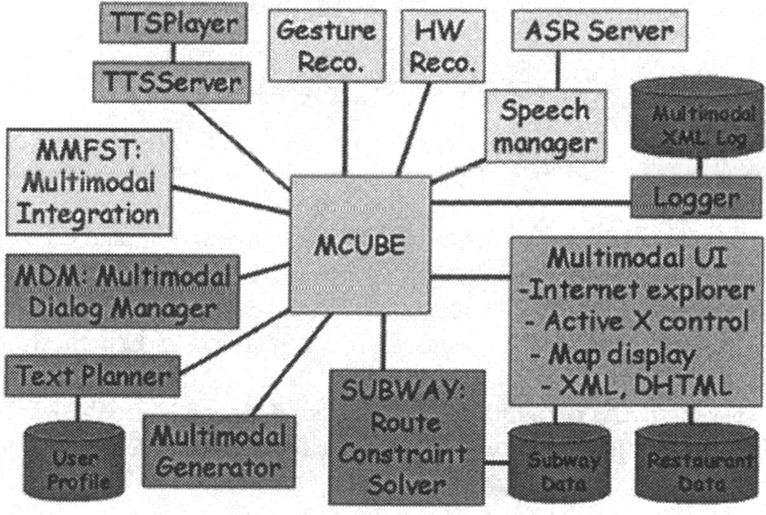

Figure 2. Multimodal architecture.

accessing the set of retrieved options, it may also be hard for users to remember information relevant to making a decision. Thus our research focus has been this critical information presentation problem. Specifically we attempt to devise improved algorithms for: (1) **Option Selection**: selecting the most relevant subset of options to mention or highlight, and (2) **Content Selection**:

choosing what to say about them (Walker et al., 2002; Stent et al., 2002; Whittaker et al., 2002).

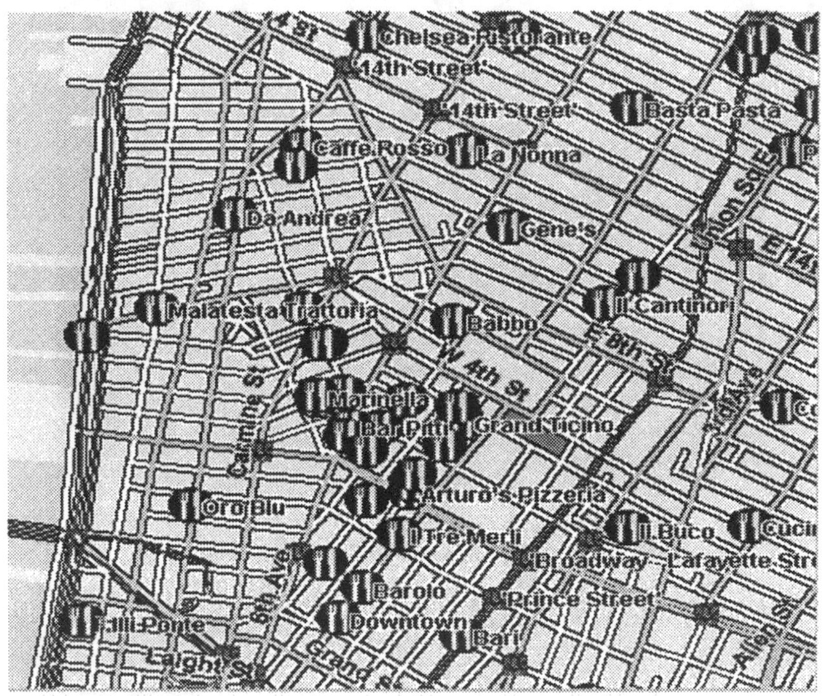

Figure 3. MATCH's graphical system response to "Show me Italian Restaurants in the West Village."

Our solution to this problem is to try to reduce the amount and complexity of the information, by focusing on identifying: (a) the options that are relevant to the user; (b) ensuring that we restrict the information we present about the options to attributes that are of direct interest to the user. Our hypothesis is that a solution to these problems can be provided by quantitative user models of user preferences based on multi-attribute decision theory (Keeney and Raiffa, 1976; Edwards and Barron, 1994). We base our dialogue strategies on the user model when providing information (Carenini and Moore, 2000; Carenini and Moore, 2001). The model of user preferences addresses the content selection problem by providing a means to rank the options returned by the database, predicting that the most relevant subset of options are those that are most highly ranked. The same model also addresses the content selection problem by identifying the attributes that should be mentioned when describing the option, namely those attributes that are predicted by the model to be most convincing to a particular user.

We have followed an iterative design approach. It has been necessary to evaluate different potential designs for response generation and dialogue management before the whole system was robust enough for data collection with real users. This chapter describes experiments utilising two complementary evaluation methods that can be applied to the design process that allow evaluation of system components before the whole system is built: (1) a *Wizard-of-Oz* data collection and evaluation using a novel Wizard tool we developed; and (2) an *Overhearer* evaluation experiment utilising logged interactions with the MATCH system. We describe in detail our Wizard Interaction Tool (WIT) and the required functionality of such a tool, as well as the design of the Overhearer evaluation. We discuss the advantages and limitations of both methods. We then summarise how these two experiments have informed our research on dialogue management and response generation for the MATCH system.

The structure of the chapter is as follows. Section 2 provides details about requirements for, and design of the Wizard Interface Tool, describes how we used the tool to collect data during the early design phase of the system, and summarises what we learned from the Wizard experiment. Section 3 describes the Overhearer evaluation paradigm that we developed to support evaluation experiments on response generation in spoken dialogue systems and summarises the findings from this experiment. Section 4 compares what can be learned from these two evaluation methodologies and summarises the chapter.

2. Wizard-of-Oz Experiment

One problem in developing information presentation algorithms for complex information gathering dialogues is that we lack detailed information about (a) the types of tasks and the strategies employed by users when seeking information and (b) the techniques employed by human experts in providing information about those complex domains. We also wanted to explore the effects of user models on users' information seeking behaviour, and various strategies for the presentation of complex information. The Wizard-of-Oz technique is well-suited to generating corpora from which information about tasks and strategies can be derived. It also allows us to collect early data about the effectiveness of various information presentation strategies without actually implementing these in a working system. The goals of the Wizard-of-Oz experiment were to: (a) acquire user models (b) generate representative domain tasks (c) understand the requirements for designing and building a Wizard interface; (d) evaluate dialogue strategies that the Wizard could perform in real time that exploit the user models; and (e) collect sample dialogues to explore the utility of the user model/dialogue strategy combination, which could also be used as training material for the spoken language understanding components of the system.

We recruited a set of 18 users via email who frequently go out to dinner and had some familiarity with the neighbourhoods and restaurants in NYC. We told the users that they would be interacting with a Wizard (referred to as "Monsieur Croque"), who would simulate the functionality and strategies of the real dialogue system. We told them that the Wizard had access to information about thousands of restaurants in the New York area, derived from Zagat's reviews. Zagat's is a popular US food guide. It is based on feedback and reviews from ordinary people who have eaten at restaurants and who volunteer their views. A Zagat's entry for a restaurant includes the following types of information: food type, food ratings, locations, prices, service, decor, along with restaurant reviews that are composites of comments made by different Zagat survey participants.

2.1 Generating Representative Tasks and Acquiring User Models

We gave 18 users an illustrative example of the types of information available for all restaurants in our database and asked them to generate two sample task scenarios, according to the following description: *A scenario should be a description of a set of characteristics that would help Mr. Croque find a small set of restaurants that would match your description. Our goal is to examine the process by which you and Mr. Croque jointly identify a restaurant that you want to eat at, so please do not select a particular restaurant in advance.* The initial instructions and scenario generation were carried out in email. Fifteen users responded with sample task scenarios. Two such tasks (MS and CK) are shown in Figure 4; a dialogue generated for the CK task is shown in Figure 5. There are several points to note about the tasks. First, task scenarios often specify particular situational constraints, e.g., meal cost of $50 in MS, which override more general dispositional preferences, (for example that MS would generally only pay $30 for a meal). Second, scenarios often mention information which is not generally available from our database, e.g., wine selection in CK. One well documented problem with this type of system lies in specifying to the user exactly what data the system knows about.

Our next step was to determine a user model for each person. In order to define a multi-attribute decision model for the restaurant domain, we first had to determine the attributes and their relative weighting for particular users. Edwards and Barron describe a procedure called SMARTER for eliciting multi-attribute decision models for particular users or user groups (Edwards and Barron, 1994). This method requires users to rank attributes. It takes only a few minutes and has been shown to result in high accuracy user models (Edwards and Barron, 1994).

USER	TASK
MS	We want to go to the Indian restaurant with the best cuisine and the best service in walking distance of the Broadway theater district. We can't eat before 6, and we need to be able to leave the restaurant by 7:30 to make an 8 p.m. show near Times Square. Don and I will both arrive separately via subway, so transportation isn't an issue. We're willing to pay up to $50 each for the meal, including drinks.
CK	I'm going to see the play Chicago on May 19. It is at the Shubert Theatre. I'm going to the matinee. Since this is a birthday celebration, we want to go out for an early dinner afterwards. I think a French restaurant in walking distance from there would be nice. My friends are wine experts, so it would be good if there was an impressive wine selection. I'm not too worried about the price, but I don't want to have to mortgage my house for this meal.

Figure 4. Two sample tasks from users MS and CK.

We elicited models for 18 users; the models are stored in a database that is accessed by the Wizard programme. Figure 6 shows three of the user models. The columns show the weightings associated with continuous variables and particular likes/dislikes for categorical variables. For all of the users, food quality is important, being the highest or second highest ranked attribute for users overall. Cost is also relatively important for each of these users, with both decor and service being of lesser importance. Overall in the 18 user models, food quality and cost were generally among the top three ranked attributes, while the ranking of other attributes such as decor, service, neighbourhood and food type varied widely.

2.2 Designing a Wizard Interface

The Wizard's task of generating dialogue responses in real time based on a specified set of strategies and a user model is extremely demanding. By carrying out pilot studies using pen and paper, and accessing restaurant information web sites, we identified several requirements for a Wizard Interaction Tool:

1 It had to allow the Wizard to specify user constraints on restaurant options in a flexible way (e.g., West Village, costing $50-$80);

2 It had to respond to Wizard queries in real time;

3 It had to provide a ranking of options consistent with a user model;

4 It had to support the use of many different user models;

5 It had to allow the Wizard to easily see, for different user models, the reason why a particular option was highly ranked;

Wiz:	So there are approximately 20 restaurants that satisfy the criteria that you specified. The first one is called Lespinasse and it's a French restaurant in midtown east which has excellent food decor and service and the cost is $86.
CK:	do you have any sample menus or anything?
Wiz:	I am sorry, I have no sample menus.
CK:	are they known for their wine list?
Wiz:	again I am sorry I haven't got that information.
CK:	ok can you tell me about another restaurant then?
Wiz:	I do have, I do have reviews.
CK:	for that Lespinasse restaurant.
Wiz:	yes.
CK:	can you read me the review or part of it?
Wiz:	The much-celebrated Gray Kunz has departed, leaving the more traditional Christian Louvrier at his place behind the stove.
Wiz:	that's it.
CK:	(laughs) ok. Tell me about another restaurant
Wiz:	ok the next restaurant is called La Grenouille, it's again a French restaurant. Again it's in midtown east, the food quality decor and service are all excellent the cost of this one is $80.
CK:	ok do you have menus or reviews for this one.
Wiz:	the review says: Gorgeous flowers, fine service, rich people and a menu written entirely in French.
CK:	I think that you need better better reviews. They don't. ok the food was excellent in both those places. Can you tell me about can you tell me how far those are from the Shubert theatre?
Wiz:	That's 8 blocks.
CK:	8 blocks so that's great. Ok. Do you have anything that's tell me about the best restaurant that you have.
Wiz:	the best restaurant along what dimension?
CK:	erm
Wiz:	in terms of food quality, cost..
CK:	food quality
Wiz:	ok, erm the best quality restaurant is er Lespinasse
CK:	ok Lespinasse, that's the first one that you told me about.
Wiz:	yes
CK:	ok, erm ,then I'm happy with that one.

Figure 5. Excerpt form the Wizard dialogue with user CK, default strategy, CK task from Figure 4.

6 It had to allow the user to modify the task constraints over the course of the dialogue.

It was obviously impossible to simply use the Zagat's web site to support a Wizard-of-Oz data collection since:(1) networking delays mean that it often did not respond in real time; (2) it did not support the use of different user models;

UsrFQ	Serv	Dec.	Cost	Nbh.	FT	Nbh Likes	Nbh Dislikes	FT Likes	FT Dislikes
CK 0.41	0.10	0.03	0.16	0.06	0.24	Midtown, Chinatown, TriBeCa	Harlem, Bronx	Indian , Mexican, Chinese, Japanese, Seafood	Vegetarian, Vietnamese, Korean, Hungarian, German
HA 0.41	0.10	0.03	0.16	0.06	0.24	Upper W. Side, Chelsea, Chinatown, E. Village, TriBeCa	Bronx, Uptown, Harlem, Upper E. Side, Lower Manhattan	Indian, Mexican, Chinese, Japanese, Thai	no-dislike
OR 0.24	0.06	0.16	0.41	0.10	0.03	W. Village, Chelsea, Chinatown, TriBeCa, E. Village	Upper E. Side, Upper W. Side, Uptown, Bronx, Lower Manhattan	French, Japanese, Portugese, Thai, Middle Eastern	no-dislike
SD 0.41	0.10	0.03	0.16	0.06	0.24	Chelsea, E. Village, TriBeCa	Harlem, Bronx	Seafood, Belgian, Japanese	Pizza, Vietnamese

Figure 6. Sample user models: FQ = Food Quality, Serv = Service, Nbh = Neighbourhood; FT = Food Type.

and (3) new constraints added while executing the task entailed respecifying the whole query from the top level page.

We therefore built a Wizard Interaction Tool (WIT) to aid in data collection. WIT was built using dynamic HTML and the display was driven using XSLT transformations of the underlying database of New York restaurant information. This allowed the web browser display to be extremely fast. The database was populated with the database of New York restaurants used in MATCH and augmented with additional information that was downloadable from the Zagat's web site. WIT allows the Wizard to specify a set of restaurant selection criteria, and returns a list of options that match the users' request. The tool also supports the selection of any user model, so that the Wizard can identify restaurant options and attributes that are important to the particular user, as explained in more detail below. The Wizard used this information, along with a written schema of dialogue strategies to guide his interaction with the user in each dialogue.

Figure 7 illustrates the Wizard interaction tool (WIT). The main function of the interface is to provide relevant information to allow the Wizard to quickly identify sets of restaurants satisfying the user's query, along with reasons for choosing them, while respecting the particular preferences of that specific user. The tool contains three main panels. The right hand panel supports query specification, allowing the Wizard to specify constraints corresponding to the user's query. as a Boolean combination of constraints and database attribute values. In this example the specified query is *Japanese, Korean, Malaysian or Thai restaurants, costing between 30-40 dollars, with food quality greater than 20 and service and decor greater than 15 anywhere in Manhattan.* The right hand panel contains radio buttons allowing the Wizard to specify: cost range (using one button for upper, and one for lower limits), food quality, service, decor, cuisine and neighbourhood. Note that neighbourhood is not depicted as the user has scrolled to the top of the relevant panel. Omitting a selection (e.g., neighbourhood) means that this attribute is unconstrained, corresponding in this case to the statement *anywhere in Manhattan.*

The left hand panel shows the specific restaurants satisfying the query along with information for each restaurant including its overall utility calculated using the relevant user model, and the absolute values for food quality, service, decor and cost. For each attribute we also supply corresponding weighted attribute values, shown in brackets after each absolute attribute value. The overall utility and weighted attributes are all specific to a given user model. In this example, for the restaurant Garden Cafe (the first option in the left hand panel), the overall utility is 80, absolute food quality is 25 (weighted value 35), service is 25 (weighted value 8), decor is 15 (weighted value 2) and cost is 38 dollars (weighted value 10). So, according to the user model, the main reason why CK should like Garden Cafe is that the food quality is excellent, as indicated by the fact that this attribute contributes almost half of the overall weighted utility (35 out of 80 units).

The centre panel of WIT provides specific information about the restaurant selected in the left hand panel, including its address, neighbourhood, a review and telephone number.

Overall the tool provides a method for the Wizard to quickly identify candidate restaurants satisfying a particular user's preferences, along with reasons (the weighted attribute values) why the user should choose that restaurant. The UI also allows the Wizard to see at a glance the trade-offs between the different restaurants, by comparing the different weighted utilities. For example, the main reason for preferring the Garden Cafe over Taka (second in the list, highlighted) is that it has better service and decor (as shown by the different weighted values of these attributes).

We demonstrate the effects of the user model by showing the results for the same query for the OR user model from Figure 6. The different user model for

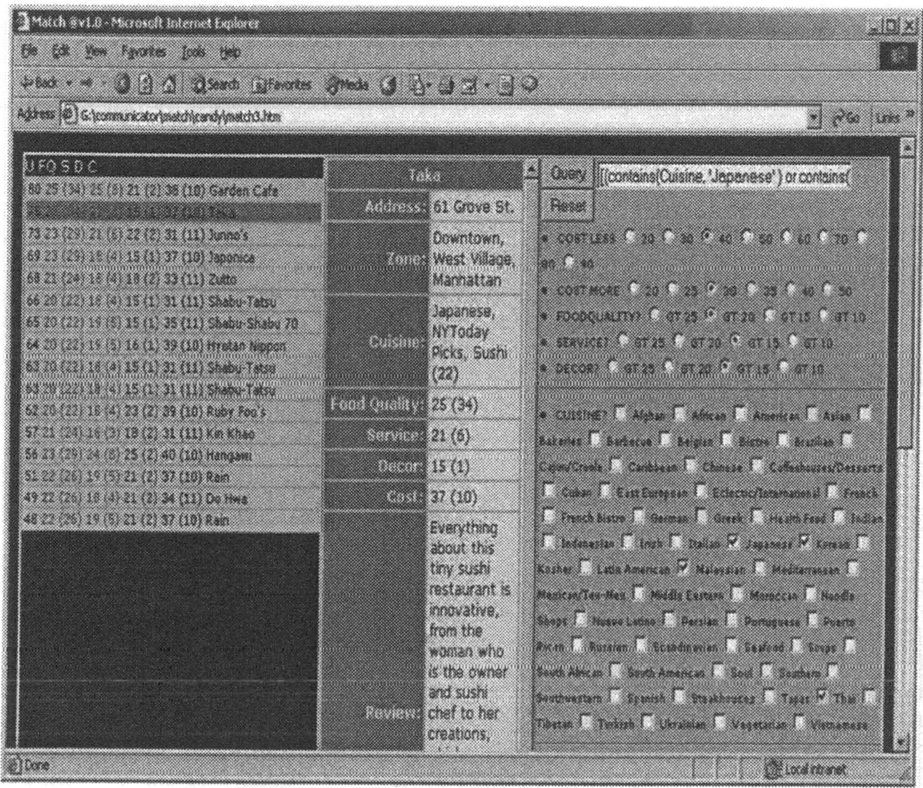

Figure 7. Wizard interface for user CK after Wizard enters query for: " Japanese, Korean, Malaysian or Thai restaurants, costing between 30-40 dollars, with food quality greater than 20 and service and decor greater than 15 anywhere in Manhattan."

OR leads all weighted utilities to change, causing a change in the ordering of the overall set of options. In Figure 7, the highest ranked restaurant was Garden Cafe, mainly because of its good food quality (the attribute most highly valued by user CK). In contrast in Figure 8, the highest ranked restaurant is Junnos because of its reasonable cost, cost being the most highly valued attribute for user OR.

It is also possible for the Wizard to easily override preferences expressed in the user model by specifying additional constraints on the query. For example, Figure 9 illustrates a dialogue with the Wizard with user HA. The user model for user HA is given in Figure 6. As the user model indicates, HA has expressed a preference for Japanese food (see column FT Likes). However during the dialogue in Figure 9, in turn HA10, HA overrides this preference in the current situation. The Wizard implements this override by clicking the

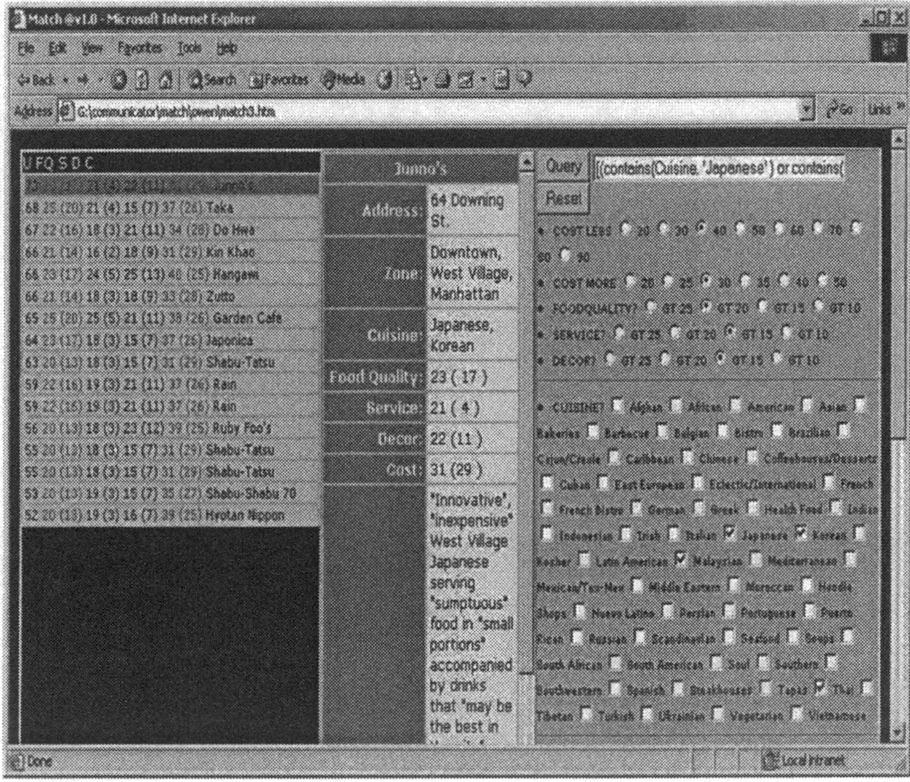

Figure 8. Wizard interface for user OR after Wizard enters query for: "Japanese, Korean, Malaysian or Thai restaurants, costing between 30-40 dollars, with food quality greater than 20 and service and decor greater than 15 anywhere in Manhattan".

"not Japanese" button in the query specification window. Similarly, when HA specifies in turn HA18, that he is also not interested in Italian food, the Wizard can simply add to the set of constraints on the query by clicking "not Italian" (selected by scrolling down the screen).

2.3 Wizard Dialogue Strategy

In addition to identifying tasks and user models, we were also interested in testing specific hypotheses about information presentation strategies. Our pilot studies with pen and paper indicated that a major problem for users was to remember and compare complex sets of options and their attributes. To reduce this complexity we therefore devised a combined SUMMARY/RECOMMEND

Wiz1: I've actually got, erm, a large number of restaurants, again this time about, 50 I'd say, erm
HA2: do you know the location of the Lucille Lortel theatre? I should know I've just been at a play there.
Wiz3: its on, erm, its between 6 and 7th avenues on, is it Nicholas? Christopher.
HA4: oh its, I see yes. Right yes, I know where it is.
Wiz5: erm, so its west village, right, west of west village.
HA6: right
Wiz7: so I have erm, the top three restaurants are erm again very similar in decor, they have different food quality service and cost. And the first one I have is er a Japanese in the west village, erm, very good food and service, erm, the cost is $37.
HA8: ok, since I just had Japanese.
Wiz9: you don't want Japanese?
HA10: I think I'll want something different today.
Wiz11: ok. erm, so I've now got about 40 erm, the top three on this occasion, erm, all have very similar decor, but they have different food quality, service and cost, erm, the top one is erm, Mexicana Mama, erm, which is west village Mexican/Tex/mex which has er very good food, er poor decor , sorry very good service, and erm the cost is $26. The next one is the Pearl Oyster Bar which is again west village, it's a seafood restaurant excellent quality food, erm, decent service, cost is $34.
HA12: can you read the review for that - does it say anything about how fresh the seafood is?
Wiz13: its just a marble counter with a few small tables, but Pearl has won over its neighbourhood with its casual charm, and Maine inspired seafood.
HA14: hmm that's Maine as in the state?
Wiz15: yes. erm the next one is erm, called the Blue Ribbon, erm this is again west village, it's a new American west with er very good food and service, the cost is $45 a head. Do you want to hear some more?
HA16: er yes
Wiz17: erm the next three I've got er again have very similar decor, they differ in terms of food quality service and cost. Er the first one is Il Mulino, which is, erm west village Italian, it has excellent food, erm, very good service, erm, the cost is $65 a head.
HA18: ok, er you can probably skip Italian as well as Japanese.
Wiz19: ok.
HA20: I've been eating too much Italian food. And er do you have a couple more?
Wiz21: yes, erm, there's Natali West, which is, erm, which is west village Indian, which has, erm, decent food, erm and service, the cost is $27. do you want to hear more?
HA22: yeah
Wiz23: erm, the the next three I have erm again have very similar er decor, they differ in terms of food quality service and cost. Erm, the first one is Little Basil which is a Thai restaurant in the West Village which has, erm, decent food and service, the cost is $27 a head.
HA24: and can you read the review for that?
Wiz25: this is not typical Thai home cooking yet the food remains true to the essence of Thai cuisine with salty sour hot and sweet flavours. do you want to
HA26: well, ok, I actually I think that I like the erm, the Oyster,
Wiz27: ok, the Pearl Oyster
HA28: Pearl Oyster bar
Wiz29: the Pearl Oyster bar
HA30: so I think, I think, that I'll go for trying to reserve that.

Figure 9. Wizard dialogue with user HA, tailored strategy, for the West Village task.

strategy, which we compared with a SERIAL presentation strategy similar to that used by current speech dialogue systems (Levin et al., 2000).

The SUMMARY provides an overview of the range of overall utility of the option set, along with the dimensions along which that set differ with respect to their attribute values. The aim is to inform users about both the set of choices, along with the range of reasons for making those choices. After entering a query corresponding to the user's choice in WIT, the Wizard examines the user selected set of restaurants and determines which attributes have the *same* values and which attributes have *different* values. Then he states for the chosen restaurants which attributes are similar and which are different. The RECOMMENDATION then describes the first restaurant including all attributes that have not been mentioned so far. The tailored strategies are applied with the relevant user model. The RECOMMENDATION strategy that the Wizard uses in the dialogues is motivated by user tailored strategies for the real estate domain described in (Carenini and Moore, 2001).

The Zagat attributes are on a scale of 1-30. The Wizard's dialogue strategy lexicalises the absolute values, as follows, in order to increase comprehensibility: 26-30 excellent; 21-25 very good; 16-20 decent; 11-15 poor. We did not lexicalise price instead using absolute value, as there was little agreement about how to describe cost among pilot subjects. Two restaurants were judged to have the same value for a given attribute if the attribute had the same lexicalisation. We did not make similarity judgements about price.

Here is an example of a SUMMARY/RECOMMEND STRATEGY: *There are 20 restaurants that satisfy your criteria. The first three have decent decor, but differ in food quality, service and cost. The first one I have is the Garden Cafe, which is in midtown east. It's Japanese, it has very good food and service and the cost is 38 dollars.*

Note that although this strategy states the total number of restaurants satisfying a query, we provide details about just three restaurants to avoid overloading the user. If there are fewer than three that satisfy the query then we obviously just provide information about these.

We contrasted this with the SERIAL strategy applied with a default user model derived by combining the average weights for the 18 user models we collected. The SERIAL strategy specified the number of restaurants satisfying the query, and then stated the attributes in sequence, stating positive before negative values and aggregating across these where possible: *There are 18 restaurants that satisfy your criteria, the first one is Nyona, which is in Chinatown, it's southeast Asian, the food quality is very good, although the decor and service are poor. The cost is 21 dollars.*

2.4 Collecting Sample Dialogues

Six subjects participated in the Wizard dialogue collection experiment resulting in a corpus of 24 dialogues. All of the subjects were familiar with Manhattan restaurants. We first examined the 30 typical tasks generated by our users. By identifying the common characteristics of these user-generated tasks, we generated two further control tasks for the domain. Each user participated in four tasks, two that they had generated themselves and two control tasks. We used this combination of user-generated and control tasks to combine ecological validity while controlling for task variability. User-generated tasks have the advantage of being both real and motivating, i.e., they are problems that the user genuinely wants to solve. At the same time, however there was a great deal of variability in the complexity and number of solutions to these user-generated tasks, and we wanted to be able to reduce this using the control tasks.

The underlying model and Wizard strategy were also varied; each user carried out two tasks with their own user model, and the tailored SUMMARY/RECOMMENDATION dialogue strategies. Each user also carried out two tasks with the default user model and the SERIAL strategy. Model/strategy and task provenance were crossed so that each user overall received four tasks: self-task/own model/tailored strategy, self task/default model/serial strategy, control-task/own model/tailored strategy, control-task/default model/serial strategy. Users carried out the four tasks in two separate sessions. Task order was randomised but each session included one user-generated and one control-task, one own model/tailored strategy and one default model/serial strategy.

A sample dialogue illustrating a control task of *Find a restaurant in the West Village* using a strategy tailored to user HA is shown in Figure 9. A dialogue illustrating the CK task in Figure 4 with the default user model and the SERIAL dialogue strategy is in Figure 5. This dialogue illustrates issues concerning what information the Wizard has available and the user's understanding of the system's capabilities. The user is trying to find a French restaurant for her friends who are food snobs. She would like to hear about the menu and wine list but this information is not available. The Wizard offers that he does have reviews, but a little later, she says that better reviews are needed. The dialogue also illustrates how the Wizard needed access to distance information. The real MATCH system can do such calculations, but this was not implemented in WIT. The Wizard kept a map of New York City next to him during the dialogue interactions, and tried to quickly make such calculations.

For each dialogue we also collected both quantitative and qualitative data. We collected quantitative information about the number of turns, words and duration of each dialogue. After each dialogue was completed, the users were asked to complete a survey. The survey first requested the users to give permission for their dialogues to become part of a public corpus so they can be distributed as part of the ISLE project. Then they were required to state their degree of agreement on a 5 point Likert-scale with three specific statements designed to probe their perception of their interaction with the Wizard (Mr. Croque): (1) I feel confident that I selected a good restaurant in this conversation; (2) Mr. Croque made it easy to find a restaurant that I wanted to go to; and (3) I'd like to call Mr. Croque regularly for restaurant information.

2.5 Results of the Wizard Study

The Wizard study allowed us to collect 30 representative tasks and 24 dialogues, along with user models for 18 users for a complex information seeking domain. We also devised a useful tool for supporting Wizard-of-Oz style data collection, that embodies user's specific preferences. This should support the collection of further data in this, and with suitable modifications, other domains.

Users' qualitative comments were useful for the further development of both the MATCH system and the strategies implemented in it. Our main experimental manipulation was not completely successful: several of our predicted effects were not supported by our data because our combined SUMMARY/RECOMMEND strategy did not improve efficiency of information access more than our control strategy. This may have been because we ran too few subjects. Nevertheless we did observe some interesting findings that confirmed our predictions: Users were more proactive with the Own Model/Tailored combination in actively supplying task constraints, and we also found correlations between task length and perceived task complexity, as well as between verbosity and likelihood of future use. Overall these findings provide some evidence for the benefits of strategies that are tailored to user requirements and that reduce the overall length of the dialogue. We next set out to define and test such strategies.

One problem with the Wizard-of-Oz method is that the cognitive demands on the Wizard mean that it is hard to test multiple strategies simultaneously. Furthermore, the fact that strategies occur in different dialogue contexts for different users makes it hard to draw definitive conclusions. We attempted to address these problems in our next study, using the Overhearer method.

3. Overhearer Experiment

The idea behind the *Overhearer* method is that the subject is an "overhearer" of a series of exchanges from several dialogues, that have previously been logged as successful interactions with MATCH. The experimental subject is asked, for each exchange, to provide feedback assessing some aspect of the quality of the system's output. Even though the Overhearer method requires our information presentation strategies to be fully implemented and integrated into the system, the use of the method: (1) allows us to get feedback during the course of the dialogue, rather than only at the end of the dialogue; (2) allows us to finesse problems with speech recognition and understanding, which may not be robust enough to support dialogue interaction with real users at the point at which we are trying to refine dialogue management and response strategies; and (3) allows us to ask the user to directly compare and contrast the use of two (or more) alternative dialogue strategies in the same dialogue context. The remainder of this section first describes the experimental setup and then summarises our results.

3.1 Experimental Method

Each dialogue involves one restaurant-selection task, but requires several exchanges to complete. Users' judgements are elicited using a series of web-pages. Each web page sets up the task by showing the MATCH system's graphical response for an initial user query, e.g., *Show Italian restaurants in the West Village*. Then the page shows the user circling some subset of the restaurants and asking the system to *summarise*, *compare* or *recommend* options from the circled subset. Figure 10 shows an example of an initial web page with the systems graphical response, followed by a screen dump showing the user circling a set in order to ask for a comparison. Each user completed 4 tasks with the system.

The subject sees one page each for SUMMARY and RECOMMEND, and two for COMPARE, for each task. On each page, the subject sees one system response tailored to her user model, and a different one tailored to the user model of another randomly selected subject. The order of the four tasks, and the order of appearance of strategies within the task is consistent across subjects. However, the order of presentation of subject-tailored and other-tailored responses is randomised from page to page.

For each instance of a RECOMMEND, SUMMARY, or COMPARE, the subject is asked to state her degree of agreement (on a 5-point Likert-scale) with the following statement, intended to determine the *informativeness*, or *information quality*, of the response: *"The system's utterance is easy to understand and it provides exactly the information I am interested in when choosing a restaurant."*.

This entire sequence of web pages is presented twice, as we wanted to compare spoken and textual presentation of information. We wanted to test the hypothesis that outputs tailored by User Models would be especially helpful for speech because the additional memory load of remembering complex information. In this study we did not test the utility of multimodal outputs. The first time the subject can only read (not hear) the system responses. The second time, she can only hear them. We used this read-then-hear approach after careful piloting because we wanted to make comparisons between text and speech that were not biased by the performance of TTS. By presenting subjects with already familiar material, we hoped that their judgements would not be prejudiced by an inability to understand poor TTS.

To summarise, each subject "overhears" a sequence of four dialogues about different restaurant-selection tasks. The entire sequence is presented twice (once for text, once for speech). The subject makes eight information qual-

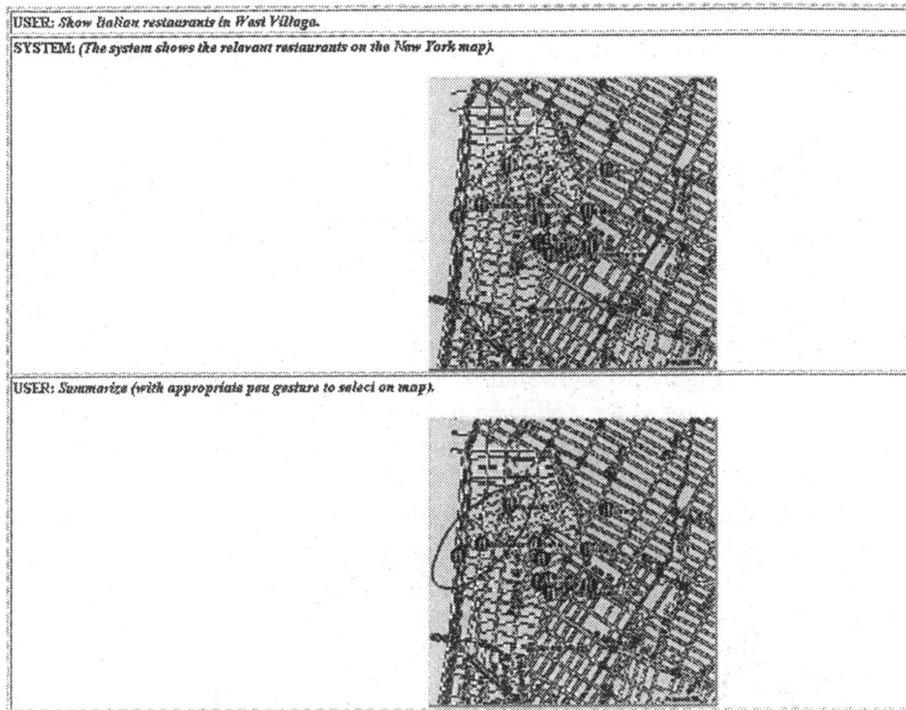
USER: Show Italian restaurants in West Village.
SYSTEM: (The system shows the relevant restaurants on the New York map).
USER: Summarize (with appropriate pen gesture to select on map).

Now please evaluate these variants of the subsequent dialog utterances by the SYSTEM in the above multimodal dialog context.

For each variant, please rate to what extent you agree with the following statement:

The system's utterance is easy to understand and it provides exactly the information I am interested in when making a restaurant selection.

1. SYSTEM: The 3 restaurants have the same price range of 28 to 33 dollars. They differ in food quality, and decor.

   The system's utterance is easy to understand and it provides exactly the information I am interested in when choosing a restaurant.
   ○ Completely disagree ○ Somewhat disagree ○ Neither agree nor disagree ○ Somewhat agree ○ Completely agree

2. SYSTEM: The 3 restaurants have the same price range of 28 to 33 dollars. They differ in food quality.

   The system's utterance is easy to understand and it provides exactly the information I am interested in when choosing a restaurant.
   ○ Completely disagree ○ Somewhat disagree ○ Neither agree nor disagree ○ Somewhat agree ○ Completely agree

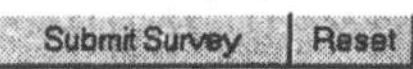
Submit Survey
Reset

Figure 10. Sample web page for Overhearer experiment.

ity judgements for each dialogue each time. The total number of information quality judgements per subject is sixty-four. The total time required to complete the experiment is approximately half an hour per subject.

3.2 Overhearer Experimental Results

Sixteen subjects completed the experiment. All were fluent English speakers. We also had them provide demographic information, about the frequency they ate out, and their familiarity with Manhattan, as we felt that these might affect their judgements. Most eat out moderately often (seven eat out 3-5 times per month, six 6-10 times). All sixteen currently live in northern New Jersey. Eleven described themselves as somewhat or quite familiar with Manhattan, while five thought they were not very familiar with it. After the experiment, ten subjects identified themselves as very interested in using a system like MATCH in the future.

To analyse the results, we first tested whether the type of user model affected subjects' rankings of the information quality of the system's responses. A one-way Analysis of Variance (ANOVA) for information quality by strategy and model indicates no overall effect of model ($F = 1.0$, $p = 0.30$ n.s.).

However, the Random model condition includes cases where the randomly assigned model is close to the User's Own model. We therefore filtered the original set of judgements to exclude cases where the distance between the Random Model and the User's Own Model was less than 0.2. This removed 9% of judgements from the original data set. To test the hypotheses, we conducted an analysis of variance with Model Type (Own,Random) * Mode (Speech,Text) * Strategy (Recommend, Compare2, Compare3,Summary) as independent variables and Judgements of Response Quality as dependent variable.

As predicted, there were main effects for Model Type ($F=6.00$, $df = 1,906$, $p < 0.02$) showing that using the User's Own Model significantly improved judgements. Again as predicted, Mode was significant, ($F=7.57$, $df = 1,906$, $p < 0.01$), with Text responses being rated more highly than Speech. There were also differences between the different Strategies ($F=117.59$, $df = 3,906$, $p < 0.0001$), with post hoc tests showing the Summary Strategy being judged as much worse than others. Finally, and contrary to our predictions, there was no interaction between Model Type and Mode ($F=0.06$, $df = 1,906$, $p > 0.05$). We expected that the additional difficulty of remembering complex spoken information would lead users to especially prefer responses generated using their Own Model in the Speech condition, given that these are explicitly tailored to their needs. The absence of the interaction term means that this prediction was not confirmed.

Thus, we were able to use the Overhearer method to test the efficacy of user tailored dialogue strategies based on the decision-theoretic user models, even though the complete system was not robust enough to support a data collection with real users interacting live with the system. Our main prediction was confirmed, namely that the user models are effective at addressing the problem of information presentation for complex problem-solving tasks.

4. Discussion

This chapter makes both technical and methodological contributions. At the technical level, we have addressed a critical problem for multimodal systems, namely presentation of information about multiple options each with complex attributes, in a way that enables users to make informed comparisons between these options. We summarise our research on information presentation techniques based on user models that are motivated by multi-attribute decision theory (Stent et al., 2002; Walker et al., 2002; Walker et al., 2004; Whittaker et al., 2002). These address the information presentation problem by allowing us to identify options that are relevant to the specific user, as well as the attributes of those options that are most important to that particular user. These are promising techniques which may generalise to speech-only interfaces, where again there are problems of complex information presentation.

Our methodological contribution is to describe how different methods can be used in iterative development of multimodal systems. We have shown how a combination of Wizard-of-Oz and Overhearer techniques can be used to derive system requirements and develop information presentation algorithms without needing to develop complete working systems at the outset. The Wizard-of-Oz technique is more open-ended: allowing us to determine user tasks and strategies as well as to pilot various expert presentation strategies. Although this data can be gathered using tools that are fairly straightforward to develop, there are nevertheless important design constraints for such tools, in that they need to support the Wizard in producing complex but plausible system behaviours in real-time. While the technique allows rich data to be collected, one limitation of this data is that it does not carefully control the dialogue context in which various strategies are generated. In contrast the Overhearer technique allows more control: once we have clear ideas about potential presentation strategies we can systematically compare and evaluate these in situations where we can control the specific dialogue context. However one weakness of the Overhearer technique is that it measures *perception* rather than observed behaviour and in the long term Overhearer data should be supplemented with this.

In conclusion, we have presented and evaluated novel algorithms for information presentation in multimodal systems, and described methods by which such algorithms can be iteratively developed. Future work will explore other information presentation techniques and evaluate other potential uses of information derived from these types of user model.

Acknowledgements

The work reported in this chapter was partially funded by DARPA contract MDA972-99-3-0003 and by the National Science Foundation under Grant No. 9910603 (ISLE) to the University of Pennsylvania. Thanks also to our colleagues on the MATCH project, Johanna Moore, Michael Johnston, Patrick Ehlen, Guna Vasireddy, Srini Bangalore, Preetam Maloor and Amanda Stent.

References

André, E. (2002). Natural language in multimedia/multimodal systems. In Mitkov, R., editor, *Handbook of Computational Linguistics*, pages 715–734. Oxford University Press.

Bangalore, S. and Johnston, M. (2000). Tight coupling of multimodal language processing with speech recognition. In *Proceedings of International Conference on Spoken Language Processing (ICSLP)*, pages 126–129, Beijing, China.

Beutnagel, M., Conkie, A., Schroeter, J., Stylianou, Y., and Syrdal, A. (1999). The AT&T next-generation text-to-speech system. In *Proceedings of Meeting of ASA/EAA/DAGA*, pages 20–24, Berlin, Germany.

Carenini, G. and Moore, J. D. (2000). An empirical study of the influence of argument conciseness on argument effectiveness. In *Proceedings of Annual Meeting of the Association for Computational Linguistics (ACL)*, pages 150–157, Hong Kong, China.

Carenini, G. and Moore, J. D. (2001). An empirical study of the influence of user tailoring on evaluative argument effectiveness. In *Proceedings of International Joint Conference on Artificial Intelligence (IJCAI)*, pages 1307–1314, Seattle, Washington, USA.

Edwards, W. and Barron, F. H. (1994). SMART and SMARTER: Improved simple methods for multiattribute utility measurement. *Organizational Behavior and Human Decision Processes*, 60:306–325.

Johnston, M. and Bangalore, S. (2000). Finite-state multimodal parsing and understanding. In *Proceedings of International Conference on Computational Linguistics*, pages 1200–1208, Saarbrücken, Germany.

Johnston, M. and Bangalore, S. (2001). Finite-state methods for multimodal parsing and integration. In *Proceedings of ESSLLI Workshop on Finite-state Methods, European Summer School in Logic, Language and Information*, pages 74–80, Helsinki, Finland.

Johnston, M., Bangalore, S., Vasireddy, G., Stent, A., Ehlen, P., Walker, M., Whittaker, S., and Maloor, P. (2002). MATCH: An architecture for multimodal dialogue systems. In *Proceedings of Annual Meeting of the Association for Computational Linguistics (ACL)*, pages 376–383, Philadelphia, Pennsylvania, USA.

Keeney, R. and Raiffa, H. (1976). *Decisions with Multiple Objectives: Preferences and Value Tradeoffs*. John Wiley and Sons, Chichester, United Kingdom.

Levin, E., Narayanan, S., Pieraccini, R., Biatov, K., Bocchieri, E., Fabbrizio, G. D., Eckert, W., Lee, S., Pokrovsky, A., Rahim, M., Ruscitti, P., and Walker, M. (2000). The AT&T DARPA Communicator mixed-initiative spoken dialog system. In *Proceedings of International Conference on Spoken Language Processing (ICSLP)*, pages 122–125, Beijing, China.

Oviatt, S. (1999). Ten myths of multimodal interaction. *Communications of the ACM*, 42(11):74–81.

Sharp, R., Bocchieri, E., Castillo, C., Parthasarathy, S., Rath, C., Riley, M., and Rowland, J. (1997). The Watson speech recognition engine. In *Proceedings of International Conference on Acoustics, Speech and Signal Processing (ICASSP)*, pages 4065–4068, Munich, Germany.

Stent, A., Walker, M., Whittaker, S., and Maloor, P. (2002). User-tailored generation for spoken dialogue: An experiment. In *Proceedings of International Conference on Spoken Language Processing (ICSLP)*, pages 1281–1284, Denver, Colorado, USA.

Walker, M., Whittaker, S., Stent, A., Maloor, P., Moore, J., Johnston, M., and Vasireddy, G. (2002). Speech-plans: Generating evaluative responses in spoken dialogue. In *Proceedings of International Conference on Natural Language Generation (INLG)*, pages 73–80, New York, New York, USA.

Walker, M., Whittaker, S., Stent, A., Maloor, P., Moore, J., Johnston, M., and Vasireddy, G. (2004). Generation and evaluation of user tailored responses in dialogue. *Cognitive Science*, In press.

Whittaker, S., Walker, M., and Moore, J. (2002). Fish or fowl: A Wizard of Oz evaluation of dialogue strategies in the restaurant domain. In *Proceedings of International Conference on Language Resources and Evaluation (LREC)*, pages 1074–1078, Las Palmas, Gran Canaria, Spain.

Chapter 15

ENHANCING THE USABILITY OF MULTIMODAL VIRTUAL CO-DRIVERS

Niels Ole Bernsen, Laila Dybkjær

Natural Interactive Systems Laboratory, Odense, Denmark

{ nob,laila } @nis.sdu.dk

Abstract This chapter discusses a series of four user-oriented design analysis problems in a research prototype multimodal spoken language dialogue system for supporting drivers whilst driving. The problems are: (a) when should the system (not) listen to the speech and non-speech acoustics in the car; (b) how to make use of the in-car display in conjunction with spoken driver-system dialogue; (c) how to identify the present driver as a basis for building user models of the driver; and (d) how to create useful online adaptive user modelling of the driver.

Keywords: In-car spoken dialogue systems; In-car multimodal interaction; Driver identification; In-car adaptive user modelling.

1. Introduction

Spoken language dialogue systems (SLDSs) are now firmly positioned in the market and appear set to become available in an increasing number of languages and for a rapidly increasing number of tasks. Current commercial SLDSs help people solve a single task or sometimes several independent tasks through spoken dialogue. The dialogue is still mostly being conducted over the phone but open microphone applications are beginning to proliferate as well. The tasks solved are mainly information retrieval and/or information entry tasks but also in this respect the field is rapidly diversifying into reservation tasks, training tasks, tasks involving important elements of negotiation between user and system, etc.

A typical commercial SLDS has speaker-independent speech recognition; up to several thousand words in its vocabulary; modest natural language pro-

W. Minker, D. Bühler and L. Dybkjær (eds), Spoken Multimodal Human-Computer Dialogue in Mobile Environments, 269-285

cessing of the recogniser's output; increasingly modular dialogue management which often interacts with a domain database; no natural language generation; and spoken output production by means of concatenated speech, i.e., through online combination of recorded sentences, phrases, and words. However, due to its superior flexibility and reflecting recent increases in perceived quality and immediate intelligibility, speech synthesis is now also starting to be used for certain languages. In order to maintain control of users' spoken input behaviour and also to support the user in actually carrying out his task, the dialogue is mostly system-directed, especially in systems intended for irregular and infrequent use. The system thus "takes the user through the task" to its completion in a structured, more or less flexible fashion (Bernsen et al., 1998).

Meanwhile, next-generation systems are gathering in the pipeline based on progress in research. These SLDSs will represent solutions to a series of next-step technical challenges, including robust speech recognition in noisy conditions; very large vocabulary speaker-independent speech recognition and understanding; recognition of the pronunciation variants produced by native speakers of different languages; confidence-adaptive dialogue through dialogue manager use of speech recogniser and natural language processing confidence scores; natural language processing of fully spontaneous spoken input, so that the SLDS no longer has to conduct system-directed dialogue when mixed-initiative dialogue or (still task-oriented) conversational dialogue is more appropriate; dialogue management of mutually dependent tasks; integration of adaptive user models built online from observations of a particular user's behaviour; situation-aware system dialogue based on knowledge of the current situation of the user-system complex; and template-based natural language generation. Moreover, next-generation SLDSs will probably no longer be mainly speech-only, or unimodal, systems but will increasingly combine speech with other modalities for information representation and exchange, enabling multimodal dialogue. Also, systems will increasingly migrate to mobile environments and devices, making location-awareness and mobile internet access highly desirable system properties in many applications.

This chapter discusses a cluster of user-oriented design analysis problems in a research prototype multimodal SLDS which addresses the next-step challenges mentioned above in the context of supporting car drivers whilst driving. Common to the problems discussed is that they concern the design of important aspects of user-system interaction for in-car environments, that they present key usability challenges during the development of the research prototype, that the problems appear to be unsolved so far, and that finding solutions to them may be of interest to designers of mobile multimodal SLDSs more generally. The research prototype system is called VICO (Virtual Intelligent CO-driver) and is being developed in the European HLT VICO project which began in March 2001 and has a duration of three years. The project partners are Robert Bosch GmbH, DaimlerChrysler AG, Istituto Trentino di Cultura, Phonetic Topographics N. V., and NISLab. NISLab is the developer of natural language understanding, dialogue management and response generation components in three languages: English, German and Italian for the VICO prototype discussed in this chapter.

In the following, Section 2 provides a general description of VICO functionality and architecture. Sections 3 through 6 discuss the following problems: when should VICO listen? (Section 3), why use multimodal speech-graphics output in the car? (Section 4), how to identify the driver? (Section 5), and which aspects of the driver's behaviour should VICO model online? (Section 6). Section 7 concludes the chapter by discussing some of the issues for which additional research seems clearly needed.

2. The VICO System

The car driver's environment is both a challenge and an opportunity for next-generation SLDSs developers. Important challenges include noise, from the car itself (engine, air flow, tyres, in-car climate regulation, etc.), traffic, rain, passengers, and in-car entertainment systems; very large vocabulary recognition, such as of +100.000 names of German regions, cities, streets, etc.; traffic safety; and ease of use by a large and heterogeneous user population. The opportunities are equally important. Car driving is a safety-critical, heads-up, hands-occupied activity in which the driver is mostly free to speak to fellow passengers and equipment but can only to a very limited extent expend valuable attention resources on GUI (graphical user interface) devices, such as screens, hand-held remote controllers, or keyboards. The car industry and user need studies concur that navigation is the "killer application" task for in-car SLDSs but that spoken interaction might be useful for many other tasks as well (Manstetten et al., 2002). Moreover, there are strong indications that spoken car navigation and use of speech in the car more generally, cannot useably be realised by command-based SLDSs (Minker et al., 2002; Salmen, 2002). The reason is that drivers are not able to remember the required, increasingly large number of spoken commands needed to operate in-car SLDSs. For reasons such as the above, the development of a usable and versatile in-car SLDS is an obvious "technology push" challenge whose "user pull" can be taken for granted.

To address this challenge, we have built the first of two planned prototypes of a natural interactive, multilingual (UK English, German, and Italian), cross-lingual (recognising accented pronunciations of proper names), confidence-adaptive, and multimodal in-car spoken dialogue system. The first prototype enables navigation assistance, including streets and street numbers, parts of cities, cities, and, when relevant, parts of country for the Trentino Province in Italy; navigation to 25 different point of interest types in this area, such as cinemas, petrol stations, doctors, and airports; information about the VICO system itself (UK English only); and hotel reservation over the internet (simulated) based on a number of driver-defined hotel selection constraints and followed by the actual hotel reservation. The first prototype also includes an observation-based user modelling module which enables VICO to adapt its dialogue behaviour to the current driver's hotel preferences. Finally, restaurant reservation is enabled in the hotel in which the user has booked a room.

The second prototype will provide additional user modelling functionality based on online gathered data on particular drivers as a basis for adaptive system behaviour; navigation to addresses and points of interest in Germany and Greater London; real hotel reservation over the internet; scenic route planning including web-based information on touristic points of interest, such as castles and churches, which will be accessed using GPS-based location awareness; car manual information; news reading; and spoken operation of in-car devices. Throughout its interaction with the driver, VICO will maintain some amount of situation awareness with respect to the car, for instance by avoiding intrusion on the driver in dangerous traffic situations. The driver-VICO dialogue is spontaneous natural interactive dialogue, allowing the driver to address any task and sub-task in any order and using any appropriate linguistic form of expression. Finally, taking into account the in-car and out-of-car (traffic) environment, VICO will incorporate aspects of multimodal communication. Thus, VICO will be activated by pushing a button on the steering wheel and the system will provide both spoken output and graphics display output.

In the following sections, we describe our approach to four key usability challenges facing VICO interaction design and development.

3. VICO Haptics - How and When to Make VICO Listen?

An in-car spoken dialogue system faces the problem of figuring out when the registered acoustics in the cabin is actually input meant for the system or just background noise. One of the really hard problems arises from potential cross-talk between the driver and the passengers while the system is listening.

Ideally, start-stop control of recognition should be performed without being noticed by the user (Furui, 2004). However, given current recognition technology and in order to reduce the amount of recognition problems and nonsense dialogues which may arise from driver-passenger cross-talk, limitation should be imposed on the periods during which the recogniser is listening. In the VICO project it has been decided to introduce a push-to-activate (PTA) button for this purpose. To start VICO and make the system listen, the user must push the button.

3.1 Button Design and Interaction

The design of the push-to-activate button has not been finally decided yet. However, it seems likely that the button will be positioned on the steering wheel. The button will be red when the recogniser is inactive and green when the recogniser is active. If the button is red and the user pushes it, it will turn green as soon as the recogniser is ready.

In addition, we will experiment with acoustic awareness so that the user will not have to look at the button to see whether it is actually red or green. Acoustic awareness may be stimulated through non-speech sound or through spoken words or phrases, such as "hello", or "good morning". We expect that a non-speech sound will be felt less intrusive during daily use of the system compared to using words or phrases to indicate that the system is ready. When the recogniser goes inactive after a period of input inactivity (see below), this may be indicated through non-speech sound as well in addition to the button turning red. Using speech for this purpose, such as saying "bye", would seem less appropriate since the system may still be talking to the driver about the task, for instance by continuing to provide navigation instructions after the recogniser has turned inactive.

The need for some kind of acoustic feedback on when the system is listening is supported by a set of Wizard-of-Oz (WOZ) experiments (see also Section 4). In those experiments, we only used a "button" on a display. The user was not supposed to push anything. The "button" would turn green when the system was ready to listen. However, users were not always aware of the state of the button because they were occupied driving the car and thus were not sure when they were supposed to start speaking. Although there is a difference between just passively waiting for the button to turn green and actively pushing a button which is then expected to become green soon thereafter, it still seems likely that acoustic feedback will be appreciated since it relieves the driver from having to keep an eye on the red/green colour of the button before speaking. The acoustics is sufficient to tell the driver when the recogniser is open and when it has closed.

3.2 When to Turn Off the Recogniser

Since we have decided that the recogniser will not just remain open once the PTA button has been pushed, we also have to find out when it is appropriate to turn off the recogniser. Clearly, it would be unacceptable that the driver has to push the button each time s/he wants to say something during an ongoing dialogue with VICO. On the other hand, however, the longer the recogniser remains open, the larger becomes the risk that it attempts to recognise speech not meant for the system, such as driver-passenger cross-talk. We have identified the following cases in which it seems appropriate to turn off the recogniser by means of a timeout function:

- a task has been completed and the driver does not initiate a new task within the following, say, 8-20 seconds;
- a driver stops interaction in the middle of a task and does not provide input for 8-20 seconds;
- a driver cancels an ongoing task and does not provide new input for 8-20 seconds.

A task is considered "completed" when the negotiation with the user is finished. A user may, e.g., have asked for route guidance to a particular address or point of interest. Once the system and the user have agreed where to go, the task is "completed" although the system may continue to provide (output-only) route guidance for the next 100 kilometres or more.

The system stacks a non-completed task in case the user wants to return to the task in order to complete it. For instance, a traffic situation may occupy the driver's attention for more than 8-20 seconds, in which case the recogniser closes down. The system must be able to easily restore the dialogue state when the user pushes the button anew in order to continue the unfinished dialogue.

Clearly, the solution just proposed does not completely remove the background noise problems caused by driver-passenger cross-talk and other hard-to-model noise factors. In particular, the driver may still be talking to passengers while at the same time trying to have a dialogue with VICO. We do not have data that tells us how often this will be a problem. The system might try to diagnose the problem, when it occurs, through out-of-vocabulary word modelling, confidence score analysis, and other means. Thus, measures to identify input which was not meant for VICO may have to be taken by system modules other than the recogniser. However, this still leaves open the question of how to deal with the problem, when diagnosed. In one approach, VICO simply ignores cross-talk input. In another, VICO applies its user modelling capabilities to remind frequent cross-talkers that driver-passenger cross-talk is counterproductive to getting the task done through spoken interaction with the system (cf. Section 6).

4. VICO Graphics - When might the Driver Look?

Existing text-and-pointing input car navigation systems include a display on which output to the driver is shown throughout interaction. In particular, the display provides feedback on the driver's input when spelling addresses. The display may be small and without map information, using an arrow to show in which direction to turn next, or it may be somewhat larger and display a map showing the present location, direction, and planned route of the car in addition to the text and iconic information which is available on the small display. Navigation information on the screen is accompanied by spoken instructions on where to turn left or right. This output combination generally seems to work quite well. Even if the driver does not have much time for studying the display, many drivers still seem to appreciate the availability of display output. The advantage is that the (static) text and graphics on the screen remains there long enough for the driver to inspect them at will, which is not the case with speech.

What is new in VICO as regards navigation is the spoken negotiation of where to go. For input, today's navigation systems require a remote control which the driver uses to specify the destination through prolonged interaction with the display, doing spelling, on-screen navigation, between-screens navigation, etc., cf. Figure 1. This is definitely not very traffic-safe to do. Spoken interaction will change that, of course, but, very likely, the spoken output during destination negotiation could benefit from being supported by output on the display as long as interaction mainly takes place through speech.

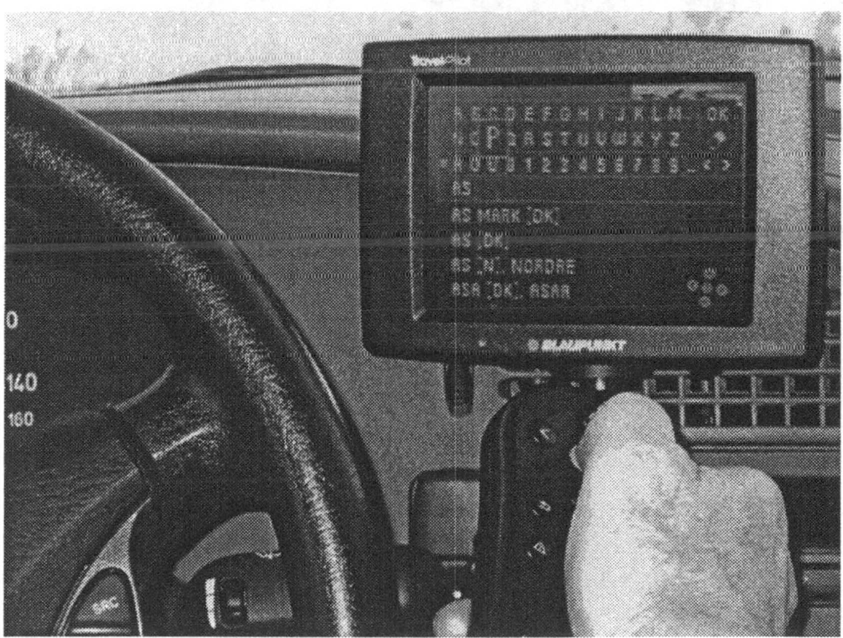

Figure 1. Inputting a destination with one of today's car navigation systems.

We decided to investigate if and when the driver might want to look at the display during a destination negotiation dialogue with VICO, as well as the kind of information users might want on the display. We made a series of

Wizard-of-Oz experiments with spoken input and spoken and text output in December 2001 (3 subjects) and January 2002 (10 subjects), see (Bernsen and Dybkjær, 2001) for details on the December WOZ experiments. To simulate driving the car in traffic we used a PC car game. Subjects were seated in front of a 42" flat screen display showing the traffic ahead in wind-screen view and the traffic behind in rear-mirror view, cf. Figure 2. To control the car, subjects had a force-feedback steering wheel and pedals (accelerator and brakes). Next to the large screen was a small portable computer simulating the in-car display and showing system output text. For the spoken output, the Festival synthesiser was used. Each user was asked to carry out three scenarios. Subjects were interviewed after their interaction with the system.

Figure 2. Driving the simulated car.

The dialogue with VICO was in English. The scenarios all concerned route planning for Danish destinations. We experimented with three different text versions on the car display. All three versions were displayed to each user (one version per scenario) but in differing order. One version was a full text repetition of the spoken output, a second version only included the key destination items of the spoken output, and the third version only provided the agreed-upon destination as text output at the end of the dialogue.

The experiments aimed to collect data on which among the kinds of information offered users would like to see on the display and in which situations they would look at the display. In the following we describe the findings.

Many subjects found it less stressful to use the car game than to drive a real car. As a major reason they indicated the fact that they knew that nothing would happen even if they crashed the car. However, some subjects found that it required much more concentration to play the car game than to drive a real car. Typically, these subjects also found it unsafe to look at the car display whilst driving.

Although most subjects found it less stressful to play the car game than to drive a real car, only a couple of them stated that they used the display quite frequently. Most subjects did not use it much, either because they found it unsafe or because they did not feel a need for it. When the display was used it was typically to cross-check the spoken output. The quality of portions of the output speech was fairly low. Danish location names pronounced by an English synthesiser are often rather difficult to understand. Moreover, as an important part of the experimental setup, the drivers were from time to time distracted by a passenger talking to them, which meant that they were likely to miss what was being said by the system. Better synthesis is certainly available which will reduce the first problem whereas the second problem is not likely to go away in real driving situations.

When subjects did not hear what the system said or were not sure that they got it right, they would typically either ask for repetition of the spoken output or look at the display. Since most subjects only used the display infrequently, these users were not aware of the changing amount of feedback provided in the different experimental conditions. A couple of users complained that there was nothing on the display when they looked. They probably checked the display when the system provided the shortest version of its text output, i.e., when only the finally agreed destination would be displayed but nothing would be displayed during the negotiation dialogue.

Although, for the reasons stated, we did not collect that much data on user preferences as to the length and contents of the text displayed, it appears from the subsequent discussions with subjects that the medium-length text version was the most appropriate. The short version does not provide sufficient support since there will not always be information available on the display when the driver has missed the spoken output. The long text output version, on the other hand, includes too much superfluous information and may be hard to interpret at a glance. The long version may therefore be deemed less safe and less to-the-point than the medium-length version which contains the key destination information expressed in as condensed a form as possible. The main functions of the text output are to allow the driver to check correctness of understanding of the spoken output and to check up on the present state of progress of the dialogue. Even if oral dialogue requires less effort from the user while driving than reading text on a display, situations may occur in which the driver stops listening to the system in order to handle a difficult traffic situation or because a passenger speaks to the driver during the spoken system output. Returning to the dialogue, the driver may either catch up by asking the system where they were at or by checking the display. Based on the WoZ results, we expect that there will be individual differences as to which of the two options drivers prefer because our subjects behaved quite differently with respect to their use of the display versus spoken dialogue. People have different driving experience and different habits, both of which are likely to influence their preferences, so both options should probably be enabled.

Inherent to the problem discussed in the present section is another, larger and more troublesome issue which we have not even begun to analyse. Whatever speech-in-the-car purists might argue, the in-car display is perhaps not likely to go away unless prohibited by law. It is simply too useful for presenting all kinds of information to the driver. If this is true, it becomes less clear exactly how much we will have achieved with respect to increasing traffic safety by replacing destination entry by remote control by destination negotiation through spoken dialogue. To be sure, something will have been achieved since destination entry by remote control is lengthy and hazardous but how much depends on the driver's additional use of the display.

5. Who is Driving this Time?

Based on its observations on the driver's behaviour, VICO incrementally builds and uses for online adaptation to the driver a user model for each driver of the particular car in which the system is installed (see Section 6). In order for VICO user modelling to be of any use, VICO must be able to determine which of the car's drivers is currently driving. Furthermore, driver identification has to be made with near-certainty. If it is uncertain that VICO has correctly identified the driver, driver misidentification will happen too often. In such cases, the driver is likely to be "mistreated" because VICO will adapt its dialogue behaviour to the driver based on a wrong user model. Similarly, the modelled behaviour of the misidentified driver will tend to fudge up the misallocated user model with misleading information. In addition, since the driver's user model cannot be invoked until the driver has been identified, VICO must identify the driver either as one already known to the system or as a new driver up front, i.e., before or, at the latest, as soon as that driver starts the dialogue. Later identification means less support for the driver, and the updated user model runs the risk of having missed to collect important information on the driver's behaviour.

In SLDSs, driver identification design is a non-trivial problem. Among the many conceivable options, we have considered the following (Bernsen, 2002):

- voice identification. Even though today's voice identification technology is not perfect, it might be possible to get near-certain identification in the car, simply because most cars, with the exception of rented cars, have rather few drivers. Voice identification is also to some extent an elegant solution because the driver does not have to do anything other than speak to VICO about some task. Voice identification happens as soon as the driver speaks. However, given its less than 100% reliability, voice identification requires the system to provide feedback, so that the user can make sure that correct identification was made. To provide feedback, the system must be taught, once and for all, to associate some output expression, i.e., a code or the driver's name, with the driver's speech signal;

- driver's code. Contrary to voice identification, the driver's code must be input to VICO explicitly. This may be done by voice, haptically through keystrokes, through personalised ignition key identification, through biometrics, such as measuring the driver's weight, etc. As we are not assuming the presence of keyboard and biometrics facilities, simplicity and traffic safety speak for acoustic or ignition key codes per driver. Correct driver identification is guaranteed, in principle, in the ignition key case which also does not require the driver to remember yet another code. Given its less than 100% reliability, voice code entry, like voice identification, demands that VICO provides code entry feedback;

- driver's spelled first name. This solution enables non-coded feedback on driver identification. However, spelling part or whole of one's name before each interaction is an awkward thing to do;

- voice name enrolment. A first-time user speaks his/her name a few times, causing a voice model of the name to be generated. During later use, the driver just has to speak his/her name to get identified. However, since the enroled name is for recognition purposes only, it cannot be used by the system for providing verification feedback to the driver.

The discussion above aptly illustrates how a range of solutions can be so densely packed in design space that it becomes hard to determine which solution is the best one. However, it may be concluded that the problem of driver identification actually can be useably solved.

An important issue which has not been discussed above, is that passengers might want to talk to VICO as well, for instance in order to relieve the driver of having to carry out a lengthy hotel reservation task. Normally, a car has fewer different drivers than different passengers. If the latter also talk to VICO, the system might come to include dozens of user models for a single car, most of which are not being used at all since they were created by one-time passengers. For this reason, an additional requirement on driver identification would seem to be that only drivers, and not passengers, should cause the creation and use of user models when speaking to the system. Several of the solutions discussed above are compatible with this requirement.

6. Modelling the Driver

Once the driver starts speaking to VICO, the system must try to identify the driver and retrieve the driver's user model, if any. If identification fails, VICO assumes that the driver is new to VICO and immediately creates a new user model (UM) for that driver. In both cases, VICO will subsequently collect relevant information on the driver's behaviour during the spoken interaction and use that information to update its model of the driver. The model itself is used to support the driver during dialogue with VICO. Slightly more systematically expressed, VICO's generic UM-related tasks are (Bernsen, 2002):

1 identify the present driver (cf. Section 5);

2 retrieve the present driver's user model;

3 optionally: create a new user model UM(Dx) for a new driver, Dx;

4 make appropriate online use of the present driver's user model during the driver's dialogue with VICO;

5 collect new information on the present driver during the driver's dialogue with VICO;

6 update the present driver's user model with the new information gathered;

7 store the user model whenever it has been updated with new information.

From a design viewpoint, and ignoring the issue of driver identification discussed above, the hardest problems in the list above probably are points 4, 5, and 6. The comparative difficulty of points 4, 5, and 6 depends on the nature of the information on the driver dealt with by the UM. Thus, before addressing those problems in more detail, decision must be made on which type(s) of information on the driver the system should collect, store, update, and use. In fact, this problem appears to be the hardest of all.

The reason is a rather general one. When embarking on adaptive user modelling in VICO, we enter a technical area fraud with difficulty and past failure. Observation-based user modelling for online adaptation appears to be among the most difficult things to do in developing interactive computer systems, independently of whether those systems use speech or other modalities of information representation and exchange. In fact, user adaptation has proved so difficult to do that it seems fair to say that, by and large, and despite numerous attempts in the past 15-20 years, research and industry have had limited success in developing useful adaptive functionality in the huge variety of interactive systems that already exist. There are successful exceptions, of course, but these tend to be functionally simple. The conclusion we should draw from that fact is that we must be extremely careful in selecting the kind of information on drivers which we want to model. It is better to succeed with one, or a few, observation-based adaptive functionalities in VICO than to fail through ignorance of the difficulties involved by trying to develop an unrealistic number of poor adaptive functionalities.

Based on analysis of some 25-30 candidate kinds of information about driver behaviour which VICO might conceivably collect and use online, we may distinguish between several different generic types of information which VICO could collect and use adaptively. According to the following, possible typology of information, at least three different generic kinds of information about particular drivers may be distinguished:

1 information on the driver's task objectives due to task goals, preferences, habits, etc.;

2 information on the driver's communication with VICO;

3 information on the driver's experience of various kinds.

In the VICO context, each generic kind of information subsumes several more specific information types, such as the driver's hotel preferences (1), the driver's difficulties in being understood by VICO due to strong accent or dialect (2), or the driver's experience in using VICO itself (3). In other words, the information typology helps generate a structured space of candidates for observation-based adaptive user modelling online.

To further constrain the design choices with respect to the user modelling capabilities of VICO, we have identified the following criteria which should be satisfied by a particular kind of driver information in order for that information to be collected and used by VICO:

1 include at least one user modelling functionality belonging to each type in the typology of generic information about the driver described above;

2 the chosen user modelling functionalities should be top quality in terms of their usefulness to all or most drivers. Some functionality may even be top quality and meet all other criteria in the present list, but if it is

only of interest to a small minority of drivers, it remains questionable whether it should be implemented;

3 the chosen user modelling functionalities should provide genuine driver adaptivity without significant drawbacks;

4 the chosen user modelling functionalities should be possible to implement without extreme or unpredictable effort. The reason for including this clause is not only the obvious one that we do not have the time for putting extreme effort into adaptive user modelling. More importantly, it seems easy to conceive of user modelling tasks which cannot be achieved without some kind of research breakthrough, hence the unpredictability clause (see also below);

5 the chosen user modelling functionalities must be based on clearly verifiable information about the driver. In particular, it is not enough that some observable property of the driver's behaviour might be due to a problem which system adaptivity could help with. We need to make sure that the property actually is due to that problem and might not be caused by some other problem which we do not address.

Space does not allow presentation of the pros and cons which we identified in the analysis of each candidate on the long list of kinds of driver information which could potentially be modelled for adaptive driver support. An example sub-type of Type (1) in the typology above, i.e., information on the driver's task objectives, is: store the driver's past hotel preferences, such as number of stars, price, location (city centre, countryside), hotel chain, and possibly other selection constraints as well. Even if not told about them by the driver, VICO could offer to use those constraints as selection criteria when looking for a suitable hotel. It is important, of course, that the driver is able to override those constraints and provide new ones. If not, all we will be doing is to produce yet another failed attempt at creating useful system adaptivity. However, in this case it is easy for the driver to override VICO's suggestions because the driver will be told that the UM has been used for selecting the hotel(s) options offered.

Let us try to evaluate the hotel preferences user modelling functionality using the selection criteria presented above. The functionality is based on clearly verifiable information about the driver (Criterion 5). Thus, the driver's hotel preferences become apparent in the driver's dialogue with VICO. Moreover, it is possible to write an update algorithm for a driver's hotel selection UM which only produces hotel selection constraints when a clear pattern can be discerned in the driver's hotel preferences. The functionality under consideration does not appear to have any significant drawbacks (Criterion 3). Also, this user modelling functionality can be implemented without extreme effort (Criterion 4). What this means is simply that, if we want to implement user modelling functionality at all, implementation of drivers' hotel selection preferences would appear very much as the standard case. So, the final question is whether information on the driver's observed hotel preferences is top quality in terms of its usefulness to all or most drivers (Criterion 2). This question is a difficult one, because the answer to the question depends on, at least, (i) how many users of VICO will actually need to book hotels, (ii) how many users will want to do so en route, and (iii) how many of those users have systematic hotel preferences. We do not know the answer to that question at this point but would clearly need to find out the best we can in order to be able to rank the user modelling option just described among its competitors.

Generally speaking, compared to the problem of identifying a user modelling candidate for information about the driver's task objectives, it would seem considerably harder to build adaptive user modelling with respect to Type (2) information on the driver's communication with VICO. An example is a system which adapts its dialogue behaviour to drivers whose strong dialect or accent makes their dialogue contributions difficult for the system to recognise and understand. One issue, of course, is that we might need two significantly different dialogue structures to accommodate both standard drivers and drivers with strong dialect or accent, making a solution relatively costly to implement (Criterion 4). A second problem is that any solution may be at risk as long as we do not have efficient ways of discriminating between different possible causes of recognition problems. Recognition confidence scores, for instance, cannot tell VICO whether the cause of repeated recognition problems is a strong dialect or accent or something entirely different, such as a driver who regularly talks to passengers whilst having a dialogue with VICO. Similarly, the measurable facts that a driver produces many out-of-vocabulary words or makes unusually many error corrections may be due to many different causes (Criterion 5). On the other hand, solutions to Type (2) user modelling problems, if we could only find them, clearly might provide genuine driver adaptivity, possibly without drawbacks worth mentioning (Criterion 3). And, even if those solutions might not benefit all or most drivers, they might benefit large fractions of exactly those drivers who might otherwise have great difficulty using spoken language dialogue systems (Criterion 2).

Type (3) information, i.e., information on the driver's experience, includes, at least, one obvious candidate for adaptive user modelling, i.e., the driver's experience with VICO itself. The idea is to offer up-front information on VICO to all new drivers independently of whether a new driver asks for it or not. VICO is a complex system both in terms of the tasks it can solve and the languages which may be used in addressing the system (cf. Section 2). New drivers are therefore quite likely to benefit from an introduction to the system which includes information on which tasks it covers and how to operate the system. Thus, provision of this information would seem to be top quality in terms of its usefulness to all or most drivers (Criterion 2) as well as providing genuine adaptivity without any significant drawbacks (Criterion 3). This assumes, of course, that drivers are identified with near-certainty, as discussed above. Implementation will be relatively simple because the system only needs to determine if the current driver is new to the system. It does not have to store a record of the driver's past behaviour nor does it need UM update algorithms, such as those needed for hotel preferences (Criterion 4). Finally, as argued in Section 5, it is clearly verifiable if the driver is new to VICO or not (Criterion 5).

7. Conclusion and Future Work

In this chapter we have discussed four issues of importance to future in-car information systems development. At the time of writing, only one-and-a-half of these issues have been resolved to our satisfaction. This is true, firstly, of the issue of which driver-system dialogue-relevant information to present on the in-car display.

The half solution found concerns observation-based user modelling for online adaptivity. We have designed and implemented the hotel selection preferences UM discussed in Section 6 above, see also (Bernsen, 2003). The functionality still needs to be tested with real users, however.

As for the two other issues discussed above, i.e., driver identification and how and when to make VICO listen, we are still investigating the pros and cons of different solutions. Thus, the duration of the time window in which the system should be listening to the driver will form the topic of future experimentation. Similarly, the problem of driver-passenger conversation while the system is listening continues to demand a more efficient solution than any we have investigated so far. As regards driver identification, we are investigating what the most elegant, useful and usable solution might be. The same applies, in part, at least, to the issue of adaptive driver modelling. Potentially, adaptive driver modelling could be extremely useful to drivers, yet the complexity of the options, trade-offs and technical issues involved would seem to make adaptive driver modelling a highly interesting research challenge which is likely to occupy researchers for some time until the terrain has been appropriately charted and useful solutions identified.

Acknowledgements

VICO is supported by the EU HLT (Human Language Technologies) Programme under Contract IST-2000-25426. We gratefully acknowledge the support.

References

Bernsen, N. O. (2002). Report on user clusters and characteristics. Technical VICO Report D10, NISLab, University of Southern Denmark.

Bernsen, N. O. (2003). On-line user modelling in a mobile spoken dialogue system. In *Proceedings of European Conference on Speech Communication and Technology (EUROSPEECH)*, pages 737–740, Geneva, Switzerland.

Bernsen, N. O., Dybkjær, H., and Dybkjær, L. (1998). *Designing Interactive Speech Systems. From First Ideas to User Testing*. Springer-Verlag, Berlin/-Heidelberg, Germany.

Bernsen, N. O. and Dybkjær, L. (2001). Exploring natural interaction in the car. In Bernsen, N. O. and Stock, O., editors, *Proceedings of International Workshop on Information Presentation and Natural Multimodal Dialogue (IPNMD)*, pages 75–79, Verona, Italy. ITC-Irst.

Furui, S. (2004). Speech recognition technology in multimodal/ubiquitous computing environments. In Minker, W., Bühler, D., and Dybkjær, L., editors, *Spoken Multimodal Human-Computer Dialogue in Mobile Environments*. Kluwer Academic Publishers, Dordrecht, The Netherlands. (this volume).

Manstetten, D., Berton, A., Krautter, W., Grothkopp, B., Steffens, F., and Geutner, P. (2002). Evaluation report from simulated environment experiments. Technical VICO Report D7, DaimlerChrysler.

Minker, W., Haiber, U., Heisterkamp, P., and Scheible, S. (2002). Design issues and evaluation of the SENECA speech-based human-machine interface. In *Proceedings of International Conference on Spoken Language Processing (ICSLP)*, pages 265–268, Denver, Colorado, USA.

Salmen, A. (2002). Multi-modal menus and traffic interaction. Timing as a crucial factor for user driven mode decisions. In *Proceedings of International Conference on Language Resources and Evaluation (LREC)*, pages 193–199, Las Palmas, Gran Canaria, Spain.

Chapter 16

DESIGN, IMPLEMENTATION AND EVALUATION OF THE SENECA SPOKEN LANGUAGE DIALOGUE SYSTEM*

Wolfgang Minker
University of Ulm, Department of Information Technology, Ulm/Donau, Germany
wolfgang.minker@e-technik.uni-ulm.de

Udo Haiber, Paul Heisterkamp
DaimlerChrysler - Research and Technology, Ulm/Donau, Germany
{ udo.haiber,paul.heisterkamp } @daimlerchrysler.com

Sven Scheible
Temic - SDS GmbH, Ulm/Donau, Germany
sven.scheible@temic-sds.com

Abstract This chapter describes a speech-based user interface to a wide range of entertainment, navigation and communication applications in mobile environments by means of human-machine dialogues. The system has been developed in the framework of the EU project SENECA. It uses noise reduction, speech recognition and dialogue processing techniques. An interesting aspect relies in the fact that speech recognition results with low confidence and word-level ambiguities are compensated by engaging flexible clarification dialogues with the user. The SENECA system has been evaluated by means of user tests. With speech input, road safety, especially for complex tasks is significantly improved. The feeling

*This chapter is an extended version of the article entitled "The SENECA Spoken Language Dialogue System" published in Speech Communication, Vol. 43/1-2, pp. 89–102, Copyright (2004), reprinted with permission from Elsevier.

W. Minker, D. Bühler and L. Dybkjær (eds), Spoken Multimodal Human-Computer Dialogue in Mobile Environments, 287-310

of being distracted from driving is smaller with speech input than with manual input.

Keywords: Clarification dialogue; Command & control dialogue; Confidence; Dialogue design; Evaluation; Grammar; Noise reduction; Robustness; Speech recognition; Text enrolment; Voice enrolment.

1. Introduction

People spend more time in their cars and want to make that time as enjoyable and productive as possible. Therefore, a large variety of electronic systems have been made available in the vehicle for comfort, ease of driving, entertainment and communications. All these systems require a rather complex human-machine interaction.

Since driver distraction becomes a significant problem, highly efficient human-machine interfaces are required. In order to meet both comfort and safety requirements, new technologies need to be brought into the car, enabling drivers to interact with onboard systems and services in an easy, risk-free way (Figure 1). Undeniably, spoken language dialogue systems, sometimes enhanced with multimodal capabilities, considerably improve safety and user-friendliness of human-machine interfaces (Gärtner et al., 2001; Green, 2000; Lamel et al., 1998; Minker et al., 2003; Temem et al., 1999; Wahlster et al., 2001).

- Free speaking microphone
- Push-to-activate in steering wheel
- Speech-operated components (radio, CD changer, tape, GSM-telephone, navigation)

Figure 1. Solution to the driver distraction problem: hands-free and eyes-free interaction with onboard systems and services (Gärtner, 2001).

The objective of the research, described in this chapter, is to integrate and further develop speech recognition technology in Spoken Language Dialogue Systems (SLDSs) for the use in cars. The research has been carried out in the framework of the EU project SENECA (Gärtner, 2001) (Speech Control modules for Entertainment, Navigation and communication Equipment in Cars) within the 4th ESPRIT programme and under Human Language Technology (HLT). SENECA has been one of the activities of DaimlerChrysler and Temic Research that was a direct follow-up of the LINGUATRONIC experience.

In 1996, Mercedes-Benz introduced the first generation of LINGUATRONIC. Developed by Temic, LINGUATRONIC is the brand name of a speech dialogue system for completely hands-free operation of the car's mobile phone, including number dialling (with connected digit dialogue), number storing, user-defined telephone directory entry name, name dialling, and directory editing. With a vocabulary of around 300 words the system allows additionally operating comfort electronics (radio, CD-player/changer, air condition etc) in different languages.

LINGUATRONIC applies speaker-independent, continuous speech recognition based on HMMs (Hidden Markov Models). For the user-specific telephone directory, an additional DTW (Dynamic Time Warping) recogniser is used. Key issues for in-car speech technology, noise reduction and echo cancellation for hands-free telephone applications are achieved by an integrated signal pre-processing module (Linhard and Haulick, 1998). Furthermore, the system automatically and imperceptibly adapts to the characteristics of the speaker's voice and the acoustic background existing in cars.

Upper-level cars are equipped with a data bus system, mostly using fibre optics. This implies that a multitude of devices can be addressed and controlled by a single and uniform speech dialogue module without requiring any extra wiring. Furthermore, the Push-to-activate (PTA) button facilitates muting of the audio and the use of the car's loudspeakers, and enables the same microphone to be used for both speech commands and telephone.

In addition to software solutions, Temic offers two hardware versions of its command & control interface, one as a plug-in board with the size of a credit card, the other as a self-contained box that interfaces directly to the bus and does not require any host processor (Figure 2). Both versions not only perform speech recognition, but also do the signal pre-processing including echo cancellation, the dialogue management, the speech coding and the storage of the speech output for the dialogue.

LINGUATRONIC is directly connected to the COMAND system in the centre console. For the driver and front passenger COMAND represents the central operating and display unit for numerous functions and end-devices. The features of the electronic unit include a large colour display (6.5 inches) in TFT technology and a fixed-installation car telephone.

In the manual operation mode, the driver and front passenger are able to select the different functions and end-devices by pressing a button next to the COMAND display. The driver is also able to input instructions using the illumi-

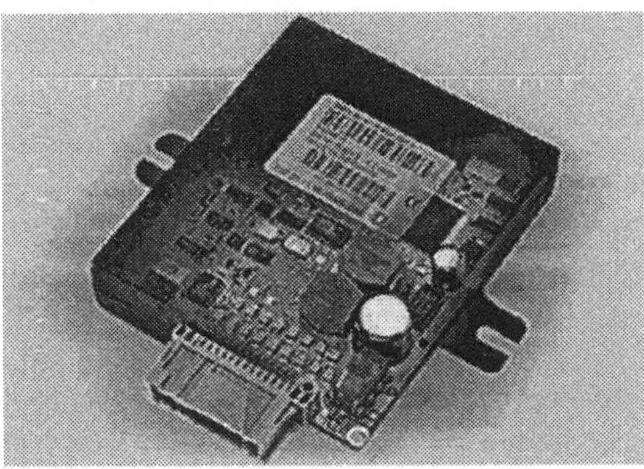

Figure 2. Hardware version of the LINGUATRONIC system (Bühler et al., 2003).

nated keys on the four-spoke steering wheel: sound volume, receiving incoming calls, ending calls, telephone directory, station search and track search in CD mode. The corresponding information is then displayed both on the COMAND display and in the central display in the instrument cluster, where it is always in the driver's field of vision.

Other features and capabilities of COMAND include a car radio, connectors for an external CD-changer, linked via the optical bus, a cassette player and, finally, dynamic route guidance based on up-to-date traffic information. The data for the navigation computer include the entire European road network as well as additional information such as the locations of gas stations, railway stations, airports, hotels or restaurants. The driver is able to choose between three route modes: dynamic route guidance, fastest or shortest route.

In this chapter we focus on the speech-based interaction with the navigation component of the COMAND system. This component represents the core application for the SENECA project. We describe the modules of the SENECA SLDS demonstrator with a particular emphasis on the speech recognition and dialogue management parts (Section 2). Some recent SLDS demonstrator evaluation results are presented in Section 3.

2. The SENECA SLDS

The SENECA SLDS architecture is shown in Figures 3 and 8. It consists of five units: the COMAND head unit is linked via an optical D2B (Domestic Digital Bus) to the GSM module, the CD changer and the DSP (Digital Signal Processing) module. The latter contains the signal and dialogue processing parts. On a notebook computer speaker-independent, connected speech recognition and navigation data access are performed. DSP and notebook computer are connected via a serial link. The system allows speech control of entertainment (i.e., radio), navigation and communication (i.e., telephone) equipment using command & control dialogues (Figure 9(b)). SENECA SLDS demonstrators have been developed for French, German and Italian.

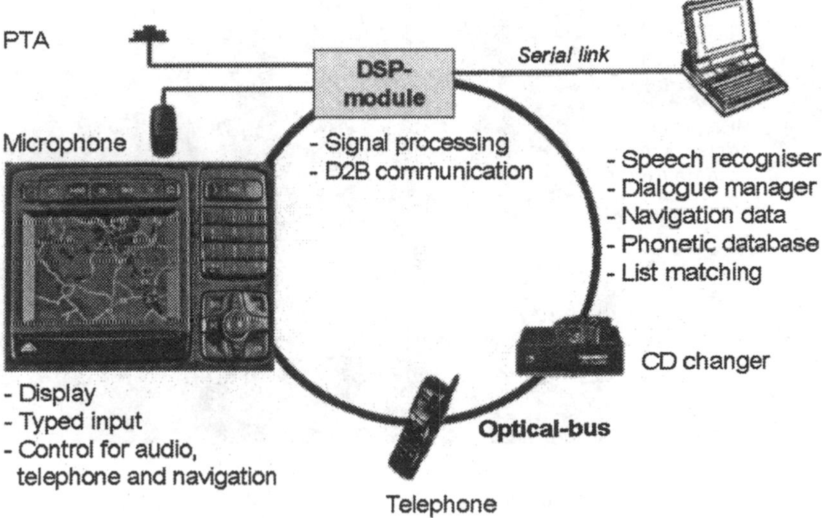

Figure 3. Architecture of the SENECA in-car SLDS demonstrator (Minker et al., 2004). The COMAND head unit featuring display and input buttons is connected to the GSM module, the CD changer and the DSP module. The notebook computer contains the SENECA SLDSs demonstrator software (i.e., parts of the system which are subject to research). Figure 8 provides a more detailed overview of the architecture.

2.1 Noise Reduction

Single and dual channel noise reduction approaches have been investigated in the project. They use several small distant microphones. The consortium collected speech data based on two different microphone arrangements.

- Both microphones have been mounted near the mirror in the car yielding a distance of approx. 4 cm. One microphone pointed to the speaker, the other into the opposite direction (Figure 4).
- Two additional microphones have been placed closely to the other two microphones. They both pointed in the direction of the speaker. This arrangement was used to investigate alternative noise reduction approaches.

A speech database including 20 sessions with 20 different speakers has been established. An experimenter guided the speaker (i.e., the car driver) through the recording session. These sessions have been recorded under specified driving conditions such as city or highway traffic.

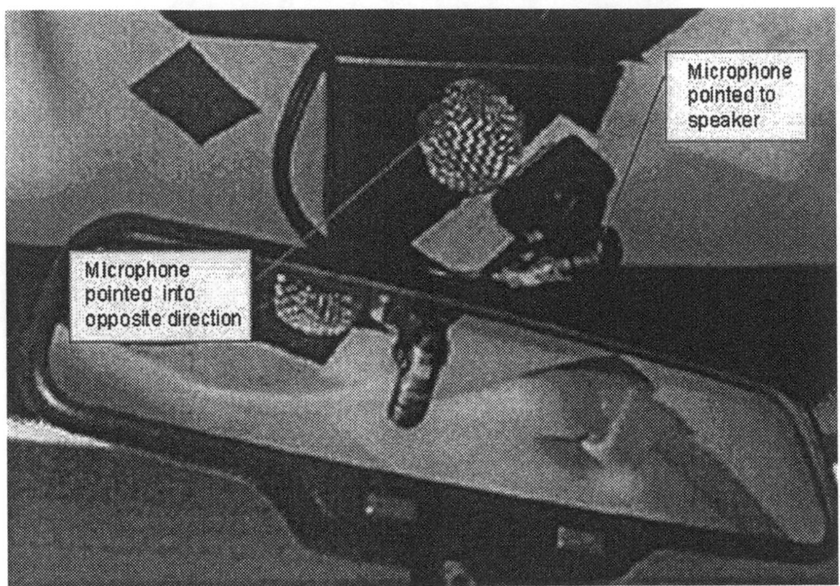

Figure 4. Metal housing with the encapsulated microphones.

In each session, the speaker uttered five sentences and spelled 55 city names. The speaker utterances have been recorded using a multi-channel platform, already applied in the SpeechDat-Car project (Moreno et al., 2000). This platform allows a simultaneous recording of four channels. The data has been sampled at 16 kHz with 16 bits. The collected speech material has been transcribed according to the SpeechDat-Car specifications.

In order to obtain information about the auditive quality of processed, noise reduced signals, an additional subjective listening test has been carried out, where speech recordings gathered under different conditions have been presented to the test persons.

2.2 Speech Recognition Technology

The SENECA SLDS is based on the standard LINGUATRONIC system. It allows about 75 different COMAND functions for audio, navigation and telephone. For activating nearly all functions, synonyms can be used either in the form of alternative words, e.g., "Radio [an]" (*switch on radio*) "Radio [ein]" (*turn on radio*) "Radio [einschalten]" (*activate radio*) or as extensions, e.g., "CD [Nummer] Eins" (*CD (number) one*).

Speaker-independent speech recogniser. The speaker-independent recogniser is organised in a client-server architecture (Figure 8). The pre-processing of the sound data is performed at the client side. Noise reduction and echo cancellation prepare the sound signal for the recogniser module on the notebook computer (server). Both client and server communicate via a serial link.

The lists of city names can be accessed on the notebook computer using a navigation library that makes use of the original (commercially available) navigation data base. To ensure a correct speech recognition process the city name entries have been extended with up to three phonetic transcriptions. The first transcription represents the correct pronunciation of the corresponding city name. The second includes a dialectal variant. The last transcription includes a commonly used wrong pronunciation. Using the pronunciation alternatives for each list entry the speech recogniser accepts a vocabulary of more than 3,000 words. Still, the memory and CPU performance requirements are sufficiently low to allow an integration of the speech recogniser into an available target system in the near future.

Confidence values. In SENECA, confidence values have been introduced to enable dialogue flow control. Calculated on different acoustic scores these values represent an estimate of the probability of a correct recognition result. Confidence values are used as thresholds. If the confidence value of a city name is too low the system asks for additional attributes, i.e., zip code, city nearby, and the region. The confidence values used in the SENECA SLDS demonstrator have been made adjustable to deal with the different environment conditions in the software laboratory and in the car.

Spell matcher. Spelling is a difficult task in speech recognition because the "words" consist of single letters. They are very short in pronunciation and often hardly distinguishable. An additional spell matcher is therefore used (Figure 5). This module uses application, language and run-time-dependent information:

- Probability of confusions between the different letters (language-dependent).
- List of all names that can be spelled (application-dependent).
- Spelled letter hypotheses (run-time-dependent).

Using original letter hypotheses, the spell matcher searches in the list of names. It substitutes those letters in the hypotheses that are easily confusable and provides a list of names matching the hypotheses with the highest probability. The names do not need to be spelled completely. The first four to five letters of city and street names are sufficient to determine the correct result within the first ten list entries produced by the matcher.

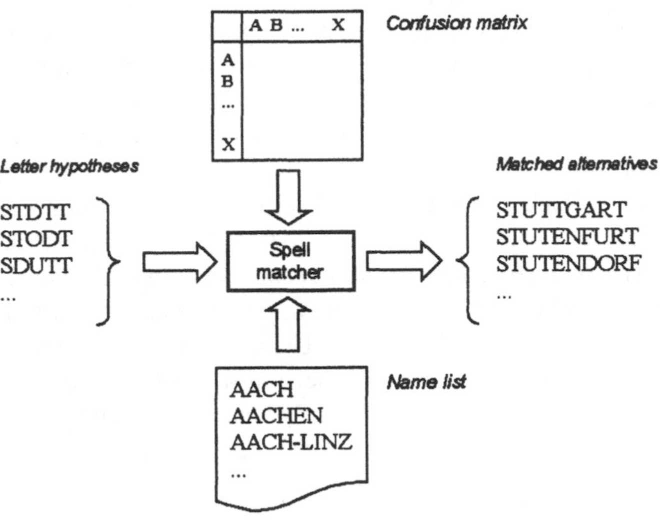

Figure 5. Spell matching process.

Grammar. The increasing demand for functionality and flexibility of speech applications and the necessity to keep complex system easy to use requires a powerful grammar format. The Java Speech Grammar Format (JSGF) from Sun Microsystems has been chosen for the SENECA speech recogniser because it is a standardised powerful grammar format that can be read and modified easily.

Temic expanded JSGF with tags to enable the usage of the parser and the introduction of elements for voice and text enrolments (cf. description below). JSGF is a Backus Naur type grammar representation. JSGF tags are strings, intended to provide additional semantic annotation and to increase the grammar flexibility. Without these tags application developers would need to parse recognition results by comparing strings in order to obtain the semantic representation. Changing the grammar would then require the dialogue to be modified accordingly. However, when using feature-value pairs as parser tags the wording in the speech recognition grammar and the semantic representation of utterances are independent. Using such a fixed feature-value pair structure enables the grammar designer to modify the wording without influencing the dialogue flow (Figure 6).

Such a parser tag feature yields another considerable advantage. Native speakers involved in the design and development process may help in keeping the speech recogniser grammar as natural and user friendly as possible while the dialogue developer implements the dialogue flow in parallel using the feature-value pairs that reflect the corresponding system functionality. If the

```
<city>              =   (Paris | Torino | Ulm){%tokens};
public <route>      =   (from <city> {$c_from}
                        to <city> {$c_to})
                        {depart = $c_from; dest = $c_to};
public <yesno>      =   (<yes> {$tag} | <no> {$tag}) {$tag};
<yes>               =   (yes | okay | yes okay) {confirm=yes};
<no>                =   (no | wrong | no wrong) {confirm=no};
```

Figure 6. Excerpt from the JSGF grammar used for speech recognition in SENECA. Given the utterance "from Paris to Torino", the parser returns the feature-value structure `[depart=[city=''Paris'']; dest=[city=''Torino'']];`.

grammar can be interchanged easily the developer is able to test the dialogue in his own native language (assuming that the recogniser is able to process this particular language).

Voice enrolments. Predecessor versions of LINGUATRONIC use two different types of recognisers for both speaker-independent command and speaker-dependent word recognition. This required a two-level dialogue processing:

- When the dialogue starts, the speaker-independent recogniser has been used.

    SYS: *Yes please?*
    USR: Dial name.
    SYS: *Name of the person?*
    USR: Smith.

- The speaker-dependent recogniser then retrieved the user-trained word.

    SYS: Smith. Dialling number.

In the current version of LINGUATRONIC voice enrolments (user-trained words) have been implemented trough a trainable Hidden-Markov-Model (HMM) recogniser. Using the voice enrolment technology, user-dependent and user-independent elements can be combined which allows flat dialogue structures. Switching between different recognisers is no more required, the user-friendliness of the system is enhanced. Input commands like "Smith wählen" (*dial Smith*) or "Zielführung zu Smith" (*route guidance to Smith*) are now possible.

SYS: *Yes please?*
USR: Dial Smith.
SYS: Smith. Dialling number.

Text enrolments. If the pronunciation of words is known the recogniser can be dynamically configured. This feature is called text enrolments and enables the grammar to be dynamically changed during run-time. The application developer provides place holders in the grammar where the desired words may be filled-in "on the fly".

In SENECA, the text enrolments are used for the city names (Figure 7). The place holders reserve memory for flexible grammar insertion depending for example on the system status or on specific user interactions. In the demonstrator the text enrolments are filled with lists of destination city names. Because of their large number only a subset of the 3,000 city names is used to keep the recognition rate as high as possible. The subsets are divided into different categories through the additional attributes zip code, city nearby, and region. For the initial recognition step at the beginning of the destination input the text enrolments contain the 1,500 biggest cities of the country and up to 1,500 cities close to the current position.

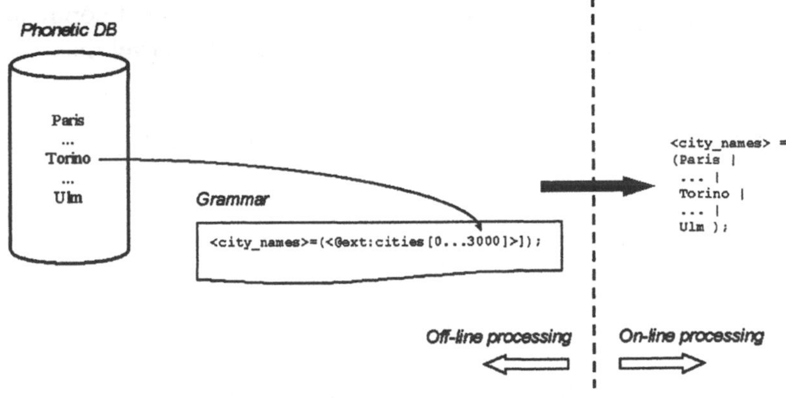

Figure 7. Text enrolments for city names.

In the SENECA SLDS demonstrator the current position has to be set manually. In a product version of such a system the position would be automatically determined by a GPS (Global Positioning System) receiver.

2.3 Dialogue Processing

The SENECA SLDS uses a menu-based command & control dialogue structure whereby any sub-function is accessible from the main function (top-down access) or directly by providing the name of the sub function (side-access).

The control commands are active at different system states. The command "Abbruch" (*abort*) can be used almost anytime, whereas the commands for correction and turn back are available only in specific dialogue states. Other general commands include "Wählen" (*dial*), "Ja" (*yes*), "Nein" (*no*), "Speichern" (*store*) and "Löschen" (*remove*). A help command "Hilfe" (*help*) is only available at the beginning of the dialogue.

Two dialogue interaction types have been implemented. A *novice* mode uses more polite and detailed prompts whereas an *expert* mode uses brief and clear prompts. The use of either mode depends on the number of recognition errors or upon initiative of the user. For the prompt design, the system offers the possibility to store up to ten minutes of pre-recorded speech. Similar commands can be used for telephone and navigation functions, e.g., for entering a new item "Neue Nummer" (*new number*) / "Neues Ziel" (*new destination*) or for switching back to the last entered item "Letzte Nummer" (*last number*) / "Letztes Ziel" (*last destination*). The entered phone numbers and destinations may be stored for later use.

Throughout the dialogue identical commands are used for getting help and aborting the interaction. Possible user commands are simultaneously displayed on the COMAND head unit display. They help the driver to remember the dialogue steps. If the traffic becomes difficult while a dialogue is in progress the system stands by for another user input. As soon as the traffic situation allows, the driver is able to retrieve the current dialogue step from the display and to resume the dialogue.

Robustness for SLDSs, especially in terms of speech recognition accuracy and robust dialogue processing, is an important research area (Hansen et al., 2000; Heisterkamp, 2001; Maier et al., 1997; Suhm et al., 1999). When activating the navigation system, the intention of the driver is usually to get a route guidance to his/her desired destination. Therefore navigation needs a unique description of this location (usually referenced by a geo-code). A well-known problem with commonly used descriptors like names of places is that its correct recognition may be difficult because of the vocabulary size (the current German navigation database contains around 69,000 city names), and because many names are phonetically confusable.

Therefore in a first prototype concept demonstrator version of SENECA the user had to distinguish between large and small cities, whereby the former ones could be uttered as an entire word and the latter ones needed to be entered in spelling mode. This solution does not seem to be user friendly since users have to guess which category their destination falls into. In the current SLDS demonstrator all city names may be uttered as entire words and the user may provide some additional information to resolve problems in the input of the city name due to misrecognition and/or ambiguities. Spelling is only used as a fallback solution in the system. Clarification dialogue strategies to enhance the robustness of SLDSs have already been applied in the Verbmobil speech-to-speech translation system (Maier et al., 1997).

In the SENECA SLDS demonstrator a straightforward approach is used to obtain a unique speech recognition output hypothesis by (repeatedly and/or recursively) applying set intersection to different candidate sets (reference word lists consisting of city names). This allows to reduce the number of candidates, so as to finally obtain a unique intersection element.

Different types of additional information may be considered to fulfil this task:

- Spelling seems not really appropriate, because people often use odd ways to spell names. It is uncomfortable for the driver, if he is forced to use only letters. Recognising single letters is difficult for the recognition component and a reliable candidate list from spelling requires lists that are too large. However, spelling may still be used as a fallback mode, if other information cannot be retrieved from the user.

- Geographical knowledge like associated words (e.g., rivers), destination distance, direction (e.g., north), destination size provided by the user also seems less reliable. For example, from the point of view of the system developer, information about size is difficult to obtain, and the user seems unable to distinguish precisely between more than three levels.

- In Europe, especially in Germany, the use of zip or area code seems appropriate, because already the first two digits yield a small candidate list. In the US, the name of the State seems to be sufficient. In addition, zip codes are widely known or easily available (e.g., through address books), which is an advantage.

Based on the analysis above, an iterative approach to destination input has been applied: in case of ambiguity and/or misrecognition the initially uttered speech input is re-recognised against a new candidate lexicon, dynamically built from the navigation database after taking the additional user information into account. Misrecognition can be detected by simply asking the user for confirmation (Figure 9 (b)). Ambiguities are revealed by cross-checking user input with the database. The type of additional information (e.g., zip code, nearby city, region name, etc.), the number of iterations, as well as the order in which the system requires this information from the user, can be flexibly adapted to different languages and countries.

In the German version of the SENECA demonstrator the following disambiguation steps are applied (Figure 9(a)) and illustrated on an example dialogue between the user and the system (Figure 9(b)):

- The first user utterance is recognised with an initial heuristic reference word list (containing 1,500 largest and 1,500 closest cities).

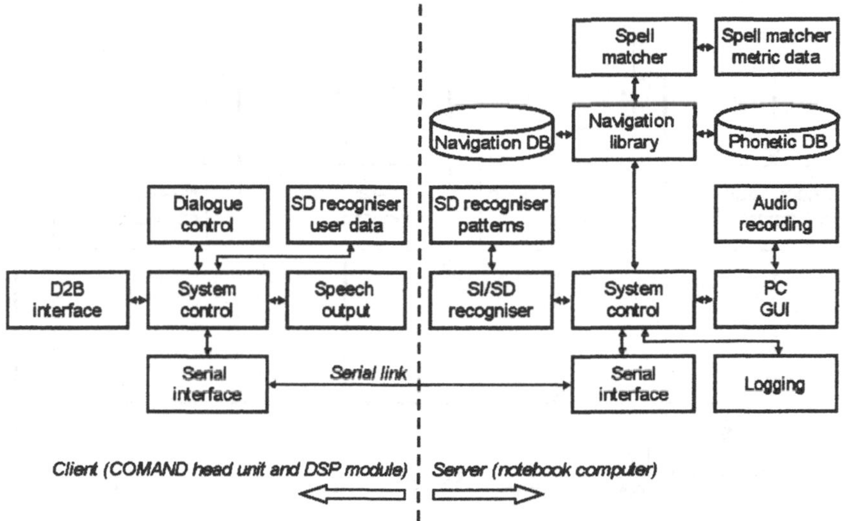

Figure 8. Client-server architecture of the SENECA SLDS demonstrator. Speech recognition is performed on both client and server side.

- If the recogniser output is ambiguous (in terms of low recognition confidence and/or ambiguity of city names) the system queries the user for the zip code. If this additional information is provided the initial user input speech is recognised using the updated word lists (re-recognition in Figure 9(a)).
- After successful recognition the system stores the city name and the iterative process terminates.
- In turn, the system proceeds with the next iteration in the following cases:
  - the user is unable to provide the requested additional information;
  - the city name is re-recognised correctly, but ambiguous;
  - the confidence of the re-recognition result is too low;
  - the re-recognition result was rejected by the user.

  Throughout these iterations the system queries the user for additional information on the zip code, the nearby city and the region.
- The spelling mode is used as a fallback anytime in the iterative process (which is not represented in the Figure 9(a)). This mode is also applied after the last iteration if the city name is still ambiguously recognised, or

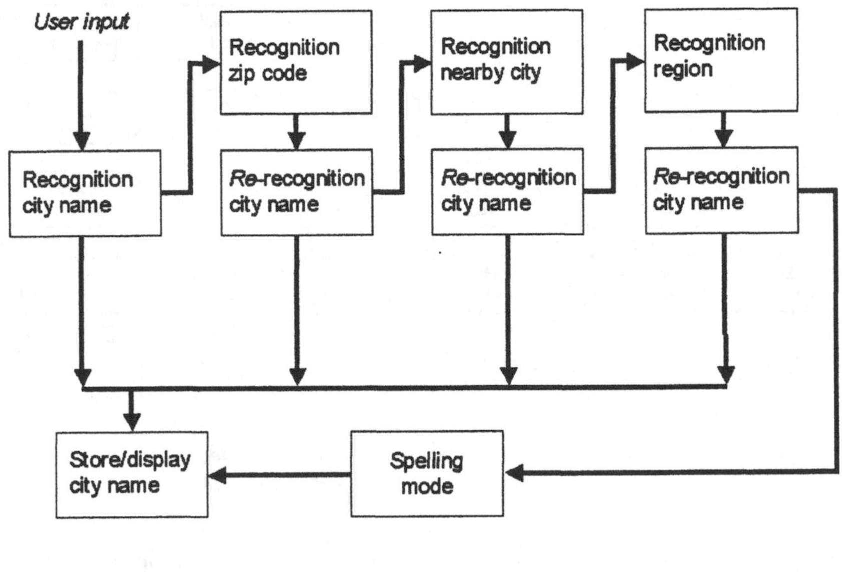

(a)

SYS: *Yes please?*
USR: Enter address.
SYS: *Name of the city?*
USR: Siegburg.
SYS: *Do you know the postal code?*
USR: No.
SYS: *Do you know a city near the destination?*
USR: No.
SYS: *Do you know the federal state?*
USR: Yes.
SYS: *Name of the Federal state or region?*
USR: North Rhine-Westphalia.
SYS: <Displays city name>
Is the name of the city correct?
USR: Yes.
SYS: *Navigation to destination started.*

(b)

Figure 9. Processing steps of the disambiguation technique in the SENECA demonstrator (a); example command & control dialogue between the user and the system (b).

should - after a successful speech recognition process - the city name not be confirmed by the user (which is not represented in the Figure 9(a)).

In summary, three recognition steps are performed throughout each iteration:

1. Query the user on whether the additional attribute (zip code, nearby city and region in Figure 9(a)) is known.
2. Recognise additional constraining information provided by the user to reduce the number of candidates in the word lists (recognise zip code, nearby city and region in Figure 9(a)).
3. Recognise the initial user input using the updated word lists (re-recognition in Figure 9(a)).

3. Evaluation of the SENECA SLDS Demonstrator

The SENECA SLDS demonstrator has been evaluated by means of user tests. The operation of the system by speech input and output was compared to the equivalent manual operation of COMAND. The results show the quality of the system and its impact on driving safety and quality. The hypotheses include the assumption that speech operation is generally better than manual operation.

3.1 Evaluation Method

A proven method for user tests of infotainment systems in cars has been adopted from earlier studies (VODIS, SENECA concept demonstrator) and improved.

The basic components of the experimental car include a passenger car (Mercedes-Benz W 220), the standard COMAND system, and a second set of pedals), the SENECA SLDS demonstrator, a notebook computer with event keys and clock, a video system (three cameras, multiplexer and digital video recorder), and a set of microphones. Three seats were reserved for the driver, a professional driving assessor and the principal investigator and one seat for the testing equipment.

A subset of 25 commands for the navigation and telephone functions was used in the experiment (each with one synonym, if available). The speech recognition transcriptions including additional user guidance are presented on the COMAND display and acoustically by speech output (if available). The notebook computer and the video recording system were installed in a rack on one of the back seats. Three soft keys of the notebook computer were used for time event recording where a log file was created for each test person.

The notebook computer's display with the system's clock were combined with the camera recordings (cf. description below) to obtain a time reference for processing the video data.

Figure 10. Camera and microphone positions in the test car (Mutschler and Baum, 2001).

The video system included three cameras which recorded the forward traffic scenery, the test person's face, and the COMAND display. The signals of the cameras and the display image of the notebook computer were mixed and digitally recorded by a Digital Video Walkman. Beside the microphone of the SENECA SLDS demonstrator an additional microphone was installed under the car roof. It picked up comments of the passengers, especially from the driver, which were recorded together with the optical data.

A professional driving assessor noted driving errors and rated the test person's driving skills. For recording the driving errors the driving assessor used a specially designed recording device. All data, including the automatically calculated times of the driving errors, were temporarily stored, and then converted to ASCII files. In dangerous situations the driving assessor warned the test person, or even intervened by using the second pedal set or taking hold of the steering wheel. This seemed particularly important since users had to perform the tasks using manual input of the COMAND head unit, which is normally prohibited during driving.

The principal investigator was responsible for the organisation and the survey of the experimental set-up. He announced the tasks which the test person had to perform and recorded the begin and end of the task as well as special not foreseen events by pressing defined keys on the notebook computer. Two driving assessors and two experimenters were employed. The two trials of a test person were conducted by the same driving assessor and the same principal investigator.

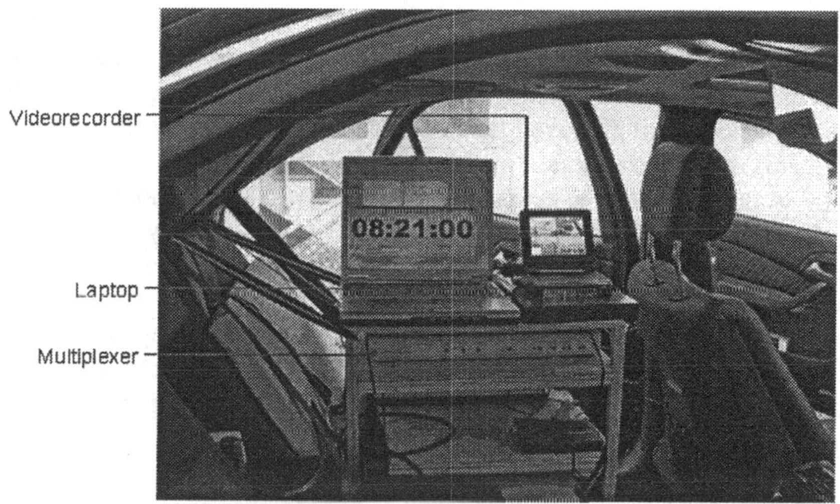

Figure 11. Position of test equipment in the test car (Mutschler and Baum, 2001).

The trials took place on a 46 km long well-established course nearby a middle size city in Germany (Tübingen). The course was composed of express roadways, highways, entrances/exits and streets across cities and villages. The test persons drove the course twice to cover both experimental conditions (speech mode/manual mode). The course was divided into 13 segments with the speech or manual system being operated during the task segments and without any system operation during the reference segments. The latter served to assess the general driving capabilities of the individual test person and also as a baseline to assess the additional mental load caused by manual and voice operation. Reference segments without any operation tasks were mixed with the task segments and served as a basis for comparison.

Before the first experimental trail a separate training phase was performed with the test persons. This was on a partly different course and took about 20 minutes, while the test person was practising the handling of the car and several exemplary tasks in the respective input modality.

For the experiment 16 test persons were recruited (experienced safe drivers), whose age and previous experience with the SENECA concept demonstrator systematically differed. Eight of them were 25 - 35 years old with and without experience in operating infotainment systems in cars. Eight of them were 50 - 65 years old with and without experience, nearly all were male.

The total of nine tasks were representative for different functions and included important complex tasks of a driver infotainment system: navigation, telephone number dialling and address book tasks. The tasks had to be performed on defined route segments. Assistance was given and noted by the experimenter if certain criteria were fulfilled.

The tasks were grouped into three types, namely destination input, dialling and address books. Destination input was most complex and included input of the city name as well as input of both city and street names. The dialling tasks included entering a given telephone number (that has been fixed on the dashboard) and entering a free number (e.g., the test person's home number). The tasks also included the actual conversation with the telephone partner. Finally, the address book tasks included activation of a previously stored destination ("go to uncle Tom") and calling a previously stored phone number ("call Smith").

The tasks were representative for different functions of a driver infotainment system. They contained typical operation actions, namely activating a main function or a subfunction, selecting an item out of a list, and input of characters ("spelling") and digits.

The tasks were given at predefined points on the course (beginning of the task segments). The test persons were instructed to start or to interrupt (break off) the task (or even refuse it, which they never did) at any time if required by the driving situation. If a task was not completed at predefined points, it was declared as aborted (latest end of the task segment). The length of the task segments were sufficient to complete the respective task at least four times (without any delays by system and user problems).

The whole trial sequence comprised written and verbal instructions, a pre-experimental questionnaire, a training of SENECA SLDS/COMAND operations and driving, the test trial including reference segments, interviews and a post-experimental questionnaire. A complete trial took about three hours.

Objective and subjective data were recorded. The Task Completion Rate (TCR) was calculated from the log file data. A task was completed when correctly and completely solved within the scheduled segment without any essential assistance. The duration of operation was measured by the experimenter. The log file contained all interesting event times and the recognitions of the speech recogniser. The driving assessor recorded the driving errors and judged the driving quality by a score from 1=very good to 6=very bad. The driving errors were categorised into the following seven main criteria: *Too low speed, too high speed, longitudinal and lateral distances, lane keeping, observation, indicating* and *braking*. The corresponding time of the driving errors were automatically measured.

Glances to the display, speedometer/steering wheel, rear mirror, aside (including the outside mirrors) were extracted from the video data. Long glances were manually measured using questionnaires and interviews. The test persons were asked about driving safety, handling of speech and manual input devices, vocabulary, acceptance and preference of input modes. They had to assess the speech input by comparing it to other extra fittings in the car with respect to driving safety and driver comfort.

3.2 Evaluation Results

Objective results. Most of the tasks show a markedly lower TCR with speech input compared to manual input. The overall average of TCR is 79% for speech input and 90% for manual input. By far the greatest part of the incomplete speech tasks is due to forgotten commands which had to be refreshed by the experimenter during the trial (those tasks were therefore counted as not completed).

However, the tasks with speech input were aborted less frequently by the experimenter at the specific course points which leaded to the lower speech input times. In fact, speech input took less time (63 seconds) on average than manual input (84 seconds), which corresponds to 75% of the manual input time. The shorter input was particularly pronounced and statistically significant for the destination input.

Concerning the accuracy of inputs, the most important user errors with speech were vocabulary errors, partly spelling errors. Vocabulary errors occur if one or several incorrect words were used for a specific function:

- Wrong commands for negative confirmation, e.g., “Falsch” (*false*) instead of “Korrektur” (*correction*).
- Wrong commands for destination input, e.g., “Adresse angeben” (*indicate address*) instead of “Adresse eingeben” (*input address*).
- Wrong paging command for list representations on the head unit display, e.g., “Nächste Seite” (*next page*), “Blättern” (*scroll*) instead of “Weiter” (*continue*).

These vocabulary errors occurred rather frequently in spite of the synonyms implemented in the SENECA SLDS demonstrator vocabulary. Vocabulary errors may also be interpreted as a system weakness: learning more than 20 commands by the user should not be necessary for advanced interfaces to car functionality.

Errors also occurred when the user did not follow the pre-defined dialogue flow:

- Instead of only confirming the ability to provide additional information with a yes/no reply, providing this information directly.
- Ignoring mis-recognitions and continuing the dialogue.

- Speaking whilst speech output is still in progress.

Push-to-activate (PTA) errors, i.e., missing or inappropriate PTA activation, are rather sparse. This may be explained by learning effects and the well elaborated feedback strategy employed by the system.

All these user induced errors increased the input time and reduced the TCR. However, with speech input there is in general a higher score for driving skill and there are fewer driving errors as compared to manual input, particularly for destination input tasks. Driving is better and safer, if infotainment systems are operated by speech and not manually.

Table 1(a) shows the driving performance, expressed by the number of driving errors for both modalities and three tasks averaged across test persons. Differences between the task and the reference segments are shown (e.g., 1.7 errors means 1.7 additional errors per minute observed during the task segment compared to the reference segment). The results basically confirm the hypothesis that the driving skills improve and there are less driving errors with speech input as compared to manual input.

Table 1. Driving skills as a function of input modality and type of task (a); types and frequencies of driving errors (b).

Task type	*Speech*	*Manual*
destination input	0.5	1.7
dialling	0.5	0.8
address book	-0.2	0.5

(a)

Driving error	*Speech*	*Manual*
distance too low	3.7	4.9
inexact lane keeping	6.6	13.9
lack of traffic observation	1.5	1.3
no indicating	0.9	1.3
sudden/late breaking	1.6	2.8
speed too high	1.5	1.7
speed too low	2.9	5.9

(b)

Table 1(b) shows the different driving errors for both modalities per trial, averaged across test persons. There are significantly less driving errors in the categories *inexact lane keeping* and *speed too low* with speech input.

Almost all other error categories show also lower driving errors with speech input. Notably *distance too low, sudden/late braking* and *speed too high* occurred less frequently with speech input. The results allow to conclude that, compared to manual input, speech not only enhances the driving safety, but also improves all technical and tactical aspects of driving. This observation holds especially for the complex tasks.

Subjective results. Safety and comfort of speech input and the other devices were individually assessed by the test persons on a six point-scale. Speech input was estimated near the top level of safety and comfort (Figure 12).

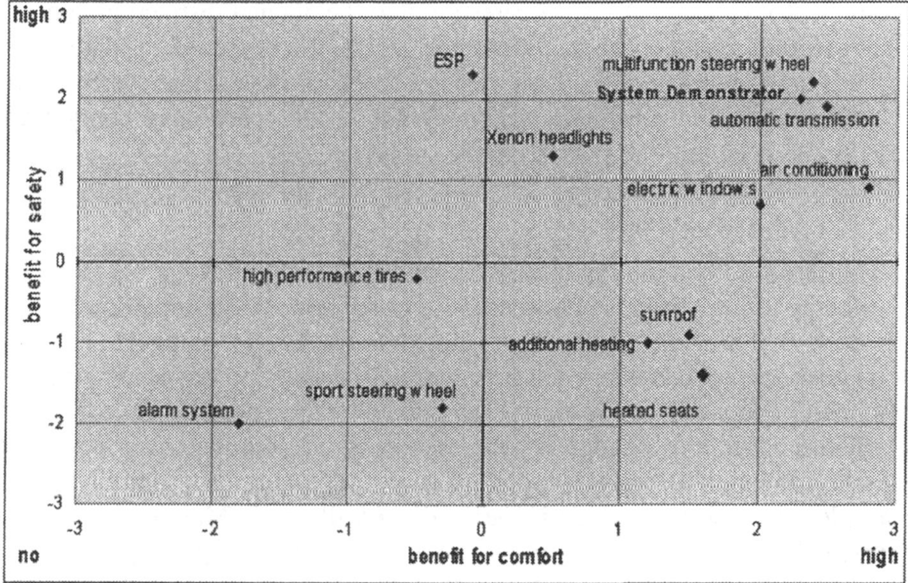

Figure 12. Subjectively assessed safety and comfort of speech input compared to other car devices (Mutschler and Baum, 2001).

Concerning the safety implications, speech input was judged to be below ESP (Electronic Stability Programme) and the multifunction steering wheel and in the range of automatic transmission. In terms of comfort, speech input was judged to be below air conditioning and in the range of automatic transmission and multifunction steering wheel.

These results show the high estimation which is subjectively accorded to speech input even compared to other car devices whose values are generally agreed upon.

To the question *What did you like with speech input?* 14 test persons praised the fact that there was no or hardly any distraction from driving. They argued that compared to manual input no glance onto display is required enabling drivers to fully concentrate on the traffic. Six test persons assessed speech input to be a simple operation or comfortable. Three test persons mentioned that the hands can be kept on the steering wheel. Other positive statements concerned easy learning, little prior knowledge necessary and good readability (each once).

The visual advantage of speech input is reflected by the statements to the question about disadvantages of manual input (*What did you dislike about manual input?*): "Distraction/less attention to traffic/higher concentration necessary" (11 test persons). It is interesting that the manual distraction is mentioned by only one test person ("Too long way to the keyboard"). In addition to these basic disadvantages many design aspects of the manual system were criticised. To the question *What did you dislike about speech input?* only three test persons criticised the speech misrecognitions.

4. Conclusion

The scientific community is well aware that speech in cars is the enabling technology to interactively and selectively bring news and information to mobile environments without causing a safety hazard. Yet, we all have seen tides of enthusiasm and reluctance towards the real-life viability of speech technology. With telephony applications now firmly established, any discussion as to whether speech technology is a commercially viable option also for use in vehicles can be abbreviated by pointing at the LINGUATRONIC and SENECA examples. Speech technology is there, and it will grow. More car manufacturers, but also system providers will soon offer more complex applications, navigation address entry being the point in question, more cars will have speech control as an option.

We have presented the SENECA spoken language dialogue system demonstrator. It provides speech-based access to a wide range of entertainment, navigation and communication applications in mobile environments. The novelty lies in the use of an intelligent dialogue strategy that allows to compensate speech recognition results with low confidence and word-level ambiguities by engaging flexible clarification dialogues with the user.

The re-design of the dialogue processing avoids the user to distinguish between large and small cities at the destination input process. The spelling mode is only necessary as a fallback solution. SENECA uses a modular systems architecture, in which type of request and number of additional loops as well as the order in which the system queries the user on the additional terms can be flexibly realised. This significantly eases porting the system to different languages. The described novelties enhance the user friendliness of the system.

The SENECA SLDS demonstrator has been evaluated by real users. The results show that the Task Completion Rate is higher with manual input and that with speech input, road safety, especially in case of complex tasks, is significantly improved. In terms of error analysis, the most frequent user errors can be explained by problems while spelling and by the selection of wrong speech commands.

Acknowledgements

The SENECA project is supported by the European Commission within the 4th framework of the ESPRIT programme "System Integration and Applications" under Human Language Technology (Contract number ESPRIT 26 981). The authors want to thank all the partners involved in the project.

References

Bühler, D., Vignier, S., Heisterkamp, P., and Minker, W. (2003). Safety and operating issues for mobile human-machine interfaces. In *Proceedings of International Conference on Intelligent User Interfaces (IUI)*, pages 227–229, Miami, Florida, USA.

Gärtner, U. (2001). The SENECA project: Speech recognition within the car for entertainment and communication systems. In *Detroit Auto Interior Show*.

Gärtner, U., König, W., and Wittig, T. (2001). Evaluation of manual vs. speech input when using a driver information system in real traffic. In *Proceedings of International Driving Symposium on Human Factors in Driver Assessment, Training and Vehicle Design*, pages 7–13, Aspen, Colorado, USA.

Green, P. (2000). Crashes induced by driver information systems and what can be done to reduce them. In *Proceedings of Convergence*, pages 26–36, Warrendale, Pennsylvania, USA. Society of Automotive Engineers.

Hansen, J. H., Plucienkowski, J., Gallant, S., Pellom, B. L., and Ward, W. (2000). CU-Move: Robust speech processing for in-vehicle speech systems. In *Proceedings of International Conference on Spoken Language Processing (ICSLP)*, pages 524–527, Beijing, China.

Heisterkamp, P. (2001). Linguatronic: Product-level speech system for Mercedes-Benz cars. In *Proceedings of International Conference on Human Language Technology Research (HLT)*, San Diego, California, USA.

Lamel, L., Bennacef, S. K., Gauvain, J. L., Dartigues, H., and Temem, J. (1998). User evaluation of the MASK Kiosk. In *Proceedings of International Conference on Spoken Language Processing (ICSLP)*, pages 2875–2878, Sydney, Australia.

Linhard, K. and Haulick, T. (1998). Spectral noise subtraction with recursive gain curves. In *Proceedings of International Conference on Spoken Language Processing (ICSLP)*, pages 1479–1482, Sidney, Australia.

Maier, E., Reithinger, N., and Alexandersson, J. (1997). Clarification dialogues as measure to increase robustness in a spoken dialogue system. In *Proceed-*

ings of ACL/EACL Workshop on Interactive Dialog Systems, pages 33–36, Madrid, Spain.

Minker, W., Haiber, U., Heisterkamp, P., and Scheible, S. (2003). Intelligent dialog overcomes speech technology limitations: The SENECA example. In *Proceedings of International Conference on Intelligent User Interfaces (IUI)*, pages 267–269, Miami, Florida, USA.

Minker, W., Haiber, U., Heisterkamp, P., and Scheible, S. (2004). The SENECA spoken language dialogue system. *Speech Communication*, 43(1–2):89–102.

Moreno, A., Lindberg, B., Draxler, C., Richard, G., Choukri, K., Euler, S., and Allen, J. (2000). SPEECHDAT-CAR - a large speech database for automotive environments. In *Proceedings of International Conference on Language Resources and Evaluation (LREC)*, pages 895–900, Athens, Greece.

Mutschler, H. and Baum, W. (2001). Final report: Evaluation of the system-demonstrator - German results. Technical report.

Suhm, B., Myers, B., and Waibel, A. (1999). Model-based and empirical evaluation of multimodal interactive error correction. In *Proceedings of Conference on Human Factors in Computing Systems (CHI)*, pages 584 – 591, Pittsburgh, Pennsylvania, USA.

Temem, J., Lamel, L., and Gauvain, J. L. (1999). The MASK demonstrator: An emerging technology for user-friendly passengers kiosk. In *Proceedings of World Congress on Railway Research*, Toulouse, France.

Wahlster, W., Reithinger, N., and Blocher, A. (2001). SmartKom: Multimodal communication with a life-like character. In *Proceedings of European Conference on Speech Communication and Technology (EUROSPEECH)*, pages 1547–1550, Aalborg, Denmark.

Chapter 17

SEGMENTING ROUTE DESCRIPTIONS FOR MOBILE DEVICES

Sabine Geldof, Robert Dale
Centre for Language Technology, Macquarie University, Sydney, Australia
{ sabine,rdale } @ics.mq.edu.au

Abstract The provision of information on mobile devices introduces interesting challenges. The most obvious of these is that ways have to be found of optimising the use of the limited available space; however, we also have to take account of the fact that, unlike many desktop-based tasks, activities carried out on mobile devices often require the user to attend to the external environment. In such cases, it is important that the device be able to provide relatively transparent assistance to the user's performance of a task in the real world. Our focus is on the delivery of route descriptions via mobile devices: our contention is that, in this context, meaningful segmentation of information is a key element in meeting both of the above challenges. This chapter describes our approach to developing a mode of interaction which supports the cognitive involvement of the user in performing the task of following a route description; we describe the technological underpinnings of the work and report on a pilot evaluation in a real task setting.

Keywords: Mobiles; Instructions; Navigation; Segmentation; Usability; Cognitive load; Language technology.

1. Introduction

A great advantage of mobile computing devices is that they allow the provision of what we might think of as 'run-time support': assistance in the physical context where a real world task is to be performed. In such contexts, the device and the environment both compete for the attention of the user, and this impacts on the design methodology for mobile devices, see (Jameson and Klöckner, 2004) for a discussion of this and related issues). Norman (1998) points out that the interaction with the device should become cognitively subordinate to performing the task at hand, arguing for the notion of the invisible

W. Minker, D. Bühler and L. Dybkjær (eds), Spoken Multimodal Human-Computer Dialogue in Mobile Environments, 311-328

computer. For applications which exhibit this property, interface design needs to be focussed on supporting the user in performing her task: an interface that complies with the way users cognitively engage with the performance of the task at hand will enhance the process of switching between the physical world and the world as represented through the device.

One such application area is broadly termed 'wayfinding' or 'navigation assistance': provided with a route description, it is the task of the route taker to apply this description to the real world in order to arrive at some target destination. The use and coordination of multiple modalities (MM) constitutes one approach towards bridging the gap between the represented and the representing world, and has been applied to the domain of route descriptions. Multi-media in-car navigation systems such as the VICO system (Bernsen and Dybkjær, 2004) present instructions through speech and graphics as the user is performing the navigation task; Stocky and Cassell's (2002) kiosk-based embodied conversational agent (ECA) uses speech, gesture and pointing to create an interaction mode where the device and the user refer to the shared physical space. Pieraccini and colleagues (2003) focus on the dialogue aspect of MM interaction; from a more theoretical perspective, Van der Sluis (2001) has extended a standard referring expression generation algorithm towards multimodality. In general, however, the text used as input for the speech modules in MM systems is derived by a fairly straightforward mapping from the application data. In contrast, our Coral system is concerned with the use of natural language generation techniques when supporting a user in this type of task: Williams (1998) describes an early version of the system for automatic generation of indoor route descriptions, and Dale et al. (2002) describe our approach to descriptions in a road network.

An increasing number of real-world navigation assistance systems now cater for pre-trip planning via the Web (see, for example, `www.mapquest.com` and `www.whereis.com.au/`) as well as for in-car GPS-based navigation; the distinction between these two types of system is blurring as the web-based systems increasingly provide functionality for downloading routes to hand-held devices. Our contention is that the type of navigation support these systems provide does not address the user's cognitive involvement in the task, which, as argued above, is required when delivery is via a mobile device. To explore this hypothesis, we compared the output of current automated navigation systems to human-generated route directions. In general, the turn-by-turn instructions produced in existing navigation systems are generated by a straightforward mapping from a graph-based representation of a route, where edges are travelable paths and nodes are turning points. This approach generally results in sequences of instructions like that in Figure 1.

However, human-generated route directions deviate significantly from this pattern in two ways.

Instruction	Street Address	Suburb	Distance	Est. Time
depart	RICHMOND ST	DENISTONE EAST	464 m	1 Min
right	LOVELL RD	DENISTONE EAST	37 m	1 Min
left	NORTH RD	EASTWOOD	360 m	1 Min
right	DONOVAN ST	EASTWOOD	380 m	1 Min
left	ABUKLEA RD	EASTWOOD	1.03 km	1 Min
left	xxxx [ROUNDABOUT]	EASTWOOD	27 m	1 Min
left	BALACLAVA RD	EASTWOOD	1.25 km	2 Mins
left	UNIVERSITY AV	MACQUARIE PARK	96 m	1 Min
arrive	UNIVERSITY AV	MACQUARIE PARK	Total 3.64 km	Total 9 Mins

Figure 1. An automatically generated route description (sourced from `http://www.whereis.com.au/`).

- Firstly, as shown in Figure 2, people select particular aspects of reality based on their salience, and leave out other details that they assume will be inferred by the route taker. The reasoning processes and underlying knowledge required here are beyond the capabilities of current systems, and although extensive research in the automatic generation of route descriptions (for an overview, see Moulin and Kettani (1999)) has produced hypotheses on how these capabilities could be developed, the cost of constructing the required underlying databases puts this out of the question for most practical purposes.
- Secondly, people tend to provide meta-information about the route, as in the following example:

  > Starting from the Macquarie campus, first get on to Lane Cove Road. The simplest way to do this is to go out of the main campus gate and keep straight ahead on Waterloo Road ... [1]

  Here, the route giver provides a high level description of a component of a route, and then provides some elaboration on how the higher level instruction might be carried out.

Focusing on salient properties of the environment and reasoning about the route at a higher level of abstraction seem to be key aspects of the way people are cognitively involved in the route guidance process, with the consequence that their understanding of instructions is a complex interaction between the instructions themselves, their understanding of the global navigation task, and their perception of the environment. Our aim is to investigate how the task of navigation can be optimally supported given the specific requirements and opportunities encountered in mobile interface design.

Leave the house and drive towards the Midway shops, at the end of the street turn right and then left at the roundabout. Drive along North road and take the third right turn, just after the first hump in the road. Go to the end of that road and then go straight ahead at the roundabout, there's a church on your left. Now go straight along Herring road for quite a way until you hit the main road (Epping Rd), go straight across at the lights and continue on until you get to the next set of lights. Turn right here into the university.

Figure 2. A human generated route description for the route in Figure 1.

- The first requirement, that of managing the obvious problem of limited real estate, holds for the development of mobile interfaces in general. Screen sizes are small, and so the presentation of information must be optimised. Note that limitations on the amount of content that can be provided also apply where voice delivery is available, since verbose messages are typically not appropriate.

- Secondly, our analysis of cognitive involvement in the navigation task needs to be translated into more precise requirements. Höppner (1995) formulated requirements for route descriptions in general: a route description needs to be both *recognisable* and *rememberable*. Both are particularly relevant in our context and relate to our analysis above. Current mobile devices do not permit the user to simultaneously attend to both the device and the real world; she needs to be able to relate the device's description of the world to the physical world (hence recognisability), and to be able to switch back and forth between the device and the real world (rememberability).

Our view is that we can begin to address both the cognitive requirements and the problem of limited real estate by introducing *segmentation* and *structuring* into the flat sequences of instructions provided by existing systems: a hierarchy of instructions that can be explored during route execution then allows the user to follow the instructions at a level that is cognitively appropriate at a given point in time. In this chapter, we demonstrate how these ideas have been implemented in the context of the Coral project.

The remainder of the chapter is structured as follows. In Section 2 we provide an outline of the approach we are exploring, with examples; in Section 3, we present the underlying technology that Coral uses to achieve this solution; and in Section 4 we describe the results of a pilot evaluation of an interface that uses these ideas. Finally, in Section 5, we draw some conclusions and point to future directions.

2. Structured Information Delivery

Given a flat sequence of instructions of the kind delivered by a typical navigation assistance system, our approach is to segment this sequence of instructions in a meaningful way, and then to augment this segmented structure with generated summaries for each segment. This approach has two distinct advantages: first, the result is a structure that lends itself to presentation within a constrained display space; and second, the use of a hierarchy reduces the cognitive load on the user and enhances the rememberability of the route description.

The following example is taken from the version of Coral that guides people around our University department: the indented italicised material corresponds to the detailed contents of segments, whereas the Roman face lines present the summaries of the segments:

- From Rolf's office go to the lift and turn left.

  From Rolf's office go left. Walk down the corridor past one room on your left and two rooms on your right. On the wall straight ahead of you, you will see the Language Technology Notice board. When you reach it, turn right. Walk down the corridor past four rooms on your left and one room on your right. On the wall on your right you will see the lift. When you reach it, turn left.

- Jim's office is straight ahead of you.

  Walk down the corridor past two rooms on your left and one room on your right. Jim's office is straight ahead of you.

The summary lines provide the route taker with a set of higher-level entities that she can choose to explore in further detail as she executes the navigation task. The segmentation structure allows her to easily memorise the overall structure of the route and to recognise progress in the execution of the task.

Using this approach to segmenting a route, we have developed an interface to a real-world route description system that allows the user to browse a route on a mobile device as she performs the navigation task. Figure 3 shows how the above example is rendered on a Palm hand-held computer.

When the route is first presented, both the map and the segment summaries are displayed; clicking on a $\oplus$ button leads to the display of the detailed instructions within the corresponding segment. To increase screen space for the text, the user clicks the 'Hide Map' button.

3. Techniques

Our solution is based on two elements. First, the route to be described needs to be segmented and summarised in a meaningful way. In an ideal world this

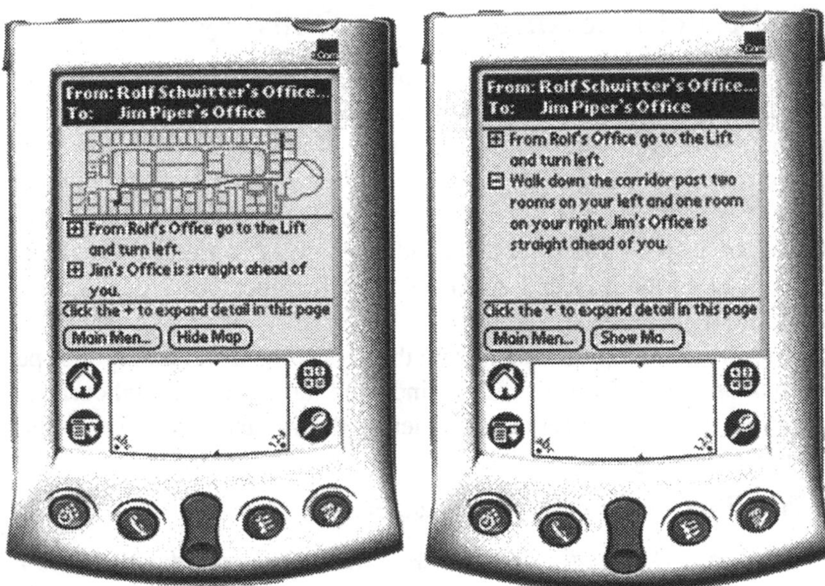

Figure 3. A segmented route description presented on a Palm hand-held computer; the second screen shows the expanded text for the second segment.

might correspond to the top-down structure developed in a hierarchical planner; however, existing systems do not make use of or provide such structures, and so we have explored the use of bottom-up heuristics for the identification of appropriate segmentations. Currently, our range of segmentation strategies makes use of both significant landmarks as segmentation points, and specific features of the constituent turns and paths (such as path length and status in the road hierarchy).

Then, we need techniques that support flexible interaction with the segmented route in conjunction with task execution. We have developed a mark-up language called RPML (Route Plan Mark-up Language) that allows for delivery via combinations of different modalities (textual, graphical, and eventually also voice): our segmentation mechanism produces RPML structures as output, and these are then rendered accordingly on different device types. The rendering device can then provide an interaction mode appropriate for the consumption of the route directions via that device. So, for example, for web delivery we use XSLT to deliver the entire route at once via a web page (see Figure 4), whereas the Palm renderer allows interactive step-by-step exploration of the description as the user performs the navigation task (see Figure 3).

The following subsections further explain each of these elements.

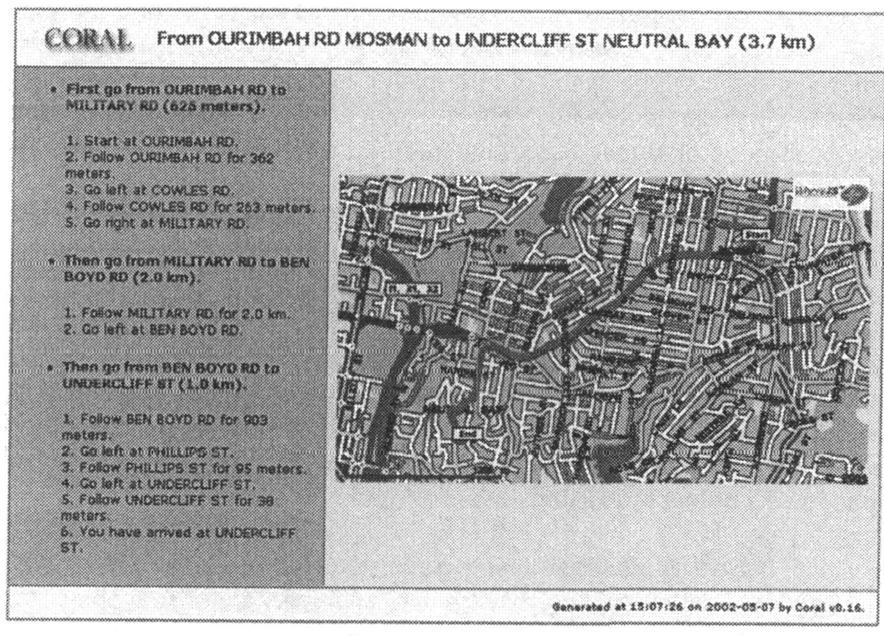

Figure 4. Example of a segmented route presentation via the Web.

3.1 Segmentation

As noted above, existing route planning systems provide flat sequences of instructions, consisting of alternating paths and turns, rather than hierarchical structures. The process of segmentation therefore consists in grouping these path and turn instructions into higher level entities that we call *segments*. The notion of segmentation we are working with here bears some relation to the notion of a discourse segment as discussed by Grosz and Sidner (1986): elements that are more related are seen as aggregating together to form constituents within a larger structure, and in theory this analysis applies recursively to produce a hierarchy.[2]

The concept of hierarchy in wayfinding is not, of course, new. The process of human spatial knowledge acquisition is often assumed to result in a hierarchical structure, referred to as the *cognitive map* by Kuipers (1978); Pailhous's (1970) observation of wayfinding behaviour by experts (specifically, taxi drivers in Paris) confirmed the hypothesis of the existence of a hierarchical strategy, where first a route between regions is constructed at a higher level before being refined into concrete path components.

As so far described, segmentation can be viewed as a way of coherently organising and structuring information. However, it can also be seen as addressing a key question in the provision of information in dialogic contexts:

how do we convey information in instalments so that the course of information exchange approximates the way humans interact? Clark and Schaefer (1989) point out that the segmentation of information in human dialogue responds to a need to decrease the cognitive effort required from the interlocutor. Similarly, in the area of human factors engineering, experiments have shown that meaningful chunking of information allows experts to use their working memory in a more efficient way than novices; see, for example, the studies cited in (Wickens and Holland, 2000, pp256ff).

Of course, only a subset of the mathematically possible segmentations of a stream of information is meaningful, and so a key task is to determine which segmentations should be used. We have explored two alternative strategies: one determines optimal break points in the sequence of paths that make up the route, and the other aggregates several paths into a higher level structure on the basis of properties of the constituent elements. These strategies have been applied to the output of existing route description systems.

3.1.1 Landmark-based segmentation. Our first strategy relies on the experimentally verified idea that landmarks at decision points constitute useful cognitive entities that improve the effectiveness of route descriptions (Lovelace et al., 1999; Denis et al., 1999; Burnett, 2000). Although what constitutes a landmark remains vague and ill-defined, attempts have been made to distinguish different categories of landmarks. Sorrows and Hirtle (1999), for example, identify visual landmarks (objects such as churches and towers which are clearly distinguishable from their environment by virtue of salient visual features), cognitive landmarks (for example, the desk of a receptionist, which may be significant because it has a particular function for a user), and structural landmarks (entities such as Trafalgar Square in London, which assist in structuring a spatial environment).

Here, we investigate how the salience of landmarks can be exploited to structure route descriptions. A landmark at a decision point delimits a part of the route to be followed, so the navigator will be aware whether she has reached that point in the route and will thus know how far she has progressed in the navigation task at hand.

We have applied this idea to the earlier version of Coral which provided indoor route descriptions for our department. The knowledge representation used in that system includes landmarks as domain objects, and these are included in the intermediate representation from which the textual route description is generated. The route plan representation consists of a sequence of alternating path and turn specifications, as shown in Figure 5.

Our segmentation strategy makes use of a separate knowledge source that indicates which domain objects are plausible landmarks; in the present case, the lift is one such object. Since this appears at a decision point (just before the

```
<start(r333), via(< >), end(p333)>,
turn(lhs),
....
<start(p2), via(<c1, pass(lhs:[4,room]), pass(rhs:[1,room]),
final(rhs:lift1)>), end(lift1)>
turn(lhs),
....
<start(p362), via(< >), end(r362)>
```

Figure 5. Part of the underlying representation for the route presented in Figure 3.

final left-hand turn in the fragment under discussion), it is selected as a segment boundary point and included in the summary for this segment. Consequently, the route is decomposed into one segment leading to the lift and a second segment from this landmark to the destination.

The intuition behind this approach to segmentation is quite straightforward: if the user is familiar with the environment, she will recognise the landmark that terminates the segment and realise that she does not need the detailed instructions for that segment. It is also easy for the user to keep this landmark in mind as an intermediary target and to remember that, once she has reached it, she should revert back to the instructions.

There are, however, limitations to this strategy, since it depends on the presence of landmarks at appropriate locations along the route. Applied blindly, it can lead to segments of significantly varying lengths, which can be confusing. Overall, then, whereas a landmark-based segmentation might be feasible for route descriptions on a small dataset (such as an indoor area), where it is relatively easy to determine which objects of the domain constitute landmarks, it becomes more difficult to apply to a larger scale environment. Raubal and Winter (2002) have demonstrated that this is possible in principle, but the measures to formally specify the saliency of various features for landmark selection require the availability of rich datasets, beyond the information available to current navigation systems.

3.1.2 Path-based segmentation. Another approach to segmentation is to investigate characteristics of the constituent paths of the route to determine whether they belong to a meaningful higher-level entity. Other work (see, for example, Höök (1991)) has explored the hypothesis that recurring higher-level patterns can be found in route descriptions provided by expert navigators. A frequently occurring pattern consists of three segments corresponding to the beginning, middle and end of a route; typically these involve, respectively, getting onto a main thoroughfare or higher-level road, travelling along that road, and then leaving that road to reach the destination via a number of lower-level roads. We refer to this route pattern as 'BME'. In the following example, we have used the subscripts B, M and E to indicate the beginning, middle and end segments of the route:

- How do I get from Macquarie University to the Queen Victoria Building, in the City?
- [Well, first you get onto Epping Road $_B$], [then you continue ahead via the freeway, following signs to the City $_M$]. [Exit at Druit Street, then the QVB is not far from there $_E$].

Given a flat sequence of paths and turns, we need to determine how these constituents are allocated to segments within such a structure. We investigated whether available information about route sequences might allow us to meaningfully segment routes. More specifically, we analysed a number of routes in a known environment and asked ourselves whether they could be segmented in a way that makes them easier to communicate and to use. This led to the hypothesis that three features of paths and turns may contribute to increase the usability of route descriptions:

Road status hierarchy: Routes often involve travelling on roads of different status within the road network, from freeways down through main roads to side roads. Our analysis demonstrated that a series of consecutive paths of the same or similar road status is likely to be perceived as constituting a higher-level entity.

Path length: For some routes, segmentation on the basis of road status alone can result in a large number of segments. In such cases, the longest such segment is the most likely candidate for the middle segment.

Turn typology: A turn that is very salient (for example, a T-junction) or that requires careful attention to driving (for example, a right turn in a drive-on-the-left road context) is a likely segment boundary candidate.

These principles are very prominent in the prototypical BME route, as demonstrated in the example above: the middle segment consists of a long stretch of one or more steps on higher level roads, and the absence of explicit or difficult turns along this middle segment reinforces the perception that it is the central part of the route. However, examination of a larger number of routes makes it clear that many variants on this pattern exist, and that these three features interact in a complex manner.

To allow for a systematic exploration of the space, we implemented a segmentation module that takes as input a route (obtained from a route planning system available on the web) augmented with road status information (derived from a widely used street directory). We used 23 routes of different length and in various suburbs of Sydney in our initial exploration.[3] Our main criterion for segmentation quality was approximation to the prototypical BME pattern. We experimented with various combinations of road status-based and length-based heuristics for segmentation; our conclusions from this study were that road status is a good indicator for segmentation (in 43% of the cases); in most other cases (another 34%), segmentation can be improved by augmenting this with heuristics that combine segments on the basis of path length. Our intuition is that turn type information could be used as an additional factor in determining segment boundaries, but further experiments would be needed to confirm this.

The two alternative segmentation strategies (landmark vs. path based) might be integrated in a system which attempts to segment a route based on one strategy and which is able to switch to the other strategy in case the first strategy fails to deliver a satisfying segmentation. The choice of one or another strategy for the first attempt might depend on the user's profile (does she like descriptions in terms of landmarks?) or in terms of the type of environment (is the environment rich in landmarks?).

3.2 A Route Planning Mark-Up Language

Our goal is to produce one route description that can be rendered via a variety of devices; in the first instance we have been exploring rendering via both standard desktop web browsers and via hand-held computers (specifically, the Palm), and we aim to extend this later to voice delivery via VoiceXML.

To support this variety of outputs, we have defined an intermediate, device-independent representation called RPML (for Route Planning Mark-up Language). Two principle features of this representation are that (a) it allows for the annotation of a route description with segmentation information that can be used for presentation by the rendering device; and (b) it allows for multimodal content, such as links to graphical representations of the described route and to voice output. Using this representation, we use XSLT to produce web pages for pre-trip planning like those found at `http://www.ics.mq.edu.au/~coral-/Routes/Sydney/Segm`, and the same input is used by a specially written renderer on the Palm that formats the output for interactive display to support incremental exploration of the route description while travelling. Figure 6 shows a fragment of RPML; this demonstrates how individual instructions can be provided both as canned output (*First go from BAY RD to PACIFIC HWY*) and as more abstracted specifications (as in the contents of the top level `<summary>` element) which the renderer can decide how to realise.

```
<route-plan context="Sydney">
<summary>
  <from>BAY RD ARCADIA</from>
  <to>UNIVERSITY AV MACQUARIE PARK</to>
  <distance>35.0 km</distance>
</summary>
<map url=
  "http://www.ics.mq.edu.au/~coral/Routes/Sydney/map302.gif"/>
&lt;segment sid="1"&gt;
  <summary>
    <string>First go from BAY RD to PACIFIC HWY.</string>
  </summary>
  <detail>
    <utterance uid="1">
      <string>Start at BAY RD.</string>
    </utterance>
...
```

Figure 6. A fragment of RPML.

4. Evaluation

At the outset of this chapter, we made the point that a key feature of applications such as the one we describe here is that the application should allow the attention of the user to be focussed on performing the task, not on interacting with the device. Consequently, the evaluation of a mobile system requires a different approach from that required for desktop systems, where the user only has to attend to the device itself; in particular, it is important to evaluate a mobile system in a real-world task setting.

In their overview of evaluation methods used for in-car navigation systems, Ross and Burnett (2001) distinguish four dimensions along which evaluation methods can be specified: the context in which the evaluation is used (task-based vs. desk-based), the technique used (task-based vs. checklist), the kinds of measures (subjective vs. objective), and the familiarity of the evaluators with the technology (expert vs. user). Their comparison of advantages of different methods as used in cited evaluation studies of navigation systems leads to a recommendation to use task-based evaluation on the road by experts, possibly followed by user evaluations to broaden the scope of the evaluation. More generally, the choice of an HCI evaluation method also depends on the stage in the development cycle at which it is to be used: in an early design stage, group discussions, questionnaires and checklists are appropriate; prototype systems might be evaluated by experts; and user trials (possibly on a larger scale) require a fully working system.

In the light of these considerations we decided to perform a small scale expert evaluation in a task-based context.

4.1 Goals of the Experiment

Our major aims were to obtain feedback on the use of segmented route descriptions and their incremental presentation on a mobile device. Although some objective information was collected, such as the number of navigation errors and the duration of travel, the form of feedback we were looking for was essentially subjective: significant quantitative evaluation would require a larger scale experiment. In this pilot evaluation, our goal was to get a feel for how the proposed delivery mode and segmented content were perceived in conjunction with navigation task execution.

4.2 Experimental Set-Up

There are a great many parameters that might influence the results of a task-based evaluation of a mobile navigation system: user acquaintance with mobile devices, familiarity with the environment to be navigated, general spatial skills, direction of travel, time and context of travel, type of route, and quality of signage, to mention but a few. In order to minimise the influence of these factors, we set up a well-defined experimental scenario, where three teams each consisting of a navigator and a driver would use route descriptions on a Palm hand-held computer to drive from the University to a particular location and back again. For safety reasons, only the navigator would use the hand-held computer, relaying verbal instructions to the driver as appropriate.

Different routes, each sourced from an online navigation system and each of approximately 30 km in length, were used for the outward and return trips. In order to compare the effect of segmented vs. non-segmented route descriptions, each team followed a segmented route description in one direction and a non-segmented in the other; Figure 7 provides examples of the two types of descriptions. The non-segmented ones consisted of a numbered (flat) list of alternating path and turn expressions ('utterances' in terms of RPML) displayed as a memo. The same routes were automatically segmented and summarised according to the method described in Section 3.1.2. Since the first pass segmentation based on road hierarchy status yielded a route description structure which approximates the BME pattern, we were confident that the quality of the segmentation could not negatively influence the outcome of our experiment.

Two observers also participated in the experiment: each accompanied a team on one of their trips. The observers' task was to observe the navigators without interfering, taking notes on any points of interest. The naviga-

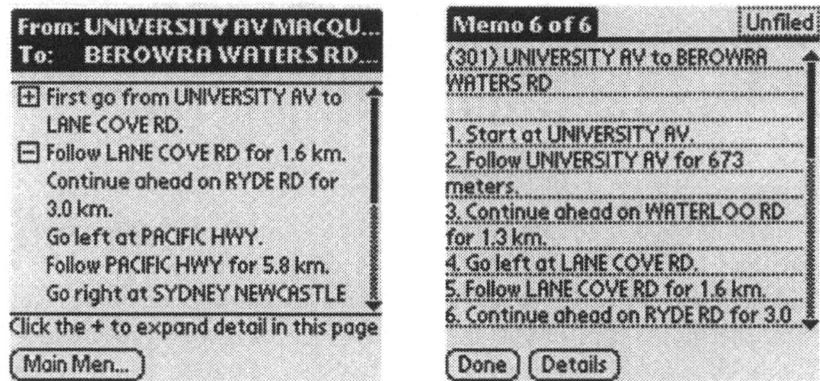

Figure 7. Segmented and non-segmented route descriptions.

tor was asked to log any events or observations related to the navigation task (such as hesitations, navigation errors, lack of information, suggestions for improvement, and so on). A post-travel questionnaire for the navigator included a question asking which presentation mode he/she preferred and why. The questionnaires, briefing and forms were carefully formulated so as to avoid a suggested preference for one or another presentation mode: for example, we used the terms 'list-based' versus 'tree-based' rather than making reference to the notion of segmentation.

4.3 Experimental Outcomes

4.3.1 Observations. In general, no major problems occurred during task execution; only one navigation error occurred, and no hesitations led to another information source being consulted. All three teams had difficulties with initial orientation, and one also with recognising the destination, but this was due to a lack of information in the source route descriptions.

The observers noted a striking difference in navigation style: whereas one navigator (N_3) systematically conveyed the distance information provided in the description (as in *Follow Lane Cove Road for 1.6km*), another navigator (N_1) did not communicate this information to his driver at all. The latter navigator explored the route description at summary level, but did not systematically provide the summary information to the driver. It was observed that the summaries themselves did not in general provide enough information for the driver to find the correct route (except on the way back to the familiar starting point).

4.3.2 Feedback from navigators. Two of the three navigators (N_1, N_2) expressed a preference for the segmented over the non-segmented presentation. Unprompted, they indicated that it seemed more appropriate for a limited bandwidth device and that it assisted in keeping track of progress in the directions. The third navigator (N_3) observed that the use of numbering in the non-segmented presentation mode was helpful and that a typographic distinction between summary and detailed information (for example, the use of a different typeface) might help to improve the usability of the segmented presentation mode.

Other feedback and suggestions for improvement related to the type of information which might be useful, such as the names of cross-streets preceding turns and confirmatory landmarks along the road.

4.3.3 Discussion. The preference for one or another presentation mode in this experiment co-occurred with the distinction noted above regarding the use of explicit distance information: that is, those who preferred the segmented description (N_1, N_2) relied less on distance information. The navigator (N_3) who relied on factual information (such as exact distance measures) was less inclined to use the structural information provided through segmentation than the navigators who used more general information, such as general orientation, topology, and road layout.

This dichotomy can be related to the often stipulated and observed difference between egocentric and exocentric spatial knowledge representation and problem solving. The former, referred to as 'navigation-based' spatial knowledge, is derived from directly observable or measurable features of the environment, such as landmarks and distances, and is typically acquired through navigation. The latter, referred to as 'survey' spatial knowledge, requires external knowledge such as insight into the overall structure of the navigation network, and is acquired by studying a map or through extensive experience with navigating the environment. Thorndyke and Hayes-Roth (1982) found through experiments that users who have acquired survey knowledge through extensive navigation experience outperform users who know an environment from studying a map only. Denis' study (1997) revealed that route descriptions provided by people who are classified as high imagers (i.e., who have rich and highly accessible visuo-spatial representations) are not rated significantly higher in terms of overall quality. Höök (1991) hypothesised that resident navigators describe routes as procedures (i.e., from the navigation-based perspective) when they assume their interlocutor is not familiar with the environment, although they construct the route using survey knowledge. Whether or not users can be classified as either type of navigator, on the basis of their experience, general spatial reasoning capabilities or perhaps gender,[4] is outside the scope of our research. However, these studies seem to support the hypothesis that survey knowledge, although not necessarily surfacing in route descriptions, plays an important role in the efficiency of a navigation process. It is this kind of spatial knowledge that our segmented and summarised routes convey, in an effort to provide navigation support in a compact and task supportive way.

5. Conclusion

Starting from limitations of existing navigation assistance systems and characteristics of human-provided route directions, we have identified two key elements that might lead to more effective navigation support systems: the emphasis of salient properties of the routes and the segmentation of these routes. The latter aspect is particularly useful in improving navigation support provided via mobile devices as it also allows optimal usage of the limited screen space, while supporting the navigator's switching back and forth between the presented information and the task at hand. We have investigated and implemented the use of segmentation and summarisation of route descriptions provided via mobile devices. A pilot evaluation of our prototype in a real-world setting is suggestive of the utility of this approach, although some navigators might prefer a non-segmented description. We are thus faced with an opportunity for customisation of route descriptions, with an emphasis either on directly observable features of the environment or on survey knowledge.

Whereas the work described here mainly aims at providing survey-like navigation support, our ongoing research is targeted towards the use of more specific natural language generation techniques to improve route descriptions along the egocentric perspective. In particular, we are investigating how currently available information about route objects can be used to generate descriptions that enhance recognisability of decision points along the route.

Another direction, alluded to earlier, is the use of voice delivery. Our RPML structures provide a source data format that can be turned into a VoiceXML document via an appropriate XSLT transformation. We envisage here the production of a dialogic structure that allows simple navigation of a hierarchical route representation via commands such as *next*, *back* and *more detail*, thus providing an interactive exploration of the route in much the same way as is offered via our Palm-based renderer.

Acknowledgements

The authors wish to thank David Hood for his work on the Palm renderer and the participants of the pilot evaluation experiment. The work described here was funded by the Australian Research Council.

Notes

1. This example is from our corpus of human generated route descriptions.
2. In practice, we have so far only found need for one level of hierarchy in our structures.
3. `http://www.clt.mq.edu.au/~coral/Routes/Sydney/Segm/`

4. Recent neurological research (Grön et al., 2000) indicating a gender-related difference in brain activation when performing navigation tasks may correspond to earlier results from psychologists' studies on gender differences in route description behaviour (Denis, 1997).

References

Bernsen, N. O. and Dybkjær, L. (2004). Enhancing the usability of multimodal virtual co-drivers. In Minker, W., Bühler, D., and Dybkjær, L., editors, *Spoken Multimodal Human-Computer Dialogue in Mobile Environments*. Kluwer Academic Publishers, Dordrecht, The Netherlands. (this volume).

Burnett, G. E. (2000). "Turn right at the traffic lights." The requirements for landmarks in vehicle navigation systems. *The Journal of Navigation*, 53(3):499–510.

Clark, H. and Schaefer, E. (1989). Contributing to discourse. *Cognitive Science*, 13:259–294.

Dale, R., Geldof, S., and Prost, J.-P. (2002). Generating more natural route descriptions. In *Proceedings of Australasian Natural Language Processing Workshop (ANLP)*, pages 41–48, Canberra, Australia.

Denis, M. (1997). The description of routes: a cognitive approach to the production of spatial discourse. *Current Psychology of Cognition*, 16(4):409–458.

Denis, M., Pazzaglia, F., Cornoldi, C., and Bertolo, L. (1999). Spatial discourse and navigation: an analysis of route directions in the city of Venice. *Applied Cognitive Psychology*, 13:145–174.

Grön, G., Wunderlich, A., Spitzer, M., Reinhard, T., and Riepe, M. (2000). Brain activation during human navigation: gender different neural networks as substrate of performance. *Nature Neuroscience*, 3(4):404–408.

Grosz, B. J. and Sidner, C. L. (1986). Attention, intentions and the structure of discourse. *Computational Linguistics*, 12(3):175–204.

Höök, K. (1991). An approach to a route guidance interface. Licentiate Thesis, Department of Computer and Systems Sciences, Stockholm University.

Höppner, W. (1995). Modularity in NLG. In *Proceedings of International Colloquium on Cognitive Science*, pages 117–121, San Sebastian, Spain.

Jameson, A. and Klöckner, K. (2004). User multitasking with mobile multimodal systems. In Minker, W., Bühler, D., and Dybkjær, L., editors, *Spoken Multimodal Human-Computer Dialogue in Mobile Environments*. Kluwer Academic Publishers, Dordrecht, The Netherlands. (this volume).

Kuipers, B. J. (1978). Modelling spatial knowledge. *Cognitive Science*, 2:129–153.

Lovelace, K. L., Hegarty, M., and Montello, D. R. (1999). Elements of good route directions in familiar and unfamiliar environments. In Freksa, C. and Mark, D. M., editors, *Proceedings of International Conference on Spatial Information Theory: Cognitive and Computational Foundations of*

Geographic Information Science, COSIT, pages 65–82, Berlin, Germany. Springer Verlag.

Moulin, B. and Kettani, D. (1999). Route generation and description using the notions of object's influence area and spatial conceptual map. *Spatial Cognition and Computation*, 1:227–259.

Norman, D. (1998). *The Invisible Computer*. MIT Press, Cambridge, Massachusetts, USA.

Pailhous, J. (1970). *La representation de l'Espace Urbain - l'exemple du chauffeur de Taxi*. Presses Universitaires de France, Paris, France.

Pieraccini, R., Carpenter, B., Woudenberg, E., Caskey, S., Springer, S., Bloom, J., and Phillips, M. (2004). Multimodal spoken dialogue with wireless devices. In Minker, W., Bühler, D., and Dybkjær, L., editors, *Spoken Multimodal Human-Computer Dialogue in Mobile Environments*. Kluwer Academic Publishers, Dordrecht, The Netherlands. (this volume).

Raubal, M. and Winter, S. (2002). Enriching wayfinding instructions with local landmarks. In Egenhofer, M. J. and Mark, D. M., editors, *Geographic Information Science*, Lecture Notes in Computer Science, pages 243–259. Springer Verlag, Berlin, Germany.

Ross, T. and Burnett, G. (2001). Evaluating the human-machine interface to vehicle navigation systems as an example of ubiquitous computing. *International Journal of Human-Computer Studies*, 55:661–674.

Sorrows, M. E. and Hirtle, S. C. (1999). The nature of landmarks for real and electronic spaces. In Freksa, C. and Mark, D. M., editors, *Spatial Information Theory*, volume 1661 of *Lecture Notes in Computer Science*, pages 37–50. Springer Verlag, Berlin, Germany.

Stocky, T. and Cassell, J. (2002). Shared reality: Spatial intelligence in intuitive user interfaces. In *Proceedings of International Conference on Intelligent User Interfaces (IUI)*, pages 224–225, San Francisco, California, USA.

Thorndyke, P. W. and Hayes-Roth, B. (1982). Differences in spatial knowledge obtained from maps and navigation. *Cognitive Psychology*, 14:560–589.

Van der Sluis, I. F. (2001). An empirically motivated algorithm for the generation of multimodal referring expressions. In *Proceedings of Annual Meeting of the Association for Computational Linguistics (ACL)*, pages 67–72, Toulouse, France.

Wickens, C. D. and Holland, J. (2000). *Engineering Psychology and Human Performance*. Prentice Hall, New Jersey, New Jersey, USA, 3rd edition.

Williams, S. (1998). Generating pitch accents in a concept-to-speech system using a knowledge base. In *Proceedings of International Conference on Spoken Language Processing (ICSLP)*, pages 1159–1162, Sydney, Australia.

Chapter 18

EFFECTS OF PROLONGED USE ON THE USABILITY OF A MULTIMODAL FORM-FILLING INTERFACE

Janienke Sturm, Bert Cranen
University of Nijmegen, Department Language and Speech, Nijmegen, The Netherlands
{janienke.sturm,b.cranen}@let.kun.nl

Jacques Terken, Ilse Bakx
TU Eindhoven, Department of Industrial Design, Eindhoven, The Netherlands
j.m.b.Terken@tue.nl

Abstract We present a study of the effect of prolonged use on the way users interact with a multimodal form-filling system. The system accepts spoken input as well as pointing input and provides output both in speech and in graphics. We measured the usability of the system in a pre-test / post-test design and analysed in detail the changes in interaction patterns due to exposure. The study shows that with practice users learn to develop interaction patterns that ensure reliable and efficient interaction, resulting in decreased dialogue duration and more user satisfaction.

Keywords: Dialogue management; Multimodal interaction; Speech/pen-based interaction; Usability evaluation.

1. Introduction

With the emergence of networked handheld devices, it has become possible to provide information services on mobile terminals that were up to now only available on desktop computers. However, interaction styles that are natural and easy to use on a desktop computer may easily become cumbersome on miniaturised devices like palmtops or mobile phones. Whereas typing or pointing on a screen in general may feel as a natural way to provide input on a desktop computer, with small devices typing and pointing may easily become

W. Minker, D. Bühler and L. Dybkjær (eds), Spoken Multimodal Human-Computer Dialogue in Mobile Environments, 329-348

tiresome due to the absence of hardware keyboards and the inherent limitations on the length of menus. In order to fully exploit the capabilities of handheld devices, an obvious solution seems to be to deploy multimodal interfaces. It is generally assumed that combining elements of graphical user interfaces and spoken dialogue systems will enable users to interact with mobile terminals in a more efficient and natural way (Maybury and Wahlster, 1998; Oviatt et al., 1997). However, it does not follow automatically that a multimodal interface will enable users to interact in the most efficient way right from the beginning. Instead, users may need practice to develop a stable interaction pattern that supports efficient use (Petrelli et al., 1997). In the present study we investigate the effect of prolonged use on the development of stable and efficient interaction patterns, using a multimodal form-filling interface for obtaining train timetable information that was developed in the MATIS project (Multimodal Access to Transaction and Information Services) (Sturm et al., 2001). The interface accepts both speech-based and pointing input and provides spoken as well as visual feedback.

Sturm et al. (2002) report the results of a usability evaluation of the multimodal MATIS interface. The goal of the evaluation study was to determine whether providing multiple modalities helps to improve the usability of the system as compared to more conventional unimodal systems, such as a spoken dialogue system and a graphical user interface (GUI). In this evaluation only novice users were asked to test the system. For public information systems this makes sense, since those systems should be suitable for use by inexperienced users without training. However, it may not be the right approach for evaluating interfaces that are used more frequently, such as those running on mobile devices that are typically used by the same person over longer periods of time. In such cases the user has the opportunity to gradually develop a preferred interaction pattern, and only monitoring the initial stage of use could lead to inappropriate conclusions. The experiments carried out by Suhm et al. (1999), Petrelli et al. (1997) and Karat et al. (2000) showed that user behaviour indeed changes as users become more experienced in using a multimodal system. In the current chapter, we therefore focus on the question whether prolonged use of the MATIS system indeed enables users to develop preferred interaction patterns, what these interaction patterns are, and whether they improve the efficiency and effectiveness of the interaction and the user satisfaction.

Multimodal interaction patterns can be characterised by means of the scheme depicted in Table 1 (Nigay and Coutaz, 1993).

The 'Fusion' property concerns the question whether the system allows the user to express a piece of information by employing different modalities for different parts of the information. For instance, zooming in on form-filling applications, where the pieces of information can be represented as attribute-value pairs (e.g. attribute: destination city; value: Amsterdam), the attribute

Table 1. Multimodal interaction.

		Use of modalities	
		Parallel	Sequential
Fusion	Combined	synergistic	alternate
	Independent	concurrent	exclusive

might be conveyed by a pointing gesture and the value by speech. The 'Use of modalities' property concerns the question whether the system allows the user to convey information in different modalities simultaneously or not. For the form-filling example it would mean that the system can or cannot handle the actions in the different modalities when they occur simultaneously. These two binary properties combine to four types of multimodal interaction: *synergistic*, *concurrent*, *alternate*, and *exclusive*. When different modalities are used in parallel, we distinguish *synergistic* use where the user employs two modalities to provide a single attribute-value pair (the "put-that-there" paradigm (Bolt, 1980)) and *concurrent* use where both modalities are used to provide unrelated information. Different modalities can also be used sequentially; here, we distinguish *alternate* use where the user conveys a single piece of information (a single attribute-value pair) stepwise, employing different modalities at each step, and *exclusive* use where the user presents one piece of information using one modality and subsequently another, unrelated piece of information using another modality. With respect to the *combined* use of modalities, it should be noted here that in fact most multimodal interaction is actually of the *alternate* rather than of the *synergistic* type (Oviatt, 1999).

In the evaluation with novice users (Sturm et al., 2002) we observed predominantly exclusive interaction patterns; the system would prompt the user for particular information and the user would reply either by speech or by a pointing gesture. That is, the initiative was with the system and the user patiently followed the requests for providing attribute values to the system. We assume that novice users feel uncomfortable taking over the initiative, for instance because they do not know how to use the facilities that are offered to interact with a graphical user interface, or out of politeness; people tend to treat computers with the same sort of politeness that they would fellow human beings (Reeves and Nass, 1996). We expect, however, that with prolonged use users will get more self-confident, start to take over the initiative and develop a preference for alternate and synergistic interaction patterns, activating an attribute by means of a pointing gesture and providing the value by speech. In the next section, we will describe and motivate the system's design. In Section 3 we describe the user test that has been carried out to study the effect of experience on the interaction. In Section 4 we present and discuss the results of the test and in Section 5 we will draw conclusions.

2. The MATIS System

We changed an existing unimodal spoken dialogue system for railway information into a multimodal system by adding screen input and output, allowing for both spoken and graphical interaction. Detailed information about the system architecture can be found in (Sturm et al., 2001).

Adding visual feedback to a spoken dialogue system has been shown to help the user in building a mental model of the task at hand and understanding the travel advice (Terken and Riele, 2001). Therefore, during the spoken dialogue, the screen shows a graphical representation of the form to be filled in (see Figure 1) and gives feedback on the recognition result, the buttons that have been pushed and other information that provides the user with the current system status, such as an hourglass that appears when the system is processing the input. Furthermore, after all fields have been filled in, the screen displays the travel advice. As mentioned earlier, the system accepts both speech and pointing input and provides output in the form of speech and graphics.

Speech input When the user activates the system, the system identifies itself and sets up a spoken dialogue to collect the query parameters. This prompting strategy supports novice users by guiding them through the task[1]. Furthermore, it creates a bias towards the speech mode, which is in agreement with the observed preference of users for the speech mode (Bilici et al., 2000; Suhm et al., 1999). The system can handle mixed initiative, i.e., situations where the user utterance contains more information than explicitly asked for in the system prompt. Speech is mandatory for providing initial values for the attributes 'origin', 'destination', 'date' (if not today or tomorrow), and 'time' (see Figure 1).

Pointing input The facilities offered to interact in the graphical mode are illustrated in Figure 1. They will be described here in terms of the classification scheme depicted in Table 1.

① The user can press radio buttons to select predefined mutually exclusive values (today/tomorrow or departure/arrival). This facility allows for *exclusive* use, where a user uses different modalities for subsequent unrelated actions. As radio buttons are active during the whole dialogue, they also allow for *concurrent* use, i.e., the user presses a radio button while also providing an unrelated value in the spoken mode.

② The user can press one of the microphone buttons to select the field that (s)he wants to fill, e.g., to correct recognition errors (pressing the microphone button will reset the field) or simply to speed up the dialogue.

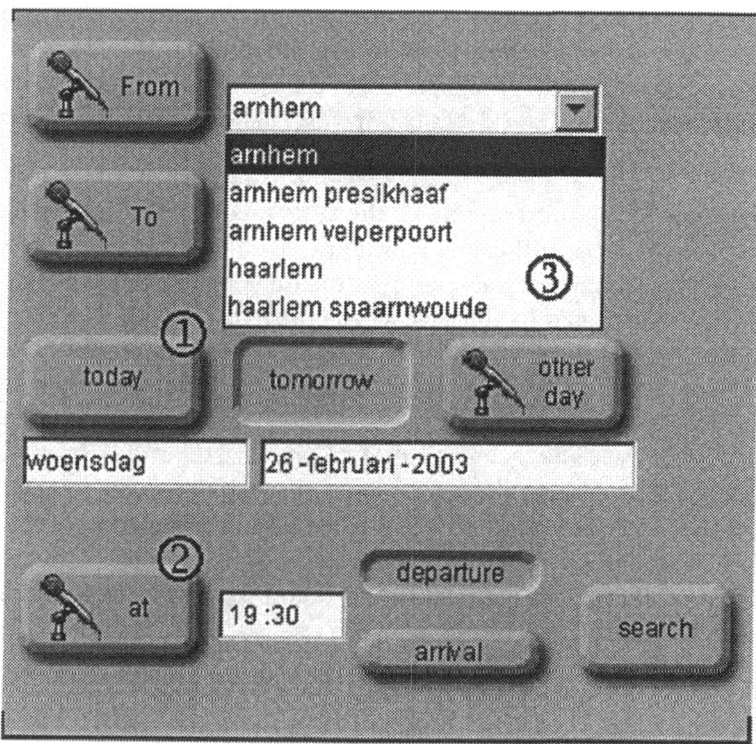

Figure 1. Screenshot of the MATIS interface (button labels have been translated from Dutch).

In the current implementation, pressing a microphone button for a given slot will interrupt the current system question and trigger a short instruction (e.g., "Say the departure station"), after which the user can enter a value for the field using speech. This allows for *alternate* use: the user can exploit two different modalities to specify one attribute-value pair. The input from the two modalities is interpreted by means of late fusion (Oviatt, 2000).

③ In case of a recognition error users can also select another station name from a drop-down list. Specifying a station name by speech and correcting the value by selecting another value from the drop-down menu would be a form of *exclusive* use in the topology of Nigay and Coutaz, although this does not do full justice to the dependency: after a recognition error, the user switches to a different modality to correct the error. Note that the drop-down list can also be used in a *concurrent* way, e.g., by selecting an alternative station name while providing unrelated data in the spoken mode. In order to keep the length of the drop-down list limited, it only contains the recognition alternatives as specified in the N-best list of the speech recogniser and all alternative stations in the cities that were in the recogniser's N-best list. When the intended station name is not in the drop-down list, the user can clear the field by pressing the microphone button (②).

Speech output The spoken output of the system consists of open questions, instructions, and verification questions. Open questions are asked to fill the slots that have no value yet. Instructions (e.g., "Say the arrival station") are triggered by the user when (s)he presses a microphone button indicating that (s)he wants to fill a certain field. Verification questions are asked when the value provided by the user has a confidence score that falls below a pre-set threshold. If the confidence score exceeds the threshold, the value is assumed to be correct and no verification question is asked. Values that are provided through the graphical interaction facilities (see ② and ③ in Figure 1) are always assigned maximum confidence; these are never verified in the spoken dialogue. The user can interrupt the spoken output of the system by pressing buttons; barge-in using speech is not possible, however.

Screen output The screen always shows the current state of the interaction. Visual feedback about the progress of the dialogue is given by showing on the screen the values that are extracted from the spoken replies of the user. In case a verification question is asked due to a low confidence level of the recognition result, the visual feedback and the spoken verification question are synchronised. Once a radio button has been pressed, it remains in that state until the user presses the alternative option. When a microphone button has been pressed, it turns green to indicate that the recording has started. When the recording has stopped, after end-of-utterance detection or a time-out, this button returns to its original colour.

When all required information has been collected, a query is sent to the information database, which returns a travel advice. The database query is done automatically when all query parameters are available and verified, but the user can also force the database query by pressing the 'Search' button, thus avoiding any remaining verification questions. The complete travel advice is shown on the screen in tabular form, while in the spoken dialogue only the main information is given (only the departure and arrival stations and the departure and arrival time).

3. Methods

3.1 System

The MATIS interface has been conceived for small devices such as palmtops or mobile phones, but for practical reasons it was implemented as a Java applet on a desktop computer with a touch screen and no keyboard. The subjects called the system using an ordinary telephone, equipped with a headset, so that they had both hands free for interaction by means of the touch screen.

3.2 Subjects and Tasks

Eight subjects (five male and three female, between 14 and 73 years of age, with mixed educational backgrounds) participated in the test. They were paid for participating. Two subjects had no or very little experience with computers. Two subjects were regular train travellers; the others were only occasional travellers (less than twice a year). To get timetable information most subjects used the booklet supplied by the railway company or asked the person at the ticket counter. Only one subject had used the commercial version of a spoken dialogue system for train timetable information before, and only one subject had used another spoken dialogue system before.

The experiment was carried out with a pre-test / post-test design (within-subjects) (see Table 2). All sessions were conducted in the usability lab of the UCE department of TU Eindhoven, which is furnished as a living room.

Table 2. Set-up of user test.

T1	*T2*	*T3*	*T4*	*T5*	*T6*
Pre-test	Practise Min. 30min	Practise M. 30min	Practise M. 30min	Practise M. 30min	Post-test

By way of introduction to the pre-test, the test leader explained and demonstrated all possible interaction styles by means of an exercise scenario. The overview and explanation of the interaction possibilities had been written down in a reference sheet to make sure all participants received the same introduction; this reference sheet was available for the subjects during all sessions. Following the explanation, the subjects took the pre-test by completing six scenarios. The scenarios were presented graphically in order to avoid influencing the manner in which people express themselves (see Figure 2).

The details of the scenarios are presented in Table 3. To ensure that the test would provide information about how users deal with speech recognition errors, some scenarios concerned station names that are highly confusable with

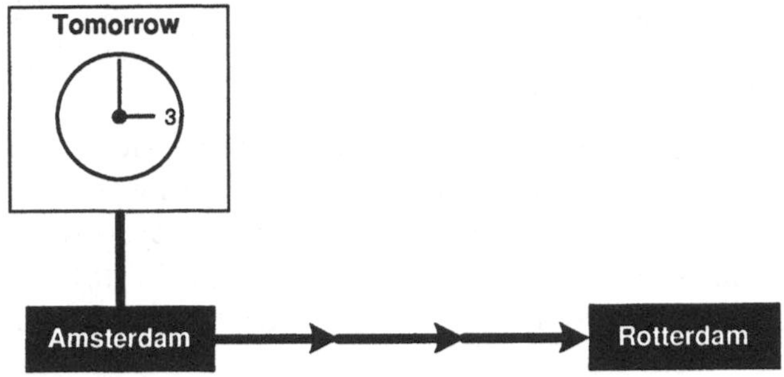

Figure 2. Example of a test scenario: "From Amsterdam to Rotterdam, leaving tomorrow at 3:00 p.m.".

one or more of the other station names in the lexicon of the automatic speech recogniser (scenarios 4, 5 and 6).

Table 3. Description of scenarios (in order of increasing difficulty).

Scenario	*From*	*To*	*date*	*Time*	*dep./arr.*
1	Eindhoven	Breda	tomorrow	15:00	depart
2	Groningen	Tilburg	today	20:30	arrive
3	Utrecht	Leeuwarden	Sunday	18:00	depart
4	Harderwijk	Zwijndrecht	tomorrow	6:30	arrive
5	Swalmen	Amsterdam RAI	tomorrow	7:30	arrive
6	Weert	Kerkrade	Saturday	15:00	depart

Once the subjects had finished the pre-test, they practised with the system during three or four sessions of at least 30 minutes each (one session a day). During these sessions they either used scenarios offered by the experimenter or they devised their own scenarios. The subjects were asked explicitly to try out all the different interaction facilities offered by the system. During the practice sessions the experimenter was available to help out in problem situations, such as the system crashing. However, the experimenter never provided hints and tips about the actual use of the system during the practice sessions. After having successfully completed 30 to 40 dialogues, the subjects were asked whether they thought they had developed stable interaction patterns. If so, the post-test was carried out, if not, they practised for another 30 minutes. In the post-test the subjects carried out the same six scenarios that were used for the pre-test (see Table 3).

3.3 Data Capture and Evaluation Measures

Speech and clicking actions of all dialogues were automatically logged (including time stamps). Additionally, all dialogues were videotaped. Based on this information, detailed analyses were made of the interaction patterns to find out whether prolonged use affected the way subjects interacted with the MATIS system. Also, effectiveness and efficiency were measured for the pre-test as well as for the post-test. Effectiveness was defined in terms of the number of dialogues completed successfully (the dialogue success rate). Efficiency was defined as task completion time (i.e., the time span between the start of the first user answer and the moment at which the query is sent to the information database). Both after the pre-test and after the post-test the subjects completed a usability questionnaire containing statements concerning different aspects of the system, such as "*The combination of speech and graphics is useful*" and "*The system is slow*" (see Table 9). The subjects expressed their agreement or disagreement with the statements on a five-point Likert-scale (1 = I strongly disagree, 3 = I agree nor disagree, 5 = I strongly agree). The Likert-scale judgements were used to measure user satisfaction.

4. Results and Discussion

In total, 48 dialogues were recorded both for the pre-test and the post-test. In Sections 4.1 and 4.2 we discuss objective measurements in terms of effectiveness and efficiency. In Section 4.3 we discuss whether users changed their interaction patterns as a function of prolonged use. In Section 4.4 we describe to what extent prolonged use affected the user satisfaction.

4.1 Effectiveness

The effectiveness of the interaction is defined in terms of the number of successfully completed dialogues (i.e., dialogues in which the user received the requested travel advice). Both in the pre-test and the post-test, 48 dialogues were recorded.

The overall effectiveness, measured across scenarios, increased from 87.5% in the pre-test to 93.8% in the post-test: in the pre-test six dialogues failed, whereas in the post-test only three dialogues failed. Both in the pre-test and in the post-test three dialogues failed because the subject decided to end the dialogue due to persistent recognition errors. The other three failures in the pre-test were caused by the fact that the subjects did not notice that the system recognised and filled in wrong values. Objectively, according to our criterion for a successfully completed dialogue, these must be considered failed dialogues, therefore we exclude these from further analysis, although one might also argue that, since the subjects did not attempt to correct the errors made, the dialogues should be considered to be successful. In that case there would be no difference in the overall effectiveness between the pre-test and the post-test.

All analyses in the following sections are based on the objectively successful dialogues only (42 in the pre-test and 45 in the post-test).

4.2 Efficiency

Results on the efficiency of the dialogues are shown in Table 4. For each scenario the mean duration of a dialogue is shown in seconds measured from the start of the first user utterance to the query to the information database. The scenarios are presented in order of increasing difficulty.

Table 4. Average dialogue duration (in seconds).

Scenario	*Average dialogue duration*	
	Pre	*Post*
1	66.8	37.5
2	52.1	30.6
3	69.8	50.1
4	65.5	35.9
5	134.5	45.5
6	115.2	83.8
Mean	79.8	46.5

Table 4 shows that, on average, dialogues are completed faster in the post-test than in the pre-test: the mean duration decreased from 79.8 seconds in the pre-test to 46.5 seconds in the post-test, with gains ranging from 20 seconds to 89 seconds. Two analyses of variance were conducted, one with Pre-Post and Subjects as main factors and one with Pre-Post and Scenarios as main factors. The effect of Pre-Post was significant in both analyses ($F_{1,7}$=16.76, p=.005 and $F_{1,5}$=18.29, p=.005, respectively). No interactions were significant. From this we conclude that the difference between pre-test and post-test is robust, and that the reduction in average duration from pre-test to post-test is not significantly different for different subjects (across scenarios) or different scenarios (across subjects). As can be seen, in the pre-test the two most difficult scenarios (5 and 6) resulted in durations that are substantially longer than those for the other four scenarios. In the post-test, scenario 6 still has the longest duration, but the duration of scenario 5 has decreased with 89 seconds to a level that is below the average duration. As this is a scenario where many speech recognition errors were made, obviously subjects succeeded in dealing with these errors more efficiently in the post-test. The relatively long duration for scenario 6 is probably due to a combination of factors, including the fact that subjects had to ask for a day other than today or tomorrow, so that radio buttons could not be used to provide the value for "Day".

In the next section we will explore possible explanations for the gains in efficiency from pre-test to post-test.

4.3 Interaction Styles

The MATIS interface offers two input modalities: speech and pointing. Table 5 shows the average number of actions per dialogue, split up into speech actions and pointing actions.

Table 5. Distribution of user speech actions and pointing actions per dialogue.

Modality	*Pre-test*	*Post-test*
Speech	6.3 (73%)	4.7 (68%)
Pointing	2.3 (27%)	2.2 (32%)
Total	8.6 (100%)	6.9 (100%)

Table 5 shows that both in the pre-test and the post-test, most of the interaction is done using speech. This is not surprising, as the fields for departure station, arrival station, time, and day (if day is not today or tomorrow) can only be filled using speech (as explained in Section 2 the station names can be corrected without using speech, by utilising the drop-down menu). The average number of speech and pointing actions decreased from 8.6 in the pre-test to 6.9 in the post-test. As can be seen in Table 5, this is mainly due to a decrease in the number of speech actions. In the next sections we will take a closer look at the data in Table 5 and explore three possible changes in user behaviour that may explain the observed patterns and efficiency gains:

1 Verbal behaviour: Users may change the way they speak to the system, either changing their speaking style or switching to mixed-initiative behaviour;

2 Changes in the use of modalities: users may start to use other modalities as a function of practice;

3 Changes in the temporal pattern: there may be a change in the moment at which users conduct specific actions.

4.3.1 Changes in verbal behaviour. As can be seen in Table 5, the observed decrease in average number of actions per dialogue is mostly due to a decrease in speech actions. One possible explanation is that users may learn to adjust their *speaking style* to the capabilities of the system, a tendency that has also been reported by (Karat et al., 2000). We observed, for example, that subjects tend to hyperarticulate in case of recognition errors, but return to normal speech as soon as they discover that hyperarticulating does not help. Such changes in speaking style may affect system behaviour in several ways. First, one may expect a decrease of the number of recognition errors, due to the fact that people learn to speak the way the system wants them to. Indeed, the number of misrecognitions per dialogue decreased from 1,14 (48/42 [2]) in the pre-test to 0,69 (31/45 [3]) in the post-test. This decrease can be attributed mainly to a decrease of the number of deletion errors; the number of substitution errors was almost equal in both tests. Another effect of changes in speaking style may be that the confidence level of the recognised words increases, which entails that less verification questions have to be asked. Indeed, the number of utterances that were recognised with a confidence exceeding the verification threshold increased from 2,78 (117/42) per dialogue in the pre-test to 3,13 (141/45) per dialogue in the post-test. The number of verification questions asked decreased accordingly, which partly explains the decrease in the number of speech actions.

The analyses described above show that subjects indeed adjusted their speaking style to the capabilities of the system. The data show that this already explains a large part of the observed decrease in the number of speech actions and the increased efficiency.

Also, subjects may have learned to use the *mixed initiative capabilities* of the system and provide more data in one utterance. Analyses of the recorded dialogues show that, although in most cases subjects provide only one information item at a time, the number of occasions where two or more items are provided in one utterance increased from 0,86 (36/42) per dialogue in the pre-test to 1,04 (47/45) per dialogue in the post-test. The combination used most frequently is a combination of Departure and Arrival station.

4.3.2 Changes in the use of modalities. Clearly, not only changes in verbal behaviour, but also a different usage of the multimodal interface during the post-test may account for the decreased number of speech acts and the increased efficiency. While practising subjects may have developed different preferences for choosing to use either speech or pointing in specific situations.

A first piece of evidence concerning the changes in user preferences for particular interaction patterns comes from the use of radio buttons. A number of pre-defined values can be entered both by speech and by pressing a radio button (today/tomorrow and arrival/departure, see Figure 1). Table 6 shows how often subjects used radio buttons rather than speech to provide such a value. The percentages in Table 6 are based on the total number of times this value had to be provided in the successful dialogues: arrival/departure had to be provided in all six scenarios, today/tomorrow occurred in four out of six scenarios, in the other two scenarios the radio buttons could not be used to specify the date.

Table 6. Use of radio buttons.

Modality	*Pre-test*	*Post-test*
Today / Tomorrow	16/30 (53.3%)	23/31 (74.2%)
Arrival / Departure	28/42 (66.7%)	35/45 (77.8%)
Overall	44/72 (61.1%)	58/76 (76.3%)

As can be seen, both in the pre-test and the post-test subjects used radio buttons rather than speech for those values that could be provided in both modalities; but the preference was stronger in the post-test. In the pre-test 61.1% of the values were provided using radio buttons, increasing to 76.3% in the post-test. A McNemar test for the significance of changes showed that this increase is significant (χ^2 =12.07, $p < .01$) (Siegel and Castellan, 1988). This observation not only accounts for the reduction of the number of recognition errors, as explained in the previous sections, but it also partly accounts for the decreased number of speech acts in the post-test (see Table 5). The preference for pointing rather than using speech may be accounted for both by the reliability of radio buttons compared to speech and by the minimal effort of pressing a radio button (Bilici et al., 2000).

A second piece of evidence regarding a change in user preferences for specific modalities concerns the way they deal with errors. When a wrong value has been filled in in one of the fields (either due to a recognition error or due to a mistake of the subject), the interface offers several facilities to correct this error. Subjects may correct the value by means of a spoken reaction (e.g., *"No not from Amsterdam but from Rotterdam"*). Or they may press the microphone button to clear the field and fill in a new value using speech. Or, if the misrecognition concerns a station name, they may choose the correct value from a drop-down list. Table 7 shows how often these three options were used both in the pre-test and in the post-test. As can be seen, subjects preferred pointing actions (using the microphone buttons and the drop-down lists) to speech to correct errors both in the pre-test and in the post-test. Furthermore, the use of spoken replies to correct errors decreased from 37% in the pre-test to 10% in the post-test. Unfortunately, often the speech recogniser did not find any sufficiently likely recognition alternatives, so that in practice no N-best list was available. Also, if the N-best list was available, there would be no guarantee that it contained the correct value. After a few ineffective attempts to correct an error using the drop-down list, many subjects would give up using the drop-down list at all. As a consequence the drop-down list proved not very useful: it was only used three times in the post-test.

Table 7. Preferred action types for correcting errors.

Action type	*Pre-test*	*Post-test*
Spoken dialogue	7 (37%)	2 (10%)
Microphone button	12 (63%)	15 (75%)
Drop-down list	0 (0%)	3 (15%)
Total	19 (100%)	20 (100%)

The net result of these shifts in preferences for specific modalities is a reduction in the number of speech actions. A further possibility for the user to reduce the number of speech actions is by using the microphone buttons in combination with the Search button, preventing the system from asking questions or avoiding the need to reply to questions. When a microphone button is pushed, the current system question is suppressed and the focus of the interaction is directed to the corresponding field. As a side effect, verification questions concerning values that were previously filled in are placed on a stack. When all values have been filled in and the Search button is pressed, the system will start querying the information database. So, by pressing the Search button before all fields have been verified, the user implicitly answers all verification questions remaining on the stack, thereby suppressing explicit verification questions and speeding up the interaction even more. The Search button was used in 33% of the dialogues in the pre-test and in 31% of the dialogues in the post-test, and the percentage of verification questions that was skipped by doing so was almost equal in the pre-test and the post-test, as well. Clearly, users had already discovered this possibility in the pre-test, and it can therefore not account for the decreased number of speech actions and the gain in efficiency from pre-test to post-test.

4.3.3 Changes in the temporal pattern.

Because radio buttons are always active, they can be used not only to provide input in a mode that is more reliable than speech and that takes little effort, but also as a way to make the interaction faster. Users may press a radio button in response to a system prompt asking for that value ("*exclusive* use"). Alternatively, they may decide not to wait until the system asks a question, but press a radio button while at the same time answering an unrelated system prompt ("*concurrent* use") or while waiting for a reaction from the system to their last utterance (i.e., during "idle time"). An additional advantage of using the system in this way is that it saves time because it precludes the system from having to ask for this value later on. A relevant distinction that can be made, then, is one between cases where buttons are pressed as an answer to a system question, and cases where buttons are pressed while the user is doing other things. Table 8 shows the distribution of the use of radio buttons over these two categories.

Table 8. Timing of radio buttons.

Moment	*Pre-test*	*Post-test*
As answer to system question	21/44 (48%)	14/58 (24%)
During other actions	23/44 (52%)	44/58 (76%)

Table 8 shows that in the pre-test the two options were used nearly equally often, whereas in the post-test in 76% of the cases the radio buttons were pushed while the user was engaged in another action. This indicates that with practice many subjects changed from a sequential multimodal interaction pattern to a simultaneous multimodal interaction pattern, therewith speeding up the dialogue. The arrival/departure button, for example, was pressed often while providing the time, and this would prevent a subsequent question from the system concerning the arrival/departure attribute.

4.3.4 Inter-subject variation. There were clear differences between the interaction patterns of different users. Two users who used only speech in the pre-test, still preferred to be guided by the spoken system questions in the post-test. They left the initiative completely to the computer and took over the initiative only once or twice to correct a speech recognition error by pressing the microphone button. This interaction pattern strongly contrasts with that of the other subjects, who preferred to keep the initiative themselves and use the system more in a tap-and-talk manner, pressing buttons to fill in values and skip verification questions as much as possible.

4.4 User Satisfaction

Both after the pre-test and the post-test, subjects filled out a usability questionnaire consisting of 15 Likert-scale statements. Table 9 shows a summary of the answers to the Likert-scale statements. For ease of comparison both the statement and the scores have been inverted for the negative statements 4 ("The system was slow") and 11 ("I was distracted by the display"), so that high scores always denote positive judgements.

Statements 1 through 13 in Table 9 are related to usability aspects. For 11 out of 13 questions the average score in the post-test is higher than that in the pre-test. In a sign test a score of 11 out of 13 in the right direction is significant ($z = 2.63$; $p < .01$) (Siegel and Castellan, 1988). Thus, we conclude that the usability judgements become more positive as a result of experience.

Substantial improvements (i.e., an improvement of 0.5 or more) are observed for those aspects where we expected training to be of influence. In

Table 9. Answers to questionnaire (1 = disagree, 3 = agree nor disagree, 5 = agree). Statements and scores marked with * have been inverted (see text).

Statement	*Rating*	
	Pre	*Post*
1. The system was easy to use	3.9	4.6
2. I always understood what was expected from me	4.5	4.8
3. Correcting errors was easy	2.9	3.4
4. The system was fast*	1.6*	1.5*
5. Speech and graphics were well tuned to one another w.r.t. contents	3.9	4.0
6. Speech and graphics were well tuned to one another w.r.t. timing	3.3	4.3
7. I liked being able to use speech as well as the touch screen	4.0	4.6
8. The system reacted adequately to the combined input	3.9	4.0
9. The length of the spoken utterances was good	4.3	4.0
10. Visualising the fill-in form was useful	4.5	4.8
11. I was not distracted by the display*	2.7*	3.2*
12. Visualising the travel advice was useful	4.9	5.0
13. Giving the travel advice in spoken form was useful	3.4	3.6
14. After a while I started using the system differently	2.9	3.8
15. I used the touch screen more often as I got more experienced	3.5	4.0

the post-test, subjects found the system easier to use (s1) and they were more satisfied about being able to use both speech and graphics (s7). Furthermore, during the post-test subjects judged speech and graphics to be better tuned to one another in time (s6) than during the pre-test (although objectively the timing was the same), and they felt they were less distracted by the display (s11). Apparently, while practising with the system, the subjects developed a mental model of the system from which they could understand and anticipate the system's behaviour.

For a number of aspects no substantial changes were observed nor expected. These statements, such as the transparency of the interface (s2) and the visualisation aspects (s10 and s12), were already rated very highly in the pre-test, resulting in ceiling effects.

Other aspects of the system were rated less favourably both in the pre-test and the post-test and need to be improved. Although subjects considered correcting errors to be easier in the post-test than in the pre-test (s3), this aspect is judged to be poor in general. Obviously, the lack of possibilities to switch to another modality for specifying values that are poorly recognised is considered a major flaw. Furthermore, the spoken travel advice is not considered useful in combination with the visually displayed advice (s13), and although subjects indicate that they appreciate the visualisation of the fill-in form, the mean for s11 ("I was not distracted by the display") was lower than expected. The data show, however, that there was a bimodal distribution in the judgements for this statement. Finally, the speed of the system is judged to be poor (s4). However, we consider this to be a technical implementation issue, rather than a weakness of the interface design.

Statements specifically dealing with changes in interaction styles (s14 and s15) were rated substantially higher in the post-test than in the pre-test, indicating that subjects themselves perceived an effect of prolonged use.

5. Conclusion

In this chapter we studied the effect of prolonged use on the interaction with a multimodal system. To this end we measured the usability of the interface in a pre-test / post-test design and analysed the interaction patterns. Although the interface has been designed for implementation on small mobile devices (such as a PDA), in this study it was simulated on a desktop PC with a telephone. Obviously, implementation on a real PDA will affect the details of the users' behaviour and their mode preferences. However, we found interesting observations of a more general nature, concerning the way in which users deal with the possibilities and the limitations of the interface and their ability to develop interaction patterns that ensure reliable and efficient interaction.

Comparing the way subjects interacted with the system in the pre-test and the post-test, we observed several interesting changes in their behaviour. Subjects learned to speak to the system in a way that is optimal for the speech recogniser, which unintentionally led to more efficient interaction. Also, subjects learned how to use the graphical interaction facilities to ensure more reliable data entry, for example by using the radio buttons and by using pointing actions to correct errors. Finally, they learned to speed up the interaction consciously by providing more information in one utterance, by using buttons to suppress (verification) questions, and by using the graphical interaction facilities simultaneously with other actions (concurrent use). It should be noted however, that concurrent use of the system may have been encouraged by the fact that the system was slow, creating a lot of idle time. The detailed analysis of our results shows that users find ways to utilise the idle time to speed up the interaction and make it more efficient. If the speed of the system increases, the need for and amount of concurrent use may decrease. In the pre-test all subjects were clearly trying to sort out the best way to interact with the system, generally allowing the system to guide the interaction. After about two hours of training all subjects had developed stable interaction patterns to which they would stick as much as possible. In the post-test the majority of the subjects preferred to keep the initiative thus striving for maximum control and efficiency. This observation is in accordance with findings reported in (Walker et al., 1997): in their comparison of a system driven dialogue strategy and a mixed initiative dialogue strategy it was observed that the system driven strategy was better suited for inexperienced users, whereas the experienced users preferred the mixed initiative approach. However, in our study, the interaction patterns observed after training were quite diverse. Although most subjects preferred to take more initiative, two subjects preferred to sustain their initial behaviour and be guided by the system in the spoken dialogue. Surprisingly, these were not the ones with the least computer experience.

The experiments described in (Litman and Pan, 1999) show that an adaptable interface generally performs better than an interface that is not adaptable. From the results of our study we conclude that our interface design has been successful in that respect: it enables users to sort out their own preferred interaction pattern. For each subject, the preferred interaction pattern seems to be the result of the perceived optimal balance between the effort (s)he has to put in the interaction and the efficiency with which the interaction takes place. The results also suggest however, that the interface may be improved in several respects: correcting recognition errors in the graphical domain should be made easier. Due to unexpected delays in the communication between modules, the system was perceived as very slow, so we should improve the speed of the system. Finally, the spoken version of travel advice is not considered to be useful and may be removed in an improved version of the interface.

Acknowledgements

The MATIS project is funded by the Dutch Ministry of Economic Affairs through the Innovation Oriented Programme Man-Machine Interaction.

Notes

1. One could also imagine a system in which the interaction is not guided by spoken system prompts, but by the user, who must press buttons to indicate the field that (s)he wants to fill using speech. In such a "tap-and-talk" implementation there would be no spoken dialogue at all, which would make the system faster, but possibly also less suitable for novice users. The results of a comparison between the current implementation and a tap-and-talk implementation are presented in (Sturm et al., 2003).
2. The total number of successful dialogues in the pre-test
3. The total number of successful dialogues in the post-test

References

Bilici, V., Krahmer, E., Riele, S. T., and Veldhuis, R. (2000). Preferred modalities in dialogue systems. In *Proceedings of International Conference on Spoken Language Processing (ICSLP)*, pages 727–730, Beijing, China.

Bolt, R. A. (1980). Put-that-there: Voice and gesture at the graphics interface. *Computer Graphics*, 14(3):262–270.

Karat, J., Horn, D., Halverson, C., and Karat, C. (2000). Overcoming unusability: Developing efficient strategies in speech recognition systems. In *Pro-*

ceedings of Conference on Human Factors in Computing Systems (CHI), Karlsruhe, Germany.

Litman, D. and Pan, S. (1999). Empirically evaluating an adaptable spoken dialogue system. In Kay, J., editor, *Proceedings of International Conference on User Modeling (UM)*, pages 55–64, Banff, Canada.

Maybury, M. and Wahlster, W. (1998). *Readings in Intelligent User Interfaces*. Morgan Kaufmann, San Francisco, California, USA.

Nigay, L. and Coutaz, J. (1993). A design space for multimodal systems: concurrent processing and data fusion. In *Proceedings of Conference on Human Factors in Computing Systems (CHI)*, pages 172–178, Amsterdam, The Netherlands.

Oviatt, S. (1999). Ten myths of multimodal interaction. *Communications of the ACM*, 42(11):74–81.

Oviatt, S. (2000). Taming recognition errors with a multimodal interface. *Communications of the ACM*, 43(9):45–51.

Oviatt, S., DeAngeli, A., and Kuhn, K. (1997). Integration and synchronization of input modes during multimodal human-computer interaction. In Pemberton, S., Rosson, M. B., and Preece, J., editors, *Human Factors in Computing Systems: CHI '97 Conference Proceedings*, pages 415–422. ACM, New York, New York, USA.

Petrelli, D., DeAngeli, A., Gerbino, W., and Cassano, G. (1997). Referring in multimodal systems, the importance of user expertise and system features. In *Proceedings of Annual Meeting of the Association for Computational Linguistics (ACL-EACL)*, pages 14–17, Madrid, Spain.

Reeves, B. and Nass, C. (1996). *The Media Equation: How people treat computers, television, and new media like real people and places*. Cambridge University Press, New York, NY, USA.

Siegel, S. and Castellan, N. J. (1988). *Nonparametric Statistics for the Behavioral Sciences*. McGraw-Hill, New York, NY, USA.

Sturm, J., Bakx, I., Cranen, B., and Terken, J. (2003). Comparing the usability of a user driven and a mixed initiative multimodal dialogue system for train timetable information. In *Proceedings of European Conference on Speech Communication and Technology (EUROSPEECH)*, pages 2245–2248, Geneva, Switzerland.

Sturm, J., Bakx, I., Cranen, B., Terken, J., and Wang, F. (2002). Usability evaluation of a Dutch multimodal system for railway information. In *Proceedings of International Conference on Language Resources and Evaluation (LREC)*, pages 255–261, Las Palmas, Gran Canaria, Spain.

Sturm, J., Cranen, B., and Wang, F. (2001). Adding extra input/output modalities to a spoken dialogue system. In *Proceedings of ACL SIGdial Workshop on Discourse and Dialogue*, pages 162–165, Aalborg, Denmark.

Suhm, B., Myers, B., and Waibel, A. (1999). Model-based and empirical evaluation of multimodal interactive error correction. In *Proceedings of Conference on Human Factors in Computing Systems (CHI)*, pages 584 – 591, Pittsburgh, Pennsylvania, USA.

Terken, J. and Riele, S. T. (2001). Supporting the construction of a user model in speech-only interfaces by adding multimodality. In *Proceedings of European Conference on Speech Communication and Technology (EUROSPEECH)*, pages 2177–2180, Aalborg, Denmark.

Walker, M., Hindle, D., Fromer, J., Fabbrizio, G. D., and Mestel, C. (1997). Evaluating competing agent strategies for a voice email agent. In *Proceedings of European Conference on Speech Communication and Technology (EUROSPEECH)*, pages 2219–2222, Rhodes, Greece.

Chapter 19

USER MULTITASKING WITH MOBILE MULTIMODAL SYSTEMS

Anthony Jameson
DFKI, German Research Center for Artificial Intelligence and International University in Germany, Saarbrücken, Germany
jameson@dfki.de

Kerstin Klöckner
DFKI, German Research Center for Artificial Intelligence, Saarbrücken, Germany
kloeckner@dfki.de

Abstract Users of mobile systems often simultaneously perform some other task, and multimodality tends to give them greater opportunities to do so. One goal in the design of mobile multimodal systems should therefore be the support of effective user multitasking. Previous research in several areas has made many contributions that are relevant to this goal, but some key issues require further work. Using the example of voice dialling with a mobile phone, we discuss task analyses of two voice dialling methods, showing how such analyses can help to identify possible obstacles to the simultaneous performance of voice dialling and other tasks. Detailed observations of users doing multitasking, supplemented with survey results, confirm that these analyses capture important aspects of the multitasking problem; but also that users' decisions and behaviour are strongly influenced by factors not covered by the task analyses, such as previous experience and beliefs about social acceptability. Conclusions are drawn concerning the implications of this research for design methods and for future research in support of user multitasking.

Keywords: Multimodal systems; Mobile computing; Multitasking; Task analysis; Eye tracking.

W. Minker, D. Bühler and L. Dybkjær (eds), Spoken Multimodal Human-Computer Dialogue in Mobile Environments, 349-377

1. The Challenge of Multitasking

Mobile interactive systems - for example, handheld and wearable computers, as well as motor vehicle driver interfaces - raise a usability challenge that is encountered to a lesser degree in stationary systems: Users often try to use such a system while simultaneously performing one or more other tasks that are related to their current environment. For example, while performing a *system-related task* such as retrieving information from the web, checking email, or using a navigation system, the mobile user may want to perform an *environment-related task* such as shopping, conversing, or walking down a street. Whether the user switches back and forth between the two tasks or performs both of them concurrently without interruption, we can speak of *user multitasking*.

When a mobile system is also multimodal, the possibilities for user multitasking may be especially appealing: The ability to choose among different input and output modalities for the system-related task may make it easier for a user to perform an environment-related task simultaneously.

This chapter examines the implications of user multitasking for the design of mobile multimodal systems: How can we design such systems so as to ensure that users can successfully engage in the sorts of multitasking that they want to engage in?

1.1 Relevant Research Traditions

A number of research areas have yielded concepts, theories, and empirical results that are relevant to these questions - although, as we will see, some key issues are not yet well understood.

1.1.1 Motor vehicle driver interfaces. An area that has yielded much of the most directly relevant research concerns driver distraction in connection with in-car systems for drivers. Many empirical studies have examined the ways in which the use of such systems can impair driving performance, see, e.g., (Green, 2003). Some research has yielded explicit models of the relationships between driving and the use of in-car interfaces, see, e.g., (Wierwille, 1993) and (Salvucci, 2001). One way of viewing the goal of the present chapter is as that of extending this type of research to other types of mobile multimodal system, for which the practical consequences of unsuccessful multitasking are not as dramatic - although they can seriously degrade overall usability.

1.1.2 Industrial and engineering psychology. In the broader field of industrial and engineering psychology, which subsumes the area just mentioned, designing for multitasking has been the topic of much research involving systems that are typically used when the operator is attending to more than one task. Examples include air traffic control systems and monitoring systems for industrial plants, which may consist of multiple displays. With systems like these, the operator usually receives training and acquires considerable expertise in performing the tasks involved individually and in combination - an advantage not enjoyed by users of many mobile multimodal systems. (Useful summaries of research are offered by Damos (1991), and by Wickens and Hollands (2000) - see especially Chapter 11.)

1.1.3 Wearable computing. One of the basic motivations underlying the design of wearable computers is the goal of allowing the user to operate them at virtually all times, in particular while performing various other activities, see, e.g., (Sawhney and Schmandt, 2000), for a description of a wearable messaging system and of a study of the success with which users were able to integrate it into their daily activities. This goal is reflected in the basic design of the hardware and in the choice of input and output devices. In particular, one general strategy is to choose or invent input and output methods that require little or no visual attention, see, e.g., (Brewster et al., 2003). In this field, however, there has so far been less attention to the theoretical and empirical analysis of multitasking than there has been in the first two areas mentioned above.

1.1.4 Multimodal systems. Similarly, in research on multimodal systems, the goal of supporting multitasking is often mentioned as one benefit of the availability of multiple input and output modalities. Modality Theory, see, e.g., (Bernsen, 2001), a framework for deciding which modalities are appropriate for which purposes, includes some predictions about the suitability of particular modalities for combination with particular types of environment-related activities. But as we will see in this chapter, the mere availability of a method for combining two tasks does not guarantee that users will be able to discover and use it effectively.

1.1.5 Handheld computing. Handheld computers are not as strongly associated with multitasking as wearable computers are. As Pascoe, Ryan, and Morse (2000) point out, they are often used in stationary settings (e.g., sitting in a chair), much like laptops. Accordingly, research into their usability has tended to focus more on the consequences of their limited size, capacity, and bandwidth than on their suitability for multitasking. One exception is the work of Pascoe et al. (2000), who studied software for handhelds that was specially designed to be used in conjunction with physically and mentally demanding environment-related tasks like tracking and observing animals in the wild.

1.1.6 Cognitive psychology. In experimental cognitive psychology, studies of multiple-task performance have a long tradition, see, e.g., (Meyer and Kieras, 1997), and (Kieras and Meyer, 1997), for influential analyses. A typical procedure in such a study is to investigate the ways in which two tasks interfere with each other when they are performed concurrently, with the goal of elucidating the unobservable processing mechanisms involved in one or both tasks. By contrast, when we are designing so as to support multitasking, it may be less important to understand exactly why a particular type of performance decrement arises when two tasks are performed concurrently; we may be more interested in ways of redesigning the system in question so that the decrement does not arise. Despite this difference in overall research goals, many of the theoretical concepts and specific results that have arisen from experimental research have implications for system design.

1.1.7 Human-computer interaction. In the field of human-computer interaction as a whole, multitasking has received less attention than it has in the areas mentioned above. The reason may be that until recently almost all of the systems studied were implemented on stationary computers that offered only limited opportunities to combine tasks. Most of the relevant contributions from this area concern support for task switching as opposed to simultaneous uninterrupted execution of tasks, see, e.g., (Miyata and Norman, 1986) and (Cutrell et al., 2001).

As we will see (e.g., in Sections 1.2 and 3.1), the human-computer interaction field has contributed relevant theories and modelling methods that do not specifically concern multitasking.

1.2 Central Open Issues

Because of some typical properties often shown by mobile multimodal systems, designing for multitasking in this context raises some questions that cannot be answered fully on the basis of the types of research discussed so far.

Issue 1. For any given combination of a system-related and an environment-related task that a user is likely to want to perform simultaneously, how can we ensure that there will exist some suitable method for combining these tasks?

One factor that makes this question difficult is the large number of possible system- and environment-related tasks that a user might want to combine. After all, a mobile multimodal system these days can have as much functionality as a PC of a few years ago; and its user may not be restricted to using it only while driving a car, or only while doing a certain type of field work.

Moreover, as a system becomes more complex, it becomes trickier to ensure that its use will be compatible with the execution of another task, because the number of possible courses that the interaction with the system can take becomes greater.

Issue 2. How can we make sure that the user who wants to combine two tasks can quickly discover a suitable method for doing so?

This issue also follows in part from the relatively large number of possible task combinations, which leads to a large number of situations in which the user is trying to deal with a new task combination that she has never attempted before.

Moreover, designers of a mobile multimodal system will typically offer more than one way of accomplishing each given task, partly in response to Issue 1. But such increased flexibility increases the search space of possible ways of combining the two tasks.

Finally, whereas in industrial and experimental settings users are typically given instruction and/or practice at combining a given pair of tasks, multitasking instruction is not common in other settings. Even when it is offered, it will run up against the general tendency of users to focus immediately on the tasks that they want to perform, as opposed to learning about the system, cf. the *production paradox* discussed by Carroll and Rosson (1987). Even rational deliberation about appropriate methods for performing new tasks seems to be the exception, the rule being the application of methods that have worked in similar settings in the past (cf. Carroll and Rosson's *assimilation paradox*).

Issue 3. What factors that are not directly related to effective task performance influence users' decisions about how to handle a multitasking problem; and how can the designer take these factors into account?

In industrial and experimental settings, users are typically induced to do their multitasking in some tried and tested way that tends to maximise effectiveness and - if applicable - safety. Users who are free to choose methods for performing their tasks may be influenced by more subjective considerations, including those involving social acceptability and personal comfort. Design solutions that do not take such factors into account are likely not to be used in the expected way.

In this chapter, it will not be possible to give comprehensive answers to these three questions - not only for reasons of space, but also because a good deal of further research is required. But we will provide some initial analyses and results so as to make the issues more concrete and to offer glimpses of possible answers. After Section 2 has introduced a suitable example system for analysis, Sections 3 and 4 will offer theoretical discussion based on task analyses. Section 5 will then report on two user studies that shed further light on the issues. Finally Section 6 will summarise the contributions of this chapter to the understanding of the three central issues.

2. Example System

As an especially simple example of a mobile multimodal system, we will consider a cell phone that supports voice dialling. One carefully designed phone of this sort is the Siemens S35i mobile phone. Here are the instructions for voice dialling from the manual of this phone

> In standby: To select, press the lower key on the left side of the phone ... Then say the name. The phone number will be dialled automatically.

These instructions can be seen as an instantiation of the concept of the *minimal manual*, see, e.g., (Carroll et al., 1987): They give the user enough information to start performing the task in question; but they do not specify all of the actions that the user will have to perform or exactly what the system will do. They therefore presuppose that the user will be able to discover the details of an appropriate method on her own. The user will in fact usually find it possible to discover at least one method, since the phone provides information redundantly, in two output modalities, thereby allowing considerable flexibility in the performance of the task. Figure 1 gives an overview of the dialling procedure and the feedback that the phone gives.

As we will see in Section 4, one challenge for the user is to choose a method that fits well with the environment-related tasks that she is performing. So as to be able to understand this problem better, we will now look closely at two different methods for making use of the feedback supplied by the phone.

3. Analyses of Single Tasks

3.1 Eye-Based Dialling

With the method that we will call *eye-based dialling*[1], the user $\mathcal{U}$ obtains almost all of the necessary feedback from the system via the visual channel. Accordingly, $\mathcal{U}$ holds the phone in a position that allows her to see its display throughout most of the dialling process, moving it closer to her mouth when speaking into it. The first column in Figure 1 shows a typical sequence of screens that $\mathcal{U}$ might see while voice dialling the number of Peter Miller and waiting for him to pick up the phone.

To provide a clearer picture of the ways in which the execution of this method can be combined with the performance of other tasks, Figure 2 shows a task analysis of eye-based dialling. The notation used for this and the subsequent task analyses is adapted from the notation that has been used for the CPM-GOMS model, see, e.g., (John and Kieras, 1996). This notation is in turn based on the notation for PERT diagrams, which are often used in project management. Each box denotes an elementary action that $\mathcal{U}$ has to perform (or, in the case of boxes with dashed borders, optionally can perform). The distribution of the actions over rows indicates the main perceptual, cognitive,

Display	Sounds	User's action
[Default screen]		Press button on left–hand side of phone.
Please speak Cancel	Loud beep (audible even when phone is away from ear)	Say name of callee as previously recorded for voice dialing (e.g., "Peter").
Playback P. Miller Cancel	Playback of previously recorded speech sample	Check name to see if speech recognition was correct.
[Arrow moves rightward.] P. Miller Cancel	Melody	Check that connection is being set up (optional).
[Right–hand phone flashes.] P. Miller Cancel	Ringing sounds	Check that callee's phone is ringing (optional).
		Bring phone to ear and wait for callee to answer.
[Further graphical feedback]	Ringing sounds; callee's voice	

Figure 1. User actions and system feedback during voice dialling with the Siemens S35i mobile phone. (Screen display translated from German and redrawn for legibility.)

or motor resource required by each action[2]. The dimension from left to right is chronological. A line joining two actions signifies that the first action is a prerequisite for the second one. For example, $\mathcal{U}$ has to hold the phone somewhere in front of her eyes in order to be able to read the prompt on the display; and she cannot speak the appropriate form of the name of the callee until she has retrieved it from memory.

Whereas CPM-GOMS aims to provide a fine-grained, quantitative model of parallel processing in expert users, including time estimates for individual

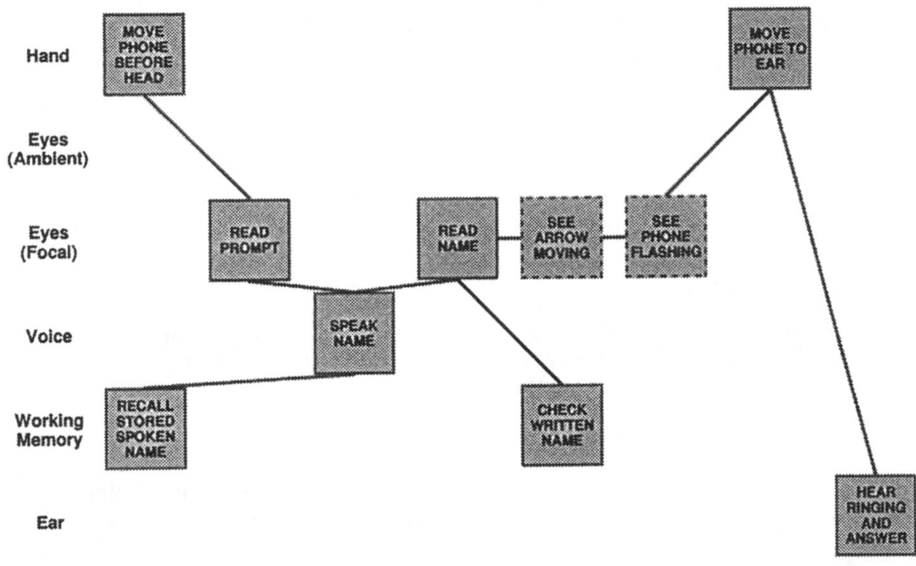

Figure 2. Analysis of the task of eye-based voice dialling. (See the text for an explanation of the notation.)

operations, the purpose of our simpler diagrams is to support the qualitative analysis of possible conflicts between concurrently executed tasks.

The distinction between *focal* and *ambient* vision, cf. (Wickens and Hollands, 2000), p. 451, will become relevant when we look at the performance of two concurrent tasks (Section 4). In the present single task of eye-based dialling, $\mathcal{U}$ uses only focal vision to read the feedback on the screen.

RECALL STORED SPOKEN NAME is included as an action that makes use of working memory (even though the name is usually retrieved from long-term memory), because it may require a conscious effort of information retrieval or even reasoning on the part of $\mathcal{U}$: As Figure 1 illustrates, the name that $\mathcal{U}$ recorded when setting up the voice dialling for Peter Miller may have been his first name, his last name, or some other variant. Similarly, the action CHECK WRITTEN NAME requires $\mathcal{U}$ to consider whether the written name that appears on the display refers to the intended person - a nontrivial task if the written and spoken forms are very different. (It is in fact important for $\mathcal{U}$ to make this comparison, since the system sometimes misrecognises a spoken name and begins dialling the number of some other person.)

The actions SEE ARROW MOVING and SEE PHONE FLASHING are optional: $\mathcal{U}$ can refrain from looking at the display while the connection is being established and the phone is ringing; the only risk is that she may bring the phone to her ear after the callee has answered the phone and begun to speak.

3.2 Ear-Based Dialling

Figure 3 describes the method called *ear-based dialling*. Throughout the application of this method, the user can hold the phone in the position that is normally used for talking. This is one respect in which the method is intrinsically simpler than eye-based dialling. The other respect concerns the checking of whether the system recognised the spoken name correctly: The phone's acoustic feedback in the case of correct recognition - the name as $\mathcal{U}$ originally spoke it - is necessarily very similar to the speech that $\mathcal{U}$ has just produced. Therefore, the process of comparing the two names involves no memory retrieval or reasoning. Accordingly, there is no action in this analysis that corresponds to the CHECK WRITTEN NAME of eye-based dialling (Figure 2).

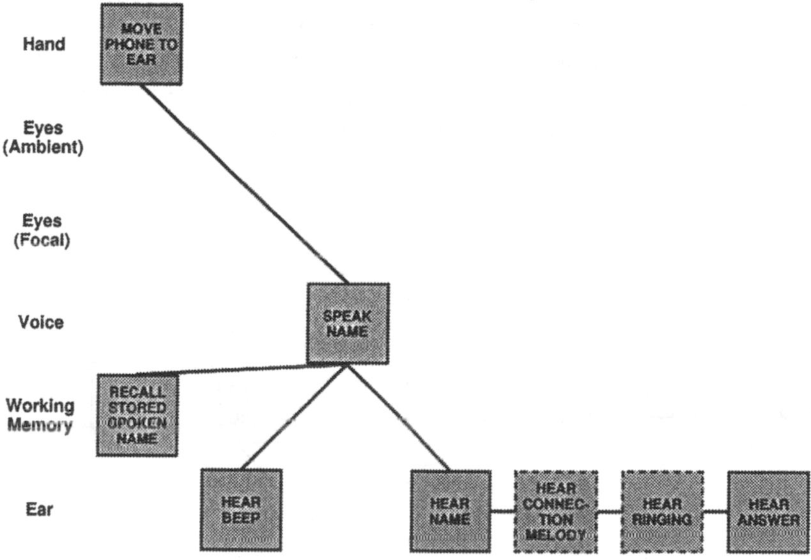

Figure 3. Analysis of the task of ear-based voice dialling.

The two methods discussed so far can be combined in various ways. For example, two of the users that we observed (Subjects 5 and 6 in Section 5.1) consistently switched from eye-based to ear-based dialling in the middle of the execution of the task (though at slightly different points). It is possible to create a different graph like the ones in Figures 2 and 3 for each such hybrid method, but when discussing such cases we will simply refer to the relevant parts of the analyses for the two pure methods.

3.3 An Environment-Related Task - Walking

The task analyses given so far already suggest some reasons why a subject might consistently prefer eye- or ear-based dialling - for example, a general preference for visual over acoustic feedback, or a desire to avoid the cognitive load imposed by the action CHECK WRITTEN NAME. But in order to analyse possible dependencies of method choice on the nature of an environment-related task, we will have to add an analysis of a typical task that people often like to perform while using a mobile phone. One such task is walking. Since this activity raises interesting issues only when there is some nontrivial navigation for $\mathcal{U}$ to perform, we will consider walking in environments that include obstacles that occasionally require some of the walker's attention.

Figure 4 shows a typical sequence in which $\mathcal{U}$ at first walks straight ahead while keeping an eye out for obstacles, then notices an obstacle, looks at it directly, makes some sort of plan for getting around it, and then executes this plan, continuing to look at the obstacle. (Of course, many other sequences can occur, but this example will be adequate for our purposes.)

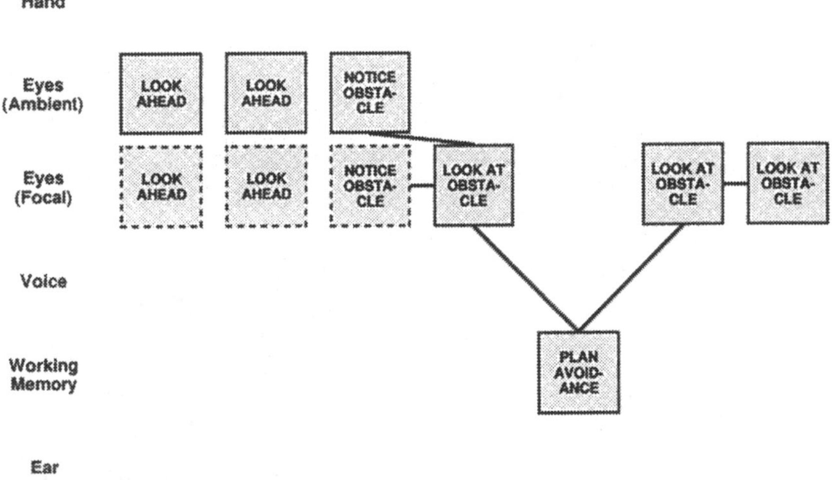

Figure 4. Simplified analysis of the task of walking through an area that includes obstacles that occasionally demand the walker's attention.

The modelling of the use of focal and ambient vision for this task takes into account the fact that a user does not in general have to fixate on an obstacle in order to notice its existence. Instead, using ambient vision to look out for obstacles is considered necessary in this analysis, whereas using focal vision is optional. Only when an obstacle is noticed is $\mathcal{U}$ assumed to fixate on it during the process of avoiding it.

It is actually often possible to navigate around an obstacle entirely without fixating on it, as was confirmed by the eye tracking study described in Section 5.1. Actions related to such easy-to-deal-with obstacles are omitted from the analysis of Figure 4, since they tend not to have much impact on the use of the mobile system.

4. Analyses of Task Combinations

We now turn to the central question of how well users can combine two tasks - in this case, voice dialling and walking. Given that the Siemens phone supports two voice dialling methods, a key question is that of which method users will (and should) choose when walking. When questions like this are discussed - whether in research articles, e.g., (Pascoe et al., 2000), or in non-scientific discussions such as product advertisements - it is customary to reason on an abstract level in terms of the resource demands of entire tasks. For example, several of the student participants in the study summarised below in Section 5.2 made comments like "With ear-based dialling, you can use your eyes to watch the street." This type of reasoning is simple enough to be applied with little effort in many situations. But with the help of our task analyses, we will see that the relevant considerations are in general more complex.

4.1 Ear-Based Dialling and Walking

One way to get an initial idea of the problems that can arise when two tasks are combined is simply to superimpose the two task analyses - as is done in Figure 5. The next step is to look for cases where required actions can interfere with each other.

One way of thinking about interference is in terms of *resource conflicts*: cases where $\mathcal{U}$ may face the necessity of simultaneously performing two actions that make use of the same input modality, output modality, or cognitive activity to such an extent that their simultaneous execution is problematic. Various theoretical conceptualisations of resource conflicts have been proposed in the literature, the best-known being Wickens's Multiple-Resource Theory, see, e.g., (Wickens, 1984). There is often some question about whether a given example of interference is best explained in terms of resource limitations, cf., e.g., (Navon, 1984) and (Recarte and Nunes, 2000). Still, thinking about task analyses in terms of resources is a useful heuristic method for identifying possible problems, even if they turn out to be explainable in other ways as well.

As an example of a type of interference that clearly does not involve only competition for a limited resource, consider a situation where $\mathcal{U}$'s environment-related task somehow produces beeps that sound like the ones produced by the

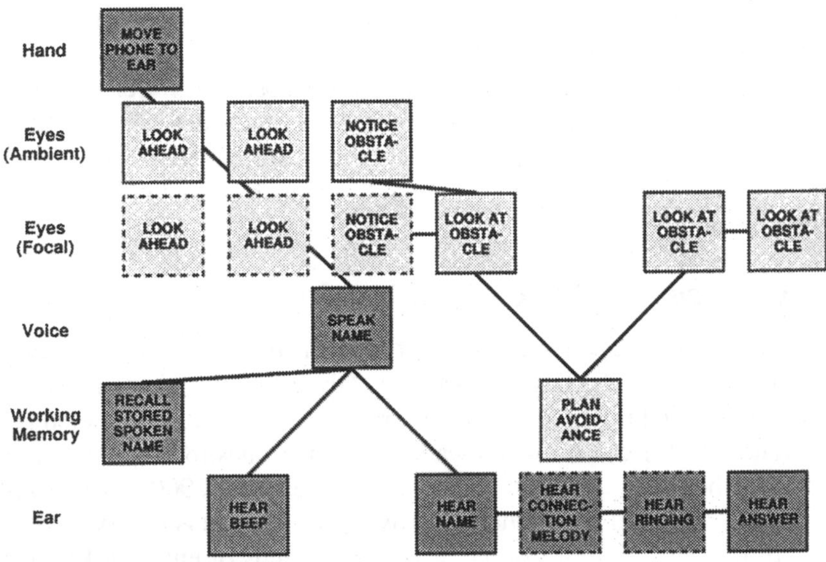

Figure 5. Superimposition of the task analyses of ear-based dialling and walking, suggesting ways in which the tasks may interfere with each other.

cell phone. $\mathcal{U}$ might have difficulty in telling whether a given beep was relevant to the system-related or to the environment-related task - even if the beeps occurred infrequently and there was no overloading of the auditory channel, cf. (Wickens and Hollands, 2000), p. 454. This sort of interference can be important when the two tasks involved have similar components (e.g., in the case of an air traffic controller who is simultaneously monitoring two airplanes and communicating with their pilots); it appears to be less frequent when a task combination involves a system-related and an environment-related task, since the two tasks are less likely to involve similar stimuli and actions.

With the task combinations that we are considering here, there is no intrinsically necessary relationship between the two tasks' timing; for example, the walking user may encounter an obstacle anywhere in the dialling process[3]. To see where interference might arise, we essentially mentally shift the uppermost analysis horizontally by various degrees and see whether any overlaps can occur between actions in the same row.

When we apply this heuristic approach to Figure 5, the intuitive expectation that few conflicts are likely is largely confirmed.

The main exception concerns the working memory conflict that can arise if $\mathcal{U}$ needs to think about how to deal with an obstacle (PLAN AVOIDANCE) just as she is about to think of the form of the name that she wants to speak (RECALL STORED SPOKEN NAME). If each of these actions is sufficiently complex to place significant demands on the user's working memory, $\mathcal{U}$ may be unable to perform both of them simultaneously without some sort of degradation of performance - for example, stumbling upon the obstacle because of having chosen an inappropriate way of dealing with it; or speaking a form of the name that the system cannot recognise.

As we will see, other task combinations often yield a larger number of instances where actions interfere with each other. But identifying these potential conflicts is just the first step. $\mathcal{U}$ may be able to anticipate a conflict more or less far in advance; and she may be able to adapt her behaviour more or less appropriately. In the most favourable case, the potential conflict may have no negative consequences. We will look more closely at these possibilities after we have seen more examples of potential conflicts.

This first example illustrates that a potential conflict may not be easy to anticipate on the basis of global task attributes such as being "eyes-free". One reason in the present case is that the conflict concerns working memory demands, which are not tied to any particular input or output channel. A second reason is that the conflict arises only in a fairly special case: when the need to recall the name and to think about an obstacle happen to coincide in time.

More generally, we can see that the variant of CPM-GOMS used here can be used as a tool for identifying possible problems with a system design - but also that the use of this tool is quite different from the application of task analysis notations to single tasks. Because the temporal relationships between the actions that are performed as parts of the system- and environment-related tasks are largely unpredictable, the analyst must consider a much larger number of possible sequences of actions and events; and predictions of global measures such as total execution time or probability of success become less feasible. The number of possible scenarios is further increased when the course of events in the system-related task is itself partly unpredictable - as is the case even with our simple system, as the following analysis will show.

4.2 Unexpected Events

More subtle conflicts can arise when unexpected events occur during the execution of a method. For example, when the system fails to recognise the name spoken by $\mathcal{U}$, instead of hearing the stored name being replayed, the user hears a loud beep; and the display visually prompts the user to restart the voice dialling process. Figure 6 shows the consequences of this event in the case of ear-based dialling. The analysis presupposes (plausibly) that $\mathcal{U}$ does not yet know on the basis of previous experience how she must respond to the beep in order to complete the voice dialling process; and that she must therefore look at the prompt on the display. In other words, the ear-based dialling method turns out to be less eyes-free than $\mathcal{U}$ might expect. If this problem arises at a moment at which $\mathcal{U}$ needs to look at an obstacle, $\mathcal{U}$ will have to figure out quickly how to resolve the conflict. Further difficulties are the natural tendencies of users (a) to respond to an acoustic warning by looking at the display for further information and (b) to carry a task (or subtask) to its completion even when there is a good reason to abort it suddenly - a phenomenon sometimes referred to as an *inertia effect*, see, e.g., (Wickens and Hollands, 2000), p. 445. In the example considered here, these tendencies can cause $\mathcal{U}$ to focus attention on the display, thereby risking a collision with an obstacle.

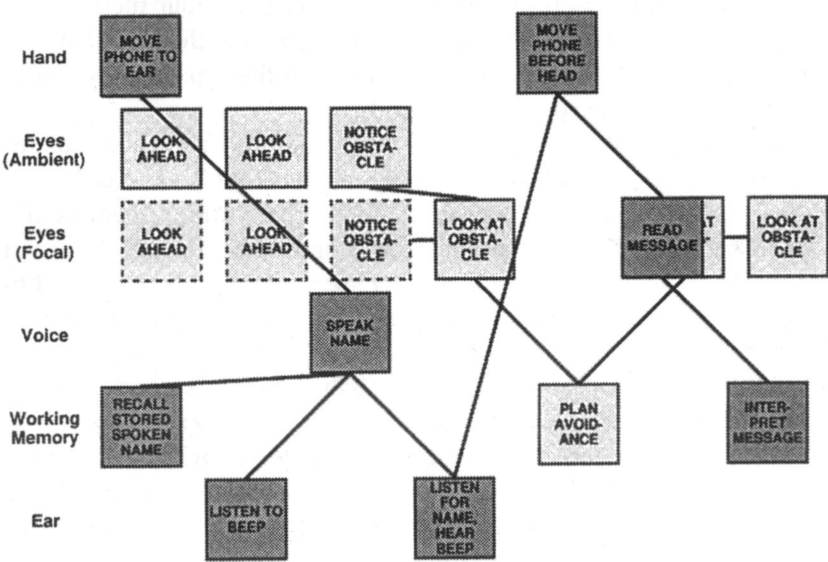

Figure 6. Superimposition of the analyses of the same tasks as in Figure 5, describing the case where the speech input is not recognised.

4.3 Eye-Based Dialling and Walking

Now let us consider the voice dialling method that seems less naturally combinable with walking: eye-based dialling (Section 3.1). A rough assessment of the resource demands would suggest that there can be problems in that both this dialling method and walking place fairly heavy demands on the visual input channel. In fact, one might expect that no-one would choose this dialling method in conjunction with walking; but as we will see (Section 5) it is actually fairly popular in this context.

Figure 7 will help us to see (a) why this combination is in fact feasible and (b) what potential problems it gives rise to. (Bear in mind that the temporal relationships among the operators of the two tasks are in general not exactly the ones that arise from the simple superimposing of Figures 2 and 4.) As we can see in the left-hand side of the analysis, an action that requires $\mathcal{U}$ to attend to the display need not lead to a problematic conflict as long as $\mathcal{U}$ is simply looking out for obstacles: $\mathcal{U}$ can then skip the optional fixation of potential obstacles (i.e., the lighter-coloured boxes with dashed borders) and rely on ambient vision.

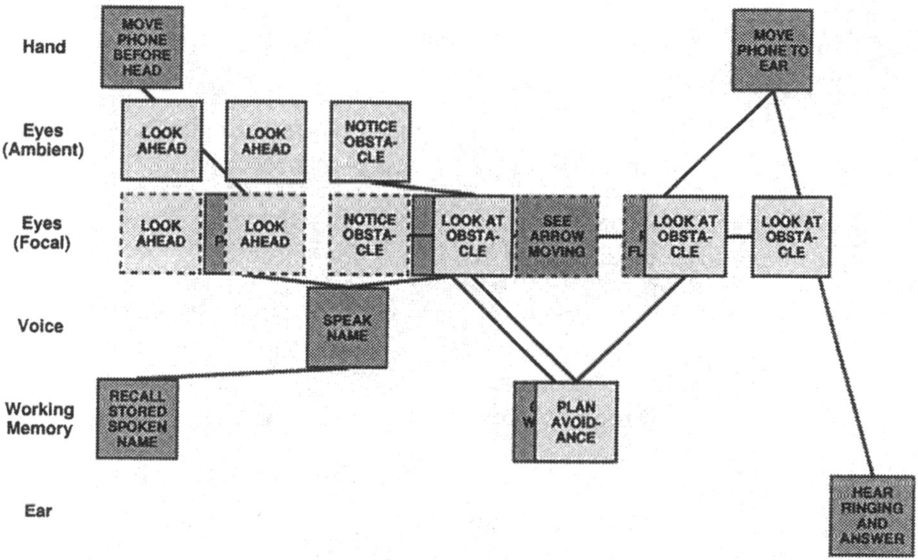

Figure 7. Superimposition of the task analyses of eye-based dialling and walking.

Similarly, as can be seen on the right, if an obstacle requires $\mathcal{U}$ to fixate on it, there need be no serious problem if the only information on the display is the feedback concerning $\mathcal{U}$'s attempt to establish a connection: Since looking at this feedback is optional, $\mathcal{U}$ can look at the obstacle, the only drawback being that she will not know exactly when she needs to move the phone to her ear. On the other hand, the decision to ignore the display in this situation may not be one that $\mathcal{U}$ finds obvious or easy to make:

- It may not be clear to $\mathcal{U}$ that this part of the feedback is less essential than the other parts.
- $\mathcal{U}$ may have established the subgoal of seeing the exact moment at which the callee answers the phone, and she may be reluctant to abandon this subtask.
- The blinking feedback on the display may be visually more salient than the obstacle.

- $\mathcal{U}$ may underestimate the extent to which fixation on the obstacle is necessary.

Probably the most serious conflict involving the visual channel occurs if the need to read the written name (READ NAME) coincides with the need to look at an obstacle (LOOK AT OBSTACLE), as is the case in Figure 7.

- Checking the name is more or less obligatory, since skipping it entails the risk of calling the wrong person.
- Checking the name cannot be postponed, since the callee's phone will start to ring within a few seconds unless $\mathcal{U}$ interrupts the call.
- Looking at the obstacle may be safely postponable only if $\mathcal{U}$ stops walking immediately - something that $\mathcal{U}$ may find difficult.

Finally, an additional working memory conflict can arise because of the need for $\mathcal{U}$ to compare the name written on the display with the name of the intended callee (CHECK WRITTEN NAME, partly obscured in Figure 7 by PLAN AVOIDANCE). Largely the same remarks apply to this conflict as to the similar conflict, involving the operation RECALL STORED SPOKEN NAME, that we already saw in connection with ear-based dialling and walking.

In sum, this approach to combining the two tasks, while basically feasible, gives rise to a number of typical problems and challenges. Before discussing such problems on a more general level, let us look at some data concerning the question: "How do people actually deal with the combination of voice dialling and walking?"

5. Studies with Users

The discussion so far has been based largely on theoretical analysis and general previous knowledge of multitasking and human-computer interaction. In order to ensure that the analyses are in touch with reality, we need to obtain data from users - specifically, to answer the following questions:

- Are our initial task analyses and theoretical considerations consistent with the ways in which users actually perform the tasks in question (individually or in combination)?

  In fact, the results to be summarised below did give rise to a number of refinements of our initial analyses; these refinements were taken into account in the presentation in Sections 3 and 4.

- Within this framework, what general tendencies and preferences do users exhibit?

Note that the task analyses allow for considerable freedom of user choice - for example, choosing between ear-based and eye-based dialling; choosing which optional operators to execute; and deciding how to prioritise and coordinate the operators of the two tasks. It has long been recognised, see, e.g., (Card et al., 1983), Chapter 5, that when a task analysis indicates that users have a choice, different users may exhibit very different behaviours, their choices being determined by a variety of factors.

We will discuss in turn two sorts of user feedback that we have obtained:

1 Fine-grained observation of individual users performing relevant tasks and task combinations.

2 More wide-ranging querying of these users as well as persons whom we have not had the opportunity to observe.

5.1 Detailed Observations

5.1.1 Preliminary considerations. One traditional way of validating task analyses such as the ones presented above is to (a) use them to derive predictions of task execution times and then (b) compare these predictions with the actually observed times for subjects who perform these tasks, see, e.g., (Baber and Mellor, 2001), and (Salvucci, 2001), for examples of such analyses involving models of multitasking. Instead of focusing on time predictions, we have chosen to make detailed qualitative observations of users' behaviour and compare them with the task analyses, for several reasons:

- The durations of many of the operators that occur in the task analyses (e.g., thinking of the stored name of the person to be called) are not known from previous studies, and they presumably show a good deal of variability from one specific case to the next.

- What we seek is not an overall validation of the models but (a) indications of how they can be refined and (b) information on how users make the many choices that are left open to them.

- The overall design goal with the types of system and task that we are looking at is not so much to minimise execution time as to help users to avoid the many potential problems that can arise with multitasking. Consequently, the ability to predict execution times accurately would not have the practical benefits that it has in some other contexts (e.g., the prediction of the time that telephone operators require to handle calls, as in the classic study of (Gray et al., 1992)).

5.1.2 Method. Recently, various methods have been developed for the collection of detailed data about the behaviour of mobile users. One ambitious data collection infrastructure was presented by Oviatt (2000): With equipment worn by a roaming user, recordings were made of the user's speech and gestural input and of the system's output. Somewhat more recently, Lyons and Starner (2001) introduced into a similar data collection system a way of capturing the user's view of the current environment: an eyeglasses-mounted video camera that shows the user's field of view. (Other cameras can be added, for example, to record the movements of the user's hands.)

While these methods can yield useful data for the analysis of problems such as those discussed above, what is still lacking is detailed information on what the user is looking at. This information can be obtained with an eye tracker. Eye tracking has a long tradition in studies of driving and the use of in-car systems for drivers, see, e.g., (Sodhi et al., 2002), but handheld and wearable computers raise somewhat different methodological challenges. For our studies, we used an ASL 501 Mobile eye tracker, which is mounted on the subject's head and transmits its data to a stationary control unit via radio waves.

Each of six subjects was first introduced to voice dialling on the Siemens S35i mobile phone. With the experimenter's help, the subject recorded the spoken names of several persons in nearby offices so as to be able to reach them via voice dialling. While the subject was seated at a table, the experimenter introduced the task of voice dialling and demonstrated explicitly that the necessary system feedback could be perceived through either the auditory or the visual modality; but the experimenter gave no instructions or hints about the use of particular modalities. After the mobile eye tracker had been calibrated, the subject was asked to use voice dialling to place a call, (a) while standing still, (b) while walking around a small room filled with a table, some chairs, and various cables, (c) while answering questions asked by the experimenter, and (d) while walking and answering questions simultaneously[4]. In some of the attempts, the phone was actually answered.

When all of the tasks had been performed, the subject watched the video recordings that had been made with the eye tracker. Each recording showed the subject's field of view and direction of gaze during the performance of one task (cf. Figure 8). The subject was asked questions about particular events in the recordings and about his or her general habits and preferences in connection with mobile phones.

Later, for each video recording, the experimenter listed the recorded actions and events along with the time intervals during which they occurred.

5.1.3 Subjects 1, 2, and 3: eye-based dialling. Subjects 1, 2, and 3 used the eye-based dialling method for all task combinations[5]. Figure 8 shows two images that indicate the focus of Subject 1's attention as he

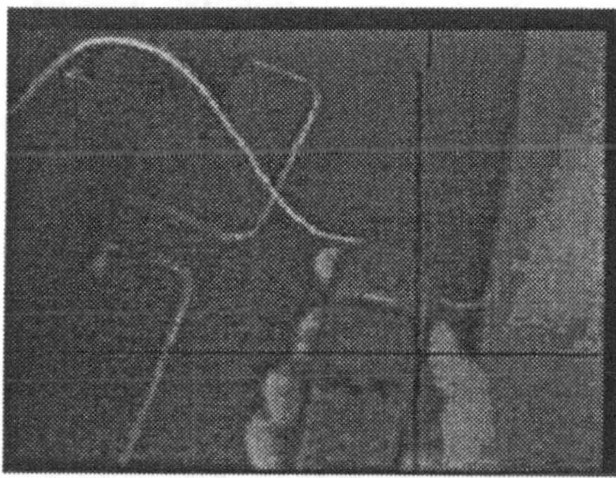 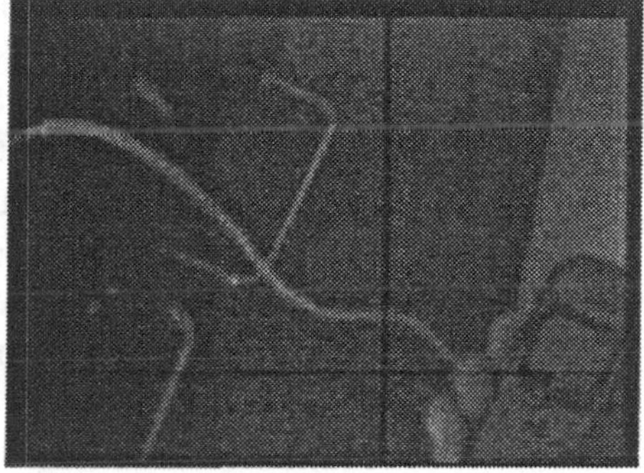

Figure 8. Typical frames yielded by the mobile eye tracker as Subject 1 performed voice dialling while walking through a room filled with obstacles. (The intersection of the two black lines indicates the subject's current point of gaze.)

dialled while walking around the room. Overall, he showed a strong and consistent tendency to fixate on the display, using at most ambient vision to obtain visual feedback from other sources, including information about obstacles. He only occasionally glanced away from the display briefly, apparently to look at an obstacle such as an electric cable.

The interview revealed that this tendency is by no means the result of lack of experience with such tasks: This subject had owned exactly this model of mobile phone for more than 1.5 years, and he reported having used the voice dialling functionality frequently, always with eye-based dialling. When asked about its use during driving, he admitted that he sometimes held the phone in front of his eyes with one hand while steering with the other hand.

When asked why he did not sometimes use ear-based dialling, he said that the acoustic feedback "got on his nerves", because it was "too loud". On the whole, he characterised the ear-based method as "stupid". He admitted that he had sometimes walked into objects while performing eye-based dialling, but he said that he had gotten used to doing so and therefore no longer worried about it.

Subject 2 likewise showed a general preference for eye-based dialling, but she was less strongly inclined to look at the display continually. While walking, she sometimes glanced away from the display to look at obstacles. Like Subject 1, she explained her general preference for eye-based dialling in terms of a consideration that is not represented in the theoretical analyses presented above (but which has been mentioned by several other subjects): It is not customary to hold a mobile phone to one's ear while dialling a number manually, because it is not possible to depress the keys accurately in this position. Subject 2 felt influenced by this habit, even though of course voice dialling is possible in the phone-to-ear position.

Subject 2 also creatively extended the method of eye-based dialling by making some use of the acoustic feedback even while holding the phone in front of her: She said that she was able to hear the playback of the recorded name faintly, thereby being able to benefit from its directness and simplicity while still looking at the display. In fact, further exploration shows that the phone can be usefully held in a large number of positions between the two extremes considered so far (at the ear vs. far enough in front of the eyes to allow easy focusing on the display). Each intermediate position yields a different point in the tradeoff between the legibility of the information on the display and ability to hear the details of the acoustic feedback. This example illustrates a general challenge for the analysis and prediction of users' behaviour where multitasking is concerned: Users cannot be counted upon to restrict themselves to the limited set of elementary actions that are explicitly supported by the system. When they try to operate the system while performing some environment-related task that was not specifically (or successfully) taken into account in the design of the system, they may be inclined to distort the usual actions - or invent new ones - in a creative attempt to fulfil the set of constraints posed by the task combination. Moreover, the number of possible action variants of this sort may be large: Whereas the user of a conventional stationary application like a spreadsheet can hardly perform any actions other than the ones foreseen by the designer (e.g., looking at the screen, selecting menu items, and pressing keys in the normal way), mobile multimodal systems can be held in a variety of positions relative to the user's body and to the environment, and they can be operated in a continuum of ways (e.g., the user's speech can have different speeds, volumes, and styles of articulation). Accordingly, any set of task analyses such as the ones presented above should in general be viewed as representing a sample of the possible methods; and the analyst should be willing to include actions and methods that do not necessarily correspond to the designer's intentions.

Subject 3 likewise used eye-based dialling consistently. He explained later that he was sceptical about the accuracy of the speech recognition. In terms of the task analyses of ear-based dialling presented in Section 4, this subject appeared to believe that the course of events shown in Figure 6, in which the user has to deal with a recognition failure, was sufficiently frequent to constitute a reason to avoid ear-based dialling.

This subject avoided possible interference between walking and eye-based dialling simply by beginning to walk only after he had spoken the name and confirmed that a connection had been established.

5.1.4 Subject 4: Ear-based dialling.

Whereas the results described so far would suggest a general preference for eye-based dialling for all task combinations, Subject 4 showed the opposite tendency: He used ear-based dialling for all task combinations - even those that involved the environment-related task of conversing with the experimenter, which produces a good deal of auditory input. Two of the reasons that he gave for this preference during the interview correspond to considerations taken into account in our analysis of ear-based dialling (Figure 3):

1 He noticed that the acoustic confirmation of the callee's name is simpler and more natural to interpret than the printed confirmation.

2 He reasoned that ear-based dialling involves less movement of the arm, since the phone is held in just one position throughout the procedure.

Note that these two points concern only the properties of ear-based dialling itself, not its relationships with the methods for environment-related tasks.

Another reason that Subject 4 gave was similar to Subject 2's reference to previous experience, although it referred to a different experience: Subject 4 said that it had never occurred to him before to hold a phone in front of his eyes while speaking into it, since he had never used voice dialling before.

5.1.5 Subjects 5 and 6: Hybrid methods. Subject 5 quickly learned to use eye-based dialling for the first part of the task and ear-based dialling for the second part: While speaking the name, he always looked at the phone. During the performance of his first task, he continued to look at the display after speaking the name, but he was irritated by the discrepancy between the spoken name ("Sebastian") and the printed name ("Müller"). In subsequent tasks, to avoid further confusion, he moved the phone to his ear immediately after having spoken the name. That is, his reason for switching to ear-based dialling was the same as the first reason given by Subject 4; but instead of using ear-based dialling throughout, he continued to begin the task with the eye-based method.

This subject (like Subject 3) avoided interference between walking and the eye-based part of his method by either standing still or walking slowly while executing this part of the method. Similarly, during the ear-based part of the method, if the spoken name was not recognised at all, the subject immediately stopped walking and looked back at the display (cf. Figure 6).

Subject 6 likewise used a hybrid combination of eye-based and ear-based dialling. Unlike Subject 5, he continued to look at the phone until the recognition of the name had been confirmed; only then did move the phone to his ear (and begin walking, if walking was required).

5.1.6 Conclusions from the detailed observations. Although we cannot generalise confidently on the basis of the observation of six subjects, it is striking that each subject consistently used one method (whether eye-based, ear-based, or hybrid), regardless of whether they were walking, conversing, or standing still. Some of the reasons for their method choices can be understood in terms of the task analyses, while others involve previous experience or subjective factors; but considerations related to the relationships between voice dialling and the environment-related tasks evidently did not influence their choice of a method.

Although each subject stuck to one method for all environment-related tasks, their behaviour did in some respects take into account the possible interferences between the system-related and the environment-related task. For example, when the environment-related task was walking, they would sometimes slow down or stand still while performing a complex part of the dialling task. The general strategy of suspending execution of one task while dealing with a demanding part of another task has great generality, and subjects have presumably applied it in countless previous situations. By contrast, choosing the most suitable modality for a particular task combination is a more novel problem, whose solution cannot make such direct use of previous experience. Hence the ways in which our subjects took into account the demands of multitasking are consistent with the previous research on learning and method choice mentioned above in Section 1.2.

An alternative to the type of observation performed here would be more longitudinal observation during which users were given numerous opportunities to deal with each specific task combination. It would be interesting to see to what extent method choices became more sensitive to the nature of the environment-related tasks. But the brief observations reported here are actually more relevant than longitudinal studies to the many situations in which users have to deal with a novel combination of system- and environment-related tasks.

5.2 Survey of a Larger Sample of Potential Users

To get a broader picture than is possible with the necessarily limited number of subjects that we can observe in detail, we elicited questionnaire responses from 22 technically sophisticated students from the University of Applied Sciences of Zweibrücken, Germany. Although 21 of the respondents owned a mobile phone, only 1 of these had used any form of voice dialling regularly, and only 3 had done so even occasionally.

The two methods of voice dialling were demonstrated to these respondents with the help of projected slides. They were asked to state on a questionnaire which method they would use in each of several situations and to write down their principal reasons.

The results concerning the choices (in Table 1) suggest a sensitivity to the demands of the environment-related tasks that is generally consistent with the sort of task analysis that we have presented above - but inconsistent with the inflexibility of method choice that was shown by the six subjects whom we observed. This discrepancy can be understood in terms of the difference between the demands placed on subjects by a questionnaire study and real task performance, respectively: The questionnaire study may encourage subjects to indicate a preference for different methods for different task combinations and to deliberate rationally about the considerations underlying their choices; subjects actually using the system are likely to be more concerned about performing their tasks successfully.

Table 1. Expressed preferences for eye-based or ear-based dialling among 22 questionnaire respondents.

Task Combination	Eye-Based Dialling	Ear-Based Dialling	No Overall Preference	Would Not (Voice-)Dial at All
Sitting still	10	7	5	
Walking down a street	5	17		6
Driving a car		22		
Conversing with a friend	16	4		2

Although the responses concerning method choice should not be seen as reliable predictors of actual behaviour, they do give us a picture of the relevant knowledge and ideas that people have - especially when supplemented with the reasons that the respondents gave for their choices. Since the reasons given overlap considerably with those mentioned by the six subjects that we observed, an overview covering both groups is given in Table 2. (Considerations that apply only when the environment-related task is walking down stairs, driving, or conversing, are omitted from the table, because the relevant task analyses have not been presented in this chapter.) Respondents' comments sometimes suggest new hypotheses about factors that may influence behaviour, which can be checked through observation of behaviour in systematically varied conditions. Also, perhaps users' understanding of possible types of interference among tasks can be leveraged in training and instruction, even if they do not apply it spontaneously.

It can be seen that several of the reasons mentioned correspond to considerations that can be derived from the task analyses presented earlier in this chapter. An approximately equal number of reasons, however, concern different factors. The implications of these results will be discussed in the final section.

6. The Central Issues Revisited

By way of summary, let us look back at what we have learned about the three central issues introduced in Section 1.2.

Table 2. Overview of reasons mentioned by 28 subjects for preferring eye-based or ear-based dialling.

Reasons for Preferring Eye-Based Dialling	
In General	**In Combination With Walking**
Reasons related to task analyses	
The information on the display is less ambiguous, and it's easier to understand. I have to look at the display anyway if the spoken name is not recognised	I think I can see the obstacles well enough just with peripheral vision.
Reasons not related to task analyses	
The beeps are funny / too loud; they get on my nerves ... I find it uncomfortable / silly to hold my arm up for several seconds while waiting for a connection. I'm not used to holding a mobile phone to my ear while dialling a number.	There's too much noise on the street for me to hear the acoustic feedback.

Reasons for Preferring Ear-Based Dialling	
In General	**In Combination With Walking**
Reasons related to task analyses	
As soon as the person I'm calling picks up the phone, I have to bring the phone to my ear anyway. I find it more natural to have the name confirmed by speech, because I entered it by speech in the first place; and the printed name may be entirely different anyway.	You need your eyes in order to be able to look at the street and the environment.
Reasons not related to task analyses	
I'm used to holding a phone to my ear when speaking into it.	

Issue 1: For any given combination of a system-related and an environment-related task that a user is likely to want to perform simultaneously, how can we ensure that there will exist some suitable method for combining these tasks?

The discussion of the task analyses in Section 4 showed that a simplified version of the CPM-GOMS notation can help us to find potential problems with a method for the handling of a combination of tasks - even if the system's design explicitly took that particular combination into account, as is the case with the task of walking, which is quite well supported by ear-based dialling. Note that some of the potential problems uncovered in this way actually occur with only a low frequency (e.g., when two independent events happen to coincide in time, or when some exceptional individual event occurs). That is, this sort of problem can escape the attention of even the diligent empirical researcher and the experienced user.

In some cases the potential problem could be eliminated through a relatively minor design improvement (e.g., eliminating system prompts that the user has to respond to within a certain time window); in other cases, a solution would require the user to adopt a somewhat different method - or an appropriate task-switching strategy.

Issue 2: How can we make sure that the user who wants to combine two tasks can quickly discover a suitable method for doing so?

Improvements to the methods offered by the system will in general also make it easier for users to discover a suitable method for a given situation: If the available methods are largely free of hard-to-anticipate traps and drawbacks, the challenge of finding a suitable method is more surmountable.

But even if, say, the methods of eye-based and ear-based dialling were optimised, we could not assume that users would consistently choose the more appropriate method. The subjects in our studies showed some intuitive awareness of the properties of methods that are relevant to multitasking, but their understanding fell far short of a full grasp of the relevant considerations - as indeed we would expect. Their decisions about which method to use in a given situation were influenced by previous experience with similar phones and by the subjective factors discussed in connection with Issue 3.

The question of how to encourage appropriate method choice is too complex for thorough treatment in this chapter, and it requires further research in connection with mobile multimodal systems. A number of relevant more general strategies were already proposed in the seminal paper by Carroll and Rosson (1987). A thorough discussion with regard to a very different type of system (computer-aided design systems) can be found in recent works of Bhavnani and colleagues, see, e.g., (Bhavnani and John, 2000). The most obvious idea is to provide a certain amount of instruction about method choice (e.g., "When you are voice dialling while walking, it is usually best to hold the phone to your ear throughout the process"). Another strategy is simply to limit the number of available methods: For example, a single method that is at least minimally suitable in all situations may be preferable to a set of methods that includes an optimal method for each situation but which also makes it likely that the user will choose methods that are poorly suited to the current situation.

Issue 3: What factors that are not directly related to effective task performance influence users' decisions about how to handle a multitasking problem; and how can the designer take these factors into account?

One type of subjective factor that emerged in our interviews and survey results concerned social acceptability considerations, for example, the notion that a certain way of holding a phone looks silly. It has long been recognised that considerations of this type are especially important with wearable and handheld computers, because these are often used in a variety of social contexts. We see that these acceptability constraints concern not only the basic appearance of a device (e.g., the conspicuousness of a head-mounted display) but also the specific ways in which a device is used - which may be evaluated differently by different users.

Other subjective considerations are related to the user's physical comfort, such as the ideas that the beep tones are too loud or that the position in which the phone must be held is uncomfortable. Such properties may fall outside of the acceptable range especially frequently when mobile multimodal systems are involved. For example, it is harder to find a single optimal beep volume when a device is used in a wide range of physical environments; and allowing users to control these aspects of the interaction can be problematic because of the relatively small communication bandwidth and the frequency with which changes would be required. Therefore, designers should consider the possibility that a basically suitable method for handling a given task in a given context will sometimes be found unacceptable for reasons involving physical comfort and therefore be rejected by the user in favour of an intrinsically less suitable method.

A great deal of further work is required on the questions raised in this chapter. We hope to have convinced the reader of their importance, provided some initial methods and results, and given some concrete ideas about the next steps to be taken.

Acknowledgments

This chapter was prepared in the contexts of the Evaluation Center for Language Technology Systems of the DFKI project COLLATE, which is funded by the German Ministry of Education, Research, Science, and Technology (BMB+F) and the project READY of Saarland University's Collaborative Research Center 378 on Resource-Adaptive Cognitive Processes, which is funded by the German Science Foundation (DFG). Marie Norlien helped to develop the methodology employed in the eye tracking studies. We thank the 22 students of the University of Applied Sciences of Zweibrücken, who participated as subjects in the study described in Section 5.2.

Notes

1. In connection with speech-based systems, terms such as *eyes-free* are often used. For our analyses, it is clearer to name the primary perceptual channel that is used with a given method.

2. As is shown in Figure 1, the user actually initiates each task by pressing the button on the left-hand side of the phone; this action is omitted from the task analyses for reasons of space.

3. Sometimes users combine tasks which are related in content, such as walking around in a city and consulting a handheld navigation system. With such task combinations, relationships between events in the

two tasks tend to be more predictable; for example, the walker is relatively likely to consult the navigation system upon reaching a point where she has to choose between two or more directions.

4. These last two task combinations have been analysed with models such as the ones presented above, but reference to these task analyses must be omitted here for reasons of space.

5. For clarity of exposition, we discuss the results for the six subjects in a different order than the order in which they were observed.

References

Baber, C. and Mellor, B. (2001). Using critical path analysis to model multimodal human-computer interaction. *International Journal of Human-Computer Studies*, 54:613–636.

Bernsen, N. O. (2001). Multimodality in language and speech systems—from theory to design support tool. In Granström, B., editor, *Multimodality in Language and Speech Systems*, pages 93–147. Kluwer Academic Publishers, Dordrecht, The Netherlands.

Bhavnani, S. K. and John, B. E. (2000). The strategic use of complex computer systems. *Human-Computer Interaction*, 1(2/3):107–137.

Brewster, S., Lumsden, J., Bell, M., Hall, M., and Tasker, S. (2003). Multimodal 'eyes-free' interaction techniques for wearable devices. In Terveen, L., Wixon, D., Comstock, E., and Sasse, A., editors, *Human Factors in Computing Systems: CHI 2003 Conference Proceedings*, pages 473–480. ACM, New York, New York, USA.

Card, S. K., Moran, T. P., and Newell, A. (1983). *The Psychology of Human-Computer Interaction*. Erlbaum, Hillsdale, New Jersey, USA.

Carroll, J. M. and Rosson, M. B. (1987). The paradox of the active user. In Carroll, J. M., editor, *Interfacing Thought: Cognitive Aspects of Human-Computer Interaction*, pages 80–111. MIT Press, Cambridge, Massachusetts, USA.

Carroll, J. M., Smith-Kerker, P. L., Ford, J. R., and Mazur-Rimetz, S. A. (1987). The minimal manual. *Human-Computer Interaction*, 3:123–153.

Cutrell, E., Czerwinski, M., and Horvitz, E. (2001). Notification, disruption and memory: Effects of messaging interruptions on memory and performance. In *Proceedings of Interact*, pages 263–269, Tokyo, Japan.

Damos, D. L., editor (1991). *Multiple-Task Performance*. Taylor and Francis, London, United Kingdom.

Gray, W. D., John, B. E., and Atwood, M. E. (1992). The precis of Project Ernestine or an overview of a validation of GOMS. In Bauersfeld, P., Bennett, J., and Lynch, G., editors, *Human Factors in Computing Systems: CHI '92 Conference Proceedings*, pages 307–312. ACM, New York, New York, USA.

Green, P. (2003). Motor vehicle driver interfaces. In Jacko, J. A. and Sears, A., editors, *Human-Computer Interaction Handbook*, pages 844–860. Lawrence Erlbaum Assoc., Mahwah, New Jersey, USA.

John, B. E. and Kieras, D. E. (1996). The GOMS family of user interface analysis techniques: Comparison and contrast. *ACM Transactions on Computer-Human Interaction*, 3:320–351.

Kieras, D. E. and Meyer, D. E. (1997). A computational theory of executive cognitive processes and multiple-task performance: Part 2. Accounts of psychological refractory-period phenomena. *Psychological Review*, 104(4):749–791.

Lyons, K. and Starner, T. (2001). Mobile capture for wearable computer usability testing. In Martin, T. and Bahl, V., editors, *Proceedings of the Fifth International Symposium on Wearable Computers*, pages 69–76. IEEE Computer, Los Alamitos, California, USA.

Meyer, D. E. and Kieras, D. E. (1997). A computational theory of executive cognitive processes and multiple-task performance: Part 1. Basic mechanisms. *Psychological Review*, 104(1):3–65.

Miyata, Y. and Norman, D. (1986). Psychological issues in support of multiple activities. In *User Centered System Design: New Perspectives on Human-Computer Interaction*, pages 265–284. Lawrence Erlbaum Assoc., Mahwah, New Jersey, USA, Hillsdale, New Jersey, USA.

Navon, D. (1984). Resources — a theoretical soup stone? *Psychological Review*, 91(2):216–234.

Oviatt, S. (2000). Multimodal system processing in mobile environments. In *Proceedings of Annual ACM Symposium on User Interface Software and Technology*, pages 21–30, San Diego, California, USA.

Pascoe, J., Ryan, N., and Morse, D. (2000). Using while moving: HCI issues in fieldwork environments. *ACM Transactions on Computer-Human Interaction*, 7(3):417–437.

Recarte, M. A. and Nunes, L. M. (2000). Effects of verbal and spatial-imagery tasks on eye fixations while driving. *Journal of Experimental Psychology: Applied*, 6(1):31–43.

Salvucci, D. D. (2001). Predicting the effects of in-car interface use on driver performance: An integrated model approach. *International Journal of Human-Computer Studies*, 55:85–107.

Sawhney, N. and Schmandt, C. (2000). Nomadic Radio: Speech and audio interaction for contextual messaging in nomadic environments. *ACM Transactions on Computer-Human Interaction*, 7:353–383.

Sodhi, M., Reimer, B., Cohen, J. L., Vastenburg, E., Kaars, R., and Kirschenbaum, S. (2002). On-road driver eye movement tracking using head-mounted devices. In *Proceedings of ETRA 2002: Eye Tracking Research and Applications Symposium*, pages 61–68. New Orleans, Louisiana, USA.

Wickens, C. D. (1984). Processing resources in attention. In Parasuraman, R. and Davies, D. R., editors, *Varieties of Attention*, pages 63–102. Academic Press, Orlando, Florida, USA.

Wickens, C. D. and Hollands, J. G. (2000). *Engineering Psychology and Human Performance*. Prentice Hall, Upper Saddle River, New Jersey, USA, 3rd edition.

Wierwille, W. W. (1993). Visual and manual demands of in-car controls and displays. In Peacock, B. and Karwowski, W., editors, *Automotive Ergonomics*, pages 299–320. Taylor and Francis, London, United Kingdom.

Chapter 20

SPEECH CONVERGENCE WITH ANIMATED PERSONAS

Sharon Oviatt, Courtney Darves, Rachel Coulston, Matt Wesson

Oregon Health & Science University, Center for Human-Computer Communication, Department of Computer Science & Engineering, Beaverton, Oregon, USA

{ oviatt,rachel,wesson } @cse.ogi.edu, courtney@uoregon.edu

Abstract A new dimension of speaker stylistic variation was identified during human-computer communication: the convergence of users' speech with the text-to-speech (TTS) heard from an animated software partner. Twenty-four 7-to-10-year-old children conversed with digital fish that embodied different TTS voices as they learned about marine biology. An analysis of children's amplitude, durational features, and dialogue response latencies confirmed that they spontaneously adapt basic acoustic-prosodic features of their speech 10-50%, with the largest adaptations involving utterance pause structure and amplitude. Children's speech adaptations were bi-directional, and dynamically readaptable when introduced to a new software partner's voice. In the design of future conversational systems, the spontaneous convergence of users' speech could be exploited to guide it within system processing bounds, thereby enhancing robustness. The long-term goal of this research is the development of predictive models of human-computer communication to guide the design of next-generation conversational interfaces, in particular ones that are adaptive and focussed on audio exchanges in mobile usage contexts.

Keywords: Conversational interfaces; Adaptive and mobile interfaces; Speech recognition; Text-to-speech; Human-computer adaptation; Animated software partners; Children's educational software.

1. Introduction to Conversational Interfaces

During the past decade, advances in spoken language technology, natural language processing, dialogue modelling, multimodal interface design, and mobile applications all have stimulated interest in a new class of conversational interfaces (André et al., 1996; Cassell et al., 2000; Karat et al., 2002; Lai

W. Minker, D. Bühler and L. Dybkjær (eds), Spoken Multimodal Human-Computer Dialogue in Mobile Environments, 379-397

and Yankelovich, 2002; Oviatt, 1996; Oviatt, 2002). In contrast with command or dictation-style interfaces, conversational interfaces support large-vocabulary spontaneous spoken language that is exchanged as part of a fluid dialogue between a user and computer. They also permit the user to take initiative in shaping the interactive dialogue. To accomplish these goals, next-generation conversational interfaces support parallel natural language processing for both input (e.g., speech recognition) and output (e.g., TTS) between human and computer.

Apart from being an information exchange, human conversation also is a social activity that is inherently reinforcing. As such, new conversational interfaces are social interfaces, and when we participate in them we respond to the computer linguistically and behaviourally as a social partner (Nass and Lee, 2000; Nass et al., 1994). In order to engage a user and manage their conversational exchange with a computer, researchers have begun developing animated software "personas" as a social metaphor and interface vehicle for facilitating interaction. However, very little research has explored users' actual interaction with such characters, or developed techniques for designing animated characters that promote a task-appropriate behavioural impact on users (Dehn and van Mulken, 2000). Exceptions include recent studies demonstrating that high-fidelity moving lips on a talking head can improve TTS intelligibility (Massaro et al., 2000), and gaze and gestural output can improve dialogue efficiency (Cassell and Thorisson, 1999). Other recent studies have shown that characters can be designed that influence users' product preferences and purchasing behaviour (Nass and Lee, 2000), and that effectively stimulate learning-oriented behaviour during tutorial exchanges (Darves and Oviatt, 2004; Moreno et al., 2001). However, more research is needed to explore different design concepts of animated characters, and to assess the impact of their basic features (i.e., animation, TTS) on users' language and performance when interacting with conversational systems.

Conversational interface design also has stimulated the development of text-to-speech research. State-of-the-art TTS systems recently have breached the intelligibility threshold, and are beginning to be applied widely for telephony, mobile, and other tasks. In a recent empirical study involving a conversational interface, 7-to-10-year-old children who listened to TTS responses asked the computer to repeat less than 1% of the time (Darves and Oviatt, 2004; Oviatt and Adams, 2000). As a result, TTS evaluation issues now focus less on basic intelligibility, and more on "naturalness" and related suprasegmental prosodic features (e.g., duration, pitch, intonation). There is agreement that future TTS research needs to conduct more actual human assessments of synthetic speech, and to gain a better understanding of human perception and behavioural reaction to TTS (Pisoni, 1997; Pols and Jekosch, 1997). In addition, future research needs to explore whether the parameters of TTS output have an influence on users' spoken input to a conversational system. Unfortunately, past research has tended to focus either on input technologies (e.g., speech recognition) or output technologies (e.g., TTS), and has ignored the overall interactive cycle between human and computer.

The cognitive science literature on Communication Accommodation Theory (CAT) has examined adaptation of linguistic and nonverbal behaviour between two interlocutors during conversation. This theoretical viewpoint acknowledges that interpersonal conversation is a dynamic adaptive exchange. Basically, a speaker's lexical, syntactic and speech signal features are tailored to their conversational partner in a manner that fosters the predictability, intelligibility and efficiency of communication, and also manages social impressions (Burgoon et al., 1995; Giles et al., 1987; Leiser, 1989). Both children and adults adapt features of their speech to more closely match their partner, including amplitude, pitch, rate of articulation, pause structure, response latency before initiating a conversational turn, and phonological features (Burgoon et al., 1995; Giles et al., 1987; Smith et al., 1995; Street et al., 1983; Welkowitz et al., 1972).

In spite of this interpersonal literature, research on human-computer interaction (HCI) has yet to investigate whether users of a conversational interface likewise adapt their speech to converge with a computer software partner. Earlier research involving keyboard or spoken interaction with text-based query systems demonstrated that users will adopt the vocabulary and syntactic structures displayed as graphic responses on a computer screen (Leiser, 1989; Zoltan-Ford, 1991). However, research has yet to explore linguistic convergence in conversational interfaces in which a user speaks to the computer and receives TTS responses, often mediated by an animated persona. If users' speech does converge with the computer in such cases, then further studies need to determine which speech features adapt, what magnitude and rate of change occurs, and what the implications are for designing robust conversational interfaces. Since the variability in users' speech signal can be substantial, it is a major cause of system recognition failure. To the extent that conversation with a computer partner does involve speech signal convergence, it may be possible to design interfaces that proactively guide users' speech to remain within system processing bounds. That is, this natural conversational behaviour could be exploited to design better synchronised and more reliable systems.

In addition, linguistic convergence during children's spoken interaction with computers has yet to be explored. Recent research has estimated that speech recognition for children's applications is subject to error rates two-to-five times higher than for adults (Potamionos et al., 1997; Wilpon and Jacobsen, 1996). Children's speech production is more challenging because many basic features are less mature, more variable, and in a state of developmental flux (Yeni-

Komshian et al., 1980). As a result, the development of conversational interfaces for children requires special design strategies to manage their higher levels of speech signal variability. However, to the extent that speech signal convergence can be elicited in child users, any design strategies that leverage from it also can expect to reap proportionately greater improvements in system robustness.

2. Research Goals

The present research was designed to explore whether the basic acoustic-prosodic features of users' speech are influenced by the TTS they hear when interacting with a computer partner. Given the cognitive science literature, it was hypothesised that a variety of features involving duration and amplitude would adapt toward a computer partner's TTS. It was predicted that when users converse with a computer character embodying an extrovert TTS voice, their amplitude would become higher, utterance durations shorter, and dialogue response latencies between conversational turns would become shorter, while the reverse patterns would be elicited when speaking with an introvert TTS voice.

It is well known that extrovert and introvert voices are associated with different speech signal characteristics. Extrovert speech typically is higher in amplitude, higher in pitch with expanded pitch range, shorter in duration with a faster rate of delivery, and displays correspondingly shorter dialogue response latencies before initiating a conversational turn. Introvert speech presents the opposite speech signal profile (Nass and Lee, 2000; Scherer, 1979; Smith et al., 1995). In designing this research, the strategy was to present users with two opposite TTS voices, ones representing the upper and lower bounds of speech signal features (e.g., amplitude, duration), in order to determine whether users' speech could be influenced by a TTS target voice when an optimal degree of contrast is present. A related research goal was to maintain natural TTS voices with an identifiable social presence. To achieve this, features of the extrovert and introvert TTS voices were manipulated together as they tend to co-vary in real speakers' voices.

One specific objective was to investigate whether users' amplitude and duration during human-computer interaction would be equally likely to adapt by increasing or decreasing in response to these different TTS voices. It was predicted that users' amplitude and duration would readapt if a contrasting computer voice was introduced part of the way through their session. In short, users' speech was expected to be dynamically adaptable to the voice of different conversational partners. In addition, the relative magnitude of adaptation was observed for different acoustic-prosodic features of speech. Finally, the generality of results regarding speech adaptation also was assessed across different types of user groups and TTS voices, and implications of the research findings were distilled for conversational interface design.

The research objectives described above were examined with a large corpus that represented children conversing with animated fish as they learned about marine biology. The I SEE! (Immersive Science Education for Elementary kids) science application used in this study was designed to engage children as learners and to support their question asking skills. Other research has detailed the impact of the I SEE! science application on children's learning-oriented behaviour (Darves and Oviatt, 2004). The average child in this study spontaneously asked over 150 questions while conversing with marine animals during a one-hour session, and children reported that they "liked talking to the animals" (Darves and Oviatt, 2004). From an applications standpoint, a further goal of this research is the design of high-performance conversational interfaces that effectively support educational exchanges.

3. Method

3.1 I SEE! Application, Interface and Simulation Environment

I SEE! is an application designed to teach children about basic marine biology, simple data tabulation, and graphing. The I SEE! educational application runs on a hand-held PC that can be used while mobile or in natural field settings (e.g., home, science centre). The interface permits children to use speech, pen, or multimodal input while conversing with animated software characters as they learn about marine biology. It also permits them to control video displays, and to tabulate data about the animals in graphs. Figure 1 illustrates the I SEE! interface.

During the study to be described, children used the I SEE! application to view rich National Geographic video images of 24 different marine animals (e.g., octopus shown in Figure 1). When they stopped the videotape, the animal displayed became animated and available as a conversational partner who could answer questions about itself using TTS output. In addition, an animated Spin the Dolphin software character, shown in the lower right corner of Figure 1, was co-present on the screen. Spin also could converse with the child, answering questions and assisting as needed with the interactive activity (e.g., starting and stopping videotapes, telling jokes). One general goal of this conversational interface was to create a sense of directness and immediacy regarding children's interaction with the characters and educational content. Details of the effectiveness of I SEE! at engaging child users has been documented elsewhere (Darves and Oviatt, 2004).

The I SEE! interface is a simulated conversational system that was designed to support the prototyping of conversational interfaces. Using this research in-

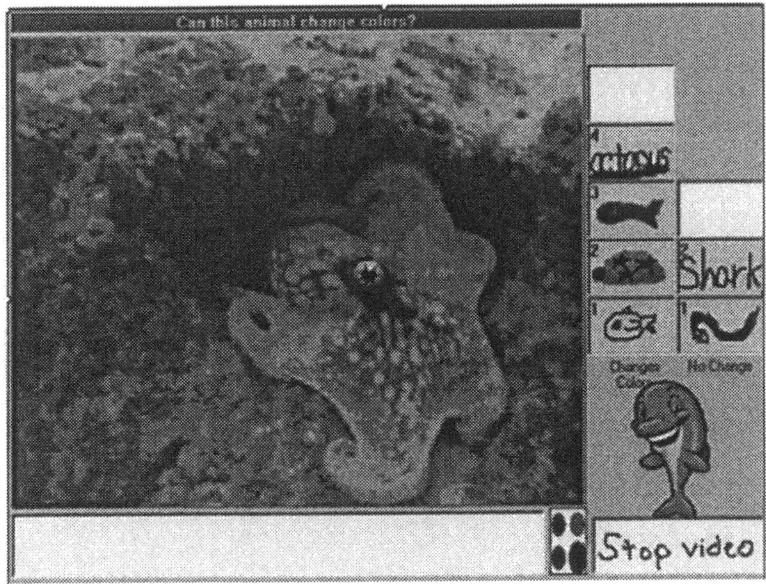

Figure 1. I SEE! user interface.

frastructure, children's input was received by an informed assistant, who then interpreted their queries and provided system responses. System responses to frequent child queries were pre-loaded into a database, a feature that supported rapid simulated responding for the majority of children's questions. During testing, children believed that they were interacting with a real system. The simulation environment ran on a PC, and it received input from a Fujitsu Stylistic 2300. Details of the simulation infrastructure and its performance characteristics have been summarised elsewhere (Oviatt and Adams, 2000).

3.2 Participants, Procedure and Test Materials

Twenty-four elementary-school children participated in this study. The participants were evenly divided into two age groups, younger children (mean age 8 years, 2 months), and older ones (mean age 9 years, 7 months), with each age group gender balanced. All participants were native American English speakers.

Before starting their session, each child received instructions and practice with a science teacher on how to use I SEE! Then the teacher left, and the child spent approximately one hour alone in a quiet classroom playing with the educational software. During this time, he or she conversed with 24 marine animals, which were organised into three task sets of eight animals apiece. Figure 2 illustrates a child talking to a marine character.

Figure 2. Child at school asking an animated character questions about itself.

During each encounter with a new animal, the child was encouraged to collect information about it, to ask any questions he or she wished, and to have fun learning new things about the animals. Children's conversations with the animals primarily were self-initiated and reflected their own curiosity and interests. The marine animals were responsive, but did not direct the conversation. In addition, no teacher or adult was present to influence what children asked, or how long they interacted with the animals in I SEE!. At the end of each session, the science teacher returned and interviewed the child.

Text-to-speech voices from Lernout and Hauspie's TTS 3000 were used for the animated characters' spoken output, including an American English male and female voice. These voices were tailored to represent opposite ends of the introvert-extrovert personality spectrum, as indicated by the speech signal literature (Scherer, 1979; Smith et al., 1995). Therefore, a total of four different TTS voices were used: Male extrovert (ME), Male introvert (MI), Female extrovert (FE), and Female introvert (FI). Table 1 summarises the differences in speech signal profiles for these different voice samples. Due to pre-loading of system responses, the lexical content in these different voice conditions was controlled. For each test session, the marine animals were assigned one of these four TTS voices during practice and task sets 1 and 2. However, the introvert-extrovert dimension of the TTS voice then was switched for task set 3 (i.e., MI switched to ME).

Table 1. Average acoustic-prosodic differences between TTS voice conditions.

TTS Voice Type	Mean Amplitude (dB)	Mean Pitch Range (Hz)	Utterance Rate (syl/sec)	Dialogue Response Latency (sec)	Mean Pause Duration (sec)
FE	60	186	5.2	1.65	.09
ME	58	106	5.2	1.65	.13
FI	45	71	3.3	3.36	.22
MI	44	58	3.3	3.36	.20

3.3 Research Design

The research design for this study was a repeated measures factorial, with type of TTS voice (Introvert, Extrovert) the main within-subject factor. This factor remained constant during tasks 1 and 2, but switched during task 3 (from I to E, or E to I), as shown in Figure 3. To assess the possibility of change in dependent measures across this switch, analyses were conducted repeatedly as the child progressed through all task sets. The different marine animals that were presented during the three task sets and the order of presentation of the task sets were counter-balanced across subjects. To test the generality of any TTS effects, the main introvert and extrovert voice types also were tested using male and female gender instantiations. Two additional between-subject factors were the child's gender and age. For the latter, a median split was performed to categorise children into the younger (mean age 8 years, 2 months) and older (mean age 9 years, 7 months) half of the 24 participants.

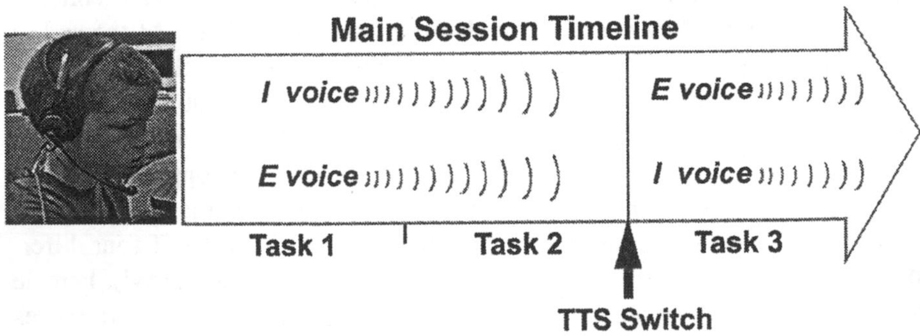

Figure 3. TTS voice for animated characters before and after switch task.

3.4 Transcription, Data Coding and Reliability

All human-computer interaction was videotaped, and the entire conversational interaction was transcribed. For each user utterance, a trained linguist measured average amplitude in vocalic regions using Praat speech signal analysis software[1]. For measurement details, see (Coulston et al., 2002). Likewise, the speech segment and total utterance duration were scored to the nearest 100th of a second, as was the total duration of pauses longer than 17 milliseconds (ms). Inter-speaker dialogue response latencies were measured between the end of an animated character's spoken utterance and the beginning of the user's next utterance to the same character, as detailed in (Darves et al., 2002).

Second scoring of dependent measures was completed for 10-15% of the data. Inter-rater reliabilities indicated that 80% of amplitude measures matched to within 0.4 dB. For durational measures, 80% of speech and total utterance durations matched to within 21 ms, whereas 80% of total pause durations matched to within 77 ms. For longer dialogue response latencies between conversational turns, 80% of the measures matched to within 0.08 seconds.

4. Results

The main focus of the analyses was to compare children's speech while interacting with the marine animals during tasks 1 and 2, as opposed to after the TTS voice shift in task 3. Data were analysed for about 2,000 utterances. Figure 4 shows an example of a transcribed subdialogue between a child and a marine animal (i.e., slipper lobster), followed by a subdialogue between the child and Spin the dolphin.

Marine Animal	Child	Spin the Dolphin
	Where do you live?	
I'm common in tropical waters and on rocky reefs.		
	What do you eat?	
I eat small creatures and dead things that I find on the ocean floor.		
	What eats you?	
Turtles, sharks, and big fish eat me. Sometimes dolphins eat me too.		
	Spin would you eat that slipper lobster?	
		Not me.
	You're nice. Okay, I'm done.	
		Would you like to hear a joke?
	Sure.	

Figure 4. Typical question-answer exchange between child and animated characters.

4.1 Amplitude

As predicted, children's vocalic amplitude differed when users conversed with an animated character that spoke with an extrovert versus introvert voice. As shown in Table 2, their average amplitude increased from 57.19 dB when interacting with the introvert voice to 58.29 dB with the extrovert one, which was a significant difference by repeated measures ANOVA, $F = 15.04$ ($df = 1, 17$), $p < .001$. This change represented a +29% relative increase in energy between the introvert and extrovert conditions. Children's accommodation of amplitude also was bi-directional. An a priori paired t-test indicated that amplitude decreased significantly when the TTS voice switched from extrovert to introvert (means 58.15 and 57.44, respectively), $t = 3.08$ ($df = 10$), $p < .006$, one-tailed. It likewise increased significantly when the TTS voice switched from introvert to extrovert (means 56.95 and 58.43, respectively), $t = 2.69$ ($df = 10$), $p < .015$, one-tailed. Table 2 summarises these amplitude means and the percentage change in energy between I to E and E to I conditions.

Table 2. Average amplitude in dB for extrovert versus introvert TTS voice conditions, and percentage change during bi-directional shifts.

	Introvert Voice (dB)	Extrovert Voice (dB)	% Change in Energy
Grand Mean	57.19	58.29	+29%
E to I	57.44	58.15	-15%
I to E	56.95	58.43	+41%

4.2 Speech and Total Utterance Duration

Children's total utterance duration also differed when they conversed with an extrovert versus introvert animated character. As shown in Table 3, their average utterance duration increased from 1.22 seconds when interacting with the extrovert voice to 1.34 seconds with the introvert one, which was a significant difference in total utterance duration (log transformed) by repeated measures ANOVA, $F = 13.66$ ($df = 1, 11$), $p < .004$. This change represented a +9.4% relative increase between the extrovert and introvert conditions. Similarly, total speech segment duration (i.e., excluding pauses) increased from 1.18 seconds in the extrovert condition to 1.28 seconds in the introvert condition, or a +9.1% relative increase. This increase in the speech segment alone (log transformed) also was significant by repeated measures ANOVA, $F = 9.96$ ($df = 1, 11$), $p < .009$. In addition, children's accommodation of utterance duration was bi-directional. A paired t-test indicated that utterance duration decreased significantly when the TTS voice switched from introvert to extrovert (means 1.38 and 1.23 seconds, respectively), $t = 3.73$ ($df = 7$), $p < .0035$, one-tailed. It increased significantly when the TTS voice switched from extrovert to introvert (means 1.20 and 1.29 seconds, respectively), $t = 1.95$ ($df = 7$), $p < .045$, one-tailed. Table 3 summarises these utterance duration means and the percentage change in duration for I to E and E to I conditions.

Table 3. Average utterance duration for extrovert versus introvert TTS voice conditions, and percentage change during bi-directional shifts.

	Introvert Voice (sec)	Extrovert Voice (sec)	% Change in Duration
Grand Mean	1.34	1.22	+9.4%
E to I	1.29	1.20	+7.5%
I to E	1.38	1.23	-10.9%

4.3 Utterance Pause Structure

As predicted, both the number and duration of children's pauses differed when they conversed with extrovert versus introvert TTS voices. The average number of pauses per utterance increased from .25 when interacting with the extrovert voice to .32 with the introvert one, which was a significant difference by repeated measures ANOVA, $F = 9.88$ ($df = 1, 16$), $p < .006$. This change represented a +26.4% relative increase in number of pauses during the introvert condition. Similarly, total pause duration for utterances that contained a pause increased from .204 seconds in the extrovert condition to .304 in the introvert condition, or a +49.0% relative increase in pause duration. This increase also was significant by repeated measures ANOVA, $F = 7.03$ ($df = 1, 13$), $p < .02$. Users' accommodation of pause structure also was bi-directional. Table 4 summarises bi-directional shifts in the average number of pauses and percentage change between I to E and E to I conditions. A paired t-test confirmed that the number of pauses decreased significantly when the TTS voice switched from introvert to extrovert (means .30 and .23, respectively), $t = 3.35$ ($df = 9$), $p < .005$, one-tailed. It likewise increased significantly when the TTS voice switched from extrovert to introvert (means .27 and .33, respectively), $t = 1.94$ ($df = 9$), $p < .05$, one-tailed.

Table 4. Average number of pauses per utterance for extrovert versus introvert TTS voice conditions, and percentage change during bi-directional shifts.

	Introvert Voice	Extrovert Voice	% Change in Pauses
Grand Mean	.32	.25	+26.4%
E to I	.33	.27	+22%
I to E	.30	.23	-23%

4.4 Dialogue Response Latency

Children's response latencies also differed when they conversed with extrovert versus introvert animated character TTS voices. As shown in Table 5, their average conversational lags increased from 4.29 seconds when interacting with the extrovert voice to 5.07 seconds with the introvert one, which was a significant difference in duration (log transformed) by repeated measures ANOVA, $F = 6.52$ ($df = 1, 16$), $p < .025$. This change represented a +18.4% relative increase in duration during the introvert condition. A priori paired t-tests confirmed the prediction that this change in latencies was bi-directional. Children's latencies increased significantly when first exposed to the extrovert voice and then switched to the introvert (mean 4.23 and 5.04 seconds), $t = 2.04$ ($df = 11$), $p < .035$, one-tailed. Likewise, their latencies (log transformed) decreased significantly when exposed to the introvert voice, but later switched to the extrovert (mean 6.00 and 5.24 seconds), $t = 1.82$ ($df = 11$), $p < .05$, one-tailed. Table 5 summarises the relative increase in latency for the introvert condition for this split comparison by task order.

Table 5. Average response latencies in seconds for extrovert versus introvert TTS voice conditions, and percentage change during bi-directional shifts.

	Extrovert Voice (sec)	Introvert Voice (sec)	% Change in Latency
Grand Mean	4.29	5.07	+18.4%
E to I Order	4.23	5.04	+19.1%
I to E Order	5.24	6.00	-12.7%

4.5 Generality of Effects

The main effects outlined above in children's speech signal convergence (i.e., in amplitude, duration, and dialogue response latencies) with the introvert and extrovert TTS voices generalised across children of different ages, genders, and specific TTS voices. That is, the main effect of TTS voice type generalised across these variables. However, some variations were observed in the magnitude of speech signal convergence for different parameters as a function of children's gender. For example, the repeated measures ANOVA revealed a significant TTS voice type by child gender interaction for amplitude, $F = 8.52$ ($df = 1, 17$), $p < .01$. Follow-up comparison showed that females adapted their amplitude toward that of their conversational partner to a greater degree than males, independent t-test (separate variances), $t = 3.17$, ($df = 16.4$), $p < .006$, two-tailed. In contrast, the repeated measures ANOVA revealed a significant TTS voice type by gender interaction for pause duration, $F = 9.45$ ($df = 1, 13$), $p < .009$. Follow-up comparison revealed that males adapted their pause duration to a greater degree than females, independent t-test (separate variances), $t = 2.33$, $(df = 7.2)$, $p < .05$, two-tailed.

5. Discussion

This research explored a new dimension of speaker stylistic variation – whether the acoustic-prosodic features of users' speech converge with the text-to-speech heard from a software partner. As summarised in Table 6, 7-to-10-year-old children adapted the amplitude and durational features of their speech by a substantial 10-50% when interacting with animated characters representing different TTS voice styles. These changes in their speech patterns also were bi-directional. That is, when exposed to an extrovert voice, child speakers increased their amplitude and decreased utterance duration and dialogue response latencies. Conversely, when interacting with an introvert voice, they decreased amplitude and increased utterance duration and response latencies.

Table 6. Summary of average relative magnitude change in linguistic features of accommodation from extrovert to introvert TTS voice.

Acoustic-Prosodic Features	Magnitude Change
Pause Duration	+49.0%
Number of Pauses	+26.4%
Amplitude	-22.4%
Dialogue Response Latency	+18.4%
Speech & Utterance Duration	+9.1-9.4%

All features represent statistically significant change.

Children were most sensitive to accommodating the patterns of silence within their software partner's utterances. Although utterance duration primarily consists of the speech segment, the largest adaptations that children made to a partner's speech actually involved pause structure, or the silent intervals within an utterance that provide temporal context for processing it. When children switched from conversing with an extroverted character to an introverted one, they interjected +26.4% more pauses, and total pause duration increased by a substantial +49%. As shown in Table 6, these changes were the largest magnitude adaptations observed among the speech features analysed. Changes in children's pause structure also were bi-directional. That is, when exposed to an extrovert TTS voice followed by an introvert one with more pauses, child speakers increased their average number of pauses per utterance from .27 to .33, or by +22%. Likewise, when interacting with an introvert TTS voice followed by an extrovert one with fewer pauses, they decreased the average number of pauses from .30 to .23, or by -23%.

Apart from within-utterance pause structure, the silent intervals between turns within a conversation also showed strong adaptive patterns. Children lengthened their response latencies +18.4% when interacting with a slower-paced introverted character, compared with a rapid extroverted one. Once again, these changes were bi-directional. When exposed to an extrovert voice followed by a slower introvert one, children correspondingly increased their lag from an average of 4.23 to 5.04 seconds, or by +19.1%. When interacting with an introvert voice followed by a faster extrovert, the direction of change reversed with a decrease in lag from 6.00 to 5.24 seconds, or -12.7%. These flexible adaptations in dialogue response latencies underscore the dynamic nature of children's ability to adapt and readapt their speech patterns to synchronise with different conversational partners.

Children also were highly sensitive to accommodating their partner's level of acoustic energy. When a child switched from conversing with an introverted partner to an extroverted one, the average amplitude increased from 57.19 to 58.29 decibels, or a relative increase of +29% in linear energy. This adaptation of energy level was the second largest observed in magnitude among the linguistic features analysed. Like pause structure, adaptations in children's amplitude also were bi-directional. When exposed to an introvert TTS voice followed by an extrovert one that was higher in amplitude, child speakers increased their own average amplitude from 56.95 to 58.43 dBs, or by +41%. Likewise, when interacting with an extrovert TTS voice followed by an introvert one, they decreased their amplitude from 58.15 to 57.44 dBs, or by -15%. These findings indicate that future conversational interfaces with TTS could be designed to actively and flexibly guide features of users' speech that otherwise would be problematic for a speech recogniser to process. For example, a higher amplitude target TTS voice could be used to increase low amplitude speech of the younger children in order to avoid recognition failure and support application success.

Users' inclination to adapt speech to accommodate their computer partner was a general phenomenon. No significant differences were observed between younger and older children in this adaptive capability. Likewise, no difference was detected in children's speech adaptation due to the specific gender instantiation of the TTS voice they heard. With respect to child gender, both male and female children adapted their speech for all measures, although males adapted pause duration to a greater extent than females, whereas females engaged in larger adaptations of amplitude. Finally, since children interacted with 24 visually distinct characters, speech adaptations were not limited to a specific visual appearance. Users' speech signal adaptations generalised across all of these variables when interacting with the introvert and extrovert TTS voices.

These research results underscore the need for more dynamic, adaptive, and user-centred approaches to conversational interface design. Since current recognition technology remains sensitive to variations in amplitude and duration (Junqua, 1993; Mirghafori et al., 1996), future interfaces with TTS output could be designed to manage these acoustic-prosodic features. That is, the design of future animated characters could exploit speakers' natural inclination to converge with the TTS voice of a software partner, and in a manner that would provide an effective tool for transparently guiding users' speech to fall within a range that is easily processed by the recogniser without any explicit instruction, training, or error messages. Further empirical research will be needed to model the most important dynamic changes in users' speech, and to formulate effective approaches for adaptive processing in future conversational systems. In fact, in one recent study user-adapted TTS speaking rates were implemented for a telephony application based on modelling of users' own rate, and users preferred this system to a non-adaptive alternative (Ward and Nakagawa, 2002). In future work, systems should be designed to support continuous and mutual speech adaptation between user and computer, which is what characterises high-quality synchronised exchanges typical of interpersonal conversation.

Auditory interface design, including the auditory personification of animated characters as social metaphors, will be especially important aspects of future mobile interfaces. These results underscore the power of auditory embodiment alone, independent of animated characters' visual appearance or the content of what they say, to influence users' spoken interaction with a conversational system. Some mobile interfaces will adapt visual displays to eliminate them at least periodically while mobile, relying instead on auditory speech and non-speech output for user feedback. As a result, future research should explore the presence and magnitude of users' speech convergence with software partners represented by voice alone, without any visual embodiment. In addition, according to the interpersonal literature speech adaptation to a partner increases with age (Welkowitz et al., 1972; Welkowitz et al., 1976), which suggests that larger adaptations than those observed in this study may be typical of adults. Future research should explore speech adaptations during human-computer communication involving adult users. Finally, in addition to amplitude and durational features, future research needs to investigate users' adaptation of pitch, intonation, and other parameters of speech.

6. Conclusion

The design of new conversational interfaces, including their auditory and visual embodiment, is both an art and an emerging science. In this research, a new dimension of speaker stylistic variation was identified during human-computer communication: the convergence of users' speech with the text-to-speech (TTS) heard from an animated software partner. From the present results, it is clear that child users consistently adapt the basic acoustic-prosodic features of their speech to converge with their computer partner, and they do so in a dynamic and bi-directional manner while conversing with animated characters that represent different TTS voices. In the design of future conversational systems, this spontaneous convergence of users' speech could be exploited to guide it within system processing bounds, thereby enhancing system robustness. The long-term goal of this research is the development of predictive models of human-computer communication to guide the design of next-generation conversational interfaces, especially ones that are adaptive or focussed on mobile usage contexts.

Acknowledgements

This research was supported in part by NSF Grants IRI-9530666, IIS-0117868, Special Extension for Creativity IIS-9530666, and a gift from the Intel Research Council to the first author. Thanks to Jason Wiles for providing marine biology expertise and serving as the science teacher during testing, to John Paul Hosom for assisting with speech signal analyses, and to Cynthia Girand for reliability scoring. Finally, special thanks to our elementary school students for their enthusiastic participation and curiosity about science and technology.

Notes

1. `http://www.praat.org/`

References

André, E., Müller, J., and Rist, T. (1996). The PPP persona: A multipurpose animated presentation agent. In *Proceedings of Workshop on Advanced Visual Interfaces (AVI)*, pages 245–247, Gubbio, Italy.

Burgoon, J., Stern, L., and Dillman, L. (1995). *Interpersonal Adaptation: Dyadic Interaction Patterns*. Cambridge University Press, Cambridge, United Kingdom.

Cassell, J., Sullivan, J., Prevost, S., and Churchill, E. (2000). *Embodied Conversational Agents*. MIT Press, Cambridge, Massachusetts, USA.

Cassell, J. and Thorisson, K. R. (1999). The power of a nod and a glance: Envelope vs. emotional feedback in animated conversational agents. *Applied Artificial Intelligence Journal*, 13(4–5):519–538.

Coulston, R., Oviatt, S. L., and Darves, C. (2002). Amplitude convergence in children's conversational speech with animated personas. In *Proceedings of International Conference on Spoken Language Processing (ICSLP)*, pages 2689–2692, Denver, Colorado, USA.

Darves, C. and Oviatt, S. L. (2004). Talking to digital fish: Designing effective conversational interfaces for educational software. In Ruttkay, Z. and Pelachaud, C., editors, *Evaluating Conversational Agents*. Kluwer Academic Publishers, Dordrecht, The Netherlands.

Darves, C., Oviatt, S. L., and Coulston, R. (2002). Adaptation of users' spoken dialogue patterns in a conversational interface. In *Proceedings of International Conference on Spoken Language Processing (ICSLP)*, pages 561–564, Denver, Colorado, USA.

Dehn, D. M. and van Mulken, S. (2000). The impact of animated interface agents: A review of empirical research. *International Journal of Human-Computer Studies*, 52:1–22.

Giles, H., Mulac, A., Bradac, J., and Johnson, P. (1987). Speech accommodation theory: The first decade and beyond. In McGlaughlin, M. L., editor, *Communication Yearbook 10*, pages 13–48. Sage Publishers, London, United Kingdom.

Junqua, J. (1993). The Lombard reflex and its role on human listeners and automatic speech recognizers. *Journal of the Acoustical Society of America*, 1:510–524.

Karat, C. M., Vergo, J., and Nahamoo, D. (2002). Conversational interface technologies. In Jacko, J. and Sears, A., editors, *The Human-Computer Interaction Handbook: Fundamentals, Evolving Technologies and Emerging Applications*, pages 286–304. Lawrence Erlbaum Assoc., Mahwah, New Jersey, USA.

Lai, J. and Yankelovich, N. (2002). Conversational speech interfaces. In Jacko, J. and Sears, A., editors, *The Human-Computer Interaction Handbook: Fundamentals, Evolving Technologies and Emerging Applications*, pages 698–713. Lawrence Erlbaum Assoc., Mahwah, New Jersey, USA.

Leiser, R. G. (1989). Improving natural language and speech interfaces by the use of metalinguistic phenomena. *Applied Ergonomics 20*, 3:168–173.

Massaro, D., Cohen, M., Beskow, J., and Cole, R. (2000). Developing and evaluating conversational agents. In Cassell, J., Sullivan, J., Prevost, S., and Churchill, E., editors, *Embodied Conversational Agents*, pages 287–318. MIT Press, Cambridge, Massachusetts, USA.

Mirghafori, N., Fosler, E., and Morgan, N. (1996). Towards robustness to fast speech in ASR. In *Proceedings of International Conference on Acoustics, Speech and Signal Processing (ICASSP)*, pages 335–338, Atlanta, Georgia, USA.

Moreno, R., Mayer, R., Spires, H., and Lester, J. (2001). The case for social agency in computer-based teaching: Do students learn more deeply when they interact with animated pedagogical agents? *Cognition and Instruction*, 19(2):177–213.

Nass, C. and Lee, K. L. (2000). Does computer-generated speech manifest personality? An experimental test of similarity-attraction. In *Proceedings of Conference on Human Factors in Computing Systems (CHI)*, pages 329–336, The Hague, The Netherlands.

Nass, C., Steuer, J., and Tauber, E. (1994). Computers are social actors. In *Proceedings of Conference on Human Factors in Computing Systems (CHI)*, pages 72–78, Boston, Massachusetts, USA.

Oviatt, S. L. (1996). User-centered design of spoken language and multimodal interfaces. *IEEE Multimedia*, 3(4):26–35. Reprinted in Morgan-Kaufmann Readings on Intelligent User Interfaces, M. Maybury and W. Wahlster, Eds.

Oviatt, S. L. (2002). Multimodal interfaces. In Jacko, J. and Sears, A., editors, *The Human-Computer Interaction Handbook: Fundamentals, Evolving Technologies and Emerging Applications*. Lawrence Erlbaum Assoc., Mahwah, New Jersey, USA.

Oviatt, S. L. and Adams, B. (2000). Designing and evaluating conversational interfaces with animated characters. In Cassell, J., Sullivan, J., Prevost, S., and Churchill, E., editors, *Embodied Conversational Agents*, pages 319–343. MIT Press, Cambridge, Massachusetts, USA.

Pisoni, D. (1997). Perception of synthetic speech. In van Santen, J., Sproat, R., Olive, J., and Hirschberg, J., editors, *Progress in Speech Synthesis*, pages 541–556. Springer-Verlag, Berlin/Heidelberg, Germany.

Pols, L. and Jekosch, U. (1997). A structured way of looking at the performance of text-to-speech systems. In van Santen, J., Sproat, R., Olive, J., and Hirschberg, J., editors, *Progress in Speech Synthesis*, pages 519–527. Springer-Verlag, Berlin/Heidelberg, Germany.

Potamionos, A., Narayanan, S., and Lee, S. (1997). Automatic speech recognition for children. In *Proceedings of European Conference on Speech Communication and Technology (EUROSPEECH)*, pages 2371–2374, Rhodes, Greece.

Scherer, K. R. (1979). Personality markers in speech. In Scherer, K. R. and Giles, H., editors, *Social Markers in Speech*, pages 147–209. Cambridge University Press, Cambridge, United Kingdom.

Smith, B. L., Brown, B. L., Strong, W. J., and Rencher, A. (1995). Effects of speech rate on personality perception. *Language and Speech*, 18:145–152.

Street, R., Street, N., and Vankleeck, A. (1983). Speech convergence among talkative and reticent three-year-olds. *Language Sciences*, 5:79–86.

Ward, N. and Nakagawa, S. (2002). Automatic user-adaptive speaking rate selection for information delivery. In *Proceedings of International Conference on Spoken Language Processing (ICSLP)*, pages 549–552, Denver, Colorado, USA.

Welkowitz, J., Cariffe, G., and Feldstein, S. (1976). Conversational congruence as a criterion of socialization in children. *Child Development*, pages 269–272.

Welkowitz, J., Feldstein, S., Finklestein, M., and Aylesworth, L. (1972). Changes in vocal intensity as a function of interspeaker influence. *Perceptual and Motor Skills*, 35:715–728.

Wilpon, J. and Jacobsen, C. (1996). A study of speech recognition for children and the elderly. In *Proceedings of International Conference on Acoustics, Speech and Signal Processing (ICASSP)*, pages 349–352, Atlanta, Georgia, USA.

Yeni-Komshian, G., Kavanaugh, J., and Ferguson, C. (1980). *Child Phonology, Volume 1: Production*. Academic Press, New York, NY, USA.

Zoltan-Ford, E. (1991). How to get people to say and type what computers can understand. *International Journal of Man-Machine Studies*, 34:527–547.

Index

Text, Speech and Language Technology

1. H. Bunt and M. Tomita (eds.): *Recent Advances in Parsing Technology.* 1996 ISBN 0-7923-4152-X
2. S. Young and G. Bloothooft (eds.): *Corpus-Based Methods in Language and Speech Processing.* 1997 ISBN 0-7923-4463-4
3. T. Dutoit: *An Introduction to Text-to-Speech Synthesis.* 1997 ISBN 0-7923-4498-7
4. L. Lebart, A. Salem and L. Berry: *Exploring Textual Data.* 1998 ISBN 0-7923-4840-0
5. J. Carson-Berndsen, *Time Map Phonology.* 1998 ISBN 0-7923-4883-4
6. P. Saint-Dizier (ed.): *Predicative Forms in Natural Language and in Lexical Knowledge Bases.* 1999 ISBN 0-7923-5499-0
7. T. Strzalkowski (ed.): *Natural Language Information Retrieval.* 1999 ISBN 0-7923-5685-3
8. J. Harrington and S. Cassiday: *Techniques in Speech Acoustics.* 1999 ISBN 0-7923-5731-0
9. H. van Halteren (ed.): *Syntactic Wordclass Tagging.* 1999 ISBN 0-7923-5896-1
10. E. Viegas (ed.): *Breadth and Depth of Semantic Lexicons.* 1999 ISBN 0-7923-6039-7
11. S. Armstrong, K. Church, P. Isabelle, S. Nanzi, E. Tzoukermann and D. Yarowsky (eds.): *Natural Language Processing Using Very Large Corpora.* 1999 ISBN 0-7923-6055-9
12. F. Van Eynde and D. Gibbon (eds.): *Lexicon Development for Speech and Language Processing.* 2000 ISBN 0-7923-6368-X; Pb: 07923-6369-8
13. J. Véronis (ed.): *Parallel Text Processing.* Alignment and Use of Translation Corpora. 2000 ISBN 0-7923-6546-1
14. M. Horne (ed.): *Prosody: Theory and Experiment.* Studies Presented to Gösta Bruce. 2000 ISBN 0-7923-6579-8
15. A. Botinis (ed.): *Intonation.* Analysis, Modelling and Technology. 2000 ISBN 0-7923-6605-0
16. H. Bunt and A. Nijholt (eds.): *Advances in Probabilistic and Other Parsing Technologies.* 2000 ISBN 0-7923-6616-6
17. J.-C. Junqua and G. van Noord (eds.): *Robustness in Languages and Speech Technology.* 2001 ISBN 0-7923-6790-1
18. R.H. Baayen: *Word Frequency Distributions.* 2001 ISBN 0-7923-7017-1
19. B. Granström, D. House and. I. Karlsson (eds.): *Multimodality in Language and Speech Systems.* 2002 ISBN 1-4020-0635-7
20. M. Carl and A. Way (eds.): *Recent Advances in Example-Based Machine Translation.* 2003 ISBN 1-4020-1400-7; Pb 1-4020-1401-5
21. A. Abeillé: *Treebanks.* Building and Using Parsed Corpora. 2003 ISBN 1-4020-1334-5; Pb 1-4020-1335-3
22. J. van Kuppevelt and R.W. Smith (ed.): *Current and New Directions in Discourse and Dialogue.* 2003 ISBN 1-4020-1614-X; Pb 1-4020-1615-8
23. H. Bunt, J. Carroll and G. Satta (eds.): *New Developments in Parsing Technology.* 2004 ISBN 1-4020-2293-X; Pb 1-4020-2294-8

24. G. Fant: *Speech Acoustics and Phonetics.* Selected Writings. 2004
ISBN 1-4020-2373-1; Pb 1-4020-2789-3
25. W.J. Barry and W.A. Van Dommelen (eds.): *The Integration of Phonetic Knowledge in Speech Technology.* 2004 ISBN 1-4020-2635-8; Pb 1-4020-2636-6
26. D. Dahl (ed.): *Practical Spoken Dialog Systems.* 2004
ISBN 1-4020-2674-9; Pb 1-4020-2675-7
27. O. Stock and M. Zancanaro (eds.): *Multimodal Intelligent Information Presentation.* 2004 ISBN 1-4020-3049-5; Pb 1-4020-3050-9
28. W. Minker, D. Bühler and L. Dybkjaer (eds.): *Spoken Multimodal Human-Computer Dialogue in Mobile Environments.* 2004 ISBN 1-4020-3073-8; Pb 1-4020-3074-6

9 781402 030741